A Reader's Guide to the Novels of *Louise Erdrich*

DATE DUE

GAYLORD   PRINTED IN U.S.A.

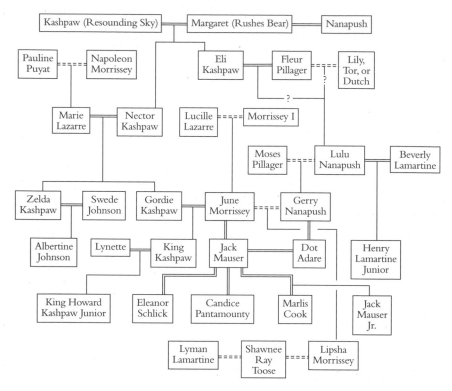

The relationships of some of the central characters in Louise Erdrich's Matchimanito novels.

Some relationships are not shown because to do so would unduly complicate the chart. For example, this chart does not show that Lyman Lamartine is the child of Lulu Lamartine and Nector Kashpaw or that Margaret, Marie, and Lulu have other children than those indicated. For such details, see the individual family charts in Part I. Unbroken double lines (═══) indicate either Indian or Western-style marriage; broken double lines (====) indicate nonmarital sexual liaisons; single lines (───) indicate children resulting from these unions. When exact relationships are unclear, we have indicated those uncertainties with question marks.

A Reader's Guide

to the **Novels of**

Erdrich

Beidler

rton

University of Missouri Press *Columbia and London*

Library of Congress Cataloging-in-Publication Data

Beidler, Peter G.
    A reader's guide to the novels of Louise Erdrich / Peter G.
Beidler and Gay Barton.
        p.   cm.
    Includes bibliographical references and index.
    ISBN 0-8262-1212-3 (alk. paper)
    1. Erdrich, Louise—Characters—Handbooks, manuals, etc.
2. Erdrich, Louise—Plots—Handbooks, manuals, etc.   3. Indians in
literature—Handbooks, manuals, etc.   I. Barton, Gay, 1946–   .
II. Title.
    PS3555.R42Z59   1999   99-12592
                                                              CIP

⊗ ™ This paper meets the requirements of the
American National Standard for Permanence of Paper
for Printed Library Materials, Z39.48, 1984.

Text Design: Elizabeth K. Young
Jacket Design: Susan Ferber
Typesetter: Bookcomp, Inc.
Printer and binder: Thomson-Shore, Inc.
Typefaces: Bembo, Helvetica

For Louise,
who drew us into her worlds

Contents

Acknowledgments

We are grateful to four people at Baylor University for bringing together the initial information for the dictionary entries on several of the characters as they appeared in Louise Erdrich's first four novels. Jennifer Alston wrote the initial entries for Celestine James, Dot Adare, Fleur Pillager, and Marie Lazarre Kashpaw; Alan C. Jones wrote them for Albertine Johnson, Eli Kashpaw, Lyman Lamartine, and Nanapush; Kateřina Prajznerová wrote them for Karl Adare, Lipsha Morrissey, Margaret (Rushes Bear) Kashpaw, and Wallace Pfef; and Alisan Stevenson wrote them for Gordie Kashpaw, Lulu Nanapush Morrissey Lamartine, Mary Adare, and Shawnee Ray Toose. We subsequently revised and expanded these entries to fit the style and scope of this book. In addition, Alisan Stevenson helped with revision, editing, and proofreading, and L. Tamara Kendig and William A. Meiers helped with proofreading. Harry J. Brown did most of the work for the index. We are especially grateful to Trent Duffy, who copyedited *The Bingo Palace, Tales of Burning Love,* and *The Antelope Wife* for Louise Erdrich and who kindly offered to check an early draft of the manuscript of this book. He called to our attention a number of large and small matters that we had missed or misunderstood. Finally, we want to express our thanks to Julie Schroeder at the University of Missouri Press for her careful copyediting of a book full of confusing details.

PGB and GB

A Reader's Guide to the Novels of *Louise Erdrich*

Introduction

Louise Erdrich is one of the most important Native American writers of the past fifteen years and one of the most accomplished and promising novelists of any heritage now working in the United States. Her fiction has won many awards and has attracted a devoted readership among lay as well as academic readers.

The daughter of Chippewa (Ojibwa)[1] and German parents, Erdrich was born in June 1954 in Minnesota. She is related through her Chippewa/French mother to Kaishpau Gourneau, who in 1882 became the head of the Turtle Mountain Band of Chippewa. An enrolled member of the North Dakota Turtle Mountain Chippewas, Erdrich spent much of her youth in Wahpeton, North Dakota, where her parents taught at a Bureau of Indian Affairs school. Her mother and father encouraged her, even as a small child, to write stories.

In 1972 Erdrich entered Dartmouth College, where she met Michael Dorris, a mixed-blood of Modoc descent, who had just become an assistant professor of anthropology. Eventually they fell in love and married. Dorris had already adopted three Indian children, and together they had

---

1. The terms *Chippewa* and *Ojibwa* (also spelled *Ojibway* and *Ojibwe*) are virtually interchangeable. Both are European renderings of a native word, sometimes transcribed as *Otchipwe,* about whose meaning scholars disagree (see Gerald Vizenor, *The People Named the Chippewa* [Minneapolis: University of Minnesota Press, 1984], 17–19). In his *Dictionary of the Otchipwe Language* (Cincinnati: Hemann, 1853; facsimile, 1970), the nineteenth-century missionary and lexicographer Frederic Baraga rendered the word as "Chippewa." Twentieth-century anthropologists have preferred some form of "Ojibwa" (see Victoria Brehm, "The Metamorphoses of an Ojibwa *Manido,*" 699, n. 1). The term by which this people traditionally referred to themselves is *Anishinabe* (or *Anishinaabe,* "person"; pl. *Anishinaabeg*). (This and subsequent Ojibwa definitions are from either John D. Nichols and Earl Nyholm, *A Concise Dictionary of Minnesota Ojibwe* [Minneapolis: University of Minnesota Press, 1995] or Basil Johnston, *Ojibway Language Lexicon for Beginners* [Ottawa: Indian and Northern Affairs Canada, 1978].)

In modern times, different bands of the Anishinabeg have often adopted either the name Chippewa or Ojibwa. In her interviews, Erdrich uses both words but tends to refer to her own family heritage as Chippewa. This is also the term used most often in her first five novels. The narrators of *The Antelope Wife,* set primarily in Minneapolis, favor the word Ojibwa.

three more children. Erdrich and Dorris encouraged and helped each other with their writing, coauthored two books (*The Crown of Columbus* and *Route Two* [both 1991]), and dedicated most of their works to one another. They seemed, for a time, an ideal Native American couple. They gave a large number of interviews, many of which were published. Their marriage eventually disintegrated, however, and Dorris committed suicide in April 1997.

Erdrich is best known, however, for her own stories and novels, which have earned for her a steadily growing readership. Her reputation as a fiction writer is now firmly established. By 1996 she had published five novels set on and around an unnamed Chippewa reservation in North Dakota, which is modeled in a general way on the Turtle Mountain Reservation where she is enrolled. These novels include *Love Medicine* (1984, 1993), *The Beet Queen* (1986), *Tracks* (1988), *The Bingo Palace* (1994), and *Tales of Burning Love* (1996). In 1998 she added a sixth novel, *The Antelope Wife*, set primarily in Minneapolis, Minnesota.

Erdrich's skill in creating and developing fictional characters is a central aspect of her success as a writer. She can fruitfully be compared with William Faulkner, who peopled the imaginary Yoknapatawpha County in Mississippi with a rich variety of men and women of several races. Similarly, in what we might call the Matchimanito saga of her first five novels, Erdrich has created an imaginary region centered around her fictional North Dakota reservation, whose heart is Matchimanito Lake, and peopled it with a varied group of men and women of white, Indian, and mixed-blood heritage. In *The Antelope Wife* she introduces a whole new set of characters with a similarly complex ancestry.

Erdrich's narrative technique is equally skillful. She handles multiple points of view, intertextual allusion, and temporal dislocation with skill rivaling that of the best of modern and postmodern writers of the Western tradition. At the same time, she weaves these techniques seamlessly with narrative elements from the Chippewa oral tradition.

Reviewers are typically enthusiastic, if not downright ecstatic, about Erdrich's fiction. They hail her as a bright new light—a courageous writer willing to break new narratological ground, a stunningly effective stylist, and a woman who courageously confronts the realities of Native American life in the twentieth century. Yet the narrative scope and depth of characterization that critics praise sometimes render her fiction bewildering. The bewilderment is especially troubling for readers who pick up her books out of sequence, or who, if they have read earlier works, do not remember who the characters are or what they did in previous novels. Even reviewers, who are typically careful and informed readers, at times find themselves perplexed by Erdrich's characters and story lines. The following quotations from reviews and articles illustrate the perplexity that many readers experience when they pick up an Erdrich novel:

> I found *Love Medicine* a hard book to penetrate. The episodes, most of them dramatic monologues, are loosely strung together and the relationships of the various narrators and characters are so confusing that one must constantly flip back to earlier sections in an effort to get one's bearings.—Robert Towers[2]

> Although I read [*The Beet Queen*] three times, I am still not sure which characters are of Indian ancestry except for Celestine, who is half-Indian, and her half-brother, Russell, who is full-blood. Apparently Mary is part Indian, but I never figured out whether her glamorous irresponsible mother, Adelaide, was part Indian. . . . —Leslie Marmon Silko[3]

> The stories [in *Tracks*] are circular and continuous and serpentlike. —Jennifer Sergi[4]

> *Tracks* is a transformational text which cavorts in the margins and flirts with danger because it plays with different parts of traditional myths, pulls stories this way and that and threatens to alter the shape of the oral tradition by bringing it into a new, written pattern. —Joni Adamson Clarke[5]

> *The Bingo Palace* is thick with characters from Erdrich's previous book and loaded with background. . . . The string of begats and the tangled skeins of relationships are so complex that they make the reader wish that instead of giving us a first chapter that is less drama than summary, Erdrich had simply provided a genealogical chart. —Kit Reed[6]

At first, the structure of *Tales of Burning Love* seems as shaggy and chaotic as something from Chaucer. The stories pop up seemingly at random, over-

2. "Uprooted," *New York Review of Books*, April 11, 1985, 36.
3. "Here's an Odd Artifact for the Fairy-Tale Shelf," 181.
4. "Storytelling: Tradition and Preservation in Louise Erdrich's *Tracks*," 282.
5. "Why Bears Are Good to Think and Theory Doesn't Have to Be Murder: Transformation and Oral Tradition in Louise Erdrich's *Tracks*," 35.
6. "A Continuing Tangle of History and Myth," *Philadelphia Enquirer*, February 6, 1994, sec. K, p. 2.

lapping, circling back and forth through time and crossing one another in ways that are often ingenious and occasionally confusing. —Mark Childress[7]

In *The Antelope Wife,* Erdrich has written her most cryptic and unfathomable book thus far, and one has a hard time telling whether she is aiming to show us the secret hand of destiny or has taken on more than she knows how to handle. . . . If in the earlier books you needed a genealogical chart to keep track of characters, in *The Antelope Wife* you need a computer program to stay on top of them all. —Mark Shechner[8]

"Confusing." "Circular." "Continuous." "Serpentlike." "Thick with characters." "Tangled." "Shaggy." "Chaotic." "Overlapping." "Circling back and forth." "Cryptic." "Unfathomable." If these are the words used by professional readers, we can imagine how students and lay readers might feel as they try to make their way through an Erdrich novel. Who are all these characters? How are they related? What do they do? When do they do it? Such basic questions are troubling enough when we read one novel, but they become even more bewildering when we encounter other novels in which some of these same characters and incidents appear, mixed with new ones.

The purpose of this book is to offer a guide to Louise Erdrich's world, bringing information from all six novels together in one place. (Our book deals only with Erdrich's single-author novels, not works she coauthored with Dorris.) This guide is intended primarily for first-time readers of Erdrich's fiction. It will also be of interest to more advanced scholars who wish to compare its geographical notes, genealogies, chronologies, and dictionary entries with their own interpretations. There have been earlier attempts to chart the characters and events of Erdrich's novels, but they have been limited in scope and are often too compressed for clarity.[9]

7. "A Gathering of Widows," *New York Times,* May 12, 1996, sec. 7, p. 10.
8. "*The Antelope Wife,* Erdrich's Indian 'X-Files,'" *Buffalo News,* May 24, 1998.
9. See, for example, figure 1, "Central Biological Relationships in *Love Medicine, The Beet Queen,* and *Tracks,*" in Hertha D. Wong's "Adoptive Mothers and Thrown-Away Children in the Novels of Louise Erdrich," 178; Peter G. Beidler's "Three Student Guides to Louise Erdrich's *Love Medicine*"; the chart called "Family Trees in *Love Medicine*" in Kenneth Lincoln's *Indi'n Humor: Bicultural Play in Native America,* 225; and Margie Towery's "Continuity and Connection: Characters in Louise Erdrich's Fiction." This last article is particularly useful, even though the appendices conflate the characters from the various novels into single charts. In the present book, except for our frontispiece chart, which integrates genealogical information from four of the six novels, we have operated on the assumption that it is more useful to have the information on each novel kept separate.

This book grows out of our own conviction that beneath the seeming chaos of story and character in Erdrich's novels lies a series of interlocking patterns, a carefully crafted web of more-than-Faulknerian complexity—as mazelike as life itself, yet ordered by Erdrich's genius. Our attempt to trace patterns through this complexity seems warranted by certain images within the novels themselves, images that invite the reader to look for connections and order within apparent chaos. In *The Bingo Palace,* for example, Gerry Nanapush recognizes that the seeming randomness of chance events actually reveals a pattern when seen from the right perspective:

> He knew from sitting in the still eye of chance that fate was not random. Chance was full of runs and soft noise, pardons and betrayals and double-backs. Chance was patterns of a stranger complexity than we could name, but predictable. There was no such thing as a complete lack of order, only a design so vast it seemed unrepetitive up close, that is, until you sat doing nothing for so long that your brain ached and, one day, just maybe, you caught a wider glimpse.[10]

Similarly, in *Love Medicine* Albertine Johnson discerns a meaningful pattern in the throbbing tumult of the Northern Lights:

> Pale green licks of light pulsed and faded across it. Living lights. Their fires lobbed over, higher, higher, then died out in blackness. At times the whole sky was ringed in shooting points and puckers of light gathering and falling, pulsing, fading, rhythmical as breathing. All of a piece. As if the sky were a pattern of nerves and our thought and memories traveled across it. As if the sky were one gigantic memory for us all.[11]

For Nanapush in *Tracks,* all the stories are connected, like a snake swallowing its own tail:

> I shouldn't have been caused to live so long, shown so much of death, had to squeeze so many stories in the corners of my brain. They're all attached,

10. *The Bingo Palace* (1994; New York: HarperFlamingo, 1998), 226. Subsequent quotations, cited parenthetically in the text, are from this edition, identified as *BP.*

11. *Love Medicine* (1993; New York: HarperFlamingo, 1998), 37. This is the 1993 "New and Expanded Version," not to be confused with the original, shorter 1984 edition, though the wording of this passage has not changed. Subsequent quotations are from the 1993 version, identified as *LM.*

and once I start there is no end to telling because they're hooked from one side to the other, mouth to tail.[12]

In the closing paragraph of *The Antelope Wife* the narrator seeks to understand the nature of the pattern in the seemingly random beadwork of human existence:

> Did these occurrences have a paradigm in the settlement of the old scores and pains and betrayals that went back in time? Or are we working out the minor details of a strictly random pattern? Who is beading us? Who is setting flower upon flower and cut-glass vine? Who are you and who am I, the beader or the bit of colored glass sewn onto the fabric of this earth?[13]

That Erdrich gives us no definite answers to such questions suggests that the confusion her readers sometimes experience results as much from the disarray of the human condition as from the complexity of style of the writer seeking meaning within it.

This guide is designed to help readers trace the patterns and connections in the seemingly chaotic vista of Erdrich's world. A book such as this, however, should never be allowed to tame the rich complexity of human experience that Erdrich provides for us. We would not wish to strip her fiction of its beauty nor to deprive readers of the fun of figuring out for themselves what is going on in her narratives. We would thus urge our readers to use this guide only after reading, enjoying, and puzzling out the novels for themselves. We do hope, however, that those who, after their own encounter with Erdrich's texts, still have questions about her story lines and characters will find in these pages some sense of direction.

As the group-narrator in the first chapter of *The Bingo Palace* tells us, "no one gets wise enough to really understand the heart of another, though it is the task of our life to try" (*BP,* 6). Our primary purpose in the charts and summaries, the dictionary and bibliography of this guide is to provide assistance to those readers who are trying to understand the hearts of Louise Erdrich's characters.

12. *Tracks* (1988; New York: HarperFlamingo, 1998), 46. Subsequent quotations are from this edition, identified as *Tr.*

13. *The Antelope Wife* (New York: HarperFlamingo, 1998), 240. Subsequent quotations are from this edition, identified as *AW.*

For *The Beet Queen,* quotations are from the HarperFlamingo edition (New York, 1998) and are identified as *BQ.* For *Tales of Burning Love,* quotations are from the HarperPerennial edition (New York, 1997) and are identified as *TBL.*

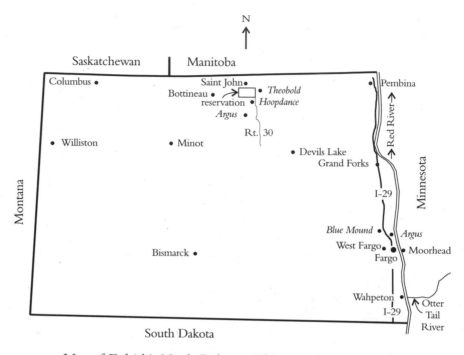

Map of Erdrich's North Dakota. This map shows in regular
type the names of the real towns and cities Erdrich mentions in
her novels. The names of fictional towns are given in italics.

Geography, Genealogy, and Chronology

I

The following geographical notes, genealogical charts, and chronologies of central events are intended to help readers find their way through the often mazelike narratives of Louise Erdrich's novels. This section traces the overarching patterns in the relationship of place to place, character to character, and event to event. To fill in these broad outlines, our readers should refer to the entries for individuals and families in the Dictionary of Characters.

In the present section we first offer a map of Erdrich's North Dakota, along with an account of our decisions about where to locate some of its fictional places, particularly the reservation that figures so prominently in *Love Medicine* and *Tracks* and the off-reservation town of Argus. In the remainder of the section, which is subdivided by novel, we give a brief overview of each novel, present a series of genealogical charts of its most prominent families, and attempt to unscramble and put into roughly chronological order its central events.

GEOGRAPHY

Readers will find the map on the adjacent page helpful as they make their way through Erdrich's novels, particularly the first five, which are set primarily in North Dakota. This map shows the outline of that state and indicates the principle places in it—along with a few just over the Minnesota line—that are mentioned in the novels.

Several of the towns and cities are real places known to anyone familiar with the geography of North Dakota: Williston, Minot, Devils Lake, Grand Forks, and Fargo (embracing West Fargo and, across the Red River in Minnesota, Moorhead). We also show on the map smaller towns mentioned in the novels, like Saint John (where Nanapush gets a Jesuit education), Columbus and Bottineau (through which Lyman Lamartine and Henry Lamartine Junior travel on their way home from Alaska), and Pembina (where Henry Junior drowns in the Red River; also the

9

region of origin of the woman wearing blue beads seen by young Zosie [II] Shawano).

We have put on the map only the highways specifically mentioned in the novels, Route 30 and I-29. The state's other major interstate highway, I-94, which runs west from Fargo through Bismarck and into Montana, is not mentioned in the novels and thus does not appear on the map. The map also does not show towns and cities that Erdrich names but which are located in neighboring states and provinces: Aberdeen, South Dakota; Minneapolis–Saint Paul ("the Twin Cities" or just "the Cities"); Silver Bay, Minnesota, on the northern shore of Lake Superior; and Winnipeg, Manitoba, in Canada.

The reservation itself, shown on our map as a small rectangle in the north-central part of the state, is never named in the novels, though most readers assume that the fictional reservation is modeled on Erdrich's own Turtle Mountain Indian Reservation. Indeed, its location in *Love Medicine* is rather precise. Lyman reports that he and Henry Junior drive "across Idaho then Montana and very soon we were racing the weather right along under the Canadian border through Columbus, Des Lacs, and then we were in Bottineau County and soon home" (*LM*, 184–85). The site of the reservation in *The Bingo Palace* is apparently the same. It is clearly not far from Canada, since Lipsha Morrissey and Shawnee Ray Toose drive up to the Canadian border for their supper date. In both novels, it seems to be a long way from Fargo. In *Love Medicine* Albertine is said to go "all the way down to Fargo on the Jackrabbit bus" (*LM*, 167), where she runs into Henry Junior. Toward the end of *The Bingo Palace* as Lipsha and his father, Gerry Nanapush, flee Fargo and head back toward the reservation, Lipsha plans to "check the oil in Devils Lake" (*BP*, 252), suggesting that the reservation is farther in the same direction. We have thus placed the fictional reservation on the map in approximately the same location as the Turtle Mountain Indian Reservation.

This location is complicated, however, in *Tales of Burning Love*. Toward the end of that novel, Jack Mauser describes the route of Gerry and Lipsha's escape from Fargo differently. Jack speculates that they would drive "toward the home reservation and beyond, to Canada. *Due north*" (*TBL*, 377, emphasis added). In an attempt to catch up with them, Jack himself then heads out of town north on "the interstate" (*TBL*, 380). The Turtle Mountain Reservation is northwest of Fargo, not due north, and is not close to an interstate. Thus, though the "home reservation" referred to in *Tales* is the same as the one in *Love Medicine* and *The Bingo Palace,* in the later novel, Erdrich seems to have changed her mind about its location.

Two fictional towns are mentioned as being near the reservation, but their exact location is not revealed. The near-reservation town most frequently mentioned is Hoopdance. In the opening chapter of *The Bingo Palace,* Erdrich's reader might take Hoopdance to be the name of the on-reservation town, since immediately after visiting the post office at "the heart of the reservation" (*BP,* 1), Lulu Lamartine buys a picture frame from "the fanciest gift shop in Hoopdance" (*BP,* 4). In other references to the town in both this novel and *Tracks,* however, Hoopdance appears to be off-reservation, a few miles away. *The Bingo Palace* places it "straight south" (*BP,* 67). *Tracks* also mentions the fictional town of Theobold as being near the reservation, although we are not told the direction. We have placed it somewhat north of Hoopdance. The town on the reservation—site of the Sacred Heart Convent, the Senior Citizens, the Indian agent's office, and the Coin-Op laundry where Lipsha picks up Shawnee Ray—is never named.

The most problematical town of all is Argus. It is always depicted as being fairly close to the reservation, but like the site of the reservation itself, its location shifts. Argus is not mentioned in *Love Medicine,* but it figures prominently in *Tracks,* where it is said to be "a few miles south" of the reservation (*Tr,* 12). It is apparently not too far, since Bernadette and Napoleon Morrissey come "down [from the reservation] to Argus one day" in a wagon to get supplies (*Tr,* 63), and when Fleur Pillager returns home from Argus, she walks (*Tr,* 34). In *The Beet Queen,* as well, the distance between town and reservation is not great. When Celestine James, Mary Adare, and Dot Adare leave the reservation and return to Argus, Mary says, "We drove twenty miles in silence . . . until around the turnoff to Argus" (*BQ,* 203).

Two references to Argus in *The Beet Queen* also locate the town up north, near the site of the Turtle Mountain Reservation. When Sita Kozka Bohl is kidnapped from her Argus wedding and taken to the reservation, the kidnappers' route is "north on Highway 30" (*BQ,* 98), and when Karl Adare leaves Argus, Celestine assumes that he takes a bus or hitchhikes "down Highway 30 south" (*BQ,* 139). Highway 30 runs due south from the eastern side of the Turtle Mountain Reservation. It comes nowhere near Fargo.

Throughout most of *The Beet Queen,* however, near Fargo is just where Argus is located. In the opening pages of the novel, the town is said to be "in eastern North Dakota" (*BQ,* 1). It is apparently not too far north of Fargo, since Jimmy Bohl, while he is courting Sita Kozka, drives "down from Argus" (*BQ,* 83) to Fargo whenever Sita is modeling in a style show. This would be a regular occurrence, since modeling for DeLendrecies is Sita's job, and he would be unlikely to make such frequent trips if Argus were up near the Canadian border. The novel also refers to a new bypass "that connected the town with the interstate" (*BQ,* 312), and as mentioned, the north-central reservation site is not near an interstate. The interstate referred to is presumably I-29, running north and south through Fargo along the eastern border of the state. The proximity of Argus to Fargo is also suggested by the route of Father Jude Miller as he comes to town by train from Minneapolis. After the train crosses the border into North Dakota, it turns "upward in a long curve that brought him to Argus" (*BQ,* 312). The primary train lines from Minneapolis into North Dakota cross the state line at Moorhead-Fargo. One of these lines veers to the north at the western edge of Fargo and runs parallel to I-29. Father Miller's route thus also suggests a location for Argus to the north of Fargo along I-29.

The association of Argus with I-29 is made more explicit in *Tales of Burning Love.* In 1992 Jack Mauser's construction company is about to begin "an overpass and access road down near Argus" (*TBL,* 151; see also 12). Two years later, Jack's name is mentioned specifically in connection with I-29 (*TBL,* 126). Moreover, the Argus in *Tales of Burning Love,* like that of *The Beet Queen,* is not a great distance from Fargo. When Jack and Dot Mauser drive up from Fargo to Argus to pick up Eleanor Schlick Mauser, they go and return in the same day (see *TBL,* 70–78). In both *The Beet Queen* and *Tales of Burning Love,* the fictional town of Argus may be modeled roughly after the real town of Argusville, just fifteen miles or so due north of Fargo. Like the fictional Argus, Argusville is on a railway line and is connected by a short link with I-29.

Because the reservation is consistently depicted as being just a short distance north of Argus (about twenty miles, according to Mary Adare's account), this second location for Argus reinforces the idea of an alternate location for the reservation. Thus, while *Love Medicine, Tracks,* and *The Bingo Palace* appear to place the reservation in the area of the real Turtle Mountain Reservation, *The Beet Queen* (with two exceptions) and *Tales of Burning Love* suggest that it is close to the eastern border of North Dakota, not far north of Fargo. On our map, however, we have shown only one reservation. We have indicated the ambiguity of its location by showing two fictional towns of Argus. We placed the fictional town of Blue Mound near the southeasterly Argus, since it is mentioned in *The Beet Queen* as being "the next town over" from Argus (*BQ*, 126) and "thirteen miles" away (*BQ*, 266). The other fictional near-reservation towns we placed near the north-central reservation site.

Readers should not be upset by the indeterminate location of the reservation and Argus. It may well be that Erdrich did not want us to identify the reservation in her novels with the Turtle Mountain Indian Reservation and thus purposefully worked in some inconsistencies. The world she creates is, after all, a fictional world. Like Garrison Keillor's Lake Wobegon, it need not be expected to coincide exactly with real locations in real states.

We do show on the map one real town that Erdrich does not mention in her novels, the town of Wahpeton, on the eastern border of the state. Because her parents taught in a Bureau of Indian Affairs school in Wahpeton, Erdrich spent much of her youth there. It is worth mentioning that just across the river from Wahpeton, Minnesota's Otter Tail River empties into the Red River. In *The Antelope Wife*, the dog carrying the baby who is later named Matilda Roy runs off onto "the vast carcass of the world west of the Otter Tail River." Scranton Roy, the cavalry soldier, "followed and did not return" (*AW*, 3). Thus it would seem that some of the key events even of her sixth novel take place not in Minnesota but in what is now North Dakota, close to the border country that Erdrich knew well from her youth.

GENEALOGY AND CHRONOLOGY

Just as the above map and geographical notes are meant to help readers negotiate Erdrich's spaces, so the following genealogical charts and chronologies are "maps" to help them untangle the knots of her intertwined family relationships and interwoven strands of time and event. Because any attempt to create an all-encompassing chronology or set of genealogical charts for the six novels might create a product more bewildering than the novels themselves, we generally base the charts for each novel only on information in that novel. Where the information for a given family is inconsistent from novel to novel, the genealogical charts reflect those inconsistencies. Also, information about a character's family not available in one novel is omitted from the charts for that novel, but may be revealed in the charts for another novel—Lulu's paternity, for example, or Marie's real parents (compare Charts 2 and 3 with Charts 7 and 8).

In a similar effort to avoid confusion, the genealogical charts group characters into separate families, even though some of these characters appear in more than one chart. In the *Love Medicine* charts, for example, Chart 1 shows where Nector and Marie Kashpaw fit into the Kashpaw family, while Chart 2 shows their relationship with the Lazarre clan. Not all family members appear in a given genealogy. Of Lulu's nine children and many liaisons, for example, only those specifically referred to in *Love Medicine* appear in Chart 3. Henry and Beverly Lamartine's older brother Slick is also omitted from that chart, because he does not figure significantly in the novel.

In all genealogical charts double lines between two boxes (===) indicate either Indian or Western-style marriage; broken double lines (====) indicate nonmarital sexual liaisons; single lines (——) indicate children resulting from these unions. Thus, for example, the broken and unbroken double lines emanating from Lulu in Chart 3 indicate that she had six unions that we know of, some of which were marriages and some nonmarital relationships, and the single lines issuing from those double lines indicate the five children who are specifically mentioned in *Love Medicine*: her first son by Moses Pillager, Gerry, Henry Junior, Lyman, and Bonita.

When exact relationships are unclear, we have indicated those uncertainties with question marks. Thus, the question marks on Charts 7 and 9 indicate the uncertainty of Lulu's paternity.

LOVE MEDICINE

Love Medicine is a series of stories, many of which had been previously published, that first appeared as a novel in 1984. It was revised and expanded in 1993. The various stories fit together into a narrative about several interconnected families that live on and near Erdrich's fictional Indian reservation in northern North Dakota. To understand *Love Medicine* we need to understand the complex interrelationship of three families: the Kashpaws, the Lazarres, and Lulu Nanapush's extended family. Although she freezes to death in the early pages of the first story, June Morrissey is in some ways the central character in the novel since she is connected in important ways to all three families.

One of the central plots of the novel is the rivalry between Lulu Nanapush and Marie Lazarre for the affections of Nector Kashpaw. Marie marries him and has five of his children, but Lulu has an affair with him and has one child by him. Several subplots enrich the novel: Gerry Nanapush's relationships with June and, later, Dot Adare; Beverly Lamartine's love for Lulu resulting in the birth of Henry Junior; Gordie Kashpaw's grief at his ex-wife's death; Albertine Johnson's difficulties in adjusting to her family after June's death; Lyman Lamartine's early efforts as an entrepreneur; and Lipsha Morrissey's surreal efforts to administer love medicine to Nector and to discover who his parents are.

The order of events in *Love Medicine* at first seems confusing. Although Erdrich often gives dates along with the titles to the various stories, and although after the first one, these stories are presented in chronological order, many of them include references to earlier incidents whose dates are unspecified. Thus, in the following summary we have rearranged the novel's most important events and presented them in chronological order. The dates are taken either from the chapter heads or from internal evidence. Where we have guessed at a date we include a parenthetical indicator (?) of the uncertainty. Dates that are uncertain in *Love Medicine* but are revealed in another novel (without contradicting *Love Medicine*) are supplied in square brackets—[1919]. Readers may also be confused by the fact that in the expanded (1993) edition of *Love Medicine* Erdrich has not only added new material but changed some of the old. In the first edition, for example, Eli and Nector are twins, while in the expanded edition Eli is said to be Rushes Bear's "youngest son" (*LM,* 101). That fact is in turn contradicted by information in *Tracks,* where Nector, born about 1908, is said to be the "younger brother" (*Tr,* 39) of Eli, who is born around 1898. There is no question that Erdrich intended the revised and expanded 1993 edition of *Love Medicine* to be definitive, and our guide accordingly uses this version as its standard text. To indicate where large blocks of new material are added in the expanded 1993 edition, we put those events in italics.

Chronology of Events in *Love Medicine*:

1898–1908(?) Nector and Eli Kashpaw are born to the original Kashpaw and Margaret (Rushes Bear).

[1919] Young Lulu Nanapush finds the body of a dead man in the woods.

c. 1920 Marie Lazarre is born.

[1924] *Lulu returns from an off-reservation boarding school as a result of letters written by Nanapush.*

1934 Marie goes to stay at the convent, where Sister Leopolda scalds her

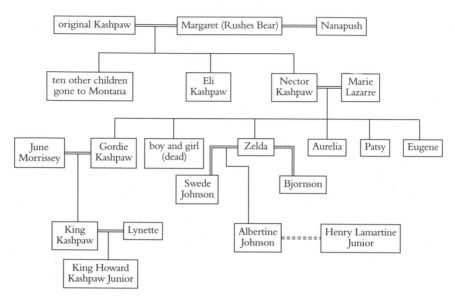

Chart 1. Kashpaw family in Love Medicine.

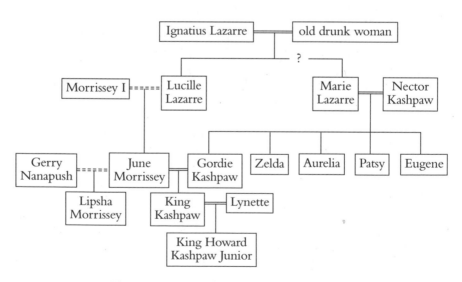

Chart 2. Lazarre family in Love Medicine.

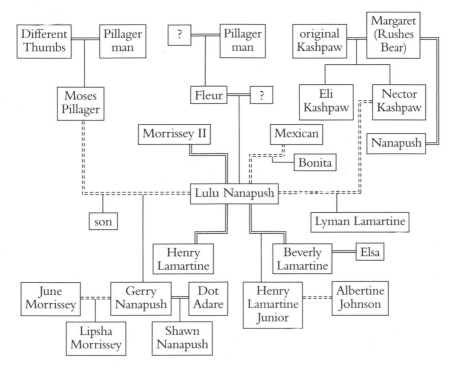

Chart 3. Lulu's extended family in Love Medicine.

back and stabs her in the hand. On her way down the hill not long afterwards, Marie is accosted by Nector Kashpaw.

1934–1935 Marie and Nector marry. Lulu goes to Moses Pillager's island, where she becomes pregnant. Before the baby is born, Lulu leaves Moses and returns to town. Marie and Nector's first child, Gordie, is born.

1935–1936 Lulu's first son by Moses Pillager is born (we do not know his first name, but his last is Nanapush).

1936–1940(?) Son and daughter born to Marie and Nector. (Both die of a fever sometime before 1948.)

c. 1939 June Morrissey is born to Lucille Lazarre and Morrissey I.

1941 Zelda Kashpaw is born to Marie and Nector.

c. 1945 Gerry Nanapush is born to Lulu and Moses.

1948 Lucille Lazarre dies, leaving her daughter June, age nine, to survive on tree sap. Lucille's mother and Morrissey I bring June to Marie to raise. Gordie and Aurelia Kashpaw try to hang June. June goes to live with Eli. *Rushes Bear moves in with Marie and helps her give birth to her last child, a son (Eugene).*

1950 Henry Lamartine is killed by a train. His brother Beverly comes to the funeral and makes love to Henry's widow, Lulu, in a shed after the wake. A boy named Henry Lamartine Junior is born to Lulu nine months later.

1952 Lulu and Nector begin an affair.

c. 1953 Lyman Lamartine is born to Lulu and Nector.

195_(?) *Gordie and June honeymoon at Johnson's motel.*

1957 The Lulu-Nector affair ends, and Lulu marries Beverly, who has come to take Henry Junior home with him. Lulu discovers that Beverly is already married and sends him back to the Twin Cities to get a divorce. Marie takes Zelda to visit Sister Leopolda. Nector burns Lulu's house, and Lulu is made bald as she rescues their son, Lyman, from the fire.

c. 1958 Albertine Johnson is born to Zelda and Swede Johnson.

196_(?) King Kashpaw is born to June and Gordie.

c. 1963 Bonita is born to Lulu and a Mexican man.

1965(?) Gerry kicks a cowboy in the groin and starts the first of many jail terms.

c. 1965 Lipsha Morrissey is born to Gerry and June, then taken to Marie and Nector to be raised.

1969(?) Henry Junior and Lyman buy a red convertible.

1970 Henry Junior goes to Vietnam.

1973 Henry Junior returns from Vietnam. He and Albertine chance to meet in Fargo, where Albertine loses her virginity to him.

1974 Henry Junior drowns himself in the Red River, watched by Lyman, who is unable to save him. *Lyman goes on a one-year drinking binge before starting to work for the Bureau of Indian Affairs and becoming involved in tribal politics and business.*

1979–1980(?) King Howard Kashpaw Junior is born to Lynette and King Kashpaw.

1980 Shawn Nanapush is born to Gerry and Dot (Adare) Nanapush. Gerry kills(?) a trooper.

1981 June is picked up in Williston by a mud engineer who says his name is Andy. June tries to walk home, but freezes to death. King buys a new car with the insurance money. The Kashpaw family assembles at the old Kashpaw place. Gordie gets drunk, hits a deer with his car, and believes that he has killed June.

1982 Lulu, Marie, and Nector all live at the Senior Citizens. Nector chokes to death on a raw turkey heart brought by Lipsha as love medicine. Marie moves back into the Kashpaw house for a time. *Gordie comes home drunk, drinks Lysol, and apparently dies.* Marie helps Lulu after Lulu's eye surgery.

1983 *Lyman's tomahawk factory venture ends in an interfamily brawl. Lyman makes plans for a bingo hall on the reservation.*

1984 Lipsha learns from Lulu that Gerry and June are his parents and that Lulu is his grandmother. Lipsha visits his half brother, King, in Minneapolis, wins King's insurance-money car in a poker game, helps Gerry escape to Canada in the car, and then brings "her" home.

THE BEET QUEEN

The Beet Queen is a loosely structured episodic novel. Like *Love Medicine,* it is a compilation of stories or chapters, some of which had been previously published as separate stories. Some of the cameo characters— Fleur Pillager, Eli and Russell Kashpaw—are reservation Indians, but they play only a small role in the novel. Key characters such as the Adares, the Kozkas, and Wallace Pfef are white. Celestine James, the mixed-blood daughter of a Chippewa woman and a white man, is the mother of the "Beet Queen," Dot Adare (the same Dot who is married to Gerry Nanapush in *Love Medicine* and Jack Mauser in *Tales of Burning Love*). Karl Adare is Dot's father. Thus Dot is part Chippewa, but she has virtually no on-reservation experiences apart from a few visits to her uncles Eli and Russell. (Eli and Russell are said to be half brothers in this novel, although in the genealogies of *Love Medicine* and *Tracks* they appear to be uncle and nephew.) Nevertheless, even though *The Beet Queen* is mostly about white characters in a white setting, it is in some ways informed by an Indian consciousness and an awareness of Indian history in a community now dominated by white values. The novel is set in the forty-year period from 1932 to 1972, mostly in the fictional town of Argus, North Dakota.

Although we find a characteristic Erdrichian humor in *The Beet Queen* (particularly in the tales of Chez Sita, the naughty box, the Christmas pageant, and the birthday party), there is also a pervasive note of loneliness and dislocation. Its characters and families are separated and do not much love one another. Letters are written but not sent, sent but delivered to the wrong people, or delivered too late. Gifts are sent but intercepted or used for the wrong purposes. The three Adare children in particular— Karl, Mary, and Jude—are in a state of perpetual dislocation. After being abandoned first by their father and then by their mother, they are separated and spend the rest of the novel not quite getting back together again.

The dislocation of the characters is offset, however, by the growing love that Celestine feels for her daughter. That love is expressed, with an image characteristic of Erdrich, as a web. As Celestine feeds her newborn baby she notices a spider in Dot's hair: "It was a delicate thing, close to transparent, with long sheer legs. It moved so quickly that it seemed to vibrate, throwing out invisible strings and catching them, weaving its own tensile strand. Celestine watched as it began to happen. A web was forming, a complicated house, that Celestine could not bring herself to destroy" (*BQ*, 176). Sixteen years later, the developing web of love that joins Celestine with her infant daughter draws Dot to her mother: "In her eyes I see the force of her love. It is bulky and hard to carry, like a package that keeps untying. . . . I walk to her, drawn by her, unable to help myself" (*BQ*, 337). Love ultimately triumphs in this novel, if not for the white family that never finds its way back together, then for the part-Indian characters, who discover the medicine that joins them.

Chronology of Events in *The Beet Queen*:

c. 1918 Karl Adare is born.

c. 1920 Sita Kozka is born.

c. 1921 Mary Adare is born.

1932 Mr. Ober dies, possibly by suicide. Adelaide Adare, pregnant with her third child by Ober, moves with Karl and Mary to Minneapolis. At the Orphans' Picnic she flies away with stunt pilot Omar, abandoning her three children. Martin and Catherine Miller steal the baby and name him Jude. Karl and Mary take a train to Argus, where Mary stays with Pete, Fritzie, and Sita Kozka. Karl leaps from the boxcar and breaks his feet. Fleur Pillager cares for him and takes him to the nuns on the reservation. They send him to Minneapolis to Saint Jerome's orphanage. Later that year, Mary causes a "miracle" image of Christ to appear in the ice at the school playground in Argus.

19__(?) Russell Kashpaw returns "from a war," wounded. Mary falls in love with Russell, but he does not cooperate. [For chronological problems, see the dictionary entry on Russell Kashpaw.]

1941 Pete and Fritzie Kozka move south because of Fritzie's health, leaving their butcher shop to Mary. Sita moves to Fargo and starts a modeling career.

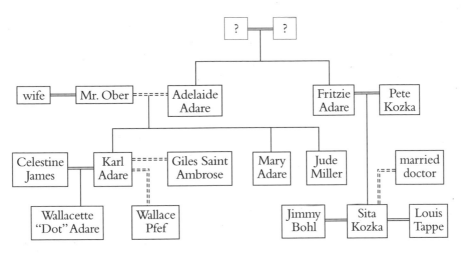

Chart 4. Adare family in The Beet Queen.

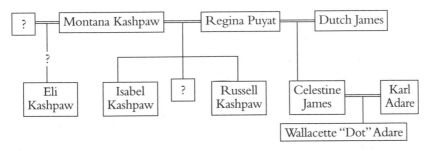

Chart 5. Kashpaw-James family in The Beet Queen.

1948 Karl sees his brother, Jude Miller, in Minneapolis, for the first time since 1932.

1950 Sita ends a three-year affair with a married doctor. After reading a letter addressed to her parents from Catherine Miller, Sita goes to Jude's ordination as a deacon (later to become a priest) but does not introduce herself. Sita writes Catherine Miller a letter but never mails it.

1950(?) Sita marries Jimmy Bohl, a restaurant owner.

1952 Wallace Pfef meets Karl Adare in Minneapolis, and they make love in Karl's hotel room. Karl injures his back in a fall.

1953 Russell Kashpaw, even more wounded from military service in Korea, is released from the VA hospital. Karl Adare comes to Argus to look for his sister Mary, but meets Celestine James instead. He and Celestine have a brief affair, and she becomes pregnant. Russell goes to live with Eli Kashpaw on the reservation. Divorced from Jimmy Bohl, Sita opens Chez Sita. Sita marries Louis Tappe.

Winter 1953–1954 Russell has a stroke.

January 1954 Wallacette ("Dot") Adare is born to Celestine, who marries Dot's father, Karl, merely as a formality and returns to Argus without him.

1960 Dot is in first grade. She attacks another schoolchild, is put in the teacher's "naughty box," and is avenged by her aunt, Mary.

Summer 1961 Karl sends Dot a wheelchair, which her mother gives to Russell.

1964 Dot plays the role of Joseph in an ill-fated school Christmas play. Adelaide bloodies her feet in a glass-breaking rage in Florida.

19__(?) Sita loses her voice but is "cured" in the mental hospital. [For chronological problems, see the dictionary entry on Sita Kozka Bohl Tappe.]

1965 Wallace Pfef has a birthday party for the eleven-year-old Dot.

1968 Karl comes to Argus and has breakfast with Celestine and the fourteen-year-old Dot.

1972 Celestine dreams that Sita is sick, and she and Mary go to Blue Mound to help her. Celestine finds and mails Sita's 1950 letter to Catherine Miller. On the day of the Beet Parade (July), Sita takes an overdose of pain pills and dies. Celestine and Mary go to the Beet Festival, with Sita's body propped in the front seat of the delivery truck. Father Jude Miller and Karl Adare come to town and attend the festival, where Karl is reunited with his former lover Wallace. Dot is crowned Beet Queen.

TRACKS

Tracks takes us back to a time before the events of either *The Beet Queen* or *Love Medicine*. It reveals such background material as the origins of Marie Lazarre and Lulu Nanapush, two of the dominant women in *Love Medicine;* the early activities of Nector as he learns the politics of dealing with the dominant white society; Sister Leopolda's early life under a different name; and the loss of a large portion of reservation land to the lumber companies. The alternating narrators of the story are Nanapush, a survivor of the consumption epidemic of 1912, and Pauline Puyat, a mixed white-Indian girl ashamed of her Indian blood.

Nanapush is a generally truthful narrator who is telling Lulu, now a young woman, the story of her family background. His motives are to convince her that she should not hate her mother, Fleur Pillager, for apparently abandoning her and that she should not marry the Morrissey man she is planning to wed. Pauline's motives in narrating her chapters are not so clear, but she seems to want to justify or cover up her own fanatical, and even murderous, actions. She seems as eager to distort the truth as to reveal it. Both narrators focus on Fleur, who has an uncanny ability to survive death herself while attracting others to their own deaths.

Tracks is set in the twelve-year period from 1912 to 1924, mostly on the reservation but partly in fictional Argus, North Dakota. Some of the relationships among its main characters are difficult to pin down. Nanapush tells us that Fleur and Moses Pillager are cousins, but "far cousins, related not so much by blood as by name and chance survival" (*Tr*, 33), and he describes his own heritage in these terms: "I was a vine of a wild grape that twined the timbers and drew them close. Or maybe I was a branch, coming from the Kashpaws, that lived long enough to touch the next tree over, which was Pillagers" (*Tr*, 33). The primary relationships between Nanapush and the Pillager family are also in name rather than blood, as indicated in the first two charts below. Nanapush names Fleur's daughter after himself, although he is not the father, and after the nickname of his own daughter, "Lulu," who had died in 1912. This second Lulu, whose paternity is in question, is a central character in *Love Medicine* and appears again in *The Bingo Palace*.

Chronology of Events in *Tracks*:

c. 1862 Nanapush is born.

c. 1895 Fleur Pillager is born.

c. 1898 Pauline Puyat is born.

c. 1898 Eli Kashpaw is born to Kashpaw and Margaret.

Early 1900s Fleur nearly drowns the first time. Russell Kashpaw is born to Regina Puyat and one of the Montana Kashpaws.

c. 1908 Nector Kashpaw is born to Kashpaw and Margaret.

c. 1910 Fleur nearly drowns the second time.

Spring 1912 Pauline goes to Argus and works in Pete and Fritzie Kozka's butcher shop.

Winter 1912–1913 Consumption ravages the reservation, wiping out Nanapush's and Fleur's families. Nanapush rescues the nearly dead Fleur and nurses her back to life.

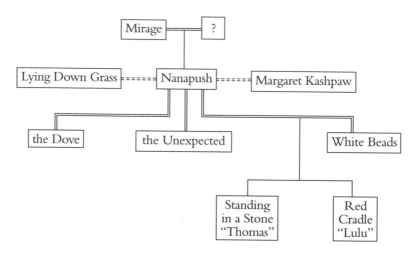

Chart 6. Nanapush's extended family in Tracks.

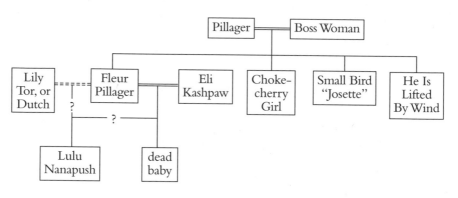

Chart 7. Fleur's family in Tracks.

Summer 1913 Fleur goes to Argus, works at Kozka's, and in off-hours plays poker with Lily Veddar, Tor Grunewald, and Dutch James. After weeks of her winning, the men get drunk and attack her. When a tornado strikes the next day, the three men seek shelter in the freezer, where Lily and Tor freeze to death. Dutch James survives but loses parts of his arms and legs.

Fall–Winter 1913 Fleur returns to Matchimanito Lake. Eli Kashpaw falls in love with Fleur and goes to Nanapush for a love medicine. Eli

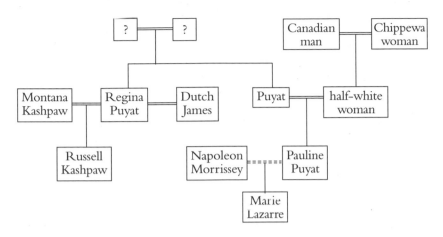

Chart 8. Puyat family in Tracks.

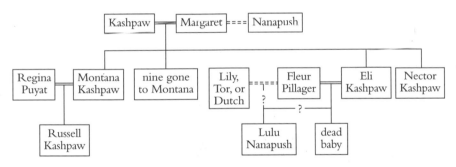

Chart 9. Kashpaw family in Tracks.

and Fleur's relationship begins. In December, Pauline returns to the reservation, where she lives with Bernadette Morrissey's family.

1913–1914 Pauline begins to accompany Bernadette Morrissey on her missions to care for the dying.

Spring 1914 Lulu is born to Fleur.

Autumn 1917 Pauline bewitches Sophie Morrissey and Eli Kashpaw so that they make love. Sophie goes into a trance in front of Fleur's house, and Fleur banishes Eli, who goes to live with Nanapush.

Winter 1917–1918 During this famine winter, Nanapush sends Eli off to hunt moose and sends his own spirit to guide him. Pauline begins a sexual relationship with Napoleon Morrissey. Boy Lazarre and Clarence Morrissey capture Margaret Kashpaw and Nanapush

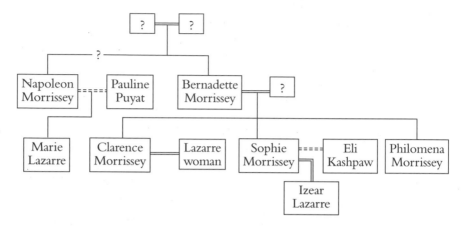

Chart 10. Morrissey family in Tracks.

and shave Margaret's head. In the struggle Margaret bites Lazarre's hand, giving him a case of blood poisoning that eventually kills him. Nanapush snares Clarence with a piano wire. By Ash Wednesday, Nanapush and Margaret are keeping company.

1918 Pauline, pregnant by Napoleon, tries to abort the baby but eventually gives birth to Marie. She abandons the baby and enters the convent. Bernadette keeps Marie to raise.

Winter 1918–1919 Pauline believes she hears a message from Jesus. She mortifies her flesh in a variety of ways. Fleur gives birth prematurely, and her baby dies. Going for help, Lulu suffers frostbite. In this second famine winter, Margaret and Nanapush stay with Fleur and Eli. The Kashpaw-Pillager families are saved from starvation by government commodities. They work together to collect money for fee payments on their land allotments.

Spring 1919 The Kashpaw-Pillager families send Margaret and Nector to town with the cash for land fees, but Nector pays the fees only on the Kashpaw land. Pauline goes out on Matchimanito Lake to confront the devil. Later, ashore, she kills the drunken Napoleon. Lulu finds his body in the woods, but keeps it a secret. Surveyors eventually find Napoleon's corpse.

Fall 1919 The lumber company begins cutting timber on Pillager land, and Nanapush learns that Nector has not paid the fees on the Pillager land. Fleur tries to drown herself (her third near-drowning), but Eli rescues her. Margaret sends Nector and Fleur sends Lulu away to government school. Fleur sabotages the lumber company's equipment and leaves the reservation.

1924 Nanapush, who has become tribal chairman, uses his influence to bring Lulu back from the off-reservation school.

[1940s(?)] Lulu is about to marry a Morrissey man, and Nanapush tells her the story of her family.

THE BINGO PALACE

The Bingo Palace appears to pick up a few years after the last events recounted in the expanded *Love Medicine*. Gerry Nanapush, who has been at large, is recaptured; Lipsha Morrissey, who is drifting aimlessly through life, returns to the reservation at the summons of his grandmother Lulu Lamartine; Zelda Kashpaw has become the family tyrant; and Lyman Lamartine continues his ambitions to get rich regardless of the cost. To these familiar faces Erdrich adds some memorable new characters, particularly Shawnee Ray Toose and her small son, Redford.

The dominant plot of *The Bingo Palace* is Lipsha's Quixotic love for Shawnee Ray, a love complicated by the rivalry of Lipsha's kinsman and employer, Lyman, and by Shawnee Ray's own uncertainty. Several important subplots enrich the novel, such as Xavier Toose's unrequited burning love for Zelda and Lipsha's continued resentment of his dead mother, June Morrissey. The latter subplot culminates in a sometimes comic winter chase in which Gerry and Lipsha follow June's ghostly lead across the snow-engulfed plains—an incident that recalls June's death in the opening sequence of *Love Medicine*.

The Bingo Palace takes place in the course of about a year. Abandoning her usual practice of dating the chapters, however, in this novel Erdrich does not specify the time of the action. At one point Zelda remembers watching Lulu's house burn thirty years earlier, an event that happened, as we know from *Love Medicine*, in 1957. Thus, in relation to the events in *Love Medicine*, *The Bingo Palace* seems to be set in the late 1980s. In relation to the events in the next novel, *Tales of Burning Love*, however, the events in *The Bingo Palace* take place in 1994–1995. There is no way to bring the events of all three novels into perfect sequence, nor should we try to do so. We should, rather, accept each novel on its own terms and not worry overmuch about disjunctions in the three-novel narrative sequence.

In addition to the "present time" events in *The Bingo Palace*, which take place between one midwinter and the next, earlier events are

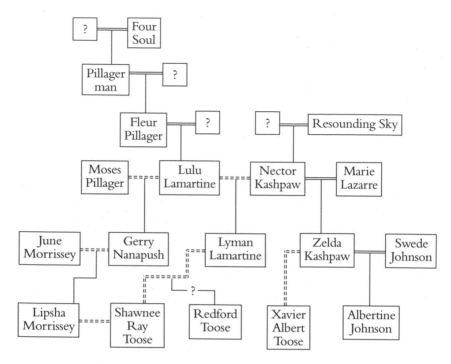

Chart 11. Lipsha's family in The Bingo Palace.

also related as memories or flashbacks. Even though the exact times of the events in this novel are uncertain, the sequence of its present-time events is the most straightforward and unambiguous of any of the six novels.

Summary of Events before the "Present Time" of *The Bingo Palace*:

[1930s(?)] Fleur Pillager returns to the reservation in a fancy Pierce-Arrow car with a little white boy and, in a poker game with the retired Indian agent, wins back the Pillager land on Matchimanito Lake.

[1940s] As a child, June Morrissey is raped by Leonard, her mother's boyfriend.

[Late 1950s] Xavier Albert Toose woos Zelda Kashpaw, but she spurns him. In his final effort to win her one snowy winter night, several of Xavier's fingers freeze.

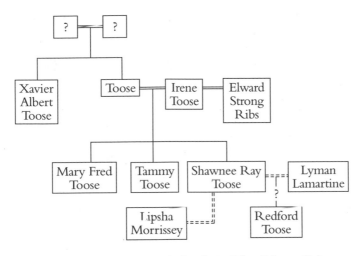

Chart 12. *Shawnee Ray's family in* The Bingo Palace.

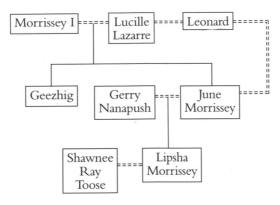

Chart 13. *June's family in* The Bingo Palace.

[c. 1965] According to one story (Zelda's), Lipsha Morrissey's mother,
   June, tries to drown him as a baby, and Zelda rescues him.

19__(?) As a teenager, Shawnee Ray Toose becomes pregnant while
   dating four different men. The presumed father is Lyman Lamartine.

19__(?) As the novel opens, Shawnee Ray's father is dead, her mother
   has remarried and moved to Minot, and Shawnee Ray and her son,
   Redford, are living with Zelda, who is Lyman's half sister. Shawnee
   Ray is attending junior college.

Sequence of "Present Time" Events in *The Bingo Palace*:

Lulu Lamartine sends to her grandson Lipsha, now living in Fargo, a photocopy of a Wanted poster of his father, Gerry Nanapush. Lipsha returns to the reservation in "June's car" on the night of the winter powwow, where he falls in love with Shawnee Ray.

Marie Kashpaw gives Lipsha the ceremonial pipe of his adoptive grandfather, Nector. On his first date with Shawnee Ray, Lipsha is held at the Canadian border, suspected of transporting hashish. Lyman rescues him and gives him a job at the bingo parlor.

Zelda tells Lipsha her "tale of burning love" about the courtship of Xavier Toose and the story of how she rescued the infant Lipsha from the slough. That night, the ghost of Lipsha's mother, June, shows up and gives Lipsha bingo tickets in trade for "her" car.

Lipsha angers the gas station clerk, Marty, and makes love to Shawnee Ray in a motel room. Playing with June's bingo tickets the next night, Lipsha wins the bingo van, which Marty and his friends vandalize. Lyman gambles away a large amount of tribal money at a Nevada casino and cheats the gullible Lipsha out of his bingo winnings. Lipsha goes to see Shawnee Ray at Zelda's house, where they make love on her bedroom floor.

Shawnee Ray leaves Redford with her sisters while she is gone to dance in a powwow competition. Lyman and Zelda get a court order giving them custody and have Redford forcibly removed from the Toose sisters.

Lipsha asks Fleur for a love medicine. Instead, Fleur—in the form of a bear—instructs him about love and the sacred value of the land.

Shawnee Ray returns home and is staying again with Redford at Zelda's house. Lipsha and Lyman go on a vision quest, but Lipsha's "vision" is a skunk. Shawnee Ray leaves Zelda, takes Redford, and enrolls in the university.

In January, Gerry Nanapush escapes again and calls Lipsha. In Fargo Lipsha and Gerry steal a car for a getaway vehicle, then discover a baby in the back seat. They evade the police, and in a blizzard the ghost of June shows up in "her" car. Gerry abandons the stolen car and goes off with June. Lipsha zips the baby inside his jacket.

Zelda has a heart attack—or at least a change of heart—and goes to Xavier Toose. Shawnee Ray, now at the university, acknowledges her love for Lipsha.

In the last chapter, just before men come to seize her land, Fleur takes her death-walk across the frozen lake to the Pillager's island. The ending is ambiguous. Fleur takes the place of "the boy out there" (*BP*, 272) on death's road, and Shawnee Ray hears a radio announcement that a "hostage" is found "in good condition" (*BP*, 268), but the reader does not know if this "boy"/"hostage" is Lipsha or the baby. Like Shawnee Ray, readers have to stay tuned.

TALES OF BURNING LOVE

Erdrich's fifth novel, *Tales of Burning Love*, resolves some of the action left hanging at the close of *The Bingo Palace*, which had ended with Lipsha Morrissey and an unidentified baby about to freeze to death in a snowbound car stolen by Gerry Nanapush, who has fled into the blizzard with the ghost of his former lover, June Morrissey. We discover in the course of *Tales of Burning Love* that the protagonists of this novel—Jack Mauser and his five wives—are connected to Gerry, Lipsha, and the baby in a variety of surprising ways. In fact, connections between this and Erdrich's previous novels abound: the opening chapter recapitulates from a different point of view the opening of *Love Medicine*; a character who was near death in *Love Medicine* reappears here, ancient but alive; one of Jack's wives is the protagonist of *The Beet Queen*; and so on. In no other novel does Erdrich weave together so many strands from her five-novel Matchimanito web of plot and character.

Yet despite this interweaving, the chronology of the events in *Tales of Burning Love* cannot be completely coordinated with the events of the previous novels. For example, we learn in *Love Medicine* that Lipsha was born in about 1965, which would make him close to thirty in January 1995, the date of the blizzard in *Tales of Burning Love*. When Jack Mauser rescues him, however, he notices that Lipsha's face is "young, just past twenty maybe" (*TBL*, 386). There is a similar problem with the age of Sister Leopolda. She is said to be 108 when she dies in 1994 in *Tales of Burning Love*, which would put her birth around 1886. By that chronology she would have been around twenty-seven in 1913 when, as Pauline Puyat, she went to Argus to work in the Kozkas' butcher shop. Yet we remember from *Tracks* that in 1913 "I was fifteen, alone, and so poor-looking I was invisible to most customers" (*Tr*, 15). (Another chronological discrepancy is noted in the overview of *The Bingo Palace*, above.)

Some of these inconsistencies might be explained as the misperceptions of characters or as the falsifications of unreliable narrators. Some may reflect the dislocations and misunderstandings that naturally result from the oral transmission of tales from character to character. And some, no doubt, reflect authorial changes of mind or rethinking of certain characters and events. We get the sense that Erdrich herself, working close to an oral tradition, is discovering more about her own characters as she hears tales about them in her own mind and writes their stories. In addition, the indeterminacy of time in *The Bingo Palace* may be seen as something of a transition between the chronology of *Love Medicine, The Beet Queen,* and *Tracks* and the rather different chronology of *Tales of Burning Love.* We point out the discrepancies only to warn readers that they exist and to encourage confused readers not to worry overmuch about them. Erdrich herself has larger truths to tell as she allows her Matchimanito saga and its people to develop.

Tales of Burning Love is set mostly in Fargo, North Dakota, where Jack Mauser, the focal character, has his construction business. Some key scenes, however, take place in fictional Argus, and minor scenes take place on the reservation. Although Jack's father is of German ancestry, his mother is from the reservation, and Jack himself is an enrolled member of the reservation tribe.

Much of the narrative concerns Jack's various loves, told largely from the point of view of his four surviving wives in a narrative setting vaguely reminiscent of Chaucer's *Canterbury Tales.* Because of his experience with five wives, Jack emerges as a kind of modern-day male Wife of Bath. *Tales of Burning Love* is a broadly comic novel with an unrealistically cheerful set of ending sequences. No one freezes to death; characters find or regain true love; even our old friend Sister Leopolda, after dying in the course of the novel, seems at the end headed for beatification.

Many narrative threads interweave in *Tales of Burning Love.* Listed below are some of the events that stand out as keys to an understanding of the development of the narrative. Most of the primary events of the novel take place between the summer of 1994 and the following summer, many of them in the first week of January 1995, but much is revealed along the way about various events from the past.

Chronology of Events in *Tales of Burning Love*:

c. 1962 Eleanor Schlick is born.

c. 1968 Six-year-old Eleanor is rescued from her burning home by her mother.

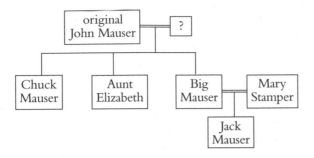

Chart 14. *Jack's family of origin in* Tales of Burning Love.

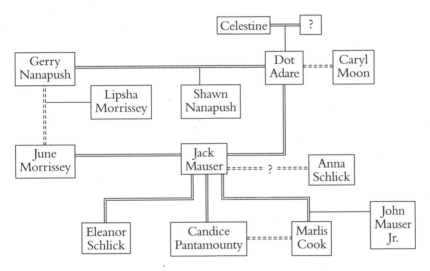

Chart 15. *Jack's wives in* Tales of Burning Love.

c. 1970 Jack Mauser studies engineering at North Dakota State University. In November he nearly freezes to death fighting a fire. Anna Schlick saves his life. Assuming Anna's unfaithfulness, Lawrence Schlick casts out both Anna and their daughter, Eleanor.

1970s Jack leaves school to make money in the construction business. He "blows" his aunt's money.

Late 1970s The teenage Eleanor stomps Jack's hand into broken glass in a store. Later they have a date and make love in his pickup truck. Eleanor and Jack begin an on-and-off relationship, during which she sends him away from time to time.

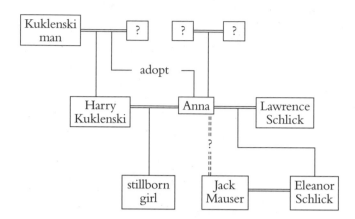

Chart 16. Eleanor's family in Tales of Burning Love.

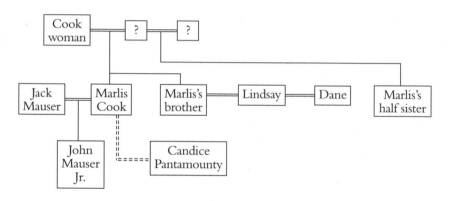

Chart 17. Marlis's family in Tales of Burning Love.

1980–1981 During one of his absences from Eleanor, Jack works for a
   year in western North Dakota, doing construction work in the oil
   fields.

Easter 1981 On Holy Saturday Jack meets June Morrissey Kashpaw in
   Williston, North Dakota. They drink together and get married in a
   bar. June freezes to death attempting to walk home to the reservation.
   The next day Jack helps the police find her body.

Fall 1981 Jack has returned to Fargo. Eleanor pretends to be pregnant
   with his child, and this announcement brings her parents back together. Jack and Eleanor get married in Florida.

1981–198_(?) Jack and Eleanor's marriage is rocky from the start. They fight continually until Eleanor goes to London for a year as an exchange student.

1983 On a winter night Lawrence Schlick sneaks home early from a funerary trade show in Minneapolis, suspicious that his wife may be having an affair with Jack. (She is not.)

Early(?) 1980s Jack begins his own construction company, Mauser and Mauser. Shortly thereafter, Jack encounters Candice Pantamounty at the city dump. A few months later he and Candice marry.

Mid–late(?) 1980s Jack buys Chuck Mauser's land west of Fargo and begins trying to get funding to build a housing development.

Summer 1992 Jack and Candice divorce. Jack performs mouth-to-mouth resuscitation on Marlis Cook after she is electrocuted in an accident. She sues him for not doing it correctly.

August 1992 Jack gets the first check of his housing development loan. Celebrating in a local bar, he runs into Marlis, and they drink together. That night at a motel she steals his loan check. They drive to South Dakota to get married. Marlis deposits Jack's check in her own account. They hide out for a month in Eugene.

September 1992 Jack returns to Fargo, looking for his car. Candice drives him to work and takes his car keys. In anger, Jack bulldozes his uncle Chuck Mauser's sunflowers.

Fall 1992–early 1994 Jack and Marlis travel to various cities as a musical duo. At the same time, Jack continues to oversee his highway construction and housing development projects near Fargo.

Fall 1993 Eleanor Schlick Mauser, now a college professor, seduces one of her undergraduate students. When he reports her for sexual harassment at the end of the semester, she loses her job. Shortly thereafter (perhaps early 1994) she goes to Argus, where she stays at Our Lady of the Wheat Priory and does research on the aged nun Sister Leopolda.

Near Christmas 1993 In Detroit, Marlis realizes that she is pregnant.

Early 1994 (still winter) On their way to Billings, Montana, Marlis tells Jack about her pregnancy. He reacts to the announcement abusively, and in Billings she humiliates him and leaves him.

Early spring 1994 Candice invites Marlis to take a trip with her to northern Minnesota. On that trip she tells Marlis that she wants to adopt the baby Marlis is carrying.

May 1994 Dot Adare Nanapush goes to work for Jack, keeping books for his construction company. Sometime later, after Caryl Moon overturns a Mack truck on Jack's Cadillac, Dot and Jack have their first date.

Spring–summer 1994 John Mauser Jr. is born to Marlis. (Exact date is not given, but he is born by June 1994.) Marlis and Candice become lovers.

June 1994 Without having divorced Gerry Nanapush, Dot marries Jack and brings him to Argus to meet her mother. Eleanor (now in her early thirties) is still living at the Argus convent. One June night about a week after his marriage to Dot, Jack visits Eleanor at the convent, where they make love. Sister Leopolda dies and, in the lightning storm that night, disappears. Two or three weeks later, Eleanor collapses and is hospitalized in Argus.

August 1994 Six weeks after Jack and Dot's wedding, they drive from Fargo to Argus to bring Eleanor back from the hospital. On this trip Dot learns that she is Jack's fifth wife and that he has a child by an earlier wife.

December 31, 1994 Jack's house burns down. Jack escapes, naked, out a basement window, after leaving clues to suggest that he burns to death.

January 1, 1995 The freezing Jack is rescued and then beaten by Caryl Moon. Jack manages to walk to his company's garage, where he slowly recovers.

January 4, 1995 Jack's banker, Hegelstead, visits him in the garage. They agree that Jack should work with Lyman Lamartine on his reservation casino project.

January 5, 1995 Three of Jack's wives attend his funeral at Schlick's Funeral Home. A radio bulletin announces the crash of the small aircraft transporting prisoner Gerry Nanapush. During his own funeral, Jack steals Candice's car and drives off with his son, John Jr. At the railway station, Gerry and his son, Lipsha Morrissey, steal the car, with the baby inside, just as a blizzard breaks. Jack pursues them in a snowplow, heading north on the interstate.

After the funeral, Eleanor, Candice, and Dot drive to the B & B in West Fargo, where they find Marlis. Dot buys pizza for a large Indian woman. Jack's four wives start back to Fargo in the blizzard, pick up a hitchhiker, and about midnight, become stuck in a snowdrift.

January 6, 1995 In the small hours of the morning the four wives keep each other awake and alive by telling scorching stories. Eleanor blows away into the storm, arrives at the airport, and reports the plight of the women in the car. Snowmobilers rescue Dot, Marlis, Candice, and the hitchhiker, but the hitchhiker (Gerry Nanapush) "falls off" on the way to the hospital. Gerry visits his daughter, Shawn, and escapes again on a neighbor's snowmobile. Eleanor, Marlis, and Candice go home, while Dot is kept in the hospital for treatment and observation.

Just before dawn, guided by the ghost of June, Jack rescues his son, John Jr., and June's son, Lipsha Morrissey, from Candice's car, where they are snowbound. They drive north to the reservation.

January 6–(?), 1995 Dot's mother, Celestine, and her Aunt Mary take turns staying with Dot in the hospital.

January 7, 1995 Jack and Lyman agree to work together on Lyman's casino project.

February 1995 Jack calls Dot at her Aunt Mary's and asks to come to see her. She refuses to see him.

March 1995 Jack has leased Chuck Mauser's land back to him, and Chuck once again plants sunflowers. One Saturday morning Jack visits his son, and he and Marlis make love. The same afternoon Jack visits Candice in her dental office.

April 1995 Jack is nearly crushed by a stone statue of the Blessed Virgin that is being delivered to the Argus convent, but he miraculously receives only minor injuries.

July 6, 1995 Father Jude Miller writes to the bishop announcing a miracle connected with the stone Virgin at Argus.

August 1995 Anna Schlick dies, and her husband cremates himself along with her body. Eleanor continues her investigations into the life of Sister Leopolda, funded in part by Lyman. Jack visits Eleanor at her house near the reservation, where they make love. His closing thought compares the pain of June's death by freezing with the pain of his own resurrection to the heat of love.

THE ANTELOPE WIFE

Erdrich's sixth novel, *The Antelope Wife,* takes us away from the characters and settings that have become familiar to us in her five Matchimanito novels. The new novel is set primarily in present-day Minneapolis; in a nineteenth-century Ojibwa village to the west, probably in the eastern Dakotas; and on a reservation somewhere "up north" of Minneapolis. A vague reference to "a Pillager woman" (*AW,* 35) is its one potential connection with the characters from earlier novels. In *The Antelope Wife*

Erdrich gives us a whole new set of intertwined characters and families. Three families dominate: the Roy family, starting in this novel with a Pennsylvania Quaker named Scranton Roy who joins the U.S. Cavalry and takes part in a bloody raid on an Ojibwa village; the Shawano family, descended from Everlasting and his daughter, Magid, an Ojibwa girl who receives an unexpected visit from an Ivory Coast slave; and the Whiteheart Beads family, starting when the grandson of Scranton Roy trades for a wife some red whiteheart beads that give their name to an Indian child.

The central consciousness of *The Antelope Wife* begins the narration with the account of a cavalry soldier who, following a dog with a baby strapped to its back, disappears onto the western prairie: "What happened to him lives on, though fading in the larger memory, and I relate it here in order that it not be lost" (*AW,* 3). The "I," though not identified here, is probably Cally (Whiteheart Beads) Roy, the great-great-granddaughter of that cavalry soldier. Cally later reports that "I am a Roy, a Whiteheart Beads, a Shawano by way of the Roy and Shawano proximity—all in all, we make a huge old family lumped together like a can of those mixed party nuts" (*AW,* 110). Cally believes that "I was sent here to understand and to report" (*AW,* 220) these families' intermingled histories. She appears at the bottom of each of the charts below, though the family relationships that explain her being there are sometimes vague and tangled.

Although the "mixed party nuts" that Cally tells about in this novel are new, many of the approaches, themes, and ambiguities are familiar. We have seen multiple levels of narration in the earlier novels; here we have episodes recounted by dogs. We have seen humanlike animals; here we find people who have deer and antelope for ancestors. We have seen gender-crossing in previous novels; here we have a soldier who suckles two babies. We have seen confused chronology before; here we find only a single reference to a specific year (1945) to help anchor us. We have seen confusing family relationships before; here we have some eight generations of entangled families, including different characters with the same names.

We have also seen Erdrich's use of the Ojibwa language in her earlier fiction; this novel seems to presuppose that the reader has an Ojibwa-English dictionary. We have seen Erdrich's humor; here it takes on new shades and flavors, all sprouting from the conviction that a sense of humor is "an Indian's seventh sense" (*AW,* 115). We have seen

her use of extended metaphors; here we follow from first page to last
the metaphor of DNA-like bead-stitching, making and remaking the
patterns of people's lives.

The genealogical charts for the families in *The Antelope Wife* are more
problematic than those in earlier novels, partly because of the number
of generations involved and partly because Erdrich leaves out many
connections and explanations. For more detail and possible alternate
relationships between characters and families, see their entries in the
Dictionary of Characters.

Although the sequence of some specific events is unclear, it is not
difficult to follow the general order of events in *The Antelope Wife*.
We are assisted by the occasional reference to the age of a character

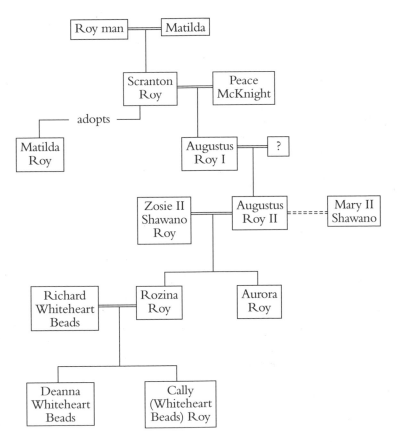

Chart 18. Roy family in The Antelope Wife.

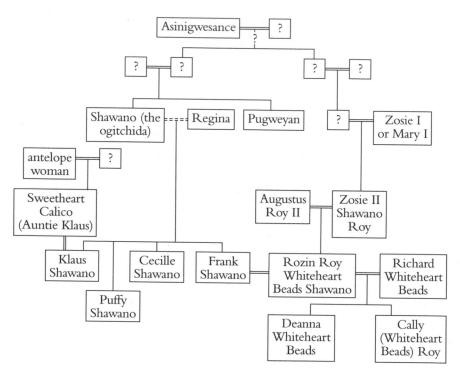

Chart 19. Shawano family in The Antelope Wife.

and by allusions to either history or technology, which suggest general time periods. When we read, for example, about the electronic bar-code scanner at a grocery store or the screen saver on a computer monitor, we assume that the surrounding events take place during the 1990s.

Erdrich also seems to drop some clues about the undated cavalry raid that begins the action. We are told, for example, that Scranton Roy enlists in the U.S. Cavalry at a fort "on the banks of the Mississippi in St. Paul, Minnesota" (*AW*, 4), that the raided village is "due west" of there, that Scranton wears a "dark blue uniform" (*AW*, 4), and that the raid takes place "during the scare over the starving Sioux" (*AW*, 3). Erdrich may be referring obliquely to the time of the U.S. Civil War, specifically to what is sometimes called Little Crow's War in 1862 and its aftermath in 1863. The Santee Sioux, deprived of rations and money promised them in treaties, tried under the leadership of Little Crow to mitigate their plight by attacking towns (especially New Ulm) and forts (especially Fort Ridgely) in Minnesota. Colonel Henry H. Sibley led troops west

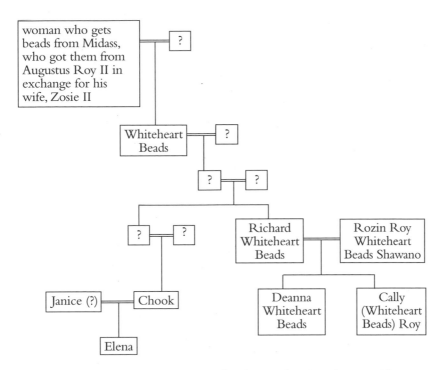

Chart 20. Whiteheart Beads family in The Antelope Wife.

from Fort Snelling in Saint Paul in 1862 (renamed "Ft. Sibley" in the novel). He defeated the Sioux and took many prisoners, thirty-eight of whom were subsequently executed.[1]

That early date and the events of Little Crow's War, however, do not fit precisely with other information in the novel. For one thing, the historical events took place somewhat further south than the likely site of the cavalry raid in *The Antelope Wife,* during which dog, baby, and Scranton flee the village into the open prairie "west of the Otter Tail River" (*AW,* 3). Furthermore, counting back from the 1990s through the generations referred to suggests that the raid took place a good deal later, in the 1880s or 1890s, although we know of no specific historical events so late that match those referred to in the novel. For the purposes

1. These events are summarized in chapter 3, "Little Crow's War," in Dee Brown's widely accessible *Bury My Heart at Wounded Knee: An Indian History of the American West* (New York: Holt, Rinehart, and Winston, 1971; also available in Bantam and other editions).

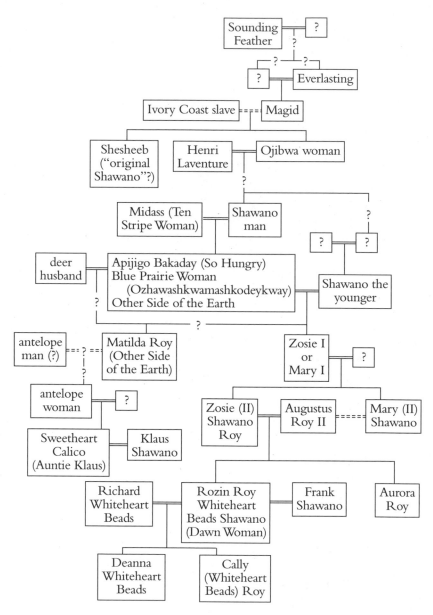

Chart 21. Shawano and Roy families in The Antelope Wife.

of this chronology, we assume the later date for the fictional raid in order to maintain consistency within the chronology.

Rather than attempting to assign specific dates to actions, we have listed them in estimated groupings of decades.

Chronology of Events in *The Antelope Wife*:

1880–1890s(?)

Apijigo Bakaday goes to the woods to forage, cook, and eat. She meets a stag and becomes his wife. Her brothers shoot the stag and bring her back to her people, who name her Blue Prairie Woman.

Scranton Roy is part of a U.S. Cavalry company that attacks Blue Prairie Woman's village, west of Saint Paul, Minnesota (probably in autumn). He kills two children and a grandmother. During the raid, a dog runs west into the open prairie with Blue Prairie Woman's infant daughter tied to its back. Scranton follows the dog.

After continuing west for several days, Scranton settles on the Great Plains. He nurses the baby, whom he names Matilda, at his own breast.

Blue Prairie Woman suckles a puppy of the bitch who had carried off her baby. She is grieving, but when her Shawano husband returns to the village, they become passionate lovers. After a starvation winter, the next spring or summer she gives birth to twin girls, Mary (I) and Josephette (Zosie I). She leaves the babies with her mother, Midass, and sets out to retrieve her first daughter.

Matilda Roy, now six years old, goes to school and meets Peace Mc-Knight, the schoolteacher. Scranton and Peace marry, and Peace becomes pregnant. While pregnant, she falls ill with a fever.

Blue Prairie Woman finds Matilda during the time of Peace's illness, and Matilda, now seven, leaves with her. Matilda falls ill, and then Blue Prairie Woman does also and dies the same day. Matilda recovers and follows a small herd of antelope.

After a difficult labor, Peace gives birth during a blizzard to a boy named Augustus (I). Peace dies, and Scranton nurses his son.

1940–1950s(?)

Scranton Roy, now an old man, receives a dream summons from the old woman he had killed. He sets out to find the remnants of her village, taking his grandson Augustus Roy (II) with him. The villagers are now confined to a reservation.

Augustus (II) falls in love with Zosie (II) Shawano, granddaughter of Blue Prairie Woman. In exchange for Zosie, he gives her great-grandmother Midass red whiteheart beads.

Augustus and Zosie marry, but he also has an ongoing affair with his wife's twin, Mary (II). Zosie becomes pregnant, and Augustus disappears mysteriously. While pregnant, Zosie sees a vision of Blue Prairie Woman and the blue beads. She gives birth to twins, Rozina and Aurora.

1945 Shawano the ogitchida comes home from the war. To avenge the death of his cousin, he captures the German prisoner of war Klaus, who bakes the "blitzkuchen." The clan adopts German Klaus, and Shawano's unborn son is named for him.

When Rozina Roy (Rozin) is five, her twin sister Aurora dies.

1970–1980s(?)

Rozin marries Richard Whiteheart Beads. Their twins, Deanna and Cally, are born.

Klaus Shawano sees an antelope woman and her three daughters at a powwow in Elmo, Montana. He falls in love with her, kidnaps her, and takes her back to Minneapolis. She tries to leave, but can't find her way out of the city. In the city, she is called Sweetheart Calico.

When Deanna and Cally are five, Rozin and Richard move to Minneapolis, where Rozin meets Sweetheart Calico and Frank Shawano. Rozin begins an affair with Frank. Walking in the park, Richard and the twins see Frank and Rozin together. Richard eventually confronts Rozin, and the affair ends.

Richard and Klaus begin a waste disposal company, apparently on the reservation. Richard engages in illegal dumping practices. He gives Klaus and Sweetheart Calico a free trip to Hawaii. On the trip, the couple is shadowed by government agents, who arrest Klaus, mistaking him for Richard.

Klaus and Sweetheart Calico both disappear for several years, then Klaus disappears for several more, leaving Sweetheart Calico in Minneapolis for his family to take care of. An explosion throws Sweetheart Calico through a window, and street people help her.

The puppy Almost Soup is born in Bwaanakeeng (Dakota-land) and is rescued from being cooked by Cally Roy, who is visiting relatives there.

When Deanna and Cally are eleven, Frank Shawano is diagnosed with terminal cancer. In March, Rozin tells Richard that she is taking the girls and moving in with Frank. Richard's unsuccessful suicide attempt results in Deanna's death.

Rozin moves back to the reservation to stay with her mothers, Zosie and Mary. The following February, Cally becomes ill. Her mother, grandmothers, and dog help keep her alive until an ambulance can come.

Richard becomes a street drunk, along with Klaus Shawano, who has returned to Minneapolis. Frank takes radiation treatments and recovers from his cancer.

1990s(?)

Zosie and Mary leave the reservation and move to Minneapolis.

At age eighteen, Cally moves to Minneapolis. She works in Frank's bakery and lives above the store. She tries unsuccessfully to find her grandmothers. One day Zosie comes to the bakery, followed shortly by Richard and Klaus, both drunk.

When Cally is twenty, Rozin moves to Minneapolis. She lives with her mothers, works in a food co-op, and goes to night school. Frank comes to the co-op, then calls Rozin until she agrees to go to the state fair with him. After the Gravitron ride, Rozin and Frank become lovers again.

Klaus continues to drink. Whenever Sweetheart Calico leaves him, he is visited by Windigo Dog.

Richard and Klaus check into a recovery lodge. Klaus stops drinking and gets a job, but Richard cries constantly and invents fictitious pasts. A priest tries unsuccessfully to comfort him.

In autumn (Cally is probably twenty-one), Frank and Rozin marry. Richard interrupts the ceremony and the reception and finally kills himself outside Frank and Rozin's hotel room. Rozin stays alone in her mothers' apartment, where she talks to ghosts and sees dream visions. After ten days Frank comes to care for her.

That Christmas the family gathers at Frank and Rozin's apartment. After dinner Cally talks with Zosie, who reveals that she is Rozin's mother, explains Cally's spirit name, and tells the story of the blue beads. Sweetheart Calico takes beads out of her mouth and speaks her first words in the novel. Cally accompanies Sweetheart Calico to the outskirts of the city.

A lawn mower runs over Klaus's head, and he decides to change his life. He takes Sweetheart Calico to the open spaces west of the city and releases her.

The next autumn, Frank plans a surprise first-anniversary party for Rozin, while Rozin plans an intimate surprise for him. The result is a surprise for everyone.

Dictionary of Characters

II

This dictionary is designed to help readers of Louise Erdrich's first six novels find their way through her always interesting but sometimes confusing cast of characters. It is a large cast. In *Love Medicine* alone there are some 75 different characters. In all six novels there are many hundreds. In the main part of this dictionary we have described around 450 characters. In the separate section at the end that we call "Miscellaneous Minor Characters," our readers will find another 200 characters or groups of characters. Although many of these individuals are distinctly minor, taken together they make up a rich and varied cast in a complex drama involving men and women of various races, ages, and generations.

In many cases, the snatches of narrative and allusion through which readers come to know these characters are scattered unchronologically through several novels. Sorting the people and events of Erdrich's world is further complicated by the fact that different narrative points of view may provide contradictory pictures, and also the fact that Erdrich's own conception of her characters has changed and developed over time.

HOW TO USE THIS DICTIONARY

This dictionary identifies each major character and most minor ones, tells briefly what they do, and gives every chapter in Erdrich's first six novels where they appear. It will be particularly helpful when used alongside the map, charts, and chronologies in Part I of this guide. Issues of place, relationships, and time sketched broadly there are addressed in more detail in this section.

Characters are listed under the name by which they are most frequently known—most often the *first* name. Our decision to list characters alphabetically by their first names was carefully considered. Readers will recognize names such as Marie, Nector, Lulu, or Gerry, but not always remember last names, especially those of female characters whose names change. It seemed best, for example, to list Lulu Nanapush Morrissey Lamartine under the name **Lulu** rather than under one of her surnames.

She is not, after all, a Nanapush by blood, and her marriages to Morrissey and the two Lamartine brothers are brief. In addition, Erdrich almost always uses only Lulu's first name. Characters for whom Erdrich has not given first names we have identified by last names. When there is more than one character with the same name we use Roman numerals, such as **Morrissey I** and **Morrissey II.** We have generally listed characters under their English rather than their Indian names, unless the Indian name is the primary one used in the novels. Thus, for example, the entry for the mother of Moses Pillager appears under **Different Thumbs** rather than Nanakawepenesick, whereas the woman who has a deer husband is listed as **Apijigo Bakaday** rather than So Hungry. Wherever we thought confusion might result, we have cross-listed characters' alternate names, with references back to the main-entry names. Thus, **Boss Woman**'s Indian name, **Ogimaakwe,** is cross-listed, since on two occasions it is the only form given. Asasaweminikwesens, however, the Indian name of Fleur's sister **Chokecherry Girl,** is not cross-listed, since it never appears apart from its English translation.

For help in determining family relationships, members of the major family groups are also cross-referenced under family names. For example, **Marie Lazarre** is cross-listed under both **Lazarre family** and **Kashpaw family. Lulu Nanapush Morrissey Lamartine** is cross-listed under **Nanapush family, Morrissey family,** and **Lamartine family,** as well as **Pillager family,** since she is a Pillager by blood. There are also family entries for the Adare, Kuklenski, Mauser, Pukwan, Puyat, Roy, Shawano, Toose, and Whiteheart Beads families.

The family connections of several of the characters are uncertain. **Nanapush,** for example, is a confusing case. He is referred to as the grandfather, father, and uncle of various other living characters, some of whom carry his name, but in fact, as the sole survivor of the consumption epidemic that carried off the rest of his family in 1912, he has no living blood relatives. The ancestry of **Marie Lazarre Kashpaw** is also confusing because she appears to have one set of parents in *Love Medicine,* but we learn in *Tracks* who her real parents are. The paternity of some characters—most notably **Lulu Nanapush** and **Redford Toose**—remains uncertain.

Where a character has no name, we use a descriptive designator—e.g. **Cowboy, Massive Indian woman, Old drunk woman.** We do not list the names of radio, television, and movie personages, such as Jimi Hendrix and Patti Page, or of other real people mentioned in passing.

We do not normally list animals unless they have specifically human traits or play a significant role in the narrative. Thus we created an entry for the **Antelope and deer people** who intermarry with humans in *The Antelope Wife,* but not for the moose that Eli stalks in *Tracks.* The speaking dogs **Almost Soup** and **Windigo Dog** have entries, as does **Pepperboy,** whose life and death play an important role in the marriage of Jack and Candice Mauser, but Lily Veddar's dog, Fatso, does not. We do list the humanlike spiritual or mythical personages who in the minds of some characters act as people in their lives—such as **Misshepeshu, Christ, Satan,** and two **Statue**[s] **of the Virgin.**

With only a few exceptions, the various references to each character are gathered into one entry, with alternate names for the same person cross-referenced. Exceptions include characters (such as **Andy, Father of Fargo baby,** and **Sister Leopolda**) whose alternate names and identities Erdrich does not at first reveal. In order to avoid giving away Erdrich's secrets prematurely, we have created separate entries for each of these characters' identities, without cross-referencing to alternate identities. When readers look up all of the chapter references in these entries, however, the double identities will be come clear. (Readers using this guide who want to avoid uncovering Erdrich's secrets prematurely can limit their tracing of references to those novels that they have already read.)

In addition to the leading players and their family members, lovers, and associates, a multitude of unnamed "extras" brush through Erdrich's pages. We find clerks and customers, photographers and reporters, factory workers and construction workers, drivers of various vehicles and people just out walking their dogs. To list each of these personages separately would be tedious, and yet calling attention to them makes us realize more fully the vastness of Erdrich's canvas, the breadth as well as the depth of her characterization. Even an anonymous white doctor, for example, who appears only briefly in chapter 7 of *Tracks,* gives readers a sharp glimpse into the racial prejudices of Erdrich's North Dakota. Most of these bit-part players we have grouped together at the end of the dictionary in a potpourri section, "Miscellaneous Minor Characters," subdivided by novel.

Some such minor characters, however, fall within categories that appear often enough to be significant as types. Group entries on **Doctors** and **Nurses,** for example, highlight the frequency with which medical personnel appear in the novels. Even smaller groupings such as **Bartenders** and **Jewelers** call attention to types of characters that a first-time reader would normally overlook. Some small groupings are connected with certain central characters, such as **Dot Adare's classmates** and **Fleur Pillager's customers.** All such groupings are alphabetized into the main dictionary. Perhaps the most significant of these group entries are those for persons who have taken orders within the Catholic Church, which figures so prominently in Erdrich's fiction. These individuals are grouped into entries for **Priests** and **Nuns.** The latter category is divided by convent to help readers get a sense of what goes on over a period of time at individual locations, such as Sacred Heart on the reservation or Our Lady of the Wheat in Argus.

Entry titles and references to entry titles are in **boldface roman** type. Characters who have no separate entry but are introduced within a group entry are given in ***boldface italics.*** In addition to these group entries, some minor characters are introduced in individual-character entries, whenever this placement seems most efficient and logical. The entry for **Stan Mahng,** for example, also includes ***Stan's baby*** and his ***girlfriend,*** and the entry for the **Gravitron operator** includes the ***Gravitron riders*** whom he endangers and the ***woman*** and ***people watching,*** who respond to his dangerous behavior.

We have designed this dictionary to serve as an index for the characters, a guide to the stories and chapters that contain significant references to them. We do not give page number references. Instead, we use story titles for *Love Medicine* and *Tales of Burning Love* and chapter numbers for the other four novels to refer readers to the chapters in which portions of a character's story appear. Our use of story or chapter references is somewhat complicated, however, by the fact that Erdrich designates sections differently in her various novels. In *Love Medicine* she gives no chapter numbers, only story titles. She breaks *The Beet Queen* into four large parts and gives continuous chapter numbers for all but the opening chapter, "The Branch." Most of these chapters, however, are divided into separately titled subchapters. Thus, for example, our "chapter 2" designation for *The Beet Queen* refers to all four of the short subchapters within that chapter. In *Tracks* Erdrich provides chapter numbers, along with the year and season in English and a month or season name in Ojibwa, with an English translation. In *The Bingo Palace* she gives both chapter numbers and chapter titles. In *Tales of Burning Love* she breaks the novel into four large parts but gives no chapter numbers, only individual chapter titles. In *The Antelope Wife* she gives us a four-part structure with chapters numbered consecutively throughout.

For all of her novels except *Tales of Burning Love* Erdrich provides a table of contents. To help readers locate chapters in this long and complex novel, we have created a table of contents, which appears immediately following this introduction; the page numbers listed refer to the 1997 HarperPerennial edition. For references to *Tales of Burning Love* in the entries, we provide our own chapter numbers in brackets following the chapter titles.

We have generally listed the activities of the various characters chronologically within each entry rather than in the order in which those incidents appear in the novels. When the characters appear as ghosts, we discuss their spirit-presences, logically enough, after they have died. Because little in Erdrich's fiction does not break out of its own mold, when in doubt we have followed where her shifting currents seemed to lead us.

CHAPTERS IN *TALES OF BURNING LOVE*

A

Adare family. See **Adelaide Adare; Dot Adare Nanapush Mauser; Jude Miller; Karl Adare; Mary Adare;** and **Shawn Nanapush.**

Adelaide Adare. Mother of Karl Adare, Mary Adare, and an unnamed infant later named Jude Miller; mistress of Mr. Ober in *The Beet Queen*. Adelaide is probably Polish (her sister marries a Kozka, and Erdrich refers to the protagonists of *The Beet Queen* as Poles and Germans [Allan Chavkin and Nancy Feyl Chavkin, eds., *Conversations with Louise Erdrich and Michael Dorris,* 237]).

In chapter 1 Adelaide lives in Prairie Lake, near Minneapolis, with her and Mr. Ober's two children, fourteen-year-old Karl and eleven-year-old Mary. Mr. Ober visits them regularly and provides for them financially, but when he dies in 1932, Adelaide and her children are left destitute and homeless. They move to Minneapolis, where Adelaide cannot find work and discovers that she is pregnant. She pawns her jewelry and steals a dozen silver spoons from her landlady. When Adelaide gives birth, the landlady discovers the theft and gives her a four-week notice to move. Near the end of that four weeks, she and the children wander into the Saint Jerome's Orphans' Picnic, where she flies away with a stunt pilot, The Great Omar, abandoning her three children. The baby is kidnapped at the Orphans' Picnic; Karl lives at Saint Jerome's until he is on his own; and Mary moves in with Adelaide's sister, Fritzie Kozka, in Argus.

Adelaide never returns to see her children. References to her in the remainder of *The Beet Queen* present her as either admirably free-spirited or irresponsible and selfish, depending on the point of view. In chapter 2 Fritzie's daughter, Sita Kozka, admires her Aunt Adelaide as a woman with style that other family members fail to appreciate. In chapter 3 Karl justifies his mother's actions by fantasizing that Omar has abducted her. Adelaide's sister Fritzie and daughter Mary, however, have washed their hands of her. In chapter 3 Adelaide sends a postcard to Fritzie from Jacksonville, Florida, inquiring about her children. Mary sees the card and, pretending to be Fritzie, sends a reply that all three children have starved to death. By the time Mary's postcard reaches them, both Adelaide and Omar have been injured in an airplane crash. Adelaide presumably sees the postcard after Omar places it on her nightstand in the hospital.

Some twenty years later (1953), in chapter 7, Adelaide, apparently unconvinced by Mary's ruse, sends her daughter a sewing machine, but Mary gives it to her cousin, Sita. Possibly another eleven years after that, in chapter 11, Adelaide, still in Florida and still with Omar, throws a glass-breaking tantrum.

This is the last reference to Adelaide herself, but her spirit lives on in her garnet necklace, which Sita redeems from a pawn shop, and in the memories of Sita, Karl, and—through Sita's stories—Karl's daughter, Dot Adare (see chapters 5, 13, 14, 15, and 16).

Adelaide Adare's baby. See **Jude Miller.**

Adelaide Adare's landlady. Woman who rents rooms to the destitute Adelaide Adare and her children in chapter 1 of *The Beet Queen.* Adelaide steals a dozen silver spoons from her to buy coats and food for the children. She is a kind enough woman, but when she finds one of the stolen spoons while helping Adelaide give birth, she gives them notice that they must move in one month.

Adrian. Boy who helps out at The House of Meats (alias Kozka's Meats) in Argus. Celestine James says in chapter 7 of *The Beet Queen* that he is supposed to be her cousin. He watches the shop when Celestine and Mary Adare take a wheelchair to Russell Kashpaw in chapter 10. He is mentioned again twice in chapter 13.

Agent. Indian agent to the Chippewa in *Tracks.* Different men may hold this position in different chapters, but the agent is generally depicted as a tool of the government for seizing Indian land. Some of the Indians, such as the Morrissey, Pukwan, Hat, and Lazarre families, cooperate with him; others, including the Pillagers and Nanapush, oppose him. When the agent tries to collect allotment fees from Fleur Pillager in chapter 1, he gets lost and spends the night following elusive lights, apparently ghosts. After his second attempt, he is found living in the woods, eating roots and gambling with ghosts. When the agent attempts to make up a tribal roll in chapter 3, Nanapush refuses to give his name. Nevertheless, because Nanapush can read, the agent designates him in chapter 5 as the person to receive letters from the land court, and in chapter 7 Father Damien urges Nanapush to deal with the agent in order to help protect the tribe. In chapter 4 Bernadette Morrissey uses the agent as conduit for a letter sent to an aunt in Grand Forks, and in chapter 7 she goes to work for him as housekeeper, secretary, and accountant.

We learn in chapter 7 that the agent has made a list and map of fees owed and foreclosure notices on reservation allotments. Kashpaw, Pillager, and Nanapush land is in jeopardy; the land of their government-cooperating enemies is not. The agent receives the fee money collected by the Pillager and Kashpaw families, but in chapter 9 he explains to Nanapush that Nector and Margaret Kashpaw have paid the fees only on Kashpaw land and that the Pillager land has been sold. See also **Jewett Parker Tatro.**

Aintapi, old lady. Old woman said to sell love medicines. Nanapush mentions her to the lovesick Eli Kashpaw in chapter 3 of *Tracks*.

Albertine Johnson. Only child of Zelda Kashpaw Johnson and Swede Johnson, born about 1958. She is named after Zelda's first suitor, Xavier Albert Toose. We learn in "The World's Greatest Fishermen" in *Love Medicine* that Albertine is born less than nine months after Zelda's marriage to Swede and that Zelda considers it Albertine's fault that she could not become a nun as she had wished. Albertine knows her father only from pictures, because he went AWOL shortly after the marriage and was never seen again. As Albertine grows up, she and her mother live in a trailer near her Grandma Marie Kashpaw, who helps take care of her. Albertine goes through a long rebellious phase. At age fifteen (1973), in "A Bridge," she runs away by bus to Fargo. There she is picked up by a young Chippewa soldier from her own reservation, Henry Lamartine Junior, who has just returned from Vietnam. That night in a hotel, the frightened Albertine has sexual relations with him.

Seven years later, in "Scales," Albertine is still involved with alcohol and drugs but wanting to make a change. In the summer of 1980, she falls in with prison-escapee Gerry Nanapush and Dot Adare, who is pregnant with Gerry's child. Albertine and Dot work together in a truck weigh-station at a construction site. When Dot goes into labor in October, Albertine joins Gerry in the hospital waiting room, and she records the birth of Shawn and Gerry's subsequent escape from the police.

Albertine is a nursing student in 1981 ("The World's Greatest Fishermen") when she receives a letter from her mother the week after Easter telling of her aunt June Morrissey's death. Albertine is bitter that Zelda did not notify her before the funeral, because she had been fond of Aunt June. Although still angry with her mother, she drives home two months later when her classes are finished. During a gathering of the Kashpaw clan, Albertine tries unsuccessfully to tell Lipsha Morrissey that June is his mother, and she prevents King Kashpaw from drowning his wife, Lynette. The following year, in "Love Medicine," Albertine sits with Lipsha at her Grandpa Nector Kashpaw's funeral. She has by this time decided to continue beyond her nurse's training and become a doctor. In "Crossing the Water" Lipsha says that Albertine is like a sister, the only girl he has ever trusted, and in chapter 9 of *The Bingo Palace* he recalls that she once loaned him money from her own school loan.

In chapter 1 of *The Bingo Palace* Albertine is pushing herself hard at her medical studies, but she also dances at the powwows on the reservation. In her trademark blue costume, she is dancing at the winter powwow with her friend

Shawnee Ray Toose when Lipsha returns to the reservation in chapter 2. At a naming ceremony in chapter 3 conducted by her original namesake, Xavier Albert Toose, Albertine receives the traditional name of Four Soul. The name is appropriate since Albertine is studying to be a doctor and the original Four Soul had been a Pillager healer, four generations earlier.

Zelda complains in chapter 10 that Albertine never comes home to stay, but Shawnee Ray says that it is Zelda's fault. On one of her brief visits home in chapter 19, when Zelda tries to control Shawnee Ray, Albertine comes to her friend's defense. She confronts her mother with the truth that Zelda has never gotten over her love for her rejected suitor, Xavier Toose. In chapter 20 Albertine advises Lipsha to leave Shawnee Ray alone until he gets himself together, advice he recalls in chapter 22.

Almost Soup. Cally Roy's white dog, who narrates chapters 8 and 9 of *The Antelope Wife.* Almost Soup claims some coyote and Dakota blood mixed with his Ojibwa reservation dog blood. He is born on the prairie, "out in Bwaanakeeng" (i.e., Dakota-land). His birthplace may be in the same general area as the original Ojibwa village attacked by Scranton Roy in chapter 1, which is near a portion of open Dakota prairie "west of the Otter Tail River." One of his ancestors is Blue Prairie Woman's dog, Sorrow, who left puppies behind in the village before heading west with Blue Prairie Woman.

Almost Soup acquires his name (Bungeenaboop in Ojibwa) in chapter 8 when he barely escapes being cooked. He is saved by the advice of *his mother,* the mercy of Original Dog, the wit he inherited from Sorrow, and the love of the girl child Cally, who is visiting her relatives in Bwaanakeeng. Shortly thereafter, he is taken to the Ojibwa reservation where Cally's grandmothers live. Later, Cally also saves him from castration. Much of chapter 8 is Almost Soup's survival advice to younger dogs, perhaps his descendants, since he speaks of *his puppies.*

In chapter 9, Almost Soup recounts the incidents following the death of Cally's twin sister, Deanna. About a year later, Cally falls ill after playing outside with Almost Soup on a sunny but freezing day. On the second night of her fever, the black dog (i.e. death) draws near (chapter 8). Almost Soup calls upon *his ancestors* for help, and he takes Cally's life for safekeeping until her body revives. After Cally moves to Minneapolis in chapter 11, she misses her dog, who would sometimes sleep with her. See also **Windigo Dog.**

Andrea. Candice Pantamounty's hygienist who X-rays Jack Mauser's rotten teeth in "Candice's Tale" [25] in *Tales of Burning Love.*

Andy

Andy. Mud engineer in "The World's Greatest Fishermen" in *Love Medicine* (see **Mud engineer**). Andy beckons June Morrissey into a bar in Williston, gives her an egg, and gets her drunk. Later, they drive out from town, and he seems to fall asleep while attempting to have sex with her in his pickup. In "Easter Snow," the opening chapter in *Tales of Burning Love,* it is revealed that "Andy" is not his true name.

Anna Kuklenski Schlick. Wife of Lawrence Schlick and mother of Eleanor Schlick Mauser. In "White Musk" [4] in *Tales of Burning Love,* Eleanor recalls Anna as a doting mother, and in "The Meadowlark" [7] she mentions her too-close relationship with her mother and says that Anna had once been an acrobat.

The story of Anna's life is told primarily in "Eleanor's Tale" [20]. A young barrel rider in Montana, Anna runs away with a small circus and is taken in by the Flying Kuklenski family, who train her as a trapeze artist. She and young Harry Kuklenski marry, but when Anna is seven months pregnant, Harry dies in a terrible accident. Anna survives, but her baby, a girl, is born dead six weeks later.

Lawrence Schlick visits Anna in the hospital and falls in love with her. When they marry, Anna grows into her role as the superwife of Fargo's most successful businessman, involved in all sorts of cultural, civic, and charitable works. When their house burns down, Anna rescues her six-year-old daughter, Eleanor, by leaping from the house with her. One bitterly cold November night, Anna helps to thaw out a nearly frozen young part-time fireman named Jack Mauser by crawling naked into bed with him. It is not clear whether they have sex— the evidence suggests that they do not—but the next morning her husband finds them asleep in bed together and disowns her and Eleanor. Despite their subsequent poverty, however, Anna feels more liberated than deprived, and she recovers her original flamboyant personality.

Anna and Lawrence never formally divorce, and after many years of separation, as recounted in "The Red Slip" [21], they become reconciled when Eleanor tells them of her engagement to Jack Mauser. Living with Lawrence again, in "The Box" [22] Anna concentrates on her church work, feeding the cast-off elements of society. Lawrence's jealous suspicions linger, however, and one night in late winter 1983 he sneaks home early from a funerary trade show to see if Anna is still seeing Jack. She is not.

Anna sends her daughter a worried note in "Night Prayer" [6] when Eleanor's health declines while staying at the Argus convent. When Anna comes to Jack's funeral in "Memoria" [10], although she is weak, suffering from a heart condition, she retains her flair and is dressed in an eye-catching sequined gown. The following August, in "A Light from the West" [43], she dies and is cremated by and with her husband.

Anna Schlick's landlord. After Anna is expelled from her husband's mansion in "The Red Slip" [21] in *Tales of Burning Love,* this landlord is said to offer her alternative ways to pay her rent without using money.

Anna Schlick's parents. Just before she dies, in "A Light from the West" [43] in *Tales of Burning Love,* Anna remembers her parents fishing off a dock. Presumably these are her biological parents, not the Kuklenskis, who adopted her.

Anne, Sister Saint. Nun at the Sacred Heart Convent in *Tracks.* She is keeping a vigil in chapter 4 when Clarence Morrissey rushes into the church and steals the statue of the Virgin Mary. She chases him back to Fleur's cabin, where she finds Clarence's sister Sophie in catatonic stupor. Sister Saint Anne is the one who tells Pauline in chapter 6 that no Indian girls may be accepted into the order at the convent. She feeds Pauline soup in chapter 8 when Pauline's hands are burned. For thanks, Pauline tells the sister that she stinks.

Antelope and deer people. In *The Antelope Wife* these people include full-blooded antelope and deer who marry or adopt humans, their animal-human descendants, and humans with deer and antelope characteristics. In chapter 6, the *deer people* who are family to Apijigo Bakaday's deer husband love her and come when she calls them, even after her deer husband dies. One of them, a *slender doe,* warns the woman (now called Blue Prairie Woman) of an impending cavalry attack. Later, a *band of antelope* adopts Blue Prairie Woman's seven-year-old-daughter, Matilda (recorded in chapter 1). Chapters 1 and 2 mention the curiosity of antelope people and chapter 2, the ease with which they can be confined by fences. See also **Apijigo Bakaday; Cally Whiteheart Beads Roy; Deanna Whiteheart Beads; Deer husband; Frank Shawano; Girl who lived with the antelope; Matilda Roy;** and **Sweetheart Calico.**

In addition to the deer and antelope people of *The Antelope Wife,* the *doe* hit by Gordie Kashpaw's car in "Crown of Thorns" in *Love Medicine* also takes on human qualities, at least in Gordie's intoxicated mind.

Apijigo Bakaday. Daughter of Midass; possibly windigo. Her name means So Hungry. In chapter 6 of *The Antelope Wife* she marries a deer husband, whom her brothers later shoot. See **Blue Prairie Woman.**

Arnie Dotzenrud. Ticket taker at the Beet Festival in chapter 14 of *The Beet Queen.*

Art. Owner of Art's Arcade, a twenty-four-hour video-game establishment in Fargo where Lipsha goes to wait for the newly escaped Gerry Nanapush in chapter 22 of *The Bingo Palace.* Art insists that Lipsha must either play or leave.

Asian woman. Woman that Henry Lamartine Junior sees in Vietnam dying from a bayonet wound. Her eyes look like Chippewa eyes, and when he is with Albertine Johnson in a Fargo motel in "A Bridge" in *Love Medicine,* he confuses his memory of the woman with Albertine.

Asinigwesance (Asin). Formerly judicious old man in *The Antelope Wife* who in chapter 13 irrationally wishes to execute the German prisoner of war Klaus.

Augustus Roy I. Son of Scranton Roy and Peace McKnight in chapters 1 and 23 of *The Antelope Wife.* After a difficult labor, Peace dies in childbirth, and baby Augustus almost succumbs, too. His father nurses him at his own breast. Augustus later has a son, also named Augustus.

Augustus Roy II. Grandson of Scranton Roy; husband of Zosie (II) Shawano Roy in *The Antelope Wife.*

Raised alone by his grandfather somewhere on the Great Plains, Augustus is bookish and shy. As a very young man, in chapter 23 he accompanies his grandfather east to find the remnants of an Ojibwa village Scranton had once raided. The survivors now live on a reservation. (For notes about its location, see **Rozina [Rozin] Roy Whiteheart Beads Shawano.**) There Augustus falls in love with Zosie Shawano, great-great-granddaughter of a woman Scranton had killed. In exchange for Zosie, Augustus offers her great-grandmother, Midass, red whiteheart beads and agrees to take care of Zosie's twin sister, Mary. Chapter 18 tells the story of their ill-fated marriage, which ends when Augustus disappears without a trace. Rumor has it that the windigo (i.e., cannibalistic) Shawano twins have eaten him. Before he disappears, he impregnates Zosie with twins.

Aunt Elizabeth. Jack Mauser's aunt on his German father's side, mentioned in "The Owl" [17] in *Tales of Burning Love.* This aunt, whom Jack refers to as *Tante,* takes care of six-year-old Jack while his mother is taking cold-water shock treatments. Aunt Elizabeth is strict and thinks Jack's Ojibwa mother has spoiled him. As a young man, Jack squanders money she apparently has given him. According to "Best Western" [28], Jack feels that she has stolen him away from his mother, and he eventually runs away to his uncle—her brother, Chuck Mauser.

Aunt Fritzie. See **Fritzie Kozka.**

Aunt Mary. See **Mary Adare.**

Aurelia Kashpaw. Daughter of Nector and Marie Kashpaw, younger sister to Gordie and Zelda. While they are children, in "The Beads" in *Love Medicine,* Gordie and Aurelia try to hang their cousin June Morrissey, at June's instigation, but Zelda runs to tell Marie. In "The Plunge of the Brave" Aurelia and Zelda share a rollaway cot in the crowded Kashpaw cabin. In "Flesh and Blood" Aurelia watches her two youngest siblings (Patsy and Eugene) and the neighbor woman's baby when Marie and Zelda visit Sister Leopolda in 1957. She would prefer to be hunting with June, Gordie, and Gordie's friend, whom Aurelia "likes."

Years later, after Nector and Marie move into the Senior Citizens in town, Aurelia moves back into the old family house, although it remains a kind of communal Kashpaw property. In about 1979, Aurelia has an addition tacked onto the house, containing a toilet, laundry, and kitchen sink. In "The World's Greatest Fishermen" (1981), Aurelia and Zelda are in Aurelia's kitchen, preparing food for a Kashpaw family gathering. As the two sisters visit, the narrator, Albertine, observes their differences. In contrast to Zelda, who criticizes everyone, Aurelia defends both Albertine and the dead June. Unlike her plain sister, Aurelia is a "looker"—plump with high, round cheeks, permed hair, tight jeans, and a fancy shirt. She works nights managing a bar, and her wink at Albertine as she leaves to go "see a friend" later that evening suggests an interest in men.

When the scattered family members come for Nector's funeral in "Love Medicine," some stay with Aurelia. Afterwards, in "Resurrection," Marie returns to the house and Aurelia moves out.

Aurora Roy. Daughter of Zosie (II) Shawano Roy and Augustus Roy II; twin sister of Rozina Roy in *The Antelope Wife.* According to chapter 3, Aurora dies of diphtheria at age five and must be pried from her sister's arms. The effect of her death on Rozin is alluded to in chapter 18.

B

Baby Kuklenski girl. Stillborn daughter of Anna and Harry Kuklenski in "Eleanor's Tale" [20] in *Tales of Burning Love.* In a trapeze accident, her father is killed, and her mother, seven months pregnant with her, is injured. She is born dead six weeks after the accident and is buried in Fargo. She would have been the half sister of Eleanor Schlick Mauser, who recalls seeing her grave.

Baby Miller boy. Three-day-old infant of Martin and Catherine Miller who dies in 1932. He is referred to in chapters 1 and 2 of *The Beet Queen*. They seek to "replace" him with Adelaide Adare's baby, whom they name Jude Miller.

Baby Pillager. Fleur's baby who is born prematurely and then dies, in chapter 6 of *Tracks*. Pauline apparently could have prevented the miscarriage, but does not do so. The baby's father, Eli Kashpaw, places its body in a shoe box high in a tree. Fleur mourns the baby's death in chapter 7 and shelters its resting place with her black umbrella. In chapter 9 she is said to have assigned the dead child to guard Matchimanito Lake. On her own death walk in chapter 24 of *The Bingo Palace*, Fleur once again sees the child, along with the other dead of her family.

Baby stolen in Fargo. Baby in the car that Gerry Nanapush and Lipsha Morrissey steal in front of the Fargo train station in chapter 24 of *The Bingo Palace*. Later, snowbound in the car, Lipsha zips the baby into his own jacket in an effort to protect it from the cold. In chapter 26, a radio broadcast the next morning announces that a "hostage" has been found in good condition, which may or may not refer to the baby. The baby's identity is revealed in "Funeral Day" [23] and "Blizzard Night" [35] in *Tales of Burning Love*.

Bank president in Fargo. Friend of Lawrence Schlick who has an apparently upsetting conversation with Schlick about his financial losses in "The Red Slip" [21] in *Tales of Burning Love*. He is probably the same man as **Lawrence Schlick's banker.** He may or may not be **Hegelstead.**

Bartenders. The *bartender at the Rigger Bar* in Williston serves June Morrissey and Jack Mauser (alias "Andy") in "The World's Greatest Fishermen" in *Love Medicine* and "Easter Snow" [1] in *Tales of Burning Love*. Two other bartenders appear in *Tales of Burning Love*. The *bartender at the Library bar* (Candice Pantamounty and Jack's favorite bar) serves Jack and Marlis Cook in "The First Draw" [14] and "Marlis's Tale" [27]; and the *bartender at the B & B* is surprised when Dot orders a pizza for the large Indian woman in "The B & B" [16].

Bernadette Morrissey. Mother of Clarence, Sophie, and Philomena Morrissey in *Tracks*. We learn in chapter 4 that Bernadette is educated by French nuns in Quebec, and she passes on her French ways to her daughters. She and her children move in with her alcoholic brother Napoleon, whose homestead thrives under Bernadette's supervision. After bringing Pauline Puyat back from Argus and taking her in, Bernadette teaches her to read. In chapters 3 and 4, she takes Pauline as an assistant in caring for the dying. Also in chapter 4

Bernadette whips her daughter Sophie for engaging in sex with Eli Kashpaw and tries to send her away to a strict aunt off-reservation. Bernadette is not present when Fleur Pillager comes to the Morrissey farm to lay a curse on the family in chapter 5.

After Pauline becomes pregnant by Napoleon, in chapter 6 Bernadette prevents her abortion attempts, delivers baby Marie, and, when Pauline leaves, keeps the child herself.

When, in the last weeks of winter 1919 (chapter 7), Bernadette's children Clarence and Sophie both come home with Lazarre spouses, as well as Izear Lazarre's six children from a previous marriage, Bernadette takes Philomena and baby Marie and moves to town. After she leaves, the farm and house begin to fall into ruin. In town, although she is already showing the first signs of consumption, Bernadette keeps house for the Indian agent and becomes his secretary, organizing the tribal property records and mailing out debt announcements to those whose land fees are unpaid. There are intimations in chapters 7 and 9 that, in this position of influence, Bernadette tries to prevent Nanapush's efforts to become involved in tribal leadership and that she is complicit with the agent's efforts to seize Indian land. Bernadette is one of the assemblage in chapter 8 watching Pauline from the shore of Matchimanito Lake in the spring of 1919. As Bernadette becomes weaker from her consumption, however, her daughter Sophie (now Lazarre) increasingly takes care of baby Marie. Bernadette probably dies shortly after this time, since Marie seems to have no memory of her and grows up thinking she is a Lazarre.

Beverly "Hat" Lamartine. Brother of Henry Lamartine, third husband of Lulu Lamartine, and father of Henry Lamartine Junior in *Love Medicine*. Nector Kashpaw says in "The Plunge of the Brave" that Beverly is a Cree. In "Lulu's Boys," we learn that Beverly, Henry, and their older brother, Slick, are close-knit, defending each other in high school. Slick is killed in boot camp, but Beverly and Henry remain close, serving in the military together and getting similar tattoos on their arms. They also fall in love with the same woman, Lulu Nanapush Morrissey. After the three play a game of strip poker, Lulu chooses to marry Henry instead of Beverly. Henry, however, dies in a wreck in 1950. After his wake, Beverly and Lulu go outside for some air and end up making love in a shed. At the funeral Lulu faints and falls into the grave, and Beverly jumps in to revive her. When Henry Junior is born nine months later, Beverly is sure that the boy is his, not his brother's.

After Henry's funeral, Beverly does not return to the reservation for seven years. He lives in the Twin Cities, where he sells children's after-school

Beverly "Hat" Lamartine

workbooks door to door, using Henry Junior's school pictures as part of his sales pitch. He is married to a natural blond, Elsa, who does not like children and who hides from her family the fact that Beverly is an Indian. A hidden ache in Beverly induces him in 1957 to visit the reservation and try to bring Henry Junior back to the city to live with him. His plans change, however, when he finds himself once again attracted to Lulu. While he is staying with her, in "The Good Tears" she becomes angry with her lover of five years, Nector Kashpaw, and marries Beverly. A week later, Beverly tells her about his other wife, and Lulu sends him back to the city to divorce Elsa, accompanied by her twelve-year-old son Gerry. While there, Gerry is thrown into detention, and Lulu thinks it is Beverly who has turned him in. This is the last we hear of Beverly; there is no indication that he ever returns to Lulu. In "The Tomahawk Factory" Marie Kashpaw taunts Lulu that she had to marry Hat Lamartine to hide the illegitimate birth of her son Lyman, her child with Marie's husband, Nector.

Big Mauser. See **Jack Mauser's father.**

Bijiu, Mrs. Woman who, along with her children, is attacked by the devil in the form of a black dog made of smoke in chapter 3 of *Tracks.* This story is similar to the story of the black dog "guarding air" after the mysterious death of Josette Bizhieu's mother and her sister's daughter in chapter 12 of *The Bingo Palace.* Both incidents are believed to be connected with Fleur Pillager's power. The Bijius sell berries to the Morrisseys in chapter 4 of *Tracks.* See also **Black dog.**

Bishop Retzlaff. See **Retzlaff, Bishop.**

Bjornson. Second husband of Zelda. In 1981, in "The World's Greatest Fishermen" in *Love Medicine,* Zelda has been living with him on his wheat farm on the edge of the reservation for about a year. When Zelda reappears some time later in *The Bingo Palace,* she is apparently not still living with Bjornson. He is never mentioned in the novel, and according to chapters 4 and 9, Zelda is now living in the old Kashpaw house.

Black dog. Manifestation of death. A black dog made of smoke attacks Mrs. Bijiu in chapter 3 of *Tracks,* and a black dog appears in the road, "guarding air" in chapter 12 of *The Bingo Palace* after Josette Bizhieu's mother and niece die mysteriously. When Cally Roy almost dies in *The Antelope Wife,* in chapter 8 Almost Soup senses the presence of the black dog.

Blue Prairie Woman. Mother of Matilda Roy and the twins Mary (I) and Josephette (Zosie I) Shawano; great-grandmother of Rozina Roy in *The*

Blue Prairie Woman

Antelope Wife. Blue Prairie Woman is the daughter of Midass and an unidentified Shawano man.

As a girl in chapter 6, Blue Prairie Woman is known as Apijigo Bakaday (So Hungry) because of her insatiable appetite. While staying in the woods, she falls in love with a deer man. She travels with him and is loved by his people until her **brothers** shoot the deer husband and bring her back. She is now renamed Ozhawashkwamashkodeykway, Blue Prairie Woman, an old name that has belonged to **many powerful women,** and she marries one of the Shawano brothers, Shawano the younger.

Blue Prairie Woman's story continues in chapters 1 and 6. Soon after her first daughter is born, a doe warns her to flee. She ties her baby's cradle board to the back of a female dog and starts to leave, but too late. Bluecoats descend on the village, killing and burning. Blue Prairie Woman sees one of the men murder her grandmother and then run after the dog, which is fleeing with her baby, a necklace of blue beads swaying from the cradle board. To ease Blue Prairie Woman's impacted breasts, an **old midwife** gives her a puppy to nurse, a female named Sorrow, who is the puppy of the bitch carrying the cradle board.

The raid probably occurs in autumn. Shawano the younger is away gathering wild rice at the time, an autumn activity. (In chapter 17 Zosie [II] Shawano Roy gathers wild rice in the fall, and the Ojibwa name for the month of September is Minomini-geezis, "wild rice sun.") Also, there is famine during the ensuing winter as a result of the cavalry's burning the tribe's stockpile of buffalo meat, which would have been accumulated during the summer.

In her grief, Blue Prairie Woman eats nothing but dirt for six months. When her Shawano husband returns to the village after the raid, the two become obsessive lovers, and she conceives twins. Even so, through the ensuing winter, Blue Prairie Woman's grief deepens. By spring, the old ones know they must give her a new name if she is to survive. The namer chooses the place where Blue Prairie Woman's spirit has gone to fetch her child—Other Side of the Earth.

Other Side of the Earth gives birth to twin daughters, Mary and Josephette, leaves them with her mother, Midass, and goes in search of her firstborn, followed by the dog Sorrow. (These incidents are also mentioned in chapter 3.) She walks for years, guided by stories of a man and a young girl with blue beads. When she finds their place, she senses sickness inside, but that night she taps at the house, and her daughter (Matilda Roy) follows her. Matilda falls into a fever as they travel, and the mother gives her child her own life-restoring name, Other Side of the Earth. As she succumbs to her daughter's illness, Blue Prairie Woman kills and cooks the dog Sorrow. Within the day, Blue Prairie Woman is dead, but the meat she leaves behind nourishes her child. Similar to

Blue Prairie Woman's grandmother I (killed)

her mother, Matilda is adopted by antelope people. As she follows them, she is still wearing the blue beads.

Years later, as related in chapter 18, the spirit of Blue Prairie Woman, wearing the necklace of blue beads, appears to her pregnant granddaughter Zosie Shawano Roy in a dream. They gamble and Zosie wins the beads and the spirit woman's names. Zosie will later give these names to her own granddaughters, Blue Prairie Woman to Cally and Other Side of the Earth to Deanna.

Blue Prairie Woman's grandmother I (killed). Old woman bayoneted by young Scranton Roy in chapter 1 of *The Antelope Wife*. When Scranton's cavalry company attacks her village, the old woman charges him with a stone to protect the children (chapter 23). She dies uttering the word *daashkikaa*. (Six generations later, in chapter 18 her descendant Cally Roy will hear that word and learn its meaning—"cracked apart.") She is identified as Blue Prairie Woman's grandmother in chapter 6.

Years later, in chapter 23 Scranton falls ill, and the old woman's spirit visits him in his fever. After a hundred nights, he offers to find the remnant of her village, taking with him supplies and his grandson, Augustus II. The old woman accepts this offering, and Scranton's fever abates.

Blue Prairie Woman's grandmother II (living). Woman in chapter 1 of *The Antelope Wife* who says that the dirt Blue Prairie Woman is eating must be rich dirt.

Bonita. Last child and only daughter of Lulu Lamartine, fathered by an unnamed Mexican man, a migrant farm worker, in *Love Medicine*. According to "The Good Tears," she is born when Lulu is almost fifty. In "The Red Convertible" (1974) the eleven-year-old Bonita takes a picture of her half brothers, Lyman Lamartine and Henry Lamartine Junior, shortly before Henry Junior dies.

Bootch. One of the men called to the house of Shawano the ogitchida to see the German prisoner of war Klaus in chapter 13 of *The Antelope Wife*. Bootch suggests that they allow the young man to prepare his offering, the blitzkuchen.

Border guard. Canadian official who stops Lipsha Morrissey on his first date with Shawnee Ray Toose in chapters 4 and 5 of *The Bingo Palace*. He finds what he thinks is evidence of illegal drug possession. Lipsha wonders whether Zelda Kashpaw has instigated the search.

Boss Woman. Wife of Pillager and mother of Fleur; also called Ogimaakwe. True to her name, we learn in chapter 3 of *Tracks* that she raises her daughters to be their own bosses. She dies of consumption in chapter 1 of *Tracks* and is referred to briefly in chapter 9 of *Tracks* and chapter 3 of *The Bingo Palace*.

Boy Lazarre. Member of one of the two families who become enemies of the Kashpaws and Pillagers. Boy Lazarre is hired by Margaret Kashpaw in chapter 3 of *Tracks* to spy on her son Eli and Fleur Pillager. For this action, Fleur is said to have cut Lazarre's tongue out and sewn it in backwards. In chapter 5 Lazarre is a member of the faction that wants to sell Indian land to the Turcot lumber company. He and Clarence Morrissey abduct Nanapush and Margaret, tie them up in a barn, and shave Margaret's head. Margaret, however, manages to bite Lazarre's hand. The wound leads to blood poisoning, which eventually kills him. Before his death, Fleur takes pieces of his hair and nails to make a curse. He seems to die of heart failure the next time he encounters Fleur. His death is referred to again in chapter 7. In Pauline's death vision in chapter 6, Lazarre is among the group of men whose deaths Fleur is presumed to have caused.

Cally Whiteheart Beads Roy. Daughter of Rozina Roy and Richard White-heart Beads; twin sister of Deanna Whiteheart Beads in *The Antelope Wife*. Cally's spirit name is Ozhawashkwamashkodeykway, Blue Prairie Woman (chapters 11 and 18). She narrates chapters 6, 11, 14, and 18. Cally may also be the story's central consciousness, the "I" that opens and closes the novel.

Cally and Deanna are probably born in the mid–1970s. (Cally appears to be twenty-two at the novel's end, which, judging from allusions to certain types of technology, seems to be in the mid–1990s.) When Rozin discovers that she is pregnant with the twins, according to chapter 7 she is in the process of separating from Richard. But she is happy about the pregnancy and chooses to stay with him. Cally is born minutes after Deanna and tends to follow the lead of her "maternal" sibling. Cally seems to have a special attachment to animals, playing with plastic animal figures (chapter 3), her stuffed green crocodile (chapter 7), and later her real dog (chapters 8, 9, and 11).

The twins grow up on their parents' reservation. (For notes about its location, see **Rozina [Rozin] Roy Whiteheart Beads Shawano.**) They have twin maternal grandmothers, because Zosie Roy and Mary Shawano refuse to reveal which of them is Rozin's mother (chapters 9 and 11). Their father,

Cally Whiteheart Beads Roy

Richard, is a young tribal leader (chapter 16). When the girls are five, the family moves to Minneapolis (chapter 3).

One afternoon in early June when Cally and Deanna are still small, their father takes them to the city park (chapter 6). There they see a woman who looks like their mother walking with a man Cally describes as a "deer man." Cally's narration includes a description of the couple's lovemaking, an account that seems to fuse what she intuits about her mother with the story of Apijigo Bakaday and the deer husband. On one occasion when the grandmothers are staying with Cally and Deanna, they allow the girls to dance in the yard naked because they are "part deer." When Frank Shawano, Rozin's lover, comes to the house, Cally recognizes him, although it is not clear whether she knows him simply as the baker or as the "deer man" in the park. After Richard forces Rozin to end the affair, Cally holds her weeping "deer mother."

While visiting relatives in Bwaanakeeng, in chapter 8 Cally rescues a white puppy from being cooked. Shortly thereafter, the puppy, now called Almost Soup, is taken to Cally's home reservation, where he stays with her grandmothers (chapter 9).

One snowy March day when Cally and Deanna are eleven (chapter 7), the girls come home from school to find their parents fighting, although Cally seems not to be as aware as her sister of her parents' impending breakup. That night, because of Richard's botched suicide attempt, Deanna dies in his pickup truck from carbon monoxide poisoning.

After Deanna's death, in chapter 9 Rozin moves back to the reservation with Cally to stay with the grandmothers. Almost a year later, on a sunny but freezing February day, Cally plays outside with her dog, Almost Soup. As she plays, she loses her bead-wrapped indis, the birth cord in its turtle holder that connects her to her long line of grandmothers (also mentioned in chapters 11 and 18). That night Cally develops a high fever. Although her mother and grandmothers try to cool her, the fever remains high for three days, and a blizzard cuts off their access to medical help. At one point, Cally has a seizure and almost dies, but her mother calls her back. An ambulance finally arrives, and at the IHS (Indian Health Service) Cally recovers quickly. After this experience, Cally develops the ability to read her mother's mind.

In chapter 11, when Cally is eighteen, she begins to wander from home, a lack of connectedness she attributes to the loss of her indis. Rozin tries to contact Zosie and Mary, who have moved to Minneapolis, to see if Cally can stay with them, but the twins are never home, so Cally goes to stay with Frank Shawano. She works in his bakery and lives in the rooms above, along with Frank, his sister Cecille, and Sweetheart Calico. Frank is kind to Cally, and she

Cally Whiteheart Beads Roy

is intrigued by Cecille's creative lying. But she finds the presence of the silent and jagged-toothed "Auntie Klaus" (Sweetheart Calico) disturbing, although her scent reminds Cally of running in the summer. (The similarity of their names may suggest a connection between the women. Cally's running is also mentioned in chapter 14.)

In the city, Cally looks for her grandmothers, asking several people their whereabouts, but each gives a different story, and she apparently manages only one brief phone visit with one of them. Finally, Grandma Zosie walks into the bakery, and Cally gives her a piece of cake. Zosie announces that Cally's dad is out on the street, a bum. Cally, who is bitter about her sister's death and has changed her name to Roy, says that she never wants to see him again. As soon as she says this, Richard—sick, hungover, disreputably dressed—walks in. He mistakes Cally for Deanna and flees in terror.

When Cally is twenty, in chapter 14 her mother moves to the city to go to night school. One August evening when Cally picks her mother up from work, Frank is there, asking Rozin out. Cally's emotions are mixed. She feels possessive of her mother but wants her to be happy. When Rozin finally agrees to go with Frank to the state fair, Cally accompanies them and observes their near-catastrophic Gravitron ride.

Frank and Rozin's wedding is in the fall. (Judging from Cally's early purchase of cake plates, this is most likely the autumn of the following year, when Cally is twenty-one.) In chapter 16 Cally is in Frank's kitchen on the wedding day, making preparations with other family members. She recalls with shame her father's phone call the night before, asking why he had not been invited to the wedding. Yet when Cecille announces that Richard is coming to the wedding, Cally does not believe her.

Richard does show up at the cliffside ceremony, however, to Cally's horror. His suicide attempt at the wedding is unsuccessful, but that night, outside the door of Rozin and Frank's hotel room, he fatally shoots himself. Having already lost her twin and now faced with her father's suicide and her mother's subsequent acute depression (chapter 17), Cally is in danger of losing her entire immediate family. Frank, however, is able to bring Rozin back into connection with life.

The following December, the family gathers at Frank and Rozin's apartment for Christmas dinner. As they arrive, Cally slips on the ice and begins to hear the Ojibwa word *daashkikaa*, not knowing what it means. (This is the word uttered by her grandmother four "greats" back when the old woman was killed by Cally's great-great-grandfather Scranton Roy in chapter 1.) Cally is quiet at dinner, watching her family and thinking of family stories and deceased family members—the story of Augustus Roy and the windigo twins, Cally's dead

Cally Whiteheart Beads Roy

father, and her own lost twin. On the back porch after dinner, Cally sees Rozin and Frank walk back from the dumpster, looking at each other with love.

Later in the kitchen, Cally asks Grandma Zosie about the word *daashkikaa* (which is an old name meaning "cracked apart") and about Cally's spirit name, Blue Prairie Woman. In response, Zosie relates her long-ago dream of the original Blue Prairie Woman and the blue beads. The story reveals that Zosie, not Mary, is Rozin's mother. Cally longs for the beads, but Zosie says that if she wants them, she must trade with their owner, Sweetheart Calico. Sweetheart Calico then draws the beads from her mouth and is at last able to speak. In exchange for the beads, she wants her freedom, so Cally walks with her all night until they reach the outskirts of the city. Cally dozes as her companion continues talking, but in the morning, Sweetheart Calico is gone. Cally hears instead the chatter of the Hmong grandmas as they dig in the dirt, and she thinks of the loss of her indis, which had connected her to her own grandmothers and the earth.

Cally's own story falls silent at the end of chapter 18, but she is undoubtedly present at Rozin and Frank's anniversary party the next autumn (chapter 22), and her voice may close the novel in chapter 23.

Candice Pantamounty Mauser. Third wife of Jack Mauser, in *Tales of Burning Love*. Descriptions of Candice's supercilious, perfectionist, controlling personality appear in "Jack's House" [9] from Jack's point of view and in "Memoria" [10] in the narrator's voice. In "Candice's Tale" [25] we learn that Jack and Candice dated in high school, their last date being when Candice is a junior. Candice later recalls having shared him with girlfriends.

In college Candice dates constantly and in the mid-seventies is fitted with a Dalkon shield, which leads to a perforated uterus and hysterectomy. She finishes her two years of college, goes to dental school, and joins a class-action lawsuit against the manufacturer of the shield. After earning her D.D.S., she uses her settlement money as down payment on a house and office space. Depressed because she will never be able to bear a child, she attempts to cope by overbooking herself at work, seeing a therapist, and getting a dog, Pepperboy. She finds the dog at the dump, where Jack is about to shoot him for biting. Candice makes a deal with Jack; in return for the dog, she will fix Jack's rotten teeth.

After several months of visits to Candice's dental office, the two go out for a lunch date, where Jack reminds her of their high school relationship and proposes marriage. They marry, but Pepperboy comes between them from the start, and in "The Wandering Room" [26] their opposing attitudes toward

Candice Pantamounty Mauser

animals drive a final wedge between them. On a deer hunt together, Candice is distressed over Jack's killing of a buck, and on their way back home in the truck, they accidentally drag Pepperboy to his death. Jack recalls the incident in "Blizzard Night" [35].

Shortly after Candice and Jack divorce, in August 1992 Jack marries Marlis Cook and takes off with her for a month-long fling. Candice seems to keep track of him, because when he returns to Fargo in September in "The First Draw" [14], he finds her sitting in his car. Trying to make him act responsibly, she drives him to his construction yard and takes his car keys away.

Early in 1994, Candice contacts Marlis, who is separated from Jack and pregnant with his child. Candice wants the baby. In "Baptism River" [29] she invites Marlis to take a trip with her to a resort on Lake Superior so that they can talk. They stop for the night at a second-class motel, where Candice offers to help Marlis through the birth and then to adopt the baby. On this trip Candice begins to feel an emotional bond with Marlis. In "Candice" [30] she realizes the lesbian implications of this bond.

Although Marlis tells her to stay away, in "The Waiting Room" [31] Candice shows up at Marlis's late-term checkup, attends Lamaze classes with her, visits in her apartment, and helps her through labor. Weeks after the birth of John Jr., Marlis is still suffering severe postpartum depression. Candice moves into the apartment to take care of Marlis and the baby, and the women become lovers.

For weeks Candice and Marlis fight over custody of the baby, as recorded in "The B & B" [16]. Candice has drawn up adoption papers, but Marlis will not sign. When Candice tells her to leave, Marlis refuses but does take a job as a substitute blackjack dealer. Candice hires a nanny to take care of John Jr.

"Memoria" [10] and "Satin Heart" [12] show Candice at Jack's funeral in January 1995. She has brought Jack's baby, chiefly to attract attention to herself. She argues with Eleanor Schlick Mauser about the final disposal of Jack's ashes. Candice wants to throw them to the wind. After the funeral, Candice, Eleanor, and Dot Adare Mauser go to the B & B where Marlis is working. There Candice gets tipsy and loses money at the blackjack table. In "The Hitchhiker" [18], just as a blizzard is striking she and the other women leave in Jack's red Explorer to ride back to Fargo. Not dressed warmly, Candice complains that they should stay at the B & B rather than risk the drift-covered roads. As they try to drive beneath an overpass, the Explorer becomes stuck in a snowdrift.

In "Secrets and Sugar Babies" [19] the stranded women begin to argue about Jack, with Candice tending to belittle him. She and Marlis get into a fight but then make up. After listening to Eleanor's tale, Candice—in "Surviving Sleep" [24]—takes her turn cleaning snow away from the tailpipe, raises the

Candice Pantamounty Mauser

question of an afterlife, and recalls Jack as a man who did not like dogs. This recollection launches her own storytelling in "Candice's Tale" [25] and "The Wandering Room" [26]. At Candice's urging, Marlis takes the next turn. Candice again picks up the thread of the tale in "Baptism River" [29] and "Candice" [30], relating the development of her and Marlis's relationship. Candice and Marlis's memories in "The Waiting Room" [31] appear not to be told to the other women. In "Rotating Wild" [32] Eleanor forces Candice to admit she is in love with Marlis. Overcome with fatigue and cold, in "The Tale of the Unknown Passenger" [34] Candice and Marlis sleep in each others' arms while Dot and their "hitchhiker" (Gerry Nanapush) make love in the front seat. In "The Disappearance" [36] and "Two Front-Page Articles" [37] a snowmobile rescue squad finds the wives and transports them to the hospital. After being held for observation and treated for frostbite, Candice and Marlis are released.

After they are rescued, Candice and Marlis discover that while they were at Jack's funeral, Jack stole Candice's car—with baby John inside (the theft is recorded in "Funeral Day" [23]). After losing the baby and then rescuing him from the blizzard, Jack telephones the hysterical Candice in "Mauser and Mauser" [39].

According to "Spring Morning" [41], Candice and Marlis buy one of the houses in Jack's housing development. In "Spring Afternoon" [42] (March 1995) Candice repairs Jack's latest decayed tooth. Marlis has called her before Jack comes to the office, and Candice seems to know that Jack has made love to her lover Marlis earlier that day.

Candice's grandmother. Had warned against waking sleepwalkers, as Candice recalls in "The Waiting Room" [31] in *Tales of Burning Love.*

Canute. One of the butchers at Kozka's Meats in chapters 2 and 4 of *The Beet Queen.*

Captain. Military officer who delivers the payment of rations for an Indian-white treaty agreement and who tries to negotiate a cash deal with Nanapush in exchange for his land in chapter 3 of *Tracks.*

Caryl Moon. Truck driver at Mauser and Mauser, hired only because Jack Mauser owes some sort of debt to Caryl's father, Maynard Moon, a lawyer. Caryl is first mentioned in "The Meadowlark" [7] in *Tales of Burning Love,* where Dot Adare Nanapush recalls that she met Jack, her second husband, when he tried to kill her boyfriend, Caryl. Dot tells the story in "Caryl Moon" [8]: In May 1994 Jack fires Dot when he learns that she has falsified load records in Caryl's favor. As she leaves, Dot runs Caryl, who is driving a dump truck, off the road. When the truck rolls over and crushes Jack's Cadillac, Jack drives off with Dot—the start of their romance—and leaves Caryl trapped in the truck. Later Jack fires Caryl.

In the second chapter with the title "Caryl Moon" [13], shortly after midnight, January 1, 1995, Caryl rescues Jack, who has escaped naked from his burning house, but then beats him into unconsciousness and leaves him in the bitter cold. Moon is mentioned briefly in "February Thaw" [40] as being once again Jack's employee—another payoff to his lawyer father whom Jack owes more than ever. Caryl is the operator of the crane that drops a statue of the Blessed Virgin on Jack in "The Stone Virgin" [44].

Catherine Miller. Woman who raises the Adare infant, later named Jude Miller. Her own infant has just died when her husband, Martin, steals the new baby from Mary Adare at the Orphans' Picnic in Minneapolis in 1932, in chapter 1 of *The Beet Queen*. In chapter 2 Catherine sees in the newspaper an inquiry, placed by Pete and Fritzie Kozka, concerning the whereabouts of the missing Adare baby, but she merely cuts the notice out and saves it, along with the baby's clothes. We learn in chapter 5 that Martin dies in 1944, and in 1950 Catherine writes to the Kozkas to tell them what has happened to the missing baby and that he is about to be ordained as a priest. The letter is forwarded to Sita Kozka in Fargo. Sita writes a letter in reply but never mails it. Many years later, in chapter 13, Celestine James finds Sita's letter and mails it. In chapter 14, ill and very weak, Catherine shows Sita's letter to Jude, revealing that he has family in Argus. Catherine's revelation prompts Jude to visit Argus on the day of the Beet Festival.

Cecille Shawano. Younger sister of Frank Shawano in *The Antelope Wife*. In chapters 11 and 16, Cecille is living in the rooms above Frank's bakery, along with Frank, Sweetheart Calico, and Cally Roy. She is a thoroughly urbanized Ojibwa (she understands only a little of the old language) who operates a kung fu studio and is studying to be a radio commentator. Cally attributes Cecille's jolting personality to her uneasy mix of Irish and Ojibwa blood. Cecille is an obsessive talker whose conversation always centers on herself. She is also a creative liar, largely because she wants to get a rise out of her too-somber brother Frank.

On the day of Frank's marriage to Rozina Roy, as the family is busy with preparations, Cecille keeps trying to tell the story of her neighbor and the dishes, although everyone ignores her. When she reports that Rozin's former husband, Richard Whiteheart Beads, is coming to the wedding, no one believes her.

Cecille Shawano

According to chapter 18, Cecille continues to stay occasionally with Frank and Rozin after their wedding, although this irritates Rozin. Yet Cally observes that the two women have become more alike over time. At the family dinner the following Christmas, Cecille is her usual confrontational self, reminding the family of Richard's suicide and questioning Grandmas Zosie and Mary about the long-standing rumor that they ate Zosie's husband.

Cecille's neighbor. Woman in Cecille Shawano's story who Cecille thinks might have stolen her set of dishes, in chapter 16 of *The Antelope Wife*.

Celestine James. Daughter of Regina Puyat Kashpaw James and Dutch James; mother of Dot Adare. Celestine's story is told primarily in *The Beet Queen*. In chapter 2 we learn that Celestine is the youngest child of Regina by her second husband, Dutch, born only a month after the wedding. Celestine has two half siblings from her mother's first marriage to a Montana Kashpaw. Celestine's parents both die when she is young, and her older half sister, Isabel Kashpaw, takes care of her. Her half brother, Russell Kashpaw, lives with them on Dutch's homestead on the outskirts of Argus. Celestine and Sita Kozka, both seventh graders in 1932, are best friends until Sita's younger cousin, Mary Adare, arrives that spring and comes between them. Over time Celestine becomes Mary's best friend.

Celestine receives word in chapter 4 that her brother, Russell, has been wounded in the war. (For possible dating of these events, see **Russell Kashpaw.**) After Russell returns home, he and Celestine have supper one night with Mary and the Kozkas.

In chapter 7 (1953) Celestine is in her early thirties and works with Mary at the Argus butcher shop. Russell returns home "from his latest war, Korea," even more wounded, and their sister, Isabel, now married, dies in South Dakota. That year, Celestine, Mary, and Russell attend the near-disastrous grand opening of Sita's new restaurant. Soon afterwards, Karl Adare visits the butcher shop looking for his sister, Mary, and has sex with Celestine on Mary's kitchen floor. Two weeks later, Karl is selling knives door-to-door when he comes to Celestine's house by accident. Celestine invites him in, and Karl stays with her for several months, during which time Russell moves out. Celestine finally forces Karl to leave, even though she is pregnant with his child. As a souvenir of their relationship, she gives him a book, which Sita recognizes in chapter 8 as the New Testament Celestine had won at a raffle the previous year.

One evening that winter, in chapter 8, Celestine finds Russell in his ice-fishing hut, collapsed from a stroke. Celestine goes into labor in the middle of a January blizzard (1954) in chapter 9. Unable to get to town, she goes to Wallace

Celestine James

Pfef's house, where Wallace helps deliver her baby girl. Insisting on naming the baby after him, Celestine calls her Wallacette Darlene. The baby's Aunt Mary, however, nicknames her Dot. We learn from chapter 15 that Celestine goes to Rapid City to marry Karl shortly after Dot's birth, but only as a formality. After their wedding dinner, she goes back home without him.

In chapter 10 a rivalry for Dot's affections develops between Mary and Celestine. Mary's interference makes it more difficult for Celestine to discipline her willful, rather spoiled child. Relationships are further strained in chapter 11 (1964) when Mary moves in with Celestine and Dot for several weeks while the butcher shop is being repaired after a fire. Chapters 11 and 12 reveal Dot's heartbreaking experiences during and after her school's Christmas play. Later that night, as Celestine holds her sobbing daughter, they are, for a moment, closer than they have been since Dot's infancy.

In chapter 12 Celestine attends the party Wallace throws for Dot's eleventh birthday (1965). Three years later Karl stops briefly in Argus, and Celestine and the fourteen-year-old Dot have breakfast with him, but the meeting is strained.

In chapter 13 (1972) Celestine has a disturbing dream about Sita, and she and Mary drive to Blue Mound to check on her. They find her ill and stay with her for several weeks. While there, Celestine finds and mails a letter Sita had written to Catherine Miller more than twenty years earlier. During this time, Celestine is also helping Dot prepare for her part in the Beet Festival. In chapter 15 Celestine sends a newspaper clipping to Karl showing Dot as a Beet Queen candidate, and in chapter 14 she receives a postcard from him in reply, saying that he is on his way. In chapter 16 Celestine insists that Dot must wear to the coronation ceremony the loud green dress that Mary has bought for her.

On a hot July day in 1972, the day of the Beet Festival, in chapter 13 Celestine and Mary find Sita outside her house, dead from an overdose of medication. Because everyone, even the undertaker, has gone to the festival, they put Sita in the passenger seat of the delivery truck and take her with them to the fairground. In chapter 15 Celestine and Mary sit at the front of the grandstand to watch Dot's coronation, where they are joined by Wallace and Karl. Celestine is terrified when Dot jumps into the skywriting plane and it disappears from sight. An hour later, in chapter 16, Celestine is still waiting in the grandstand when Dot returns. That evening Celestine and Dot fall into the familiar routines of their life together, and as each lies awake in her separate room, Dot feels close to her mother.

In 1994 Celestine is still living in Argus, but Dot and her daughter, Shawn, are living in Fargo. (Dot's husband, Gerry Nanapush, is in prison.) On a sweltering June day in "A Wedge of Shade" [3] in *Tales of Burning Love*, Dot

Celestine James

comes to Argus to tell her mother of her sudden marriage to Jack Mauser (without divorcing Gerry). Celestine is dubious, but when she discovers that the Chippewa family of Jack's mother are her distant relatives, she accepts him. (She refers to herself as a Kashpaw in this chapter, although we know from *The Beet Queen* that she is a Puyat. Her half siblings are Kashpaw.) In "The Meadowlark" [7] Dot says that her mother, who usually has a seventh sense about men, likes Jack.

The following January, after Dot is stranded for a time in a snowbound car during a blizzard, Celestine and Mary take turns staying with her in the hospital while she recovers ("February Thaw" [40]). There, Celestine and Dot express their love for each other. Celestine goes along with Dot's ruse that the car's missing passenger is Celestine. (The missing person is actually Gerry Nanapush.) When Dot is released from the hospital, Celestine and Shawn cook a big dinner for her.

Celestine's mother. See **Regina Puyat Kashpaw James.**

Children who die in fire. Victims in Richard Whiteheart Beads's apocryphal story of his past in chapter 15 of *The Antelope Wife*. Since Richard's invented pasts are concocted from stories he has heard, this tale may allude to Sweetheart Calico's experience recorded in chapter 5.

Chokecherry Girl. Sister of Fleur Pillager. Also known by her Indian name, Asasaweminikwesens, she dies of consumption in chapter 1 of *Tracks*. She is also referred to in chapter 3 of *The Bingo Palace*.

Chook. Nephew of Richard Whiteheart Beads in *The Antelope Wife*. In preparation for the autumn wedding of Frank Shawano and Richard's ex-wife, Rozina Roy, (chapter 16) Chook cooks buffalo and moose meat and runs errands for the women. When Richard shows up at the reception with a letter for Rozin, Chook delivers it.

According to chapter 18, Richard is Chook's favorite uncle, and he is so upset by Richard's suicide that he speeds in a motorboat until it runs out of gas. Although he is apparently still married that autumn, by the time he shows up at the family Christmas, Chook has gone through a difficult divorce. He brings his daughter, Elena, with him. At dinner, he is pained when Cecille Shawano insists on talking about Richard, but he still jokes with the others and pretends to have a fit. He also notices Rozin's love for her new husband.

Chook's wife. Watches Chook's escapade in the motorboat after the autumn suicide of Richard Whiteheart Beads, according to chapter 18 of *The Antelope*

Wife. By that Christmas, she and Chook have divorced, and Chook has their six-year-old daughter, Elena, for the day. Chook's wife may be the "Janice" of chapter 16, since Janice is mentioned in conjunction with Chook at Frank Shawano and Rozina Roy's wedding.

Christ. Appears to Pauline in chapter 6 of *Tracks* to tell her to fetch more souls. Pauline decides in chapter 8 that Christ is weaker than Satan and believes that she herself must be his champion and savior. At the end of that chapter she marries him by becoming a nun.

Chuck Mauser. Jack Mauser's uncle on his German father's side in *Tales of Burning Love*. He is apparently the uncle who is farming near Argus when Jack is a boy or teenager, with whom Jack lives when he runs away from his Aunt Elizabeth, Chuck's sister. These events are referred to obliquely in "Best Western" [28]. In "Eleanor's Tale" [20], while a student at North Dakota State University, Jack visits Chuck's farm and helps him fix his machinery. In "The Red Slip" [21], when Eleanor wants to date Jack, she calls him at Chuck's. In "The First Draw" [14] and "The Wandering Room" [26] we learn that when Chuck gets behind financially, Jack buys his quarter section of land west of Fargo. At first Jack leases the land back to him for sunflower farming, but (apparently unknown to Chuck) Jack plans to turn it into a housing development as soon as he can get financing. By August of 1992, Chuck's wife has left him. When Jack shows him the first large check of his development loan, Chuck—who is bitter about losing fertile land to development—is not pleased. Chuck and Jack apparently have an agreement that Chuck can harvest his sunflower crop before the development begins, but, enraged by one of his ex-wives, in September Jack bulldozes Chuck's crop.

Two years later, after houses are built on the land but have not sold, in "Jack's House" [9] Chuck writes to Jack threatening to repossess and seed the land if Jack does not make his mortgage payments. Chuck attends Jack's funeral in January 1995 ("Satin Heart" [12]), apparently the only blood relative to do so. At the end of the novel, in "Spring Morning" [41] Chuck leases his land back from Jack, again planting it in sunflowers. He also buys one of the houses in Jack's new subdivision, and his wife returns.

Chuck Mauser's wife. Has left Chuck by August 1992 in "The First Draw" [14] in *Tales of Burning Love,* but she has returned by March 1995 in "Spring Morning" [41].

Circus performers. Performers who are part of the same circus as Anna Kuklenski in "Eleanor's Tale" [20] in *Tales of Burning Love. **Ali-Khazar***'s act

Circus performers

involves white Arabian horses waltzing on their hind legs; the ***Lady of the Mists*** makes herself appear and disappear; and the ***Mysterious Bernie*** folds himself into a painted cracker tin. See also **Flying Kuklenskis.**

Clarence Morrissey. Son of Bernadette Morrissey; older brother of Sophie and Philomena Morrissey. We learn in chapter 4 of *Tracks* that Clarence is a big handsome young man who has helped build a two-story house for his family on the farm of his uncle Napoleon Morrissey. When Fleur casts a spell on Clarence's sister Sophie, rooting her to the ground, rigid, for two days, Clarence steals a statue of the Virgin Mary and takes it to Fleur's cabin to break the spell. In chapter 5 Clarence avenges Eli Kashpaw's sexual liaison with Sophie by shaming Eli's mother, Margaret Kashpaw. Clarence and his companion, Boy Lazarre, abduct Nanapush and Margaret, tie them up in a barn, and shave Margaret's head. In revenge, Nanapush and Nector Kashpaw set a snare for Clarence. He survives the snare, but is left with scars on his neck and a twisted mouth. (Years later, it is probably Clarence that Marie Kashpaw is referring to in "The Tomahawk Factory" in *Love Medicine* as "the twisted-mouth.") In chapter 7 Clarence marries a Lazarre woman and—together with Sophie, her Lazarre husband, and his six children—takes over Bernadette's house. According to Nanapush, this joining of Morrisseys and Lazarres marks the beginning of a loss of status for the once-prosperous Morrissey clan.

Clarence is one of the observers from the shore when Pauline Puyat goes to Matchimanito Lake to confront the devil in chapter 8 of *Tracks*. After Napoleon's body is found, Clarence claims in chapter 9 that his uncle has appeared to him in a (drunken) vision accusing Fleur of the murder.

Cowboy. Man whom Gerry Nanapush kicks in the groin. As recorded in "Scales" in *Love Medicine,* the cowboy takes Gerry to court and gets him sentenced to prison for three years, but the sentence is prolonged indefinitely because of Gerry's repeated escapes. The original incident apparently takes place in about 1964 or 1965.

Damien Modeste, Father. Catholic priest and friend to the Indians. In chapter 1 of *Tracks* he comes to the reservation as a young man in 1912 after the previous priest dies in the consumption epidemic. He immediately begins to demonstrate his characteristic kindness when he visits Fleur Pillager and Nanapush, who have barely survived the terrible winter. Chapter 3 of *The*

Bingo Palace indicates that he keeps records of the Indians from the first decade of their westward migration to the reservation. Nanapush, however, refuses to give Father Damien his true name in chapter 3 of *Tracks*, identifying himself simply as "No Name." Later in that chapter, Nanapush does give the priest a name for Fleur's first baby—Lulu Nanapush.

In chapter 4 of *Tracks* Father Damien sees Clarence Morrissey steal the statue of the Virgin. He offers to perform a marriage ceremony for Nanapush and Margaret Kashpaw, and he takes Nanapush's confession in chapter 5. Pauline Puyat says in chapter 6 that she will tell Father Damien about Fleur's dead baby, but there is no evidence that she does so.

In chapter 7 Father Damien brings a white doctor to minister to the frostbitten Lulu, then tries to talk Nanapush into letting the doctor take Lulu back to amputate her feet. He brings rations to the Kashpaw-Pillager family during the terrible famine of 1918 and shows them the lists and charts indicating that they are about to lose their land. Father Damien contributes from his own pocket the last quarter to pay the back taxes on the Pillager and Kashpaw lands. Also in chapter 7 Father Damien finds an Indian child frozen to death, victim of its parents' alcoholism. He urges Nanapush to take a leadership position in the tribal government so that he can help protect his people, and in chapter 9 Nanapush realizes that the priest is right. Father Damien tries unsuccessfully to rescue Pauline from her leaky boat on Matchimanito in chapter 8. In chapter 9 he hears Nanapush's "confession" about Edgar Pukwan Junior, and he helps Nanapush in his effort to bring Lulu back from boarding school. (Lulu returns in 1924.)

In "The Island" in *Love Medicine*, Nanapush tells Lulu that he had six years earlier (perhaps around 1918) lost his spirit to Father Damien in a card game. Reservation rumor in "The Beads," however, reports that the priest makes his confession to Fleur, who follows the old Indian ways of spirituality. Father Damien is probably the "French priest" in "The Beads" whom Marie says she does not fear. He is also probably the reservation priest referred to in "Night Prayer" [6] in *Tales of Burning Love* as having documented a stigmata miracle at which Sister Leopolda was present. We know that he is still alive in August 1995, because he is mentioned in "A Last Chapter" [46] as someone Eleanor Mauser wants to interview about Leopolda.

Dane. Husband of Marlis Cook's ex-sister-in-law, Lindsay, in "Marlis's Tale" [27] in *Tales of Burning Love*. He does not want Marlis to live in the foundation crawl space under their trailer. Later he leaves, and Marlis can live inside the trailer with Lindsay.

Darrell

Darrell. Frank Shawano's cousin, who speaks well of Frank and Rozina Roy on the day of their wedding, in chapter 16 of *The Antelope Wife.*

Day Twin Horse. Reservation postmaster who tries to watch Lulu Lamartine the day she steals a Wanted poster of Gerry Nanapush in chapter 1 of *The Bingo Palace.*

Dead man in woods. Body discovered by the seven-year-old Lulu Nanapush in the little clearing where she plays in "The Good Tears" in *Love Medicine.* (According to the dating in *Tracks,* Lulu would be five when she finds this body.) See also **Napoleon Morrissey.**

Deanna Whiteheart Beads. Daughter of Rozina Roy and Richard Whiteheart Beads; twin sister of Cally Whiteheart Beads in *The Antelope Wife.* According to chapters 11 and 18, Deanna's spirit name, Other Side of the Earth, is given to her by her grandmother, Zosie Shawano Roy.

Deanna and Cally are probably born in the mid-1970s. According to chapter 7, Rozin discovers that she is pregnant while she and Richard are separating, but she is overjoyed about the pregnancy and chooses to stay with him. Deanna is born before her sister and continues to take the lead through their childhood. The twins grow up on their parents' reservation, where their father is a young tribal leader (chapter 16). They have two maternal grandmothers, since the twins Zosie Roy and Mary Shawano will not reveal which of them is Rozin's mother (chapters 9 and 11). When Deanna and Cally are five, the family moves to Minneapolis (chapter 3).

Rozin adores her daughters. When she realizes in chapter 3 that she is falling in love with Frank Shawano, she weeps, fearing the effect her unwanted passion may have on her daughters. They comfort her by feeding her imaginary seaweed marshmallows. Deanna and Cally are still small in chapter 6 when their father takes them to the city park one June afternoon. There they see a woman who looks like their mother walking with a man Cally describes as a "deer man." Once, when the girls' grandmothers come down from the reservation to baby-sit, they allow Deanna and Cally to dance in the yard naked because they are "part deer."

It is March in chapter 7, but a late heavy snow is falling. Deanna and Cally, now eleven, have a good day at school, but at home that afternoon, their parents are fighting. When Deanna goes downstairs to investigate, Rozin reassures her, but Deanna knows that something is badly wrong. Typically maternal, she does not tell Cally for fear of upsetting her. When Deanna wakes in the night and sees her father leave the house, she sneaks out and climbs behind the backseat of the truck, whose engine is running. Richard has intended to commit suicide, but he accidentally locks himself out of the truck and changes his mind. As we learn in chapter 9, Richard finds Deanna in the truck the next morning, dead. According to chapter 17, Rozin buries Deanna on the reservation under a traditional grave house, where she regularly leaves offerings of food, tobacco, and coins for Deanna's passage between the two worlds.

Deanna's death is a recurrent thread stitching together much of the remaining action of the novel. Blaming both Richard (chapter 16) and her own love for Frank (chapter 11) for the tragedy, in chapter 9 Rozin moves back to the reservation with Cally to live with her mothers. Her grief over Deanna causes her to neglect Cally, who is allowed to run wild so that she is chilled and becomes gravely ill.

Deanna's death has an even more devastating effect on Richard, who cannot face his guilt and becomes a drunken bum, wandering the streets (chapters 10, 11, and 15). Sparked by Rozin's marriage to Frank ten years later, Richard's emotional emptiness finally causes him to commit suicide in chapter 16. Cally, too, misses her sister deeply, as we see in chapters 11 and 18.

After Richard's death, Deanna's spirit comes back briefly in chapter 17 to ask her mother if she is coming, too. Longing to hear her daughter's voice, Rozin begs her to stay and prepares a meal for her. When death beckons Rozin in her dreams, she decides to accept the invitation to join her daughter, until Frank intervenes and reconnects her with the living.

Deer husband. Lover of Apijigo Bakaday whose love cures her insatiable hunger in chapter 6 of *The Antelope Wife*. He is killed by Apijigo Bakaday's brothers. See also **Antelope and deer people.**

Defender girl. Woman whose less-than-two-months' pregnancy Lulu Lamartine perceives just by touching her hand in "Crossing the Water" in *Love Medicine*.

Dental office receptionist. Offensively "perky" woman who makes an emergency appointment with the dentist for Jack Mauser in "Easter Snow" [1] in *Tales of Burning Love*. Instead of keeping the appointment, Jack numbs his pain with liquor and marries June Morrissey in a bar.

Devil. See **Satan.**

Different Thumbs. Mother of Moses Pillager. She fools death into not taking the infant Moses by pretending he is already dead, as told in "The Island" in *Love Medicine*. Her Indian name is Nanakawepenesick.

Doctors

Doctors. In *The Beet Queen,* **Fritzie Kozka's doctor** tells her in chapter 4 that her lungs need dry warmth and that she should not be exposed to even one more Dakota winter. A **married doctor** in chapter 5 strings Sita Kozka along for three years until she realizes he will never leave his wife. The **doctor who assists Karl Adare** in chapter 6 after Karl injures his back orders a plank to keep his spine straight. In chapter 14 **Wallace Pfef's doctor** tells him he is suffering from nervous exhaustion and recommends a muscle relaxant and a vacation.

In *Tracks,* chapter 4, **Dutch James's doctor** cares for him after Dutch nearly freezes to death and amputates piece after piece of Dutch's rotting body. The **white doctor** who comes to examine Lulu Nanapush's frostbitten feet in chapter 7 leaves in anger when Nanapush refuses to let him take Lulu away for an amputation.

In *Tales of Burning Love,* Jack Mauser summons a **doctor** in "The Red Slip" [21] when he fears that Eleanor Schlick is having a miscarriage. The doctor simply tells Eleanor to rest. (The reader knows that she is not pregnant.) Some years later, **doctors** periodically check on Eleanor while she is sleeping in the hospital after collapsing of exhaustion and starvation in "Night Prayer" [6]. **Doctor Boiseart** attends Marlis Mauser during her pregnancy and the birth of her son in "The Waiting Room" [31]. He and Candice Pantamounty have a violent disagreement about how to treat Marlis during delivery. An **emergency room crew** treats Marlis, Candice, and Dot Mauser when they are brought in by a snowmobile rescue squad in "The Disappearance" [36]. A **hospital doctor** reassures Celestine James in "February Thaw" [40] when Dot seems to be sleeping too much after her blizzard ordeal. A **Filipino doctor** examines Jack at the Argus hospital after a stone statue nearly crushes him in "The Stone Virgin" [44]. He is amazed that Jack is not seriously injured.

When Cally Roy becomes gravely ill in chapter 9 of *The Antelope Wife,* the **doctor at the IHS** (Indian Health Service) orders an I.V. for her.

See also **Psychiatrists and therapists** and **Orderlies.**

Dog people. See **Almost Soup; Black dog; Original Dog; Sorrow; Sorrow's mother;** and **Windigo Dog.**

Dorothy Ludlow. Woman who runs a charm school that Sita Kozka attends for a time in Fargo. She teaches Sita never to frown in chapter 5 of *The Beet Queen.*

Dot Adare Nanapush Mauser. Daughter of Celestine James and Karl Adare; wife of Gerry Nanapush and mother of Shawn Nanapush; fifth wife of Jack Mauser.

Dot Adare Nanapush Mauser

Dot is conceived in chapter 7 of *The Beet Queen* when Karl visits Argus for the first time in twenty years. Celestine ends her affair with Karl the same day she realizes that she is pregnant. That night Karl's sister, Mary Adare, has a vision of the baby who will be born—a willful girl with red hair. Stranded in a snowstorm the night she goes into labor, January 18, 1954, in chapter 9 Celestine gives birth at Wallace Pfef's house, assisted by Wallace. Celestine names the baby girl Wallacette Darlene in honor of him, but the baby's Aunt Mary nicknames her Dot. We learn in chapter 15 that immediately after Dot's birth, Celestine takes the baby to Rapid City and marries Karl, but then she returns to Argus without him.

In chapter 10 Celestine and Mary compete for Dot's affections throughout her childhood. As Dot's mother, Celestine is the disciplinarian, while Mary indulges Dot. After being punished in her first-grade class, Dot lies to Mary about the "naughty box." Her lie causes Mary to make a fool of herself with the teacher. Karl sends Dot an electric wheelchair the following summer, but Celestine insists that she give it to her paralyzed uncle, Russell Kashpaw. When they take the wheelchair to Russell at Eli Kashpaw's place, Dot misbehaves and is disciplined by Fleur Pillager.

Dot once tries to run away (chapter 12), but when she arrives at Wallace Pfef's house, he reasons with her until Celestine comes. When Dot is ten (1964), in chapter 11 Mary moves in temporarily with her and Celestine. Mary's intimacy with Dot during these weeks further undermines Celestine's authority and increases her jealousy. That winter Dot gets the part of Joseph in the school's Christmas play. Chapters 11 and 12 record the incidents on the ill-fated night of the play: Dot humiliates herself at the performance, and later Wallace turns her away from his door. Afterwards, at home, Dot turns to her mother rather than Mary for comfort. Over the following weeks, Dot will not speak to Wallace. In January (chapter 12) he gives a party for Dot's eleventh birthday to try to win her back. Although the adults view the party as a disaster, Dot loves it and forgives Wallace.

Also in chapter 12, Dot is a rebellious fourteen-year-old when she meets her father for the first time as Karl is passing through Argus. Dot grows angrier and more rebellious every year. When she is eighteen, in chapter 14 Wallace tries to help by planning a Beet Festival so that Dot can be honored as Beet Queen. Chapters 13–16 relate Wallace's and Dot's family's preparations for the festival, which takes place in July 1972. Although Dot is excited as her expected coronation approaches, she is mortified when she learns during the Beet Parade that Wallace has rigged the vote for her to win, and that everyone knows it. In revenge, she dunks Wallace in the dunking booth, as recorded in chapters

Dot Adare Nanapush Mauser

14 and 16. With her family watching, in chapters 15 and 16 Dot climbs aboard a plane as it takes off to write "Queen Wallacette" in the sky. When she returns an hour later, her mother is still waiting for her on the grandstand. Dot realizes Celestine's love for her and, by the day's end, feels close to her.

We learn in "A Wedge of Shade" [3] in *Tales of Burning Love* that Dot has just enrolled at the U of M (University of Minnesota) when she goes to hear the prisoner/wanted man Gerry Nanapush speak publicly. She joins the effort to raise money for his "cause." Their relationship begins one night at a Howard Johnson's in Grand Forks after one of his speeches. According to "Scales" in *Love Medicine,* in December or January 1979–1980 Gerry impregnates Dot during a prison visit. During her pregnancy, Dot works at a construction site weight station, where she is joined by Albertine Johnson, and Gerry is in and out of prison. He returns when their daughter, Shawn, is born in October but leaves immediately afterwards to escape the police. Dot must raise Shawn alone, because Gerry is recaptured and returned to prison. "Crossing the Water" in *Love Medicine* indicates that in 1984 Dot and Shawn are in Canada and that Gerry, newly escaped again, is on his way to visit them.

When Shawn is thirteen, in May 1994 Dot goes to work for Mauser and Mauser construction company in Fargo as a bookkeeper, as recorded in "Caryl Moon" [8] in *Tales of Burning Love.* Soon after she begins working there, she becomes romantically involved with one of Jack Mauser's employees, Caryl Moon. When Jack discovers that Dot has altered records in Moon's favor, he fires her. Furious, Dot plays chicken with Moon, who is driving a Mauser gravel truck. In the fiasco that ensues, the truck is disabled and Jack's red Cadillac is demolished, but Jack and Dot leave the accident scene together.

We learn in "Hot June Morning" [2] that Dot refuses to sleep with Jack unless they are married, so he marries her immediately, although they have known each other only a month. After their first weekend of marriage, Dot and Jack go to Argus to see her mother. In "A Wedge of Shade" [3] Dot tells Celestine about Jack and says that she intends neither to divorce Gerry nor to tell him about the new husband. (This statement is at variance with the reference in chapter 21 of *The Bingo Palace* to Gerry and Dot's divorce and his awareness that she has remarried.) When Jack gets to Celestine's house, he is immediately arrested for financial misconduct in his business. Dot and Celestine then go tell Aunt Mary about Jack. When they return home, Jack is waiting for them. That night, lying in the dark, Jack slips a ring on Dot's finger, and in "Trust in the Known" [5] he muses about his relationship with Dot and her daughter.

In August, when they have been married about six weeks, at the end of "Night Prayer" [6] Dot receives a phone call for Jack from Eleanor Mauser, an

Dot Adare Nanapush Mauser

ex-wife Dot knows nothing about, who wants a ride from the Argus hospital. In "The Meadowlark" [7] Dot confronts Jack with his failure to tell her about this previous marriage. After Dot and Jack pick up Eleanor from the hospital, on their return to Fargo Dot learns that Jack has had four previous wives and has a child. Both Dot and Eleanor are wounded by his revelations on this trip, and the two develop a camaraderie. The following evening, in "Caryl Moon" [8], Dot tells Eleanor how her relationship with Jack began. Dot begins paperwork to end both of her marriages, although in September she is still living with Jack.

Before the year's end, Dot leaves Jack four times, the final time on New Year's Eve ("Jack's House" [9]). She and Shawn are living in an apartment, whose location she will not tell Jack. She warns him that something bad will happen, a prophecy that seems fulfilled when his house burns down ("The Garage" [15]). In "Memoria" [10] and "Satin Heart" [12] Dot attends Jack's funeral, where she watches his history unfold as his former wives interact. After the funeral, Dot is at the West Fargo steak house–bar–casino with the other wives in "The B & B" [16] when a massive Indian "woman" enters, whom Dot recognizes as Gerry. Dot buys "her" a pizza and "she" follows Dot out of the room.

In "The Hitchhiker" [18] all the wives—Dot, Eleanor, Candice Panta-mounty, and Marlis Cook—get into Jack's red Explorer, and Dot drives toward Fargo as a blizzard strikes, overriding the others' concern about the dangerous weather conditions. As they leave West Fargo, they pick up a snow-covered hitchhiker, whom Dot knows to be Gerry. He goes to sleep in the space behind the backseat, doped with painkillers Dot had given him earlier. On the way to Fargo, the Explorer becomes stuck in a snowdrift, and Dot feels guilty that her stubbornness now imperils them all. In "Secrets and Sugar Babies" [19] she agrees with Eleanor's suggestion that each woman tell her story to help them all stay awake through the night, and she sets the rules for the exchange. Through the chapters in part 3 of *Tales of Burning Love,* Dot listens as Eleanor, Candice, and Marlis tell their stories, engages in dialogue with them, helps clean snow from the tailpipe, and periodically turns on the car's heater. Dot does not tell a tale in the car. She instead lives out her tale of burning love, for in "The Tale of the Unknown Passenger" [34] she makes love with the hitchhiking Gerry while the other women sleep.

Eventually, a snowmobile rescue squad picks up the occupants of the car in "The Disappearance" [36] and "Two Front-Page Articles" [37]. But by the time they arrive at the hospital, Gerry has disappeared. Dot claims that the missing passenger is her mother. In "February Thaw" [40] Dot stays several days in the hospital, recovering from her ordeal. After she is released, she discards

Dot Adare Nanapush Mauser

the divorce papers she had begun for her marriage to Gerry, and when Jack telephones, she tells him that he should go back to Eleanor. Later, taking a walk, Dot is overcome with longing for Gerry, lies on the ground, and weeps. Finally, she starts back to the shop and considers going into business with her aunt and mother.

Dot Adare's classmates. Children at Saint Catherine's school in Argus. The children in Dot's *first-grade class* are intimidated by her aggressiveness in chapter 10 of *The Beet Queen*. Dot knocks out the tooth of one *first-grade girl,* and the *girl's mother* phones Dot's mother, Celestine James.

Dot's relationship with her classmates has not changed much by the time she is in fourth grade in chapter 11. Dot has a crush on the *boy who plays the front end of the donkey* in the Christmas play in which Dot is Joseph. When he does not cooperate during the performance, she smacks him with her mallet. A *fat blond hysterical woman,* apparently the boy's mother, runs from the audience to rescue him. The incident is referred to again in chapter 12. The *three boys and one girl* who are invited to Dot's eleventh-birthday party in chapter 12 are said to be Dot's only friends.

Dot Adare's mother. See Celestine James.

Dove, the. Nanapush's wife with finicky tastes, apparently the first of his three wives. Also referred to by her Indian name, Omiimii, she is mentioned in chapters 3 and 9 of *Tracks.*

DuCharme. Man at the trading store in town who notices Sophie Morrissey's beauty and gives her free candy in chapter 4 of *Tracks.*

Dutch James. Second husband of Regina Puyat Kashpaw James and father of Celestine James. Chapter 3 of *Tracks* refers to him as a Dutchman. In chapter 2 he lives in Argus and works at Pete Kozka's butcher shop. On a delivery to the reservation he meets Regina, whose Kashpaw husband has moved to Montana. Dutch apparently takes Regina and her son Russell back to Argus to live with him. In the spring of 1912, Regina's niece Pauline Puyat also comes to stay with them and work in the butcher shop. When Fleur Pillager comes to work at the butcher shop in June of 1913, she, Dutch, and two of his coworkers play poker in the evenings. The men resent the fact that Fleur always wins. One August night when Pete is out of town, Dutch and his two coworkers attack Fleur. When a tornado—presumably Fleur's revenge—strikes the next day, they all three take shelter in the butcher shop's meat locker, and Pauline locks the door from the outside. They are not found for several days. Dutch is the only one who survives, but in chapter 4 he loses parts of his arms and legs, piece by piece, to gangrene. As Regina cares for him, for the first time she and Dutch seem actually to love one another. By the time cold weather comes, Dutch has more or less recovered, and he and Regina marry. Chapters 4, 6, and 8 indicate that Pauline is haunted by what she has done to Dutch.

According to Sita Kozka's account in chapter 2 of *The Beet Queen,* Dutch and Regina's daughter, Celestine, is born a month after the wedding. This account also relates that after the wedding, Regina brings down from the reservation "three other children" whom Dutch knew nothing about and that Dutch dies by freezing solid in the Kozka's meat locker. The latter two details are at variance with the account found in *Tracks.*

In chapter 6 of *Tracks* Dutch, now dead and still missing pieces of his limbs, is one of the men who gambles with Fleur in Pauline's death vision.

Dympna, Sister. Witnesses the apparently miraculous stigmata in Marie Lazarre's hand (1934) at the Sacred Heart Convent in "Saint Marie" in *Love Medicine.* She is still at Sacred Heart in 1957 and serves as doorkeeper when Marie arrives with her daughter Zelda in "Flesh and Blood," but she does not recognize Marie. See also **Nuns at Sacred Heart Convent.**

E

Edgar "Dizzy" Lightninghoop. Lyman's boss and the tribal superintendent of the Bureau of Indian Affairs in "The Tomahawk Factory" in *Love Medicine.* At one point, Lulu Lamartine occupies his office and threatens to burn his proposal for the building of a tribal souvenir factory.

Edgar Pukwan. Tribal police officer who reluctantly helps Nanapush rescue Fleur Pillager in chapter 1 of *Tracks.* Afraid of the consumption that has killed Fleur's parents, Pukwan will not touch her and tries to burn the Pillager house. He soon dies—possibly from consumption, although chapter 8 suggests that his death is caused by a Pillager curse.

Edgar Pukwan Junior. Son of Edgar Pukwan and, like his father, a tribal police officer. In chapter 1 of *Tracks* he helps Nanapush bury the bodies of the five Pillagers who die in the consumption epidemic of 1912. In chapter 5 Nanapush threatens to tell Pukwan (whom he refers to as his cousin) if Boy Lazarre and Clarence Morrissey harm Nanapush or Margaret Kashpaw, but they report that Pukwan is off in the war (World War I). Pukwan returns from the

Edgar Pukwan Junior

war in chapter 7 bringing the influenza virus with him. Chapters 7, 8, and 9 indicate Pukwan's hatred of the Pillagers, whom he blames for his father's death. Along with the Lazarres and Morrisseys, he profits from his alliance with the government and apparently plays a part in foreclosing on and selling Pillager land. When Napoleon Morrissey is found dead, Pukwan casts the blame on Fleur Pillager. But in chapter 9, Nanapush gets revenge: he publicly "confesses" Pukwan's masturbation, and he defeats Pukwan in an election for tribal chairman.

Ed Rafferty. Truck driver who seems to tease Albertine Johnson in "Scales" in *Love Medicine.*

Eleanor Schlick Mauser. Second wife of Jack Mauser in *Tales of Burning Love.* We learn in "Night Prayer" [6] and "The Meadowlark" [7] that Eleanor's appearance is dramatic, with black hair, strong eyebrows, large green eyes, and full lips. She has her mother's poise and energy.

The only child of Lawrence and Anna Schlick, Eleanor is the sole object of her parents' attention, and before their separation she has a peacefully happy childhood, as recounted in "White Musk" [4]. In "Eleanor's Tale" [20] her one-time trapeze artist mother, Anna, rescues the six-year-old Eleanor from their burning house. A year or two later, Eleanor sees Jack Mauser for the first time on the bitterly cold November night when she and her mother save his life after he has become encased in ice while fighting a fire. When her father, Lawrence, returns home from putting out the fire and finds Anna and Eleanor asleep in bed beside Jack, his jealous reaction completely changes Eleanor's life. Abandoned by Lawrence, she and her mother are reduced to poverty.

In "The Red Slip" [21] Eleanor, now a teenager, encounters Jack in a department store and takes revenge for the harm he has caused by grinding his hand into broken glass. She then decides to seduce him, believing that doing so will prove to her father that there was nothing between Jack and Anna. Her efforts have the unexpected consequence of her falling in love with this former enemy.

Eleanor and Jack begin an on-and-off relationship, with Eleanor sending him away again and again. During this time, Jack goes out to western North Dakota to work in the oil fields and stays for a year (apparently 1980–1981, since he is in Williston on Easter 1981, but back in Fargo by fall). When he returns, Eleanor observes that he drinks too much and says strange things. That fall, the now college-aged Eleanor falsely announces that she is pregnant by Jack, which precipitates her parents' reunion. She tries to end her relationship with Jack but instead goes to Florida with him, where they get married. The marriage becomes a long series of fights until Eleanor finally goes to London for a year as an exchange student.

Some years after their divorce, in "Hot June Morning" [2] Jack recalls Eleanor as a professional Catholic and an intellectual; dysfunctional, dramatic, and unpredictable. Yet, as we learn in "Trust in the Known" [5], they continue to visit each other from time to time, and according to "Night Prayer" [6] they even make love a few times.

After her divorce from Jack, Eleanor acquires two M.A. degrees and an arrest record ("Night Prayer"). As recounted in "White Musk" [4], in the fall of 1993 Eleanor is a college professor in Minneapolis, teaching a seminar on The New Celibacy. She is about thirty (she is in her early thirties in 1994, "Night Prayer"). In October Eleanor seduces one of her male undergraduate students, whose name she cannot remember ("Kim, Tim, Vim, or something like that"). When she gives him a B minus at the end of the semester, he brings sexual harassment charges against her. After losing her job, Eleanor sublets her apartment and decides to visit the subject of her latest research project, Sister Leopolda, at the convent in Argus.

In "Night Prayer" [6] Eleanor stays at the convent for some time, where she helps take care of Leopolda and finds the quiet life restorative. As she watches Jack Mauser's construction crew remove the cracked wooden statue of the Virgin from the convent yard, she thinks about Jack again. One day she receives a memo from him asking her to meet him in the garden at midnight, with no day specified. Two days later, on a hot June night (1994), Eleanor goes out into the garden and finds Jack lowering himself over the wall. When Sister Leopolda enters the garden, Eleanor disguises Jack as a statue of the Virgin. While a storm gathers, Leopolda and Eleanor talk about the nature of love. The old nun appears to die at the feet of the "statue," and Eleanor is haunted by her last words. Later, Jack finds Eleanor's room in the convent, where they make love as the storm breaks. Following this encounter, Eleanor realizes that she has fallen back in love with Jack. She loses sleep, is unable to eat, and finally collapses in nervous exhaustion and is taken to the Argus hospital. When she has sufficiently recovered, in August Eleanor calls Jack to come pick her up.

Jack comes to the hospital in "The Meadowlark" [7], accompanied by his latest wife, Dot. On the trip back to Fargo, Eleanor learns that Jack has a baby boy by one of his other wives. Both Dot and Eleanor are wounded by his revelations on this trip, and the two begin to develop a camaraderie. The following evening, in "Caryl Moon" [8] Dot tells Eleanor the story of how her own relationship with Jack began.

Eleanor Schlick Mauser

By December Eleanor has moved back to Minneapolis. Jack thinks about her in "Jack's House" [9], "The Garage" [14], and "The Owl" [17]. After Jack's supposed death by fire, of all his wives Eleanor is the most distraught. "Memoria" [10] and "Satin Heart" [12] depict the visitation room at the Fargo funeral home of Eleanor's father, Lawrence Schlick, on the day of Jack's funeral, January 5, 1995. At the funeral, Eleanor and Candice get into an argument over how to dispose of Jack's remains. Eleanor wants to bury his ashes in the cemetery, since she secretly intends to be buried beside him.

After the funeral, in "The B & B" [16] Eleanor goes along with the other wives to the steak house–bar–casino where Marlis Cook Mauser, Jack's fourth wife and the mother of his child, is dealing blackjack. That evening, in "The Hitchhiker" [18] all of the wives get into Jack's red Explorer to ride back to Fargo as a blizzard is striking. As they try to drive beneath an overpass, the Explorer becomes stuck in a snowbank. In "Secrets and Sugar Babies" [19] the stranded women begin to argue about Jack, with Eleanor tending to defend him. Faced with the possibility of dying in the blizzard, Eleanor proposes that each woman tell her story to stay awake through the night.

Eleanor's is the first of these "tales of burning love." In the small hours of the morning she tells of her childhood, especially her relationship with her mother ("Eleanor's Story" [20]), and of her relationship with Jack ("The Red Slip" [21]). Her story is interrupted occasionally by questions from the other wives.

When the women discuss life after death in "Surviving Sleep" [24], Eleanor expresses a paradoxical faith in both science and a transcendent element in human existence. She then listens to Candice's and Marlis's tales. A little before 6:00 A.M., in "Rotating Wild" [32] Eleanor criticizes Candice and insults Marlis. Enraged, Marlis suggests that it is time to clean the snow away from the tailpipe and that it is Eleanor's turn. The women form a human chain, but Marlis lets go of Eleanor's hand, and Eleanor flies away into the storm. Sister Leopolda appears to her out of the darkness in "A Conversation" [33], and her instructions save Eleanor's life. Following a row of trees, Eleanor arrives at the airport terminal. She alerts authorities to the plight of the other women, and they are rescued, as related in "The Disappearance" [36] and "Two Front-Page Articles" [37].

In "February Thaw" [40] Dot tells Jack that he should go back to Eleanor. That April, Jack sees Eleanor (and other women he has loved) in the face of the statue of the Virgin as it falls on him in "The Stone Virgin" [44].

In the months following her blizzard encounter with Leopolda, Eleanor rents an old farmhouse at the edge of the reservation, deciding to make her research on the old nun her life's work ("A Last Chapter" [46]). She rejects a search for proofs in favor of a trust in subjective reality. Although they do not to live together, Jack visits Eleanor periodically.

In August Eleanor's mother and father die ("A Light from the West" [43]), and as she dies, Anna recalls her daughter's newborn face. One lush, late-August night, Jack comes to the farmhouse, and he and Eleanor make love.

Elena. Daughter of Chook and, apparently, Chook's wife. Elena is six years old when she comes with her father to the family Christmas dinner in chapter 18 of *The Antelope Wife*. By that time, Chook and his wife are divorced. (Since Chook and his wife seem to be still married at the time of Richard Whiteheart Beads's suicide, and Chook and Janice seem to come as a couple to Frank Shawano and Rozina Roy's wedding, Janice is possibly Elena's mother.)

Eli Kashpaw. Second youngest of twelve children born to Kashpaw (Resounding Sky) and Margaret (Rushes Bear), Eli is probably born in 1898. We learn in "The World's Greatest Fishermen" in *Love Medicine* that his ten older siblings move to Montana when land is allotted. Although Margaret allows the government to put her youngest, Nector, in school, she hides Eli to keep him home. He learns the woods and the old Indian ways. As children, Russell and Isabel Kashpaw and Pauline Puyat have to track Eli down to get to know him, but find him good company, as recorded in chapter 10 of *The Beet Queen*. (There is some confusion about Eli's relationship to these Kashpaw children. In *The Beet Queen,* he is referred to as Russell's half brother, but the genealogy in *Love Medicine* and *Tracks* indicates that Eli is the younger brother of Russell's father. See **Montana Kashpaw.**) When Russell and Isabel's mother, Regina, dies after moving to Argus, Eli leaves the reservation for the first time ever to attend her funeral.

In chapter 3 of *Tracks* Eli is a shy fifteen-year-old woodsman. In the fall of 1913 he is tracking a wounded doe when he comes upon Fleur Pillager in the clearing at her cabin on Matchimanito Lake. He is captivated by Fleur and goes to Nanapush for help. Armed with advice and gifts from Nanapush, Eli returns to Fleur, and they begin an intense love affair. Margaret tries to get Eli to return home, but he will not leave Fleur. In the spring Fleur gives birth to a daughter, Lulu Nanapush, but it is not clear whether Lulu is Eli's child or the product of Fleur's possibly having been raped in Argus shortly before her return to the reservation. (For discussion of Lulu's paternity, see **Fleur Pillager** and **Lulu Nanapush Morrissey Lamartine.**)

According to chapter 4 of *Tracks,* after Lulu's birth Margaret spends much of her time with Eli and Fleur at Matchimanito, and Pauline Puyat occasionally visits. By the summer of 1917, Eli realizes that Pauline is sexually attracted

Eli Kashpaw

to him, and he rejects her. In revenge, while Eli is working during the hay harvest at the Morrissey farm, Pauline bewitches him into a torrid seduction of fourteen-year-old Sophie Morrissey. Aware of the infidelity, Fleur rejects him. As Eli recounts in chapter 5, on moonlit nights he watches her walk into the icy Matchimanito Lake and, after a time, walk back out. Suspecting that she is pregnant with the lake creature's child, he goes to live with Nanapush. As they endure that winter's famine, the nineteen-year-old Eli, guided by Nanapush's spirit, shoots a moose. Later that winter, Eli gives Fleur the scarf of fine white cloth that becomes her trademark, and they reconcile. Hearing the cries of their lovemaking, the hungry people ice fishing on the lake are warmed with hope.

The following winter, 1918–1919, brings even worse famine, as recorded in chapters 6 and 7. To conserve resources, during much of the winter Nanapush and Margaret live with Eli and Fleur, who is pregnant with Eli's child, and Pauline occasionally pays an unwelcome visit. Eli is away when Fleur goes into premature labor and the baby dies. When he returns, he buries the child in a shoe box by tying it with his own hair high in a tree. The whole family nearly starves before winter is out, for Eli can find no more game. They are saved only because Margaret, and then later Eli, go to town for government commodity rations. When they learn the danger of foreclosure on Kashpaw and Pillager land, Eli is angry, and the family spends the rest of the winter raising money for land allotment fees.

The following spring (1919), Eli is mentioned as one of the observers on the shore when Pauline goes out onto Matchimanito Lake to meet the devil in chapter 8. In the fall, chapter 9, Fleur learns that her land has been sold because Eli's brother Nector did not pay the fees on it. Eli tries to convince her to move onto Kashpaw land with him. Instead, she weights herself with stones and walks into the lake. Eli saves her, but he is frightened when she lays a curse on Nector. Ironically, in an effort to earn money to repurchase a piece of Pillager land, Eli goes to work for the very lumber company that is logging it.

When Nector returns from boarding school and various wanderings, Eli is still living with their mother at the old Kashpaw place in "The Plunge of the Brave" in *Love Medicine.* Eli and Nector hunt ducks that Nector sells in "Wild Geese" (1934). Eli is a skilled huntsman but too shy to market his kill.

Fourteen years later (1948), in "The Beads" in *Love Medicine,* Eli is living in a mud-chinked shack on the far end of Kashpaw land. It is rumored that he still goes to visit Fleur, who is living with old Nanapush at the time. He establishes a rapport with the troubled nine-year-old June Morrissey, whom Nector's wife, Marie, has taken in, and June comes to live with him in the woods. As Eli recalls in "Crown of Thorns," June sleeps on a cot beside his stove, and he hates to send her off on the government school bus on cold dark mornings. In "The World's Greatest Fishermen," Albertine Johnson recalls Eli's affection for "his little girl" June. Even after June moves out, Eli keeps a photograph of her in his cabin along with an old pencil drawing she makes as a high school student (chapter 10 of *The Beet Queen*). According to "The Beads," Eli seems to have a way with children. In chapter 19 of *The Bingo Palace* Albertine recalls her Uncle Eli's amusing them with string designs—cat's cradle, chicken foot, and such.

In 1953, in chapter 7 of *The Beet Queen*, Russell Kashpaw comes to stay with Eli on the reservation. That summer, in chapter 8, Russell apparently moves in with Eli permanently. After Russell's paralyzing stroke the following winter, Eli leaves the reservation for the second time ever in chapter 10 to sign him out of the hospital. Apparently with Fleur's help, Eli cares for Russell in his two-room house. In "Flesh and Blood" in *Love Medicine* (1957), Marie thinks about how Eli has grown even quieter and less social with the passage of time, and she assumes that he never thinks about women.

In the summer of 1961 (chapter 10 of *The Beet Queen*) Russell's half sister, Celestine James, and her daughter, Dot Adare, visit Eli and Russell to bring Russell a wheelchair. When Dot is a teenager, one of her various dreams in chapter 14 is to live on the reservation with Eli and Russell. In chapter 13, Eli watches as a hospital orderly dresses Russell in his military uniform for the Beet Parade (1972).

June remembers Eli's warm kitchen in "The World's Greatest Fishermen" as she walks to her death in an Easter snowstorm in 1981. Two months later Eli arrives with Gordie Kashpaw, June's former husband, at a family gathering at the old Kashpaw place. He refuses to ride in the new Firebird that June's son, King Kashpaw, has bought with her insurance money. Early one morning after June's death, in "Crown of Thorns" Gordie comes to Eli's house to beg a beer. Eli tries to feed him breakfast but will not give him any more beer, so Gordie leaves. Afterward, Eli sits and remembers June as a child living with him.

Elizabeth. See **Aunt Elizabeth.**

Elmo. Owner of Elmo's Landscape Systems in Texas where Karl Adare works in chapter 14 of *The Beet Queen* just before returning to Argus to see his daughter Dot crowned as Beet Queen. Karl quits this job in chapter 15 when one of the managers sneers at him for bragging about his daughter.

Elsa Lamartine. Twin Cities wife of Beverly Lamartine in "Lulu's Boys" in *Love Medicine*. She is a natural blond who hides from her family the fact that Beverly is an Indian. Although she is rigid and unaffectionate with him, Beverly

Elsa Lamartine

adores her. On a visit to the reservation in "The Good Tears," Beverly marries Lulu Lamartine without divorcing Elsa. When he tells Lulu about this other wife, she sends him back to the city to divorce Elsa, but it is doubtful that he actually does so. He apparently has Lulu's twelve-year-old son Gerry thrown into detention, and we never hear of his returning to the reservation.

Elward Strong Ribs. Second husband of Irene Toose (Shawnee Ray Toose's mother), mentioned in chapters 2 and 10 of *The Bingo Palace.*

Ethiopian woman. Young woman who answers the door when Cally Roy and Cecille Shawano go looking for Cally's grandmothers in chapter 11 of *The Antelope Wife.* Cecille embellishes the incident when she recounts it to her brother Frank.

Eugene Kashpaw. He and Patsy are the youngest of Marie and Nector Kashpaw's five children in *Love Medicine.* Eugene is the last-born, since, as recorded in "The Beads" in *Love Medicine,* Marie's youngest is a boy, born in 1948. Marie almost dies in that long labor and birth, during which she is attended by her mother-in-law, Margaret, and the medicine woman Fleur Pillager. In 1957 Marie leaves Eugene and Patsy in their sister Aurelia's care in "Flesh and Blood" when she takes their other sister, Zelda, to visit Sister Leopolda.

Everlasting. Parent of Magid and forebear of Rozina Roy in chapter 3 of *The Antelope Wife.*

Father of Fargo baby. Man who leaves his car with the motor running outside the train station in Fargo, with his baby in the backseat, in chapter 24 of *The Bingo Palace.* When Gerry Nanapush and Lipsha Morrissey steal the car, the distraught father jumps onto the trunk, but soon rolls off. This story is told from an alternate point of view in "Funeral Day" [23] in *Tales of Burning Love.*

Fleur Pillager. Medicine woman; wife of Eli Kashpaw and mother of Lulu Nanapush. Most of the story of Fleur's childhood and young adulthood appears in *Tracks.* In chapter 2 we learn that the Pillagers, who are of the bear clan and live beside Matchimanito Lake, are known for their sensitive hands, their penetrating gaze and wolf grin—and their power. From as far back as Fleur's grandmother, Four Soul, the Pillagers have had medicine power. (See also **Pillager family.**)

Fleur Pillager

Once as a child and then as a fifteen-year-old, Fleur seems to drown in the lake, but in each case she sends her rescuers on death's road in her place. Fleur is feared, and gossiped about, all of her life. Years later her power to make other souls take her place in death is still discussed (chapter 12 of *The Bingo Palace*), and a story is still told that the lake spirit, Misshepeshu, grabbed her as a girl and "had its way with her" ("Love Medicine" in *Love Medicine*). When Fleur is a child, Nanapush visits her family's home at Matchimanito, bringing peppermint, as she recalls in chapter 3 of *Tracks*.

Fleur is seventeen in chapter 1 of *Tracks* when her parents and three siblings die in the consumption epidemic in the early winter of 1912. Nanapush rescues her, nurses her back to life, and then buries her dead family. Except for her distant cousin Moses, Fleur is now the only living Pillager, and she and Nanapush barely survive that winter. In late winter, Fleur returns to her family's cabin beside Matchimanito and lives there alone. When the lumber companies and the government fee collectors come, Fleur eludes them, determined to hold onto Pillager land.

Fleur goes to Argus the following June (1913, chapter 2) and works in Pete and Fritzie Kozka's butcher shop. Fritzie teaches her to cut meat and gives her a black umbrella (which appears again later in the novel). As she works, Fleur is watched by Pauline Puyat and followed about by Russell Kashpaw. In the evenings, she plays poker with three of her fellow employees, Lily Veddar, Tor Grunewald, and Dutch James. One night in August, angered by her winnings, Lily, Tor, and Dutch attack Fleur in the smokehouse, while Pauline hides nearby and does nothing. The next day, it appears that Fleur takes her revenge. A tornado destroys the butcher shop, and her three assailants freeze when they take refuge in the meat locker. In chapter 4, Pauline is haunted by her memory of Fleur's rape.

That fall, in chapter 3 Fleur walks back onto the reservation. With her Argus earnings and winnings, she pays the fees on every Pillager land allotment she has inherited. The local gossip speculates that she has returned from Argus pregnant, but within a month, Eli Kashpaw becomes her lover, which "muddie[s] the water" for the gossips. When Lulu is born the next spring, Fleur almost dies in childbirth, but is assisted by Eli's mother, Margaret Kashpaw—and a drunken bear.

Erdrich's readers, like the reservation gossips at the end of chapter 2, cannot be certain of Lulu's paternity. The only knowledge we have of the attack on Fleur in the Argus smokehouse comes from Pauline, recorded first in chapter 2 and then repeated to Margaret and Nanapush in chapter 3. Even Pauline admits that she did not see what happened in that attack. More importantly,

Fleur Pillager

as Nanapush reminds us, Pauline is a notorious liar. In fact, when Nanapush mentions Pauline's story to Fleur, Fleur replies, "the Puyat lies." Nevertheless, there is evidence that Fleur is pregnant before becoming Eli's lover. When she returns to the reservation after the incident in Argus, in chapter 3 Nanapush notices that her dress is too small, strained across the front, although he doesn't know whether there is money or a child in the dress. The strongest evidence of an Argus paternity is Eli's description of Fleur at their first meeting as having "no curve" and being ravenously hungry. His report leads Nanapush to remark, "I was sure she was pregnant." Nanapush, however, does not see her for himself, and when Margaret sees her later in the chapter and judges that she is pregnant, Fleur and Eli are already lovers. By the time Lulu is born, at the chapter's end, Nanapush appears to think that Eli may in fact be her father, although he adds, "who knew for certain . . . ?" Despite the general uncertainly about Lulu's paternity, however, after her birth, everyone clearly accepts her as Eli's child, even her grandmother Margaret. (For the paternity issue, see also **Lulu Nanapush Morrissey Lamartine.**)

Margaret tries to get Fleur and Eli to move to the Kashpaw place in chapter 4, but Fleur will not leave Pillager land and Eli remains with her. Margaret often stays with them after Lulu's birth, and Pauline visits occasionally, envious of Fleur and Eli's passion. In the autumn of 1917, after Pauline bewitches Eli into a sexual liaison with Sophie Morrissey, Fleur gets revenge by casting a spell over Sophie, so that the girl remains immovable outside Fleur's cabin for two days. Fleur also rejects Eli.

After a short time, in chapter 5 Eli returns to Fleur's cabin, although she will still not let him touch her. On moonlit nights he sees her walk into the icy autumn lake and then emerge sometime later. Eli comes to believe that Fleur is pregnant with the lake creature's child, and he goes to live with Nanapush. In the famine winter that ensues, Eli leaves meat at Fleur's door, but she mocks him. When Clarence Morrissey and Boy Lazarre attack Margaret and shave her head, it is only the fear of Fleur that prevents their seriously harming her. In response to the attack on Margaret, Fleur shaves her own head, and her curse contributes to Boy Lazarre's death. To cover her bald head, Eli gives Fleur the scarf of fine-woven white cloth that will become one of her trademarks. Before the winter is out, Fleur accepts Eli back, and the hungry people ice fishing on Matchimanito hear their cries as they make love.

The following winter, 1918–1919, brings even worse famine. In chapter 6 Fleur, pregnant with Eli's child, is gaunt. She, Eli, Lulu, Nanapush, and Margaret are all living together, sharing their meager supply of food. Pauline comes frequently to visit, believing that she is in competition with Fleur for the souls of the Indian people. Fleur mocks Pauline but is kind to her. When Fleur goes into labor prematurely, only Pauline and Lulu are present. Lulu goes through the snow to Margaret's for help (a journey on which her feet become severely frostbitten). Pauline, however, does not help Fleur, failing to bring her the medicines needed to stop the labor. The child is born, and the enraged Fleur throws a knife at Pauline. According to Pauline's subsequent vision, Fleur walks down death's road and gambles for the lives of her children with the men whose deaths she has caused. Fleur loses the life of the baby but wins Lulu's.

In chapter 7 Fleur grieves her baby's death. One sleeting night she takes the black umbrella (given her by Fritzie Kozka) to the tree where the infant is buried, to shelter its burial box. As the winter drags on, the family almost starves, saved only by the arrival of government rations. When Father Damien explains the danger that they may all lose their land, Fleur scoffs that no one would dare to remove Pillagers from the shores of Matchimanito. Yet after the loss of her child, Fleur's power seems to wane, and she becomes overly protective of Lulu. In the spring, Nanapush and Moses Pillager conduct a healing ceremony for her.

When Pauline in chapter 8 takes a boat out onto Matchimanito to confront the devil (in the form of the lake creature), she sees Fleur, whom she considers the devil's agent, standing on the shore dressed in black. Shortly thereafter, Fleur is mistakenly held responsible for the death of Napoleon Morrissey, whom Pauline has killed.

The ultimate challenge to Fleur's power comes in the fall of 1919 (chapter 9), as loggers move onto her land and she learns that Nector and Margaret have failed to pay the Pillager land fees. At this news, Fleur loads herself down with stones and walks into the lake. When Eli saves her from her third drowning, she opens her eyes and says that Nector will take her place this time. After sending Lulu away to boarding school, Fleur returns for one last defense of her land, sabotaging the equipment of the invading lumberjacks. Afterwards, as *Tracks* closes, she leaves the reservation. Lulu's memories of Fleur and her grief at being sent away appear in "The Island" in *Love Medicine.* When Lulu as a young woman will not call Fleur mother or visit her, Nanapush tries to make her understand her mother's reasons for sending her away (chapter 9 of *Tracks*). Years later, in chapter 11 of *The Bingo Palace,* Lulu still does not talk about Fleur, but says that she understands her.

In *The Beet Queen* we learn in chapter 10 that Fleur comes to Argus for the funeral of Regina Puyat (probably in the 1920s). In chapter 3, while Fleur is away from the reservation, she makes her living as a peddler, wearing her signature white head scarf. In 1932 Fleur heals the injured and ill fourteen-year-old Karl Adare and takes him to the reservation convent.

Fleur Pillager

In chapter 12 of *The Bingo Palace* Fleur returns to the reservation for the last time. Dressed in a white suit, driving a white Pierce-Arrow, and accompanied by a young white boy, she lures the former Indian agent Jewett Parker Tatro into a poker game. Fleur's boy, acting as her surrogate, wins from Tatro all that he owns, the Pillager land he has bought and more. An explanation for Fleur's acquisition of the car and clothes may be suggested in chapter 14 of *The Bingo Palace,* which refers to her making love to high society men of Saint Paul, Minnesota.

Fleur is living on the reservation with old Nanapush in 1948 when she helps Marie Kashpaw to give birth to her last child in "The Beads" in *Love Medicine.* Rumor has it that Eli still visits her. *The Beet Queen* depicts Fleur as helping Eli, in the late 1950s through early 1970s, to care for Russell Kashpaw, who is paralyzed from a stroke. In 1961 (chapter 10) she disciplines Russell's impudent niece, Dot Adare, and on the day of the Beet Festival in 1972 (chapter 13), she helps get Russell ready for the parade.

Fleur continues to live at Matchimanito the rest of her life. In old age she is referred to variously as Old Lady Pillager, the Old Lady (Mindemoya), or just "the Pillager" ("Love Medicine" in *Love Medicine;* chapters 11 and 14 of *The Bingo Palace*). She is respected and feared as a powerful medicine woman. In chapter 3 of *The Bingo Palace,* she is present at the naming ceremony of Albertine Johnson. Reservation gossip in chapter 1 suggests that Fleur is putting off dying until she can pass on her power to her great-grandson, Lipsha Morrissey. Lipsha is aware of the stories about Fleur, as indicated by his references to her in several chapters, including "Love Medicine" in *Love Medicine* and chapters 5, 11, and 14 of *The Bingo Palace.* In 1982, he wants to ask Fleur for a love medicine for his adoptive grandmother, Marie Kashpaw, but is afraid to do so. When he needs a love medicine for himself, however, he gathers the courage to meet her. When Fleur comes into town on her "feast day" in chapter 11 of *The Bingo Palace,* Lipsha goes home with her. As darkness settles, Fleur changes into a bear and speaks to him. She speaks in the old language (chapter 22), gives Lipsha advice about love (chapter 14), and admonishes him about the enduring value of the land (chapter 13). The story of her recovery of Pillager land recounted in chapter 12 may be part of her conversation with Lipsha. Fleur may also appear to Lipsha as the skunk he encounters at Matchimanito Lake in chapter 17 and again in his room in chapter 20. Fleur also appears to Lyman in a vision, as mentioned in chapters 13 and 20.

In chapter 27 of *The Bingo Palace,* when the authorities come to Matchimanito with signed papers to confiscate Fleur's house, they find her gone. They envision Fleur as setting out across the frozen lake to the island where the souls of the Pillagers wait for her. This journey is Fleur's death walk. Having sent others in her place on death's road, she now takes the place of "the boy"— probably her great-grandson, Lipsha. Some people, however, hear her laugh as they deal their cards and see her bear tracks in the snow, and are sure that the Pillager still walks the woods of Matchimanito Lake.

Fleur Pillager's boy. Candy-munching young white boy who arrives in the Pierce-Arrow with Fleur in chapter 12 of *The Bingo Palace*. The Chippewas who watch the card game in which he wins Jewett Parker Tatro's land feel that the boy is not human, but is one of Fleur's souls cast out as bait.

Fleur Pillager's customers. Children, women, and men who buy from Fleur's peddler's cart in chapter 3 of *The Beet Queen*. They are wary of her, and she never stays more than one night anywhere. One **man with lumps on his neck** invites her to sleep in his dead wife's parlor.

Florentine. Neighbor woman with whom Lulu Lamartine is having coffee in "The Good Tears" in *Love Medicine* when Lulu realizes that her house is burning.

Flying Kuklenskis. Family of trapeze artists who adopt the Montana runaway Anna in "Eleanor's Tale" [20] in *Tales of Burning Love*. Anna later marries young Harry Kuklenski. The ***"original" Flying Kuklenski,*** Harry's uncle, was the Polish man who started the circus trapeze act. He is now buried at a circus cemetery in Milwaukee. ***Old master Kuklenski*** is apparently the leader of the troop at the time Anna joins them. The family has a history of fatal accidents. Old master Kuklenski has dropped his ***daughter,*** presumably to her death. His ***son*** (who may or may not be Harry) has also dropped his ***wife,*** also presumably to her death, since she is referred to as his "former" wife. (If the son were Harry, then the wife he drops would be Anna Kuklenski's predecessor.) See also **Anna Kuklenski Schlick; Baby Kuklenski girl; Harry Kuklenski;** and **Kuklenski Brothers.**

Flying Nice. One of the people Fleur Pillager has forced to take her place on death's road, as recorded in chapter 11 of *The Bingo Palace*.

Fortiers. Apparently a family who lives between Gordie Kashpaw's place and town. Gordie passes their "settlement" on his drunken drive in "Crown of Thorns" in *Love Medicine*.

Four Soul. Healer; grandmother of Fleur Pillager. In chapter 3 of *The Bingo Palace* the records of Father Damien identify Four Soul as being among the

Four Soul

Chippewa in the first decade of migration west to the reservation. It is her name that Albertine Johnson receives in a ceremony run by Xavier Albert Toose and attended by Fleur. The name of this healer is appropriate because Albertine is hoping to be a doctor. In chapter 27 of *The Bingo Palace* Four Soul is one of the dead Pillagers who welcome Fleur on her death walk to the island in Matchimanito Lake.

Frank Shawano. Son of Shawano the ogitchida and Regina; brother of Puffy, Klaus, and Cecille Shawano; second husband of Rozina Roy in *The Antelope Wife*. Frank is older than Klaus and Cecille, but his and Puffy's relative age is not revealed. Since Frank is the only child named in the 1945 portrait of his family (chapter 13), he is likely the oldest. We are not told his age in this chapter, but he is old enough to be sent to the store for supplies and is at an age where he resents being bossed but likes being taken care of by his relatives. (If we guess that he is five or six, that would put his birth date in about 1940.)

In chapter 13, Frank's father calls a group of men to his house to see the German prisoner of war he has kidnapped. In an attempt to save his life, the young German, Klaus, offers to bake a cake. Frank helps gather the supplies and refuses to leave during its preparation. The outcome is a heavenly confection that marks Frank for life. He becomes a baker whose quest is the exact reproduction of the blitzkuchen.

In chapter 3, probably in the late 1970s or early 1980s, Rozina Roy White-heart Beads walks into Frank's bakery in Minneapolis. Frank is immediately attracted to her. Within a week after they take their first walk together Rozin is falling in love with him, too. He is big, strong, and handsome. He is gentle and quick to grin and joke (chapters 3 and 11). Then on one of their walks, they consummate their love—in the rain, in a piece of woods near a playground. It is not clear how long their affair lasts. Once, Rozin's husband, Richard Whiteheart Beads, and her twin daughters, Cally and Deanna, see the lovers together in the city park (chapter 6). Frank appears to Cally like the "deer man" in the Shawano family story her grandmother has told her. Frank also comes to the house, bringing the girls sugar cookies cut in fancy shapes. Cally will later recall sitting on his lap and his playing games with them (chapter 11). But after one of Frank's visits, Richard finds evidence of the affair, confronts Rozin, and forces her to break off the relationship.

Six years after his and Rozin's initial meeting, in chapter 7 Frank is diagnosed with cancer and given little chance of surviving even nine months. He goes to old-time healing ceremonies, but he has also finalized his will. One snowy March morning, Rozin announces to Richard that she is leaving him, taking the girls, and going to be with Frank. The jealous Richard wonders about the attraction and concludes that Frank is perhaps a "love medicine Ojibwa," like the rabbit character in the stories. Then, suddenly, Frank's life changes again when Deanna dies that night in her father's botched suicide attempt. Rozin feels that her and Frank's love has killed Deanna, and she goes home to the reservation, leaving Frank to endure his cancer treatments alone.

Seven years later, Frank has recovered from his cancer, but as Cally notes in chapter 11, the radiation treatments have destroyed his "funny bone" along with his tumor. Meanwhile, his brother Klaus has become a street drunk, and Frank has taken in Klaus's "wife," Sweetheart Calico. Frank's younger sister, Cecille, is also living with him in the rooms above his bakery when the eighteen-year-old Cally moves back to Minneapolis and comes to stay with them. When Cally phones Rozin, Frank stays close by. Rozin, too, wishes to know how he is doing but is afraid to talk to him or even say his name. Frank's frustrated passion for Rozin is now invested in his search for the exact recipe for the blitzkuchen. He stays engrossed in his bakery work and is an easy target for Cecille's elaborate lies about the weather and the day's events. One day Klaus wanders into the bakery in terrible condition, and Frank cares for him.

About two years after Cally's arrival, Rozin moves to Minneapolis. One August evening, Frank shows up at the food co-op where she works and asks her to go out with him. She rebuffs him, but he keeps calling until she agrees to go to the state fair at the end of the month. There, an out-of-control Gravitron ride is a turning point for Rozin. The couple begins to have long talks on the phone as they are pulled back together by the gravity of their mutual attraction. Frank tells Rozin that he loves her for her practicality and strength, but he admits to himself in chapter 16 that it is the smell and taste of her that has captivated him.

Frank proposes to Rozin beside a cliff in the state park. Their wedding is in the autumn (apparently the year following Rozin's move to the city) on the site of Frank's proposal. As a horde of family members busy themselves preparing for the reception, Frank is working on the wedding cake, his latest effort to achieve the perfect blitzkuchen. Later, when Richard Whiteheart Beads interrupts the cliffside ceremony, Frank grabs him by the throat and wants to push him over the cliff. Richard shows up again at the reception with a letter for Rozin saying that he has poisoned the cake. After Richard admits that this is a lie, Frank cuts, eats, and serves his masterpiece. His quest, he discovers, has been achieved—this cake is the true blitzkuchen, and the guests experience both its gustatory and its spiritual effects. The missing ingredient had been fear.

That night, Richard comes to Frank and Rozin's hotel and fatally shoots himself outside their door. In chapter 17 the grieving Rozin isolates herself in

Frank Shawano

her mothers' apartment and will not eat. Frank knocks on the door and phones, but Rozin will not let him in nor talk to him. After ten days, Frank finally gets into the apartment. Although Rozin warns that she is now seeing ghosts and tells him to leave, Frank stays and cares for her.

Frank's patient love seems to heal Rozin. In chapter 18, they are living together in the apartment over the bakery, though not always alone. To Rozin's annoyance, Cecille sometimes stays with them. That Christmas, a few family members gather at their apartment. They sit at a table lovingly made by Frank himself, decorated with a candelabra he has given Rozin. Dessert is an elaborate twelve-layer cake Frank had toiled over the night before. The couple's profound affection for one another is obvious to their guests.

The next autumn, a year after the "kamikaze" wedding, Frank and Rozin each worry over the best way to celebrate their upcoming anniversary. Frank recalls Rozin's mentioning a big party, with all of last year's wedding guests invited. Rozin knows that Frank would prefer a private celebration, untraditional and sexy. Putting each other's wishes ahead of their own, both make their plans. These plans collide into an ending that catches everyone by surprise.

Fritzie Kozka. Wife of Pete Kozka and mother of Sita Kozka. Pete and Fritzie operate Kozka's Meats in Argus. Fritzie is described in chapter 2 of *Tracks* as a string-thin blond chain-smoker who will not tolerate her husband's talking behind her back. When Fleur Pillager comes to work at the butcher shop in the summer of 1913, Fritzie lets her live on the shop property, teaches her to cut meat, and gives her a black umbrella. While Fritzie and Pete are gone to Minnesota in August, their shop is destroyed by a tornado. When they return, Fleur is gone, and they find their three male employees—Lily Veddar, Tor Grunewald, and Dutch James—frozen inside the meat locker (only Dutch survives).

In "The Branch" and chapter 1 of *The Beet Queen*, Fritzie is referred to as the aunt of Karl and Mary Adare, who in 1932 are abandoned by their mother, Fritzie's sister, Adelaide Adare. Fritzie and Pete take in the eleven-year-old Mary. Their daughter, Sita, resents the intrusion, but in chapter 2 Fritzie has no patience with Sita's selfishness. Fritzie puts ads in the Minneapolis newspaper, where Mary's baby brother had been kidnapped, offering a reward for information leading to his recovery. According to chapters 5 and 13, Fritzie tells her friends the story of Adelaide's flight. Sometime later, in chapter 3 Fritzie shows Mary a postcard from Adelaide asking about the children. When Mary is eighteen (thus in about 1939), in chapter 4 Fritzie suffers a nearly fatal pulmonary hemorrhage and finally stops smoking. Over the following months, the wiry Fritzie softens, gaining weight and color. About two years later, she and Pete move to Arizona for her health, and they leave the butcher shop to Mary, since Sita is not interested in it.

After Fritzie and Pete leave, in chapter 5 (1950) the adoptive mother of Mary's now-grown baby brother attempts to contact Fritzie in response to her newspaper ads, but Fritzie never receives the letter. Also in chapter 5, Fritzie and Pete attend Sita's wedding to Jimmy Bohl. Sita recalls in chapter 13 that when she continues to be childless, her mother asks if she is violating the church's injunction against birth control. Fritzie is also mentioned briefly in chapters 10 and 11.

Years later, in 1995, in "A Wedge of Shade" [3] in *Tales of Burning Love,* Mary recalls Fritzie and Pete's leaving the butcher shop to her, though she does not mention them by name. Mary offers to pass the business on in the same way to her own niece, Dot Adare, and Dot's new husband, Jack Mauser.

Frog people. What the Shawano Ojibwas call the Germans, because they popped up out of nowhere on Ojibwa land, according to chapter 13 of *The Antelope Wife.*

G

Geezhig. Son of Lucille Lazarre and older brother of June Morrissey. His name means "day." In chapter 6 of *The Bingo Palace* Geezhig warns June to leave the house when Lucille's boyfriend Leonard arrives. Later, when Leonard rapes June, it seems that Geezhig has already escaped and is not present.

George Many Women. One of the guides in chapter 1 of *Tracks* who help government surveyors divide up tribal lands. In chapter 2 he witnesses the fifteen-year-old Fleur Pillager's survival from her second drowning and hears her hiss, "You take my place." The fearful Many Women stays away from water, but he ultimately drowns in a bathtub. Many Women is among the group of men in Pauline's death vision in chapter 6 whose deaths Fleur is presumed to have caused.

Germaine. Hoards the commodity flour that Lulu Lamartine mysteriously knows is wormy in "Crossing the Water" in *Love Medicine.*

Gerry Nanapush. Son of Lulu Nanapush and Moses Pillager. Gerry is not the oldest child of Lulu and Moses; their first son seems to have been born in about 1935 or 1936, while Gerry is born in 1945 (according to information

Gerry Nanapush

in "Scales," "Wild Geese," and "The Island" in *Love Medicine*). In "Lulu's Boys" we learn that Lulu's three oldest boys bear her maiden name, Nanapush, apparently because they are born before her marriage to Morrissey. One of Gerry's Nanapush brothers is in junior college when Gerry is twelve. When Lulu marries Beverly Lamartine in "The Good Tears" and then discovers that he has another wife, she sends the twelve-year-old Gerry, already grown-up and tough, back to Minneapolis with him to make sure that Beverly divorces the other wife. While he is there, Gerry is thrown into detention (probably juvenile detention). Lulu believes that Beverly has turned him in.

According to "Crossing the Water," when Gerry is just out of high school he has an affair with June Morrissey Kashpaw, which produces a son, Lipsha, born in 1965. About the time June's pregnancy begins to show, Gerry leaves. Shortly thereafter, possibly in either 1964 or 1965, Gerry kicks a cowboy in the groin in a drunken fight, as recorded in "Scales" in *Love Medicine*. The cowboy presses charges, and Gerry is sentenced to three years in prison. Gerry prolongs his sentence indefinitely, however, by continuing to escape, boasting that no prison can hold a Chippewa. Gerry's ability to escape is also referred to in "The Bridge."

Gerry's escapes turn him into a Chippewa hero, as mentioned in "Lulu's Boys" and "Crossing the Water" in *Love Medicine*. In "A Wedge of Shade" [3] in *Tales of Burning Love,* Gerry is involved in a series of speaking engagements, apparently in the brief periods when he is out of prison. He develops a following of supporters who raise money for his cause and hope to free him. One of these is Dot Adare, a student at the U of M (University of Minnesota). Gerry and Dot's relationship begins one night at a Howard Johnson's in Grand Forks after one of his speeches.

In late December or early January, 1979–1980, according to "Scales" in *Love Medicine* Gerry impregnates Dot on her visit to the state prison. He escapes at least twice that next year so that he can be with her, but he is recaptured. After the weather turns cold, Gerry shows up again at Dot's job. He stays with Dot until she goes into labor, a week past her October due date. At the hospital, just after she gives birth to their daughter, Shawn, two officers arrive, but Gerry eludes them and escapes. Dot later hears that Gerry has been recaptured and that this time he has shot and killed one of the arresting officers and has been taken to a maximum security prison in Marion, Illinois.

In "The World's Greatest Fishermen" in *Love Medicine* (1981), Gerry's son, Lipsha, wishes he knew his father. In "Crossing the Water" (1984), Lulu tells him who his father is, and Lipsha leaves home to look for Gerry. While being transferred from Marion to the North Dakota State Penitentiary, Gerry escapes.

Gerry Nanapush

He goes to the apartment of King Kashpaw, June Kashpaw's legitimate son, in the Twin Cities to even an old score—King had betrayed Gerry in prison. Gerry finds Lipsha there, and he, Lipsha, and King play a game of five-card stud for the car King had bought with June's insurance money (a Firebird). Lipsha wins the car. When the police arrive, Gerry disappears. As Lipsha is driving "June's" car toward home, he discovers that Gerry has stowed away in the trunk. Lipsha drives him to the Canadian border, where Gerry disappears into the woods, on his way to see his wife and daughter.

In chapter 1 of *The Bingo Palace* Gerry has recently been recaptured, although his Wanted poster still hangs in the post office. Albertine sees his hungry and desperate-looking face on television in chapter 3. In chapter 21, in his prison cell Gerry longs for Dot, his children, and June. (According to this chapter, Gerry and Dot are divorced, and he is aware that she has remarried. But according to "A Wedge of Shade" [3], "Caryl Moon" [8], and "February Thaw" [40] in *Tales of Burning Love,* Dot remarries without divorcing Gerry.) Because of a tribal request initiated by Lulu, Gerry is transported to a Minnesota prison, and when the small aircraft transporting him is caught in a January storm and goes down, Gerry escapes. (The year is given as 1995 in *Tales of Burning Love,* but appears to be in the late 1980s in *The Bingo Palace.*)

Gerry calls Lipsha from Fargo at midnight in chapter 22 of *The Bingo Palace,* but Lipsha does not fully understand his instructions. The two finally find each other the following night in a Fargo alley, but they are without transportation. In chapter 24 they steal a white car and are astonished when a man chases them and attempts to hang onto the trunk. Only later do they discover a baby in the backseat. Caught in a blizzard as they head north, Gerry and Lipsha follow in the wake of a snowplow. When they see the ghost of June driving her blue Firebird, Gerry follows her off the highway, gets into her car, and drives away with her into the storm. That night in chapter 25, federal marshals come to Lulu's apartment to question her about the escape, but she merely confuses and misleads them. The following day, radio news in chapter 26 indicates that the escape car has been found, but not Gerry Nanapush.

Two chapters in *Tales of Burning Love,* "Funeral Day" [23] and "Blizzard Night" [35], recount the story of Gerry and Lipsha's escape from the point of view of the man hanging onto the car, the baby's father, Jack Mauser, who is also Dot's new husband. Jack is also driving the snowplow that Gerry and Lipsha follow.

Tales of Burning Love also narrates these incidents from Dot's point of view. Although Dot has married again, she thinks about Gerry in "A Wedge of Shade" [3] and "Caryl Moon" [8]. The radio bulletin announcing Gerry's January 5

Gerry Nanapush

plane crash is recorded in "Radio Bulletin" [11], and Lyman Lamartine gives Dot the news of Gerry's escape in the next chapter, "Satin Heart," at Jack's supposed funeral. In answer to Dot's question as to Gerry's whereabouts, Lyman writes "B & B."

Dot is at "The B & B" [16] in West Fargo that afternoon when a massive Indian woman enters, covered with ice. The "woman" is Gerry ("The Tale of the Unknown Passenger" [34]). Apparently the ghost of June has driven him back to town. Dot recognizes Gerry's wolf grin, buys him a large pizza, and leaves the room for half an hour to talk to him. Their conversation is not recorded, but later chapters suggest that they devise a plan for Dot to pick him up in the car and that she gives him some painkillers.

As Jack's ex-wives head back to Fargo in Jack's Explorer with Dot driving ("The Hitchhiker" [18]), a half mile from the B & B they see a large, blanket-wrapped hitchhiker, who is later revealed to be Gerry. Dot stops for him, and he immediately goes to sleep in the space behind the backseat. For more detail, see **Hitchhiker.** About midnight the vehicle becomes stranded in the blizzard. Several hours later, in "The Tale of the Unknown Passenger" [34] Gerry revives Dot, who has been overcome by carbon monoxide, and while the other passengers sleep, Gerry and Dot make love. Dot gives Gerry a key to her apartment. When the passengers are rescued in "The Disappearance" [36], Gerry slips away. Dot protects his identity by telling authorities that the missing passenger is her mother. We learn in "February Thaw" [40] that both Dot's mother and her Aunt Mary Adare play along with this ruse.

At 7:40 that morning, in "Smile of the Wolf" [38] Gerry lets himself into Dot's apartment to spend a few minutes with their daughter, Shawn. Later, when marshals break down the door, Gerry has escaped, apparently on the neighbor's snowmobile. While she is in the hospital recovering from her ordeal in the blizzard ("February Thaw" [40]), Dot dreams about Gerry. When she wakes, her mother assures her that Gerry is all right. As she takes a walk the next month, Dot is overcome with longing for him.

Gerry's other woman. Woman on whose "mercy" Gerry is cast after June leaves him, referred to in chapter 1 of *The Bingo Palace.* It is not clear whether the reference is to June's original leaving of Gerry to return to her husband in 1964–1965, or to her death in 1981. If the latter, then this woman would probably be Dot Adare, who gives birth to Gerry's daughter in 1980. If the former, there are no hints about her identity.

Giles Saint Ambrose. Bum who befriends young Karl Adare in chapter 1 of *The Beet Queen.* He encounters Karl in a box car and gives him his first sexual experience. Shortly afterwards Karl leaps from the car, leaving the sleeping Giles behind.

Girl who lived with the antelope. Ancestor of Sweetheart Calico, according to chapter 2 of *The Antelope Wife*. Jimmy Badger tells the story of this long-ago girl who, along with her human daughters, ran with the antelope in summer and stayed at camp in winter. (The old man's use of the word "human" may suggest that she had other, nonhuman children as well.) His story is congruous with both the story of Matilda Roy in chapter 1 and that of Blue Prairie Woman (as Apijigo Bakaday) in chapter 6.

Gordie Kashpaw. Eldest child of Nector Kashpaw and Marie Lazarre Kashpaw; husband of June Morrissey; father of King Howard Kashpaw in *Love Medicine*. Gordie is born about 1935 (see "Saint Marie" and "Resurrection"). As recorded in "The Beads" and "The World's Greatest Fishermen," Gordie is jealous when his nine-year-old cousin June comes to live with his family in 1948. He and his sister Aurelia try to hang June, but they are stopped by their mother and another sister, Zelda. Yet, as Gordie recalls in "Crown of Thorns," he and June grow close and as children are always together. In "Flesh and Blood" (1957) Gordie and June are off hunting when Marie returns from seeing Sister Leopolda. When he comes home, Marie is aware of the distance between him and herself. In "Love Medicine," Marie sees a vision and subsequently warns Gordie never to ride in a car with the Lamartine boys.

Gordie and June run away to South Dakota and marry, as recorded in "Resurrection" and "Crown of Thorns." But the marriage is troubled from the outset. Gordie recalls their awkward honeymoon in "Resurrection" and his physical abuse of June in "Crown of Thorns." June's comment about this abuse appears in "The World's Greatest Fishermen." Gordie and June have one son, King Howard Kashpaw. "Crossing the Water" recounts June's brief affair with Gerry Nanapush, after which she returns to Gordie. When June gives birth to Gerry's son, Lipsha, in about 1965, Gordie cannot handle raising another man's son, and June gives Lipsha to Marie (or tries to drown him, depending on who is telling the story). June eventually divorces Gordie, according to "The World's Greatest Fishermen," but he continues to love her.

June dies in early spring of 1981, and a month later Gordie begins to drink heavily ("Crown of Thorns"). Two months after her death, in "The World's Greatest Fishermen" Gordie arrives drunk at a family gathering. His and June's son, King, is there with his wife and baby in a new Firebird that King has bought with June's insurance money. When King, himself drunk, begins smashing "June's" car, Gordie runs out to stop him and holds him as King sobs. One

Gordie Kashpaw

night, in "Crown of Thorns" the distraught Gordie calls out June's name, and she responds, first appearing outside the window and then breaking the glass and entering the house. He flees to his car and drives to town for more wine. After he hits a deer with his car and then beats it to death, he believes that it is really June he has killed. He confesses the supposed murder to a nun at the Sacred Heart Convent and is subsequently picked up by police and hospital orderlies. According to "Love Medicine," he spends some time in the Bismarck hospitals. After his father, Nector, dies and Marie moves back into the family house, in "Resurrection" Gordie comes to the house begging her for whiskey. When she gives him none, in desperation he drinks a can of Lysol. That night, sometime after midnight, it seems that Gordie dies. Marie senses that he is "chasing [his] own death" and, as his heart quits, he catches it. Lulu Lamartine refers to his death in "Crossing the Water."

Grandma Kashpaw. See **Marie Lazarre Kashpaw.**

Grandma making soup. Grandmother who almost cooks the dog Almost Soup in chapter 8 of *The Antelope Wife*. Two other **grandmas** argue about whether he should be cooked or given to Cally Whiteheart Beads, and a **grandpa** insists he be given to Cally.

Grandma Mary. See **Mary (II) Shawano.**

Grandma Zosie. See **Zosie (II) Shawano Roy.**

Grandpa Kashpaw. See **Nector Kashpaw.**

Gravitron operator. Young man, apparently high on drugs, who dangerously accelerates the Gravitron at the state fair while Rozina Roy and Frank Shawano are riding in chapter 14 of *The Antelope Wife*. Many of the **Gravitron riders** get sick. One **woman** breaks the window of the control booth, and the **people watching** bring the ride under control.

Grinne family. Lower-class family in Blue Mound to whom Sita Bohl gives Mary Adare's sewing machine in chapter 13 of *The Beet Queen*. They live on the income from selling balls of used aluminum foil.

Hadji. Foreman at the construction site where Albertine Johnson and Dot Adare work in the summer and fall of 1980 in "Scales" in *Love Medicine*. Erdrich thanks her own foreman, also named Hadji, in the acknowledgments section in *Tales of Burning Love.*

Harriss. Policeman who, with Officer Lovchik, tries to arrest Gerry Nanapush in the hospital where Gerry's wife Dot is having her baby in "Scales" in *Love Medicine.*

Harry Kuklenski. First husband of Anna Kuklenski Schlick and father of Anna's stillborn baby. The story of his life is recounted in "Eleanor's Tale" [20] in *Tales of Burning Love.* Harry is one of the Flying Kuklenskis, a family of Polish acrobats that takes in the runaway Anna and trains her to be part of their show. During a performance in Fargo, lightning strikes the circus tent, and Harry falls to his death. He is buried in a circus cemetery in Milwaukee, alongside his uncle, the original Kuklenski. His pregnant wife survives the accident, but their baby is stillborn six weeks after his death. Years later, as Anna is dying of congestive heart failure in "A Light from the West" [43], she feels Harry's hand grab hers.

Hat family. Reservation family that appears to profit from its cooperation with the government. In chapter 7 of *Tracks* the Hats are one of the few families that have been able to pay their allotment fees and thus retain their land. See also **Jean Hat** and **Two Hat.**

Hegelstead. President of the First National Bank of Fargo. He makes a huge housing-development loan to contractor and one-time friend Jack Mauser in *Tales of Burning Love.* In "The First Draw" [14] Hegelstead makes out the check for Jack's first draw on his loan. Two years later, in "Jack's House" [9] Hegelstead calls Jack the day after Christmas to warn him he must make a payment on his overdue loan by the first of January. Four days after Jack's apparent death, in "The Owl" [17] Hegelstead pays Jack a brief, secret visit and warns that the bank will foreclose the next day. Jack suggests that the only way Hegelstead can recover the bank's money is to finance Jack again in a big project with Lyman Lamartine. Although Hegelstead does not reply at the time, in "Mauser and Mauser" [39] he does in fact follow Jack's advice. He calls Lyman and makes a deal: Lyman will pay off Jack's subcontractors and Hegelstead will lend Jack (or Lyman) more money for the construction of a casino in order to recoup the bank's losses. Jack will be the contractor.

He Is Lifted By Wind. Brother of Fleur Pillager. Also known by his Indian name, Ombaashi, he dies of consumption in chapter 1 of *Tracks.* He is mentioned again in chapter 9.

Henri Laventure

Henri Laventure. Ancestor of Rozina Roy named in chapter 3 of *The Antelope Wife*. He is the bastard son of a **bastard daughter** of a **French marquis.** Henri steals gold coins from a **bishop** and then escapes to Canada. Somewhere in "the north," possibly Canada, he marries **six Ojibwa women,** the oldest of whom is the sister of the windigo Shesheeb.

Henry Lamartine Junior. Son of Beverly Lamartine and Lulu Nanapush Lamartine, born in 1950 or 1951. He is named after Henry Lamartine, Beverly's brother and Lulu's deceased husband, because he is conceived the night of Henry's wake (1950), according to "Lulu's Boys" in *Love Medicine.* His father, Beverly, whom Henry Junior knows as Uncle Hat, lives in Minneapolis, but he returns to the reservation when Henry Junior is seven with the intent of taking the boy back to the city with him. Instead, he stays briefly, marries Lulu, and then goes back to the city without his son.

Of his eight half siblings, Henry Junior is closest to his younger brother, Lyman. Their relationship is described by Lyman in chapter 14 of *The Bingo Palace* and "The Red Convertible" in *Love Medicine.* Henry is an exceptionally talented grass dancer, and he and Lyman travel the powwow circuit together. When Henry is about eighteen, he enlists in the Marines, but before he enters the service, he and the sixteen-year-old Lyman have a gloriously carefree summer (apparently 1969), driving their red Oldsmobile convertible all over the northern Midwest, and even to Alaska. When they return home, Henry goes off to training camp and shortly after Christmas is sent to Vietnam. (When his family receives his first overseas letter, the year is 1970.)

We learn from "A Bridge" that Henry Junior spends nine months in combat and about six months as a prisoner of war, released after the evacuation. After some delay because of "red tape" and being questioned by a military psychologist, he is discharged. Three weeks after his return to the States, in the spring of 1973 Henry is in Fargo when he encounters the fifteen-year-old Albertine Johnson from his home reservation. They go to a bar and then to a motel, where they have sexual relations, although Henry knows she is a minor. In the motel, Henry has flashbacks of a bayoneted Vietnamese woman whose eyes are like a Chippewa's, and he shrieks and lashes out when Albertine touches him in his sleep.

Henry Junior returns home in "The Red Convertible," changed from an easy-going youth to a withdrawn, tense shell of a man. Lyman purposefully batters their car, hoping that repairing it will bring Henry out of his shell. The strategy seems to work, and in the spring in 1974 Henry and Lyman drive to the Red River. But after drinking and fighting with his brother on the riverbank,

Henry jumps into the river and drowns. After Lyman tries unsuccessfully to rescue him, he sends "Henry's" car into the river after him. Lyman is deeply affected by his half brother's death, as recounted in "The Good Tears" and "The Tomahawk Factory." Henry Junior is mentioned briefly by Albertine and Marie Kashpaw in "Scales" and "Love Medicine."

In *The Bingo Palace,* Lyman keeps Henry Junior's memory alive by dancing the traditional grass dance in Henry's costume (chapters 2, 14, and 18). Lyman briefly sees Henry's face in a vision in chapter 13 and tells Lipsha about his relationship with Henry in chapter 14. In chapter 18, while dancing alone in the woods during a religious fast, Lyman has a visionary conversation with Henry. He finally accepts his brother's death and decides to retire Henry's old dance costume.

Henry Lamartine (Senior). Second husband of Lulu Nanapush Morrissey; brother of Beverly Lamartine. Several stories in *Love Medicine* mention Henry briefly. We learn in "Lulu's Boys" that he has an older brother, Slick, who dies in boot camp, but that he and Beverly serve in the military together. They also fall in love with the same woman, Lulu. After playing a game of strip poker with the two brothers, Lulu decides to marry Henry. In "The Good Tears" we learn that Lulu marries Henry for "fondness" and that he builds a house for her and her children, although he never gets legal ownership of the land on which it sits. Henry dies in 1950 in a car and train wreck, an event that is recounted from a variety of points of view in "Lulu's Boys," "Flesh and Blood," and "The Good Tears" (with a passing reference in "The Plunge of the Brave"). Although Lulu represents Henry's death as an accident, others see it as suicide, especially Marie Kashpaw, who believes the reason for the suicide is Lulu's promiscuousness.

Hitchhiker. Large, strange, almost spectral figure who materializes out of the storm as Jack Mauser's four living widows leave the B & B the night of Jack's funeral, in "The Hitchhiker" [18] in *Tales of Burning Love.* It is not clear at first whether the figure is a man or woman. Dot picks the person up and lets her or him ride in the small space behind the backseat in the Ford Explorer. The hitchhiker falls asleep in "Secrets and Sugar Babies" [19], and the four women seem almost to forget he or she is there. In "The Red Slip" [21] Marlis tries unsuccessfully to rouse him or her to help clear the snow around the tailpipe. In "Surviving Sleep" [24] Dot asks how the hitchhiker is, but he or she wants to be left alone. In "The Tale of the Unknown Passenger" [34] this stranger turns out to be both the pizza-eating Indian "woman" who blew into the B & B and the escaped prisoner, Gerry Nanapush. He makes love to Dot in the car while the others are asleep. It appears from their conversation that she had

Hitchhiker

known his identity all along and that they had planned the pickup. Later, when the passengers are rescued by a snowmobile squad, in "The Disappearance" [36] the hitchhiker (Gerry) "falls off" in order to evade authorities, and Dot protects him by claiming that the missing person is her mother.

Hmong grandmas. Old women whom Cally Roy hears talking as they work in their gardens the morning after she has accompanied Sweetheart Calico to the outskirts of the city in chapter 18 of *The Antelope Wife*. Chapter 11 refers to the beauty of Hmong-Ojibwas, but the old women may be full-blood Hmong, since Cally does not understand their language.

Hugo, Sister. Young Dominican seventh-grade teacher at Saint Catherine's school in Argus in chapter 2 of *The Beet Queen*. She helps Mary Adare to the infirmary after the accident on the playground slide that causes the face of Christ to appear in the broken ice.

I

Ida. Woman who sponsors the big memorial powwow (Indian dance contest) in Montana that Shawnee Ray Toose nearly wins in chapter 16 of *The Bingo Palace*. Zelda claims in chapter 10 to know Ida and says that Ida will not pay the promised prize money, but this prediction seems to be mistaken. (There are a number of similarities between Erdrich's Ida and the Ida of Michael Dorris's *A Yellow Raft in Blue Water*.)

Ignatius Lazarre. Father of Lucille Lazarre and purported father of Marie Lazarre. (Events in *Tracks* show that Marie actually has a different ancestry.) Marie refers to Ignatius as her father in "The Beads" in *Love Medicine* and calls him a "sack of brew" in "Flesh and Blood."

Irene Toose. Mother of Shawnee Ray, Mary Fred, and Tammy Toose. After her first husband, Toose, dies, in chapter 2 of *The Bingo Palace* she marries Elward Strong Ribs and moves with him to Minot, leaving her daughters on the reservation—Shawnee Ray still in high school and pregnant. Lipsha asks about Irene in chapter 4. In chapter 10 Shawnee Ray misses her mother, who now puts her new husband's needs before those of her daughters.

Isabel Kashpaw. Daughter of Regina Puyat and a Montana Kashpaw; older sister of Russell Kashpaw. As children, Isabel, Russell, and their cousin Pauline Puyat seek out Eli Kashpaw on the reservation to get to know him, as related in chapter 10 of *The Beet Queen*. (According to *The Beet Queen*, Eli is Isabel and Russell's half brother; but the genealogy in *Love Medicine* and *Tracks* indicates that he is the younger brother of their father.) Although Isabel herself is not mentioned in *Tracks,* in chapter 2 of *Tracks* Isabel and Russell's father goes to Montana, and Regina moves to Argus with Russell. Regina marries Dutch James, gives birth to his daughter, Celestine James, and, according to chapter 2 of *The Beet Queen,* brings "three other children" whom Dutch knows nothing about to Argus from the reservation. These children are apparently Isabel, Russell, and Pauline, although this account is at variance with the one in *Tracks.* Isabel and Russell never take on the James name. Regina dies when Celestine is still small, and Isabel raises her half sister. She is a lenient guardian, letting Celestine do as she pleases.

In chapter 7 of *The Beet Queen,* we learn that Isabel marries a Sioux man, moves to South Dakota, and dies violently, perhaps of a beating or in a car wreck. Russell goes to South Dakota but is unable to learn anything about her family or her death. In chapter 13 Isabel's ghost seems to beckon Russell onto the death road while he is taking part in the Beet Parade.

Ivory Coast slave. One of Rozina Roy's ancestors named in chapter 3 of *The Antelope Wife*. He crawls into Magid's house one night, and she accepts him as her lover.

Izear Lazarre. Marries Sophie Morrissey in chapter 7 of *Tracks*. He has already been married, is rumored to have killed his first wife, and brings his six unruly children to the new marriage. When he moves into Bernadette's house with his children, Bernadette moves to town, leaving the house to him, Sophie, Clarence, and Clarence's new Lazarre bride.

J

Jackie. One of Rozina Roy's two oldest cousins, close in age to her sister Ruby, who helps with the preparations for Rozin's wedding in chapter 16 of *The Antelope Wife*. She and her sister may be the cousins who put Rozin into the shower after Richard Whiteheart Beads's suicide.

Jack Mauser. Highway and housing construction contractor in *Tales of Burning Love;* husband successively to June Morrissey Kashpaw, Eleanor Schlick, Candice Pantamounty, Marlis Cook, and Dot Adare Nanapush. His legal name is John J. Mauser. Jack is described in "Candice's Tale" [25] as a big man, tough

Jack Mauser

and muscular, not fat, and in "Marlis's Tale" [27] as rugged, with brown hair and dark eyes. In the mid-1990s of the novel's present he is apparently in his forties, because when he was in college, Eleanor was still a child ("Eleanor's Tale" [20]), and in 1994 she is in her early thirties ("Night Prayer" [6]).

The little we know about Jack's ancestry is revealed through hints found in the following chapters: "A Wedge of Shade" [3]; "The First Draw" [14]; "The Owl" [17]; "The Red Slip" [21]; and "Mauser and Mauser" [39]. He is half German through his father, who is identified only as the "big Mauser" and the son of "the original John Mauser." His mother, Mary Stamper, is an Indian, her family a mixture of several tribes. She is from the reservation, and Jack himself is an enrolled member of the Chippewa nation. When Jack remembers his mother's face, it reminds him of the face of Sister Leopolda, who is a Puyat. When he sees Lipsha Morrissey, who is of Pillager, Morrissey, and Lazarre descent, Lipsha's face seems familiar, and Jack thinks that he may be a cousin. The owners—at least one of whom is a Pillager—of the land where Lyman Lamartine intends to build his new casino are said to be Jack's relatives. Jack's specific connections with these reservation families, however, are never made clear.

We learn a little about Jack's childhood through his memories. Especially painful are the memories of his mother, a strong but gentle woman, who every autumn experiences catatonic spells in which she relives the early loss of her parents. In "The Owl" [17] Jack remembers being left at his Aunt Elizabeth's house by his father while his mother is undergoing treatments. His aunt is strict, and he feels that she has stolen him from his mother ("Best Western" [28]). He eventually runs away from her to live with her brother, his Uncle Chuck Mauser, who is farming near Argus.

Although as a boy Jack is chubby and unpopular, in high school he comes into his own as a football hero, lead tenor in the choir, and ladies' man ("Hot June Morning" [2], "Candice's Tale" [25], and "Best Western" [28]). One of the girls he dates in high school is Candice Pantamounty. After graduation he goes to North Dakota State University (in Fargo), where he studies engineering ("Eleanor's Tale" [20]). While he is in college he fixes farm machines for his uncle and works as a part-time fireman in Fargo. Fighting a fire one bitterly cold November night, he is sprayed with water and nearly freezes to death. Anna Schlick, the wife of the fire chief, takes him home and thaws him out by giving him a warm bath and by crawling into bed with him. When her husband finds them in bed together, he disowns his wife and his child, Eleanor, in a fit of jealousy. This event probably takes place about 1970.

Jack leaves school because he wants to make money in construction ("Night Prayer" [6]). He is said in "The Owl" [17] to have squandered his aunt's money in the 1970s. We learn in "Satin Heart" [12] that he proposes marriage to the daughter of an old Swedish widow who is possibly his landlady.

Jack does not realize how much Eleanor Schlick resents him for his part in ruining her idyllic childhood. In "The Red Slip" [21], when Eleanor is a teenager, she sees Jack in a store and punishes him by stomping his hand into broken glass. Several weeks later, however, she calls him. On their first date she loses her virginity to him in his Silverado pickup. That is the start of their on-and-off relationship, during which Eleanor often sends him away. In one of his absences from her, Jack goes out to western North Dakota for a year (1980–1981), where he does construction work in the oil fields.

In the spring of 1981 ("Easter Snow" [1]) Jack is working a temporary job as a mud engineer (see **Mud engineer**). On Holy Saturday he comes to Williston with a toothache. There he meets June Morrissey Kashpaw in a bar. Jack realizes that she is from his mother's home reservation and tries to hide his identity from her, telling her his name is Andy. After making the rounds to several bars, Jack decides that he is in love with June and marries her in a bar. Jack tries unsuccessfully to consummate the marriage in his pickup just outside of town. June wanders off, and although Jack tries to follow her in his pickup, when she leaves the road, he abandons her. She walks into a gathering snowstorm and freezes to death. (This scene is a replay from Jack's point of view of the opening scene of *Love Medicine,* in "The World's Greatest Fishermen.") Jack is troubled by guilt and seems to spend the rest of his life seeking to replace June in new wife after new wife.

When Jack returns to Fargo, Eleanor observes that he drinks too much and says strange things ("The Red Slip" [21]). In the late fall, Eleanor tells her parents that she is pregnant by Jack (a lie), and her mother apparently tells Jack. Eleanor tries to break up with him, but he talks her into going to Florida, where they get married. (The time of these events is probably not long after Jack's return from the oil fields, since Eleanor says that on the Florida trip he is using up the money he earned out west "in the last year." Thus the time of their marriage seems to be late autumn of 1981.) This marriage, though sexually satisfying, is fraught with arguments and fighting until Eleanor leaves for a year as an exchange student in London. Over the years, through Jack's successive marriages, he and Eleanor continue to stay in contact, as we learn in "White Musk" [4] and "Trust in the Known" [5]. According to "Night Prayer" [6], they even make love on a few occasions.

Sometime after he and Eleanor separate, Jack starts his own construction company, Mauser and Mauser, based in Fargo. We learn in "The First Draw" [14] that there is no partner, that Jack simply doubles his own name. His first big

Jack Mauser

job, according to "Candice's Tale" [25], is to build an economy motel. When the company is still new, Jack meets Candice Pantamounty at the town dump, where he intends to shoot his dog. Candice offers to fix his teeth in exchange for the dog, and Jack agrees. He and Candice date and eventually marry. In "A Wandering Room" [26] they go deer hunting together, after which he accidentally causes the death of her dog, Pepperboy, an event that contributes to the disintegration of their troubled marriage. Thus, the dog that brings them together ultimately helps drive them apart. We are not told how long Jack and Candice are married, but this is the longest of his five marriages ("Jack's House" [9]).

Sometime during this period, Jack buys land west of Fargo from his uncle, Chuck Mauser, and begins trying to get a line of credit to build a subdivision on it ("The First Draw" [14]). These efforts culminate in August 1992 when Jack gets a huge loan from the bank for his housing development, just as his construction business is about to begin a big highway project near Argus. He decides to name the development simply "the Crest."

Two significant personal events also take place in the summer of 1992: Jack and Candice divorce, and Jack meets Marlis Cook. Jack's first encounter with Marlis occurs when he gives her mouth-to-mouth resuscitation after an accident, as recounted in "Marlis's Tale" [27]. She tries to sue him for her subsequent nerve damage, but he cures her. Shortly after his divorce from Candice and a few weeks after curing Marlis's twitch, one August morning Jack receives the first installment check of his development loan ("The First Draw" [14]). He shows the check to his uncle, but Chuck is bitter about losing the land. As Jack eats lunch and celebrates at a bar, Marlis walks in.

There are variations in the two accounts of what happens next. Marlis's account, which appears in "Marlis's Tale" [27] and "Best Western" [28], is more detailed. The story from Jack's point of view, which consists of two brief paragraphs in "The First Draw" [14], is much more vague, perhaps because Jack is drunk during much of this time. According to Marlis, as she and Jack drink together in the bar, he shows her his loan check and tells her he has just gotten divorced. After an afternoon and evening of drinking, they go to a motel, where he knocks himself unconscious and, unknown to Jack, Marlis steals his check. When he comes to, she threatens him with statutory rape charges. The next day (day 2) she blackmails Jack into buying her a new wardrobe. After another evening of drinking, in "Best Western" [28] Marlis drives Jack to South Dakota where they are married by a justice of the peace early the next morning (day 3). They return to Fargo later that day, and while Jack sleeps off his drunk, Marlis secretly deposits the loan check into her own bank account. They spend the next month in Eugene, hiding out from Jack's creditors.

Jack Mauser

In "The First Draw" account, however—in which the days blur somewhat into one another—Marlis's threat seems to occur on the second night they are together, rather than the first; the wardrobe-buying incident is omitted; and it seems that Jack decides to go home on his third morning with Marlis, rather than after a month in Eugene. Nevertheless, this chapter reveals that it is August when Jack meets Marlis and September when he arrives back in Fargo, which agrees with Marlis's account of a month's absence from the city. When Jack locates his car, he finds Candice sitting in the front seat, as if waiting for him. She drives him to work and takes his car keys. Enraged, Jack jumps on a bulldozer and strips one of his uncle's sunflower fields.

Over the next two years, while Jack oversees construction on the Argus interstate access and his new subdivision, he and Marlis also go on the road as a musical duo, Jack singing, Marlis playing the piano. They book gigs in hotels and nightclubs in various cities across the northern Midwest. In the winter of 1993–1994 (probably after Christmas) Jack realizes at a gig in Minneapolis–Saint Paul that Marlis has stolen his loan check, and they begin to fight. On the way to their next engagement in Billings, Montana, Marlis tells him that she is pregnant. Not believing her, he becomes abusive. Marlis gets even in a motel room in Billings. She ties him up and subjects him to some of the pain of being a woman. When their baby is born (in or before June 1994, "Night Prayer" [6]), Marlis names him John Jr. after his father, and in "The Owl" [17] Jack holds his son.

Jack's new employee Dot Adare Nanapush first catches his eye in the spring of 1994 as she charges across his construction yard, as we learn in "Hot June Morning" [2]. Dot's accounting skills temporarily save Jack's failing business. Nevertheless, Jack fires Dot for falsifying records in favor of Caryl Moon, another of his employees who is Dot's short-term boyfriend ("Caryl Moon" [8]). Shortly thereafter, Moon turns his dump truck over on Jack's prized Cadillac. Jack locks Caryl inside the overturned truck and rides away with Dot—the start of their stormy relationship.

Jack marries Dot (his fifth wife) that June, after knowing her for only a month (although they had once been in school together). The following week, in "Hot June Morning" [2] Jack comes to Argus to meet Dot's mother, Celestine James, but in "A Wedge of Shade" [3] he is arrested by Officer Lovchik as soon as he arrives at Celestine's house. Jack returns later that day. He whispers his mother's name to Celestine, but neither Dot nor we are able to hear. All we learn is that Celestine, who refers to herself as a Kashpaw, but whose Indian mother was actually a Puyat, says that he is of the "old strain" and thinks that she and he are probably related.

Jack Mauser

Within the first week of his marriage to Dot, in "Trust in the Known" [5] Jack makes plans to see Eleanor, and in "Night Prayer" [6] he visits her by night at the Argus convent where she is staying. When the aged Sister Leopolda comes into the garden, Eleanor hides Jack. He hears Leopolda predict that he will be crushed by a woman, and he inadvertently contributes to her death. Afterward, Jack goes to Eleanor's room in the convent and they make love. A few weeks later, in August, Eleanor calls Jack's house, wanting him to pick her up from the Argus hospital. In "The Meadowlark" [7] Dot accompanies Jack to Argus to get Eleanor. On their trip back to Fargo, Dot learns that she is Jack's fifth wife, and both she and Eleanor learn that he has a son.

Over the next few months, Dot leaves Jack four times, the final time on New Year's Eve. That night, as recorded in "Jack's House" [9], he gets drunk and thinks about each of his five wives. His new house catches fire, neither the smoke alarm nor sprinkler system works, and the house becomes an inferno. He leaves some "evidence" to indicate that he burns to death and at about midnight breaks naked out of a basement window. The ruse nearly works. Many of Jack's lawyers and creditors believe that he is dead.

Caryl Moon gives the naked Jack a lift in "Caryl Moon" [13] and then beats him unconscious. Jack regains consciousness and drags his nearly frozen body to his company's garage where he reflects on his life and his marriages. He slowly recovers in "The Garage" [15] and "The Owl" [17]. His banker, Hegelstead, tipped off by Caryl Moon, comes to the garage and confronts Jack about his unpaid loans. Jack suggests that the only way Hegelstead can recover the bank's money is to lend Jack more money for Lyman Lamartine's big casino project. We learn in "Mauser and Mauser" [39] that, after a phone conversation with Lyman, Hegelstead accepts this suggestion.

Others, however, including Jack's wives, still think that Jack is dead. Eleanor's father, funeral director Lawrence Schlick, hosts Jack's funeral on January 5, 1995 ("Memoria" [10] and "Satin Heart" [12]). Planning to head north from Fargo (perhaps even into Canada, as mentioned in "The Owl" [17]), Jack decides in "Funeral Day" [23] to "borrow" Candice's car while she is attending his funeral. He also wants to see his infant son, John Jr. After a battle of wits and force with the baby's nanny, the formidable Tillie Kroshus, Jack steals Candice's white Honda, reluctantly kidnaps his son, and drives to the train station. When the car and baby are stolen by Gerry Nanapush, whom Jack recognizes, Jack unsuccessfully attempts to hold onto the car. (This scene is related from the point of view of Gerry's passenger, Lipsha Morrissey, in chapter 24 of *The Bingo Palace*. There is a discrepancy between the accounts, however, because the man holding onto the car in *The Bingo Palace* is said to be small and young.)

Jack Mauser's grandfather

In "Blizzard Night" [35] Jack goes back to his garage, starts up his snowplow, and heads north in an effort to recover his son. Out on the interstate, he sees the headlights of a car behind him, driving in the wake of the snowplow. When these headlights disappear, Jack begins to wonder if his son might be in the car, and he finally turns back to search for it. With the help of June Morrissey's ghost, just before dawn the following day (January 6), Jack finally locates the white car, drags Lipsha to the cab of the snowplow, continues driving north, and only then discovers that John Jr. is zipped safe inside Lipsha's jacket.

That morning, in "Mauser and Mauser" [39] Jack, Lipsha, and the baby drive onto the reservation. Jack calls Candice and Marlis and checks into a motel. The following day (January 7) Jack makes a deal with Lyman Lamartine. Lyman will pay off Jack's subcontractors, and in return Jack will secure additional loans from Hegelstead and, as an enrolled member of the tribe, will be the contractor for Lyman's new tribal casino.

In "Spring Morning" [41] Jack leases his Uncle Chuck's land back to him. Chuck buys a house in Jack's new development, as do Candice and Marlis. One Saturday morning in March, Jack visits his son at Marlis and Candice's house. While there, he makes love to Marlis. In "Spring Afternoon" [42] Jack goes to Candice's office to have a tooth repaired.

In April, while Jack's construction crew is moving a new statue to the Argus convent in "The Stone Virgin" [44], Caryl Moon drops the statue onto Jack, but Jack miraculously survives, virtually unhurt. In "A Last Chapter" [46] Jack visits Eleanor and they make love—this time, apparently, with a difference. Having survived fire and ice, Jack is a reborn man.

Jack Mauser's ancestors. Assortment of big-shot and little-shot people, including North Dakota dirt farmers, Indians, and a railroad executive, referred to in "The Red Slip" [21] in *Tales of Burning Love.*

Jack Mauser's aunts. See **Aunt Elizabeth** and **Chuck Mauser's wife.**

Jack Mauser's father. German man referred to as "the big Mauser" in "The Owl" [17] in *Tales of Burning Love,* where Jack recalls the time his father leaves him, at age six, with Aunt Elizabeth. "Candice's Tale" [25] mentions that Jack inherited his taste for sweets from his father.

Jack Mauser's grandfather. Referred to as Jack's "big white German grandfather" in "The First Draw" [14] and as "the original John Mauser" in "The Owl" [17] in *Tales of Burning Love.*

Janice

Janice. One of the family members who, together with Chook, is supposed to bring food to Rozina Roy and Frank Shawano's wedding in chapter 16 of *The Antelope Wife.* See also **Chook's wife.**

Jean Hat. Guide who helps government surveyors divide tribal lands in chapter 1 of *Tracks.* In chapter 2 Hat rescues Fleur Pillager as a child from her first drowning and is later run over by his own surveyor's cart, thereby taking her place on death's road. In chapter 3 Hat's ghost in seen emerging from the bushes where he died, one of several uncanny occurrences marking Fleur's return to the reservation in 1913. In Pauline Puyat's death vision in chapter 6, he is among the group of men whose deaths Fleur is presumed to have caused. See also **Hat family** and **Two Hat.**

Jeesekeewinini. Name Nanapush uses when he visits Moses Pillager in chapter 7 of *Tracks* to get Moses's help in healing Fleur. The name refers to a medicine man who communes with the Manitous in order to diagnose and heal illness.

Jewelers. A *Fargo jeweler* cleans and repairs Adelaide Adare's garnet necklace, which Sita Kozka has redeemed from a Minneapolis pawn shop, in chapter 5 of *The Beet Queen.* Sita is wearing the gleaming necklace when she dies (chapter 13). Years later a *Fargo jeweler* sells Jack Mauser the expensive wedding ring that he gives to Dot. He shows up at Jack's funeral in "Satin Heart" [12] in *Tales of Burning Love,* demanding the ring back, since Jack had made only three payments on it.

Jewett Parker Tatro. Retired Indian agent. He is apparently the man—see **Agent**—who had been responsible for the Indians' losing much of their land. In chapter 12 of *The Bingo Palace* we learn that he buys the Pillager land around Matchimanito after it is stripped bare by the lumber companies. After he retires, he wants to sell it and move back to New England. Instead, trying to win a Pierce-Arrow, he loses all he owns to Fleur Pillager in an apparently bewitched card game.

Jimmy Badger. Old medicine man to whom Klaus Shawano goes for advice at the Elmo, Montana, powwow in chapter 2 of *The Antelope Wife.* (He is probably the same as the *old man singing the stick game song* in that chapter.) Jimmy Badger is leaning on *his grandson* as he leaves the gambling tent, where he has won. He gives Klaus advice on catching antelope, but warns him to stay away from the four antelope women, whose ancestry he relates to Klaus. After Klaus has kidnapped one of the women, the old man tells him to bring her back. Years later, in chapter 20, Klaus recalls Jimmy Badger's words: "*Bring her back to us, you fool.*" See also **Sweetheart Calico.**

Jimmy Bohl. Owner of several businesses in Argus and first husband of Sita Kozka. Jimmy begins dating Sita in chapter 5 of *The Beet Queen* after she breaks off her three-year relationship with a married doctor. When he proposes to her, Sita—a fashion model at the time—is not excited by the prospect of marriage to this unromantic steak house owner. At first she puts him off, then later marries him. In chapter 7 Sita constantly criticizes Jimmy for the way he runs The Poopdeck Steakhouse. He responds by overeating and gaining weight. When they divorce, Jimmy retains all of his businesses except the restaurant; Sita gets the restaurant and the house. In chapters 8 and 13 we learn more about the house, which Jimmy builds as a kind of showplace, the largest home in Blue Mound. Jimmy is also mentioned in chapter 10.

Jimmy Bohl's brothers and cousins. Jimmy's cousins and one brother kidnap Jimmy's bride, Sita Kozka, after their wedding and drop her off in front of a reservation bar in chapter 5 of *The Beet Queen*. The brothers are mentioned in chapter 13 as regularly getting drunk in Jimmy's recreation-room basement.

Joe. Muscled, tattooed fire-tender for the religious ceremony in which Lyman Lamartine and Lipsha Morrissey participate in chapter 17 of *The Bingo Palace*.

John Mauser. See **Jack Mauser; Jack Mauser's grandfather;** and **John Mauser Jr.**

John Mauser Jr. Son of Jack and Marlis Mauser in *Tales of Burning Love*. He is referred to as "John Joseph Mauser" in "The Owl" [17] and as "John James Mauser Jr." in "Two Front-Page Articles" [37]. (His father's legal name is "John J. Mauser.")

In "Best Western" [28] Marlis realizes that she is pregnant with John Jr. near Christmas time, 1993. When she tells Jack about the pregnancy, he responds abusively. She considers having an abortion. When Candice Pantamounty learns that Marlis is pregnant, however, she wants to take care of Marlis and adopt the baby ("Baptism River" [29]). After the baby's birth, which occurs in or before June 1994 ("Night Prayer" [6]), Marlis and Candice become lovers and thus his resident parents ("The Waiting Room" [31]). Over Candice's objection, Marlis names the baby after Jack, and in "The Owl" [17] Jack holds his son. Eleanor Mauser and Dot Mauser learn about his birth in August 1994, in "The Meadowlark" [7].

The following January (1995), John Jr. shows up in the care of his nanny at his father's supposed funeral in "Memoria" [10] and "Satin Heart" [12]. In "The B & B" [16] we learn that although Marlis is nursing John Jr., after the funeral Candice sends him home with the nanny before going to see Marlis at work.

John Mauser Jr.

In "Funeral Day" [23] Jack comes to see his son but, in the process of taking Candice's car, ends up kidnapping him. Almost immediately afterwards, Gerry Nanapush, newly escaped from prison, steals the car for a getaway vehicle, not knowing that John Jr. is in the backseat. Jack pursues the escape car in "Blizzard Night" [35] and several hours later rescues the baby, zipped inside the jacket of a nearly frozen young man, Lipsha Morrissey. (This story is told from Lipsha's point of view in chapter 24 of *The Bingo Palace;* see **Baby stolen in Fargo.**) Jack drives with Lipsha and John Jr. on north to the reservation, where he phones the worried Marlis and Candice in "Mauser and Mauser" [39]. As he lies on the motel bed beside his son, Jack thinks about the name of his construction company, "Mauser and Mauser."

John Jr. is still nursing in March 1995, when Jack visits Marlis in "Spring Morning" [41].

Johnson. Owner of the rundown, and closed, Minnesota lake resort where June Morrissey and Gordie Kashpaw spend their honeymoon in "Resurrection" in *Love Medicine.* They bargain with him for the use of an unfurnished cabin without running water.

Josephette Shawano. See Mary (I) Shawano and Josephette (Zosie I) Shawano.

Josette. See Small Bird and Josette Bizhieu.

Josette Bizhieu. Town gossip in *The Bingo Palace.* In chapter 12 Josette speaks to the owl at the church doorway. Both the owl and the mysterious deaths of Josette's mother and niece appear to be connected with the survival powers of the four-souled Fleur Pillager. Years later, now a resident at the Senior Citizens, Josette spies on Fleur's descendants. She sees Lulu Lamartine mail the copy of Gerry Nanapush's Wanted poster to Lipsha Morrissey in chapter 1; she watches Lipsha try to heal Russell Kashpaw in chapter 7; and in chapter 25 she is the reporting busybody when Lulu is arrested at the Senior Citizens.

Josette Bizhieu's mother and niece. Women who die mysteriously on the same day, as reported in chapter 12 of *The Bingo Palace.* Later, a black dog appears in the road, "guarding air." This story may be related to the story of the black dog made of smoke who attacks a Mrs. Bijiu in chapter 3 of *Tracks.* Both incidents are believed to be connected with Fleur Pillager's power. See also **Black dog.**

Jude Miller. Son of Adelaide Adare and Mr. Ober; younger brother of Mary and Karl Adare; adoptive son of Martin and Catherine Miller.

June Morrissey Kashpaw

Jude is conceived shortly before Mr. Ober's death in chapter 1 of *The Beet Queen*. When he is born in Minneapolis in 1932, the destitute Adelaide refuses to name him and a month later abandons him, along with Mary and Karl, at the Saint Jerome's Orphans' Picnic. He is then abducted by a young man who, as we learn in chapter 2, is named Martin Miller. Martin steals the baby to replace the newborn he and his wife, Catherine, have just lost. Catherine clips out ads that the baby's aunt, Fritzie Kozka, has placed in the newspaper offering a reward for information leading to his return. The Millers, however, keep the baby and name him Jude.

Sixteen years later, in chapter 4, Karl sees Jude—now a chubby, redheaded seminarian—at the Orphans' Picnic and recognizes him by his resemblance to Adelaide. Two years later, in chapter 5, Martin Miller has died and Jude is about to be ordained as a deacon on his way to the priesthood. His adoptive mother finally writes to the Kozkas to reveal his whereabouts, but only his cousin, Sita Kozka, sees her letter. Sita attends Jude's ordination ceremony in Minneapolis, February 18, 1950, but she neither meets him nor tells his biological family his whereabouts. She writes Catherine Miller in reply, but does not mail the letter. Thus Jude continues to be unaware that he is adopted. His sister, Mary, recalls him in chapter 7.

In chapter 14 (July 1972), when Jude is forty his ailing mother shows him the letter from Sita, which has finally been mailed earlier that same year. Drawn by the letter, he goes to Argus, arriving on the day of the Beet Festival. He is in the grandstand when his niece Dot Adare is named Beet Queen, and some of his family members notice him, but neither he nor they recognize one another.

Father Jude is visiting Our Lady of the Wheat Priory in Argus when Sister Leopolda disappears in "Night Prayer" [6] in *Tales of Burning Love*. He supports the scientific explanation that she has been vaporized by a lightning strike, attempting to quell rumors of a miraculous assumption. Later, however, in "A Letter to the Bishop" [45] Jude appears to consider miraculous certain events surrounding the convent's new stone statue of the Virgin, and he suggests that the bishop investigate the history of Sister Leopolda, presumably to consider her for sainthood.

June Kashpaw's unruly customer. Client whose hair June deliberately burns stiff green with chemicals when she is studying to be a beautician in "The World's Greatest Fishermen" in *Love Medicine*.

June Morrissey Kashpaw. Daughter of Lucille Lazarre and Morrissey I, who never church-marries Lucille; wife of Gordie Kashpaw and mother of King Kashpaw; lover of Gerry Nanapush and mother of Lipsha Morrissey.

June Morrissey Kashpaw

As the daughter of an alcoholic mother, June's childhood is a litany of abuse and abandonment. One cold night, in chapter 6 of *The Bingo Palace,* after Lucille's boyfriend Leonard shows up, Lucille ties June to the stove to prevent her from running away. Later in the night Leonard rapes June. According to chapter 4, June is at various times found freezing in an outhouse, in a ditch, or on the convent steps. In 1948, in "The Beads" in *Love Medicine,* June is alone with her mother in the woods when Lucille dies. The nine-year-old June lives on pine sap and grass until she is found by her drunken Morrissey father and an old drunk Lazarre woman, who is apparently Lucille's mother. The two drunks bring her to Marie Kashpaw (Lucille's adoptive sister) to raise. Marie sees no resemblance in June's features either to the Lazarres or to the Morrisseys. Two of Marie's children, Gordie and Aurelia, try to hang June, apparently at June's instigation. June is furious when Marie rescues her, and she elects to go to live with Eli Kashpaw.

"Crown of Thorns" in *Love Medicine* and chapter 10 in *The Beet Queen* depict the period in which June lives with Eli as the only peaceful time in her turbulent life. Eli is said to be crazy about "his little girl." June sleeps on a cot beside Eli's stove, and he teaches her to trap, hunt, and hide from game wardens. When June is in high school, she makes a pencil drawing of a deer, which Eli keeps in his cabin along with her photograph, even after she is gone.

After June moves in with Eli, she continues to play with the Kashpaw children. She and Gordie do everything together, like brother and sister, as he recalls in "Crown of Thorns." She goes hunting with Gordie and his friend in "Flesh and Blood." In "Resurrection," the teenage June and Gordie run away to South Dakota and marry, but it is an unhappy marriage and June leaves from time to time. Gordie's abuse of June is referred to in "Crown of Thorns" and "The World's Greatest Fishermen." June and Gordie have one son, King Howard Kashpaw, who seems to inherit his father's tendency to abuse women.

On one of her absences from Gordie, June has a brief affair with the teenage Gerry Nanapush, as recounted in "Crossing the Water." June and Gerry's son, Lipsha Morrissey, is born about 1965. June does not want to raise Lipsha, but what she does with the baby is open to question. Either she brings Lipsha to Marie to raise (as suggested in "The World's Greatest Fishermen" and "Crossing the Water" in *Love Medicine* and in chapters 5 and 11 of *The Bingo Palace*) or she tries to drown him by putting him into a weighted sack and throwing him into the slough (as suggested in "Love Medicine" in *Love Medicine* and chapters 5, 11, and 20 of *The Bingo Palace*). June eventually divorces Gordie, as recorded in "The World's Greatest Fishermen." She leaves the reservation and tries a number of occupations—beautician, secretary, clerk, waitress. By 1981, though

June Morrissey Kashpaw

not an outright prostitute, she sleeps with various men who give her money. People say of her in chapter 10 of *The Beet Queen* that she turned out even wilder than Eli had raised her.

As recounted in "The World's Greatest Fishermen" in *Love Medicine* and in "Easter Snow" [1] in *Tales of Burning Love,* in 1981 June is in Williston, North Dakota, worn, broke, and hungry. She has bought a bus ticket to return to the reservation. Waiting for the noon bus to arrive, June is beckoned into the Rigger Bar by an oil field mud engineer named Jack Mauser, who tells her his name is Andy. They make the rounds to several bars, and June misses her bus. After eating supper June and Jack get married on a whim in a quasi-legal ceremony. June, desperate for someone to rescue her, tells Jack that he is "the one," that he has to be different from the rest. After Jack tries unsuccessfully to consummate their marriage in his pickup just outside of town, June gets dressed and starts walking back. She then changes her mind and sets out for "home" in a gathering snowstorm, recalling the warmth of her Uncle Eli's kitchen. Jack follows for a time in his pickup, but when she heads off over a fence, he goes back to town. Later he calls the police and helps to track her. The next morning they find her frozen body leaning against a fence post.

Although on the surface June does little more than die in the opening stories of *Love Medicine* and *Tales of Burning Love,* in some ways she is the character whose spirit most unifies all five Matchimanito novels. She continues to haunt the other characters, both figuratively—in their memories and thoughts—and literally, as a ghost. "The World's Greatest Fishermen" recounts various reactions to her death: Albertine Johnson's warm memories of her aunt; the jealousy of Zelda Kashpaw; the loneliness of her former husband, Gordie; the grief and guilt of her son, King; the isolation of her second son, Lipsha, who does not know that June is his mother. Even the blue Firebird that King buys with her insurance money is infused with her spirit.

June particularly haunts her husbands, her lover, and her younger son. A month after her death, June's ex-husband Gordie begins to drink. On one of his drunken binges in "Crown of Thorns," he sees June look through the bathroom window. Later, after he hits a deer with his car and then clubs it to death, the deer seems to be transformed into June. He confesses this "murder," and the police and hospital orderlies come take him away. When Gordie gets out of the hospital in "Resurrection," he goes to his mother's house, where he drinks a can of Lysol and apparently dies as a result.

June's ghost is kinder to her lover Gerry and son Lipsha. Although she is remembered by reservation gossip in chapter 1 of *The Bingo Palace* as having left her son to die and his father to the mercy of another woman, she does not really

June Morrissey Kashpaw

abandon them. Lipsha recalls in chapter 14 that he has been visited by the form of his mother in the Northern Lights (probably a reference to the Northern Lights incident in "The World's Greatest Fishermen" in *Love Medicine*). Lipsha still thinks of her as his Aunt June in "Love Medicine," but in "Crossing the Water" his grandmother, Lulu Lamartine, tells him that June and Gerry are his parents. Lipsha joins his father, who has just escaped from prison, at King's apartment in the Twin Cities, where they play poker with King for "June's" Firebird. As the game is about to begin, Gerry recalls the events of June's life and her death, and Lipsha later realizes that "the ghost of a woman" is there with them. Lipsha wins the car, and through it, June helps Gerry escape to Canada. On the trip, Gerry and Lipsha talk about June, and afterwards, Lipsha drives June's car home to the reservation. After Gerry is recaptured, in the isolation of his prison cell he is haunted by June's memory in chapter 21 of *The Bingo Palace*.

In chapter 5 of *The Bingo Palace,* after Zelda tells Lipsha how June had tried to drown him, June's ghost visits him in the night, asking for her car. She gives Lipsha some bingo tickets, which turn out to represent a kind of car trade. We learn in chapter 7 that after leaving Lipsha, June takes the blue Firebird, but he wins a van with the bingo tickets she has given him. Driving around in his new van, Lipsha sees June in the Firebird. Even so, Lipsha continues to feel abandoned. In chapter 14 he is envious of Redford Toose, who has a loving mother, Shawnee Ray. Lipsha looks for June on his vision quest in chapter 17, but she does not show up.

In *Tales of Burning Love* Jack Mauser is also haunted by memories of June. As we learn in "Blizzard Night" [35], from time to time in the years after her death details about her surface in his mind. Throughout his next four marriages, Jack feels that he has stayed married to her ghost. In "Jack's House" [9] and in "The Garage" [15] he wonders if the manifold problems in his life are retribution for his having abandoned June to die in the snow and for his not even telling her his real name.

June's activities on the blizzard night of January 5–6, 1995, connect Gerry, Lipsha, and Jack in an uncanny web. As recorded in chapter 24 of *The Bingo Palace* and "Blizzard Night" [35] in *Tales of Burning Love,* the newly escaped Gerry is driving north through the blizzard in a stolen white car, with Lipsha in the seat beside him and Jack's baby boy in the backseat, when June in her blue Firebird begins driving alongside. Both cars are following Jack, who is driving a snowplow searching for his son. Jack sees them, and although he does not know who is in the white car, he recognizes June in his rearview mirror. Gerry follows June's car off the road and, leaving Lipsha in the white car, drives away with her in the Firebird. June apparently takes Gerry to West Fargo, because that is where he shows up later that night in "The B & B" [16] in *Tales of Burning Love*. Meanwhile, Jack turns back to see what has become of the white car. When he himself becomes lost in the blizzard, June's ghost appears, wearing a wedding dress. She guides him to the white car, where he rescues her son Lipsha and his son, John Jr.

June is mentioned three more times in *Tales of Burning Love,* first by Lyman Lamartine in "Mauser and Mauser" [39]. Then Jack sees June in the face of the statue in "The Stone Virgin" [44], and in "A Last Chapter" [46] he compares the pain of her freezing to death with the pain of his own coming back to life.

Karl Adare. Son of Adelaide Adare and Mr. Ober; brother of Mary Adare and Jude Miller; father of Dot Adare by Celestine James. Karl appears only in *The Beet Queen.* He is born about 1918. In chapter 1 we learn that until he is fourteen, Karl lives with his mother and younger sister, Mary, in Prairie Lake, where Mr. Ober, who is not married to Adelaide, visits them regularly. Karl has black hair (chapter 8), is described as spindly and sensitive, and seems to be his mother's favorite. After Mr. Ober's death in 1932, the family, now destitute, moves to Minneapolis, where Adelaide gives birth to another boy. After their mother abandons them at the Saint Jerome's Orphans' Picnic and a stranger kidnaps the baby, Karl and Mary take a freight train to Argus to stay with their aunt and uncle, Pete and Fritzie Kozka.

In "The Branch," when Karl and Mary arrive in Argus, Karl is frightened by a dog and runs back to the boxcar without Mary. In chapter 1, a tramp named Giles Saint Ambrose joins Karl in the boxcar and lets the ravenous Karl eat his food. Feeling rejected after having a sexual encounter with Giles, Karl runs out the door of the moving boxcar. In chapter 3 we learn that Karl's leap from the train has shattered his feet and that he subsequently develops pneumonia. Fleur Pillager cares for him and then transports him to the reservation convent. The nuns send him back to Minneapolis, where he stays at Saint Jerome's orphanage a year before entering the seminary. Meanwhile, in Argus Mary thinks she sees Karl's face in the shattered ice in chapter 2.

In chapter 4, Karl returns to the Orphans' Picnic in about 1948 to show off his apparent financial success to his former teachers. There he sees his younger brother, who is now about sixteen. Karl recognizes him because of his hair but does not identify himself. In 1952 (chapter 6) Karl is selling an air seeder at the Minneapolis Crop and Livestock Convention when he meets Wallace Pfef, a

Karl Adare

business promoter from Argus. Karl invites Wallace to his hotel room, where they have sexual relations and Karl injures his back in a fall. Chapter 9 records Wallace's attentions to him in the hospital.

Chapters 7 and 9 record Karl's return to Argus in 1953 to look for his sister, Mary. He first goes to the butcher shop, where he has a sexual encounter with Celestine James. He then goes to Wallace's house (he had called Wallace the previous evening), where he stays for about two weeks. Selling knives door-to-door, one day Karl accidentally knocks on Celestine's door. When Celestine lets him in, he stays, without letting Wallace know where he is. Karl lives with Celestine during their several-month-long affair. During this time, he has a reunion dinner with Mary, which goes badly. Celestine becomes pregnant with Karl's baby, but she still sends him away. After leaving Celestine, in chapter 8 Karl goes to his cousin Sita Tappe's house in Blue Mound, where Sita accuses him of stealing from her and Celestine. (Sita's accusations are false, but Wallace claims in chapter 12 that, sometime before going to Sita's, Karl has stolen some money from Wallace.)

As recorded in chapter 15, Karl sees his daughter, Dot, for the first time when he and Celestine get married in Rapid City, shortly after Dot's birth in January 1954. Celestine and the baby then return to Argus without him. He writes them and sends Dot occasional gifts, odd items that he is selling at the time. The summer after Dot's first-grade year, Karl sends her an electric wheelchair (chapter 10). Karl does not see his family again until Dot is fourteen (1968), when he stops on his way through Argus. Karl, Celestine, and Dot all go out for breakfast in chapter 12, but it is a tense reunion.

Another four years have passed when, in chapters 14 and 15, finally aware of the emptiness of his life, Karl responds to Celestine's note about Dot's part in the Beet Festival. He quits his job in Texas and drives to Argus to attend the festival. There, he saves Wallace from drowning in the dunking tank and, along with Celestine, Mary, and Wallace, watches as Dot is proclaimed Beet Queen and flies off in a skywriting plane. An hour later, in chapter 16, his car is parked in front of Wallace's house.

Kashpaw. Father of Eli, Nector, and ten older children with Margaret (Rushes Bear); also called Resounding Sky and the "original" Kashpaw. Chapter 3 of *Tracks* suggests that, in his youth, Kashpaw and his friend Nanapush are notable for their amorous pursuits (even sharing some women between them, according to chapter 9). But Kashpaw matures into a shrewd man, involved in business and politics. According to chapter 9 of *The Bingo Palace* and chapter 7 of *Tracks,* he builds the original log house onto which subsequent generations of Kashpaws will add. Chapter 5 of *The Bingo Palace* identifies Kashpaw as Resounding Sky and tells that he handed down to Nector the pipe smoked at the U.S. treaty ceremony. We know from chapter 3 of *Tracks* that he dies sometime before 1913. His death apparently occurs before the allotment of reservation land, because according to "The World's Greatest Fishermen" the primary Kashpaw allotment is granted to Margaret. In chapter 9 of *Tracks* his old friend Nanapush envisions a happy reunion with Kashpaw in the land of the dead.

The Beet Queen creates some ambiguity about Kashpaw's relationship to Regina Puyat and her Kashpaw children. Throughout this novel, Regina's son, Russell, is referred to as Eli Kashpaw's half brother, implying that Russell's father—the Montana Kashpaw who is Regina's first husband—is the same man as Eli's father, the original Kashpaw. But this conflicts with the account in chapters 2 and 3 of *Tracks*, which indicates that in 1913, a year in which Eli's father is already dead, Russell's father is living somewhere in Montana. Regina's first husband seems to be one of Kashpaw and Margaret's older children, all of whom, as we learn from chapter 3 of *Tracks* and "The World's Greatest Fishermen" in *Love Medicine,* move to Montana when reservation land is allotted. The "half brother" status of Eli and Russell may represent a general, rather than a specific, kinship. See also **Montana Kashpaw.**

Kashpaw boy and girl. Two unnamed children of Nector and Marie Kashpaw who die the same year of a fever, sometime before 1948. They are mentioned by Nector in "The Plunge of the Brave," by Marie in "The Beads," and by Lulu in "The Good Tears" in *Love Medicine.* Their loss is one reason Marie takes in the nine-year-old June Morrissey. If she had lived, Marie's daughter would have been almost the same age as June, who was born about 1939. The boy was probably older, since Nector refers to them as "a boy and a girl baby."

Kashpaw family. See **Aurelia Kashpaw; Eli Kashpaw; Eugene Kashpaw; Gordie Kashpaw; Isabel Kashpaw; June Morrissey Kashpaw; Kashpaw; Kashpaw boy and girl; King Howard Kashpaw; King Howard Kashpaw Junior; Lynette Kashpaw; Margaret (Rushes Bear) Kashpaw; Marie Lazarre Kashpaw; Montana Kashpaw; Nector Kashpaw; Patsy Kashpaw; Regina Puyat Kashpaw James; Russell Kashpaw;** and **Zelda Kashpaw Johnson Bjornson.**

Kerry. Family member of Cecille Shawano's neighbor in Cecille's story about the missing dishes, in chapter 16 of *The Antelope Wife.*

Kim, Tim, Vim. Undergraduate student in Eleanor Mauser's college seminar on The New Celibacy whom she seduces in "White Musk" [4] in *Tales of*

Kim, Tim, Vim

Burning Love. Eleanor is not sure what his name is, but thinks it ends in "–im." When she gives him a B minus for the course, he brings charges of sexual harassment against her. He tells **his parents** the details of the seduction, and **his mother** spends two hours with the **college president,** who forces Eleanor to resign. Afterward, a **group of students** from the seminar claim to have been brainwashed. A **reporter** calls Eleanor to ask about her resignation. Jack Mauser saves a newspaper article about the incident in "Jack's House" [9].

King Howard Kashpaw. Son of June Morrissey Kashpaw and Gordie Kashpaw. We learn in "The World's Greatest Fishermen" and "Crown of Thorns" in *Love Medicine* that King's parents have a troubled marriage. His father sometimes hits his mother, and June periodically leaves them. When she divorces Gordie and leaves permanently, June plans to establish herself somewhere and then send for King, but she never manages to do so. King's troubled childhood produces an abusive, violent personality. As he is growing up, he often mocks and beats up his younger "cousin," Lipsha Morrissey, and once even tries to shoot him. (Lipsha is actually King's half brother, June's illegitimate son. Although Lipsha does not know who his mother is, King apparently does, and his cousin Albertine Johnson guesses that this is the reason for his animosity toward Lipsha.) We learn in "Crossing the Water" that when Lipsha is ten, he surprises King by punching him in the face.

In 1981, in "The World's Greatest Fishermen," King is living in the Twin Cities with his wife, Lynette, and infant son, King Junior. When June dies that Easter, King buys a new sports car with her life insurance money, a blue Firebird. Two months after her death, King drives the new car to a family gathering at the old Kashpaw place. He wants his father to ride in the car, but no one will even touch it because it is June's. While he is there, King becomes drunk, beats up the car, verbally abuses Lynette, and even tries to drown her. Observing him, Albertine makes the connection between his violence and Gordie's abuse of June. She believes that, underneath his bully front, King is afraid—of what, she doesn't know.

In "Crossing the Water" we see other facets of King's cowardly personality. King claims, falsely, to have served as a Marine in Vietnam, where he supposedly used the code name "Apple" and his **Kentucky buddy,** the name "Banana." Actually, he has served time in the Stillwater prison, where he betrayed Gerry Nanapush to the authorities. Gerry's quip that King is an "apple"—that is, red (Indian) on the outside and white on the inside—gives ironic significance to King's hypothetical Vietnam nickname. In 1984, Gerry, who is newly escaped, and Lipsha, who has just learned he is Gerry's son and King's half brother, show up at King's apartment in the Twin Cities. The three men play poker for "June's car," which Lipsha wins. At his wife's urging, King surrenders the car, keys, and registration to Lipsha.

King Howard Kashpaw Junior. Son of King Howard Kashpaw and Lynette. King Junior is a baby when his parents bring him to a family gathering in 1981 in the first story of *Love Medicine,* "The World's Greatest Fishermen."

In the novel's last story, "Crossing the Water," he is in 1984 an intelligent kindergartner who has taught himself to read and is moved up to first grade. He tells *his teacher* that he prefers to be called Howard instead of King. In this story, we see King and Lynette's family violence from their son's point of view. Howard despises his father and recalls a time when the police came for him and handcuffed him. Thus when the police come to their apartment looking for Gerry Nanapush, Howard—assuming they are looking for his father—runs to the door to let them in.

Klaus, original German. Young German prisoner of war whom Shawano the ogitchida kidnaps in chapter 13 of *The Antelope Wife.* Klaus saves himself from being killed by baking the delicious and magical blitzkuchen. Afterward, he is adopted into the clan; Shawano's newborn son is named for him; and Shawano's older son Frank will spend his life trying to reproduce the blitzkuchen. Klaus is also mentioned, though not by name, in chapter 11.

Klaus Shawano. Son of Shawano the ogitchida and Regina; brother of Frank, Puffy, and Cecille Shawano; lover of Sweetheart Calico in *The Antelope Wife.* He narrates chapters 2, 4, 13, and 15.

Klaus is younger than Frank and at least one other sibling, since chapter 13 refers to Regina's "children" while she is pregnant with Klaus. Shortly before his birth (about 1945), when his mother eats the magical blitzkuchen baked by the young German prisoner of war, the unborn Klaus hears her speak to him, calling him by name. He is named Klaus after that German baker. We learn in chapter 20 that Klaus is left-handed and in chapter 12 that he gains a hard-won GED certificate, and perhaps a college degree.

Klaus begins telling his story in chapter 2, one year after his fateful trip to Elmo, Montana. Before that trip, he is apparently content with his life as a sanitation engineer in Minneapolis. On weekends, he works the western powwow circuit as a trader (chapters 2 and 11). He describes himself as an ordinary man, a bit too broad, but proud of his long, dark, curly hair. (He mentions his "Buffalo Soldier" blood in chapter 2.) At the powwow in Elmo, however, he sees four "antelope" women and asks old Jimmy Badger for

Klaus Shawano

antelope medicine. Klaus takes Jimmy's advice about how to attract an antelope, but ignores the old man's insistence that he leave the women alone. After capturing their attention with a piece of sweetheart calico cloth, Klaus invites the daughters to nap in his tent, then kidnaps their mother.

When the woman, whom Klaus calls Ninimoshe ("my sweetheart"), realizes in Bismarck, North Dakota, that she is caught, she fights Klaus, breaking her teeth on the edge of the bathtub. Klaus carries her back to Minneapolis where he guards her possessively. When he thinks that she is trying to kill him with sex, he calls Jimmy Badger but disregards Jimmy's demand that he return her. Throughout his narration, Klaus makes excuses for his possessive behavior, placing the blame on the woman herself. Both Klaus and his family refer to the antelope woman as his "wife" (thus our genealogical charts represent their relationship as a marriage), but this may simply represent another of Klaus's rationalizations, representing as wife a woman who is in fact his captive. In the city, people most often call Klaus's woman Sweetheart Calico.

The sequence of the next several incidents in Klaus's life is left vague. According to chapter 3, Sweetheart Calico drives Klaus crazy, so that he disappears for four years, leaving her behind in the city. According to chapter 11, they both disappear for four years, and when Klaus returns, he has turned into a street-walking bum.

The events of chapter 4 fall somewhere between Klaus's first bringing Sweetheart Calico to Minneapolis and his return some years later as a bum. Sweetheart Calico has already left him and returned several times, and Klaus now wears a buzz cut. He is part of a Native-owned trash collection business that Richard Whiteheart Beads seems to manage. At the business party in chapter 4, Richard offers Klaus a trip to Hawaii that Richard has won from the company. On the trip, however, Klaus and Sweetheart Calico are shadowed by two big guys in suits, who turn out to be government agents. Mistaking Klaus for Richard, they arrest him for Richard's illegal dumping practices. Ultimately Klaus loses everything—money, house, boat, and Sweetheart Calico. Hints in chapters 4 and 10 suggest that Klaus may think Richard and Sweetheart Calico are lovers.

By chapter 10 both Klaus and Richard have made their descent into the gutter. They wander about the city, drinking Listerine and cheap wine and accepting handouts. Klaus's physical and psychic misery is captured in the chapter's title, "Nibi"—water. His body is sick and dehydrated, and his spirit is "scorched" with longing. He dreams of his antelope wife, in the guise of the Blue Fairy, pouring out a glass of water in front of his eyes. As Klaus kneels and drinks the polluted water of the Mississippi, he watches the image of his Blue Fairy–antelope wife beneath the surface.

In chapter 11 Klaus and Richard wander into the bakery of Klaus's brother Frank. Klaus, speechless with thirst, passes out. When he wakes, still begging for "nibi," Sweetheart Calico mercifully gives him a cup of water. While Frank is on the phone trying to get his brother into detox, Klaus and Sweetheart Calico walk out the door with arms around each other.

Sweetheart Calico leaves, returns, and leaves again in chapter 12, sending Windigo Dog—a spirit of uncontrollable hunger—in her place. Windigo Dog tells Klaus a dirty dog joke, and in chapter 13, Klaus tells him the story of Klaus's German namesake.

In chapter 15, Klaus and Richard are finally in a recovery program, and Klaus has an early-morning industrial cleaning job. Disgusted with Richard's fits of weeping, Klaus confronts him with his dishonesty. Richard, in turn, confronts Klaus with his abduction and destruction of Sweetheart Calico. Klaus finally faces the fact that his excuses have been lies, but he remains torn between needing to let her go and wanting to cling.

At the preparations in chapter 16 for Frank's marriage to Rozina Roy, Klaus is four-months sober and struggling to stay away from the cold beer. Later, when Richard interrupts the cliffside wedding ceremony, Klaus and his brother Puffy restrain Frank from pushing Richard over the cliff. That afternoon, when Richard also disrupts the reception, Klaus hits him over the head with a frozen turkey.

Klaus's sobriety does not last, however. In chapter 20 he is again sleeping in the bushes at the park, listening to Windigo Dog tell jokes, and dreaming about a real life, when a riding lawn mower runs over his head. He escapes with his life only because a stray dog (presumably Windigo Dog) bolts toward the lawn mower, is hit, and vanishes. When the dog disappears, Klaus is finally able to master his windigo cravings. Waking, he makes two decisions—to stop drinking and to let his antelope wife go free. He carries out the later decision in chapter 21. For a week he watches for Sweetheart Calico, and when she appears, he ties her wrist to his with a band of calico and walks through the city. When they reach the open spaces to the west, Klaus, fighting back his own longing, unties the cloth and watches as the antelope woman wearily makes her way west and disappears.

Kroshus, Mrs. See **Tillie Kroshus.**

Kuklenski brothers. Brothers of Harry Kuklenski. Anna Kuklenski sends her dead husband Harry's body back to Milwaukee with them to be buried beside his uncle, in "Eleanor's Tale" [20] in *Tales of Burning Love.*

Kuklenski family. See **Flying Kuklenskis.**

L

La Chien woman. Woman whom Mary Bonne cuts after finding her in bed with Mary's husband, as recalled in "Flesh and Blood" in *Love Medicine*.

Lake man. Man-monster-cat mentioned in chapter 8 of *The Antelope Wife* who lives in Ojibwa lakes and periodically takes people, especially women. See also **Misshepeshu.**

Lamartine family. See **Beverly "Hat" Lamartine; Elsa Lamartine; Henry Lamartine Junior; Henry Lamartine (Senior); Lulu Nanapush Morrissey Lamartine;** and **Slick Lamartine.** Also wearing the Lamartine name, although not Lamartine by blood, is **Lyman Lamartine.**

Langenwalter. Argus undertaker who is attending the Beet Parade when Sita Kozka dies in chapter 13 of *The Beet Queen.*

LaRue. Nosy woman who implies to Marie Kashpaw that Eli Kashpaw is not a fit caretaker for June Morrissey in "The Beads" in *Love Medicine.*

Lawn-mowing man. Young black man on the riding lawn mower that hits a stray dog and then runs over Klaus Shawano's head in chapter 20 of *The Antelope Wife.*

Lawrence Schlick. Father of Eleanor Schlick and husband of Anna Kuklenski Schlick. In "The Meadowlark" [7] in *Tales of Burning Love,* we learn that he is an undertaker and runs Schlick's Funeral Home.

The story of Lawrence's marriage to Anna Kuklenski is told in "Eleanor's Tale" [20]. He meets Anna when he visits her in the hospital after the trapeze accident that had killed her first husband. He falls in love with her and they marry. Lawrence, a leading Fargo businessman and citizen, provides for his family in grand style. They live in a turn-of-the-century mansion, and he dotes on his daughter, Eleanor. (In "White Musk" [4] Eleanor recalls that he built her a playhouse.) After Anna saves six-year-old Eleanor from a house fire, the grateful Lawrence joins the fire department.

After putting out a terrible fire one frigid November night, however, Lawrence comes home to find his wife in bed with one of the young firemen, Jack Mauser. Anna has saved Jack's life after he nearly froze to death and has gotten into bed with him to warm him. It is not clear whether the two have had sex, but the impulsive Lawrence asks no questions. He immediately casts both Anna and Eleanor out to live a life of poverty.

This whole experience is so upsetting to Lawrence, however, that in "The Red Slip" [21] his various businesses fail until he is left with only his funeral business, which he moves into the mansion with him. He reconciles with Anna after Eleanor tells them she is pregnant with Jack Mauser's child and plans to marry him. Even so, his suspicions continue and in "The Box" [22] (1983) he sneaks home two days early from a convention to see if Anna is sleeping with Jack. She is not.

In January 1995 Lawrence Schlick hosts Jack's funeral—at a financial loss—as told in "Memoria" [10] and "Satin Heart" [12]. While Jack was alive, Lawrence considered him a rival and enemy, but after Jack's (supposed) death, he is able to forgive him. He has painstakingly gathered what seem to be Jack's charred remains from the basement of his burned house. At closing time Lawrence herds Jack's wives out the door in "The B & B" [16], but holds Eleanor for a moment before she leaves. Meanwhile, in "Funeral Day" [23] Jack imagines that Schlick is gloating over his death and resolves to specify in his will that some other undertaker should handle his real, future funeral.

In August of that year, in "A Light from the West" [43] Anna dies at home. The grieving Lawrence prepares her body for cremation and then crawls into the chamber to be cremated with her.

Lawrence Schlick's banker, lawyer, and accountant. Men who advise Lawrence the morning he finds his wife Anna in bed with Jack Mauser about how to arrange his business affairs so that she can get no more money from him, in "Eleanor's Tale" [20] in *Tales of Burning Love.* The banker is likely the **Bank president in Fargo.**

Lawrence Schlick's cousin. Realtor who helps Lawrence rent a new place and put his mansion up for sale after Schlick finds his wife in bed with Jack Mauser in "Eleanor's Tale" [20] in *Tales of Burning Love.*

Layla Morrissey. Cousin of Lipsha Morrissey who works for Zelda Kashpaw at the Indian agency. She asks Lipsha about Fleur Pillager the day Fleur comes to town in chapter 11 of *The Bingo Palace.*

Lazarre family. See **Boy Lazarre; Ignatius Lazarre; Izear Lazarre; Lazarre woman; Lucille Lazarre; Marie Lazarre Kashpaw;** and **Old drunk woman.**

Lazarre woman. Marries Clarence Morrissey in chapter 7 of *Tracks.*

Leonard. Lucille Lazarre's boyfriend. In chapter 6 of *The Bingo Palace* he rapes

Leonard

Lucille's young daughter, June Morrissey, apparently while the drunken Lucille is asleep.

Leopolda, Sister. Nun and schoolteacher. Sister Leopolda takes her orders at the Sacred Heart Convent on the reservation in 1919, at the end of chapter 8 of *Tracks*. She is assigned to teach arithmetic at Saint Catherine's school in Argus. In chapter 2 of *The Beet Queen,* she is still teaching at Saint Catherine's in 1932. When Mary Adare cracks the ice in the school yard, causing the image of Christ to appear, Sister Leopolda takes photographs of the "miracle." Several nights after the incident, Leopolda is found beside the icy image, scourging her arms with thistles. She is sent away to recuperate—apparently back to Sacred Heart, since that is where she is in *Love Medicine* from 1934 through 1957. This convent is described in "Saint Marie" as a place where nuns are sent who do not fit in elsewhere.

Leopolda appears in two *Love Medicine* stories told from Marie Lazarre Kashpaw's point of view. In "Saint Marie" she is Marie's teacher at the convent school. What primarily distinguishes Leopolda from the other nuns is her attitude toward the devil, whom she sees as her personal enemy and a ubiquitous, lurking presence. Leopolda's weapons against his inroads include, for herself, fasting to the point of starvation and, for her pupils, terror and pain. Although Marie initially tries to defeat Leopolda by siding with the devil, one day in the classroom Leopolda gets the best of them, hurling her metal-tipped oak pole through Satan's heart—actually an old black boot—and throwing Marie into the dark closet with the "dead" boot.

When Marie comes to the convent in 1934, seeking to become a nun, Sister Leopolda is her sponsor. Leopolda professes love for Marie, but it is a twisted, violent love. She pins the child to the floor with her foot and pours a kettle of scalding water over her back in order to melt her "cold" heart and boil Satan out of her. When Marie confronts Leopolda with the suggestion that the devil is in Leopolda more than in Marie, the nun loses some of her power over Marie. After Marie kicks her into the oven, Leopolda stabs Marie through the hand and knocks her unconscious. To cover up the attack, she tells the other nuns that the child has had a vision and swooned and that the stigmata have appeared miraculously in her palm. Thus, when Marie regains consciousness, Leopolda must kneel beside her and accept Marie's blessing. (As a grown woman with children, Marie will recall in "The Beads" having "faced down the raging nun.")

In 1957 Sister Leopolda seems to be dying. In "Flesh and Blood," Marie takes her daughter Zelda to visit the nun. Leopolda has shriveled to a pile of sticks and is partially deranged, yet her mind is clear enough to know who

Marie is and to remember their old enmity. The two trade insults and physically struggle. At the end of this struggle, Leopolda pulls Marie back from a vision of falling into darkness, and Marie leaves the now-quiet old woman, certain that she will be dead by the next spring.

Leopolda, however, does not die in the spring of 1958. According *Tales of Burning Love,* she is still alive in 1994 and is 108 years old ("Night Prayer" [6]). This accounting conflicts with the chronology of *Tracks,* which suggests that she would be 96 in 1994 (see chapter 2 of *Tracks*).

In *Tales of Burning Love* Leopolda's "saintly hungers" are the object of research of college professor Eleanor Mauser, who in "White Musk" [4] is teaching a seminar on The New Celibacy in the fall of 1993. Sometime after the end of that semester, possibly early in 1994, Eleanor goes to the Our Lady of the Wheat Priory in Argus, where Leopolda now resides, to observe and interview the old nun. According to "Night Prayer" [6] Leopolda does not like her young interviewer. When Leopolda goes out to pray in the convent garden one hot June night (1994), she is annoyed to find Eleanor there. Eleanor refuses to leave, however, and the two discuss prayer and the nature of love. Leopolda predicts that Eleanor's ex-husband, Jack Mauser (who is at that moment in the garden posing as the statue of the Virgin), will die screaming, crushed by a woman. After Leopolda utters her last words—"End this torment"—she appears to die in an ecstasy. After Eleanor and Jack leave, lightning strikes Leopolda's metal walker, and the nun disappears, either vaporized by the lightning or, as some of the nuns believe, the object of a miraculous assumption.

The following January, in "A Conversation" [33], Leopolda appears to Eleanor, who is exposed at night in a subzero blizzard. In this appearance, Leopolda continues her conversation about love and desire, the "holy fire" by which she is herself possessed. Her final instruction to the younger woman helps to save Eleanor's life.

Jack Mauser recalls Leopolda's vision of his death in "Jack's House" [9] and "The Garage" [15]. In "The Stone Virgin" [44] her prophecy is partially fulfilled when the statue of the Virgin falls on him, although he survives essentially unharmed. This survival and subsequent miracles surrounding the statue are the subject of Father Jude's "A Letter to the Bishop" [45], in which he suggests that Sister Leopolda's history is worth investigating, apparently with a view to her possible beatification. Miracles surrounding the old nun also lead Eleanor deeper into her research on spirituality in "A Last Chapter" [46], and she remembers Leopolda's words concerning the desire that nails God and humans to their crosses: "Only pull forth the nails."

Leo Pukwan

Leo Pukwan. Third-generation tribal policeman who, along with Zelda Bjornson and the social worker Vicki Koob, in chapter 15 of *The Bingo Palace* seizes Redford Toose from the house of his aunts, Tammy and Mary Fred Toose. Pukwan carries out his mission by knocking Mary Fred unconscious with his pistol. See also **Edgar Pukwan** and **Edgar Pukwan Junior.**

Lily Veddar. Employee at Pete Kozka's butcher shop in *Tracks.* In chapter 2 Lily plays cards with Tor Grunewald, Dutch James, and Fleur Pillager in the evenings after work. Lily's bad-tempered dog, Fatso, sits in his lap as he plays. One hot night in August 1913, enraged at Fleur's winnings, Lily leads the men's attack on Fleur. The next day the three men take shelter from a tornado in the meat locker, and Pauline locks them in. When they are found several days later, Lily is frozen to death. He reappears in Pauline Puyat's death vision in chapter 6, again playing cards with Fleur.

Lindsay. Marlis Cook's ex-sister-in-law, who lets Marlis live in the foundation crawl space under her trailer in "Marlis's Tale" [27] in *Tales of Burning Love.* Having divorced Marlis's brother, Lindsay is now married to Dane. After Dane leaves, Marlis lives in the trailer with Lindsay.

Lipsha Morrissey. Son of June Morrissey and Gerry Nanapush. As we learn in "Crossing the Water" in *Love Medicine,* Lipsha is conceived in 1964 during a brief affair between June, who is married to Gordie Kashpaw and already has one legitimate son, and Gerry, who is just out of high school. In "Crossing the Water," "Love Medicine," and chapter 5 of *The Bingo Palace* we learn that when Lipsha is born, June does not want to raise him, but it is a matter of debate precisely what she does with him. One version of the story is that she brings baby Lipsha to Marie Kashpaw to raise. Another version is that she tries to drown him, and either Marie or her daughter Zelda rescues him. (See also chapters 11 and 20 of *The Bingo Palace.*)

In any case, Marie takes in Lipsha, and in "The Beads" in *Love Medicine* and chapter 4 of *The Bingo Palace,* she thinks of her adoption of him in connection with her adoption of his mother June. He grows up confused about his origins because, although Marie tells him that his mother had tried to drown him ("Love Medicine"), she never tells him who his parents are. Some details of Lipsha's childhood appear in "The World's Greatest Fishermen" and "Crossing the Water" in *Love Medicine* and chapter 4 of *The Bingo Palace.* Lipsha is a withdrawn child who often clings to Marie and weeps for no apparent reason. His supposed foster cousin (actually, half brother), King Kashpaw, persistently mocks him and beats him up. Once, hunting gophers with Lipsha, King even

Lipsha Morrissey

takes a potshot at him. When Lipsha is ten, he surprises King by punching him in the face. Another cousin, Albertine Johnson, befriends Lipsha, who says that she is like his sister, the only girl he has ever trusted. Two months after June's death, as they watch the Northern Lights together in "The World's Greatest Fishermen," Albertine tries to tell Lipsha who his mother is, but he will not listen, angry that his mother had tried to drown him. Nevertheless, he recalls in chapter 14 of *The Bingo Palace* that he has been visited by the form of his mother in the Northern Lights.

We learn in "Love Medicine" that after his "Grandma" Marie and now feeble-minded "Grandpa" Nector move into the Senior Citizens, Lipsha often visits them. Partly because of the healing power in his hands, passed down to him from his Pillager ancestors, he is able to help Marie with Nector. Marie wants Lipsha to make a love medicine so that Nector will love her rather than his old flame, Lulu Lamartine. After hesitating at first, Lipsha decides to do so, but he takes a shortcut, substituting frozen turkey hearts for those of Canada geese, and his attempt to work a love medicine has tragic results—his Grandpa Nector chokes to death on one of the turkey hearts. Although Grandma Marie is angry with Lipsha, he is able to comfort her.

In 1983, Lipsha works briefly for his father's half brother, Lyman Lamartine, in "The Tomahawk Factory," and in 1984 he finally learns the story of his parentage from his grandmother, Lulu Lamartine, in "Crossing the Water." Lipsha leaves the reservation and tries to find his father, who he feels will soon escape from prison. By chance or fate, they meet at King Kashpaw's apartment in the Twin Cities. Lipsha wins "June's car" (bought by King with June's insurance money) in a rigged poker game and then helps Gerry escape. As Lipsha visits with his father on their way to the Canadian border, he finally experiences a sense of belonging. At the end of this story, the last in *Love Medicine,* Lipsha drives June's car back home.

The narrators of chapter 1 of *The Bingo Palace*—reservation gossips—also mention Lipsha's driving onto the reservation in the blue Firebird and his part in the tomahawk factory fiasco, although they reverse the order of these events. This narration adds that, even though Lipsha finishes high school and scores high on college entrance exams, he does not go to college or get a steady job. After a series of temporary jobs, he ends up working in a sugar beet factory in Fargo, where he is said to frequent the bars and rougher parts of town. When Lulu sends him a copy of his father's Wanted poster, however, he decides to return home.

Lipsha attends the winter powwow in chapter 2 of *The Bingo Palace* and is captivated by the beautiful Shawnee Ray Toose. Shawnee Ray, however,

Lipsha Morrissey

is engaged to Lyman Lamartine and has a son, presumably Lyman's. Zelda Kashpaw is trying to promote the relationship between Lyman and Shawnee Ray. In chapter 4 Marie gives Nector's sacred pipe to Lipsha. When Lipsha tries to take Shawnee Ray to dinner at a restaurant in Canada, they are detained at the border for possession of drugs and Nector's pipe is confiscated. Lyman arrives in chapter 5 to work out the problem with the border guards, and he tries unsuccessfully to buy the pipe from Lipsha. He also gives Lipsha a job in his bingo hall. Their relationship is complicated by the facts that Lyman is Lipsha's uncle and they are both in love with Shawnee Ray.

Also in chapter 5, Zelda tells Lipsha that his mother, June, had thrown him into a slough in a weighted gunnysack and that Zelda herself had dragged him out. (We learn in this chapter that Marie has at some point changed her version of the story, probably after Lipsha learned that June is his mother, now claiming that Lipsha's mother sorrowfully gave him up because she was too wild to take care of him herself.) Later that night, June's spirit visits Lipsha in the bingo hall bar, gives him a booklet of bingo tickets, and, as he discovers the next morning, takes "her" car, the blue Firebird. In chapter 7, Lipsha plays bingo in an attempt to win a fancy van. To finance his gambling, he starts charging for the use of his healing power, and his "touch" deserts him. He begins winning at bingo, however.

Also in chapter 7, Lipsha and Shawnee Ray make love for the first time in a motel room. When Lipsha buys condoms at a nearby gas station, he exchanges insults with Marty, the attendant. The next night, Lipsha wins the bingo van, using one of June's tickets. Driving around in the van, he sees June in the Firebird—their car trade is now complete. Later that night, Marty abducts Lipsha from a party, takes him to Russell Kashpaw's to be tattooed, and vandalizes the van.

Lipsha continues trying to win Shawnee Ray's love. When in chapter 8 Lyman again asks to buy Nector's pipe, Lipsha offers to trade it if Lyman will step aside from his pursuit of Shawnee Ray. Lyman alters the deal, persuading Lipsha to lend him the pipe in return for his promise not to tell Shawnee Ray about Lipsha's offer. In chapter 9 Lipsha is winning regularly at bingo, and Lyman persuades him that the two of them should open a joint bank account. Although Shawnee Ray tells Lipsha to leave her alone, he goes to Zelda's house (where Shawnee Ray is staying), and they make love a second time. Afterwards, in chapter 10, Shawnee Ray uses money Lipsha has given her to escape from Zelda's control.

Desperate to secure Shawnee Ray's love, in chapter 11 Lipsha decides to ask his great-grandmother, Fleur, for a love medicine. When he accompanies the

Lipsha Morrissey

old woman to her house at the far end of Matchimanito Lake, she changes into a bear and begins speaking to him. Chapter 13 indicates that Fleur speaks to him about the enduring value of the land. We learn from chapters 14 and 22 that she speaks in the old Indian language, which Lipsha does not usually understand, but that her thoughts enter his mind as pictures. When Fleur does not give him a love medicine, Lipsha considers suicide. He decides instead to go on a spiritual quest and visits Lyman for advice. The two rivals undertake a vision quest led by Xavier Toose, Shawnee Ray's uncle, in chapter 17. Instead of the dramatic vision he expects, however, Lipsha encounters a skunk, who, like Fleur, lectures him on the importance of the land. In chapter 19 the skunk-reeking Lipsha gets a ride back to town with Albertine, who advises him to leave Shawnee Ray alone for a while. The following night, in chapter 20, Lipsha remembers being saved from drowning as an infant by the lake creature of Matchimanito, and he has a vision in which the skunk is spokesperson.

In January (chapter 22) Lipsha has a dream about his father and then learns that Gerry has escaped. (The year appears to be in the late 1980s in *The Bingo Palace* although it is given as 1995 in *Tales of Burning Love.*) Gerry calls Lipsha from Fargo but his directions in the old Indian language confuse Lipsha. When they finally meet, Lipsha's van will not start. In chapter 24 of *The Bingo Palace* they steal a white car (which turns out to have a baby in the backseat) and, after evading the police, escape from Fargo. As they head north they are caught in a blizzard but manage to fall in behind a snowplow. (According to "Blizzard Night" [35] in *Tales of Burning Love,* they are now on the interstate.)

When June reappears driving the blue Firebird, Gerry goes with her. Left behind in the white car, Lipsha zips the baby into his jacket to protect him from the bitter cold. In chapter 26 the radio news the next day says that "a hostage" has been found in good condition, and in chapter 27 Fleur takes the place of "the boy" in death, but the identities of this hostage and boy are ambiguous. Thus, as *The Bingo Palace* ends, Lipsha's fate remains uncertain. In "The Tale of the Unknown Passenger" [34] in *Tales of Burning Love,* Gerry and his wife, Dot Adare, worry about Lipsha and console themselves with the conviction that Lyman has gone out to find him.

In *Tales of Burning Love* the story of this car theft and subsequent storm is told from the point of view of the baby's father in "Funeral Day" [23] and "Blizzard Night" [35]. Searching for the missing baby, the father is driving the snowplow that Gerry and Lipsha follow north on the interstate. (Although Gerry and Lipsha get a head start, they are delayed by traffic and have to evade police, so apparently by the time they reach the interstate, they are behind the snowplow.) *Tales of Burning Love* also resolves the ambiguity about Lipsha's survival. Near

Lipsha Morrissey

dawn following the night of the storm, the baby's father, Jack Mauser, finds the white car and drags Lipsha and the baby to safety. Jack notices Lipsha's Chippewa face and his one slightly crooked tooth, a feature he inherited from his mother, who—unknown to either of the men—had also been Jack's first wife. As Jack drives on up to the reservation in "Mauser and Mauser" [39], the exhausted Lipsha sleeps, with the baby still zipped against him.

Living lost. Assorted outlaws, drunks, addicts, fools, and artists—Anna Schlick's friends—whom Anna takes care of after she resumes her marriage with Lawrence Schlick. This collective term is used in "The Box" [22] in *Tales of Burning Love*.

Louis Tappe. State health inspector who comes to Chez Sita to investigate the food poisoning in chapter 7 of *The Beet Queen*. He falls in love with Sita Kozka Bohl, now divorced from Jimmy Bohl. In chapter 8, Louis and Sita marry. He quits his job as health inspector and moves to Blue Mound to live in the big house that Sita has received as part of her divorce settlement. In his new job as county extension agent, he collects data about the local entomological pests and helpers. He also observes and takes notes on Sita's psychotic behavior. After long trying to manage Sita's psychotic episodes himself, when Sita in chapter 10 pretends to be mute, Louis finally consults a psychiatrist, who admits her to the state mental hospital. After spending one night in the hospital, Sita is "cured."

Caring for Sita wears on Louis, and by the time they attend Dot Adare's eleventh-birthday party in chapter 12 (1965), he is suffering from angina and seems frail. Although Sita is largely withdrawn at the party, Louis seems to enjoy being with the children. We learn in chapter 13 that in the last years of his life, Louis stockpiles the tranquilizers to which Sita has become addicted. By 1972, Louis is dead and Sita's supply of pills is almost gone. She ends her life by taking the last half bottle of Louis's legacy on the day of the Beet Festival.

Lovchik. Ronald Lovchik is an Argus police officer in the 1950s to 1970s in *The Beet Queen*. In chapter 10 Ronald is described as a tall, sad, unassertive man who has a crush on Sita Kozka and brings her chocolates, until she marries Jimmy Bohl (c. 1950). He listens to Wallace Pfef talk about sugar beets in chapter 6 (1953). He is the officer in chapter 10 assigned to investigate the complaints made by Dot Adare's teacher, Mrs. Shumway, against Mary Adare in 1960. In chapter 13 Ronald stops Mary and Celestine James for speeding on the way to the 1972 Beet Parade and speaks to Sita, who sits between them on the front seat, not noticing that Sita is dead. He hopes to court Sita now that her husband Louis is dead, so he does not ticket them.

Lulu Nanapush Morrissey Lamartine

This may or may not be the same Lovchik who, in "Scales" in *Love Medicine,* tries several times unsuccessfully to arrest Gerry Nanapush in 1980. The Lovchik is referred to as a "local police" officer, although the setting of the story is not specified. There is also an officer Lovchik on the Argus police force in 1994 (Ronald's son?) in *Tales of Burning Love.* This Lovchik arrests Jack Mauser for financial misconduct when Jack comes to Argus to meet his latest mother-in-law in "A Wedge of Shade" [3].

Lucifer. See **Satan.**

Lucille Lazarre. Mother of Geezhig and June Morrissey by a Morrissey man (Morrissey I) who does not marry her; supposed sister of Marie Lazarre Kashpaw. Marie refers to Lucille as her sister and to Ignatius Lazarre as her—and thus presumably Lucille's—father in "The Beads" in *Love Medicine.* (The reader of *Tracks* knows that Marie's birth parents are not, in fact, Lazarres, and thus Lucille is not her blood sister as she supposes.) Marie declares Lucille to be the only Lazarre for whom she has any use. In chapter 6 of *The Bingo Palace* Lucille is described as an alcoholic who has good days and bad days. One cold night, after her boyfriend Leonard shows up, Lucille ties the child June to the stove to keep her from running away. Later in the night Leonard rapes June.

Lucille badly neglects June, who as a child is found abandoned on a number of occasions, freezing or starving, as recounted in chapter 4 of *The Bingo Palace* and "The Beads" in *Love Medicine.* Lucille dies in the woods, alone with the nine-year-old June. After her death, her drunk Morrissey "spouse" and an old drunk woman who is apparently her mother (Marie refers to the old drunk as her own disowned mother) bring June to Marie for her to raise. Lucille is also referred to, though not by name, in "The World's Greatest Fishermen" in *Love Medicine.*

Lulu, daughter of Nanapush and White Beads. See **Red Cradle.**

Lulu Nanapush Morrissey Lamartine. Daughter of Fleur Pillager; mother of eight sons, including Gerry Nanapush, Henry Lamartine Junior, and Lyman Lamartine, and one daughter, Bonita.

Lulu's paternity is uncertain. She may have been conceived when Fleur was (possibly) raped by three men in an Argus smokehouse or during Fleur's subsequent love affair with Eli Kashpaw. Pauline Puyat even suggests that she may have been fathered by the lake man, Misshepeshu. The indications that one of the Argus men is Lulu's father are strong, but never conclusive. (For speculations about Fleur's pregnancy, see **Fleur Pillager.**) According to Pauline at the end of chapter 2, the reservation folk themselves are never sure whether

Lulu Nanapush Morrissey Lamartine

Lulu was fathered in the smokehouse, or by the lake man, or by Eli. In trying to judge whether Lulu's appearance betrays a half-white heritage, we have only the testimony of the unreliable Pauline. In chapter 3 she tells us that Lulu has green eyes and "skin the color of an old penny," possibly suggesting mixed blood, but in chapter 4 she records that Lulu has "the Kashpaws' unmistakable nose." That both Erdrich and her characters intend for Lulu's paternity to remain a mystery is evidenced by the fact that, years later, when her grandson Lipsha Morrissey asks who her father is, Lulu refuses to answer (*The Bingo Palace,* chapter 11). Despite this uncertainty, after her birth everyone clearly accepts Lulu as Eli's child, even her grandmother Margaret Kashpaw, who earlier had been keen on proving the opposite. (Examples of this assumption of Eli's paternity appear in chapter 9 of *Tracks,* where Nanapush, speaking to Lulu, refers to Eli as "your father," and in chapter 11 of *The Bingo Palace,* in which Lulu refers to her "dad's" feast day.)

The first eleven years of Lulu's life are recorded in *Tracks,* primarily from the point of view of her "grandfather," Nanapush. In chapter 3 Lulu is born in the spring of 1914 in Fleur's cabin at Matchimanito Lake, after a dangerous delivery. Nanapush names her, giving her his own surname and the nickname (Lulu) of his deceased daughter. In chapter 4 Pauline records with envy the love and attention Fleur and the rest of the family lavish upon Lulu. When, in the winter of 1917–1918 (chapter 5), Nanapush and Margaret are attacked by Boy Lazarre and Clarence Morrissey, Lulu escapes and runs to Margaret's house. In the famine winter of 1918–1919 (chapter 6) the pregnant Fleur goes without food so that Lulu can eat. When Fleur goes into early labor, Lulu runs for help through the snow to Margaret's house. She almost freezes to death, but according to Pauline's death vision, Fleur wins Lulu's life in a card game in the land of the dead. In chapter 7, Nanapush cares for Lulu's severely frostbitten feet at Margaret's house and refuses to allow the white doctor to amputate. Once Lulu and her mother recover, the anxious Fleur, whose baby has died, follows Lulu everywhere. The next spring (chapter 8), Lulu is among the group on the shore watching Pauline in the leaky boat on Matchimanito Lake.

According to her recollection in "The Good Tears" in *Love Medicine,* the summer that Lulu is seven she finds a dead man by her "playhouse" in the woods. Chapters 8 and 9 of *Tracks* reveal the man to be Napoleon Morrissey. (According to the *Tracks* account, this incident takes place in 1919, when Lulu is five.) Soon afterward, Fleur, about to be evicted from her land, sends Lulu away to an off-reservation boarding school. At school, as we learn in "The Island" in *Love Medicine,* Lulu misses her mother desperately and often tries to run away. In 1924 Lulu is finally able to return to the reservation, where she

Lulu Nanapush Morrissey Lamartine

lives with Nanapush and Margaret, whose efforts have brought her home. Her return is recorded in "The Island" and in chapter 9 of *Tracks*. In "The Island" there is hostility between Lulu and Margaret after Lulu's return. In "The Good Tears," however, Lulu thinks of Margaret as her grandmother and recalls the old woman's stories about the removal of the Chippewas from their ancestral land. These stories will later be the basis of Lulu's own refusal to relinquish her land.

Lulu's first love is Nector Kashpaw (Eli's younger brother, thus possibly her uncle), as recorded in "Wild Geese" in *Love Medicine*. When Nector begins seeing Marie Lazarre, however, Lulu goes to the island home of her mother's kinsman, Moses Pillager ("The Island"). They become lovers, and in 1935 or 1936 Lulu gives birth to their son (his given name is not revealed). Moses is the father of at least one other of Lulu's sons, Gerry Nanapush (born about 1945), and possibly a third, since her three oldest sons carry her maiden name, Nanapush, and are thus probably born before her first marriage ("Lulu's Boys").

Because Moses will not come live in town with her, Lulu decides in "The Good Tears" to marry Morrissey II out of spite. At this point Nanapush takes her aside and tells her the stories about Fleur and the Kashpaw, Morrissey, and Lazarre families that are recorded in the odd-numbered chapters of *Tracks*. As indicated in chapter 9 of *Tracks,* his object is to make Lulu understand Fleur and to persuade her not to marry the Morrissey. Lulu goes ahead with the marriage, although she later regrets it.

Lulu's second marriage is to Henry Lamartine (Senior), as recorded in "The Good Tears" and "Lulu's Boys" in *Love Medicine*. Henry dies in a car and train wreck in 1950, a probable suicide. When Henry's brother Beverly comes for the funeral, he and Lulu make love in a shed after the wake. Nine months later, Lulu gives birth to Beverly's child, her seventh son, whom she names Henry Lamartine Junior.

In 1952 Lulu and Nector begin a five-year affair, as related in "The Plunge of the Brave" and "The Good Tears." Lulu has a son with Nector—the youngest of her eight boys—named Lyman Lamartine, born about 1953. (According to "Lulu's Boys," after her three Nanapush sons, the next oldest are Morrisseys, who are later renamed Lamartine, probably after Lulu marries Henry. Reservation gossips observe that Lulu's third group of sons, the younger Lamartine boys, look as if they have various fathers, which the reader knows to be the case.)

As recounted in "Lulu's Boys," "The Plunge of the Brave," and "The Good Tears," Beverly returns to the reservation from the Twin Cities in 1957 with the intention of taking Henry Junior back to the city. But he is once again attracted to Lulu, and they sleep together. While Beverly is staying with her,

Lulu Nanapush Morrissey Lamartine

Lulu receives papers evicting her from her land. They are signed by Nector Kashpaw. Furious with Nector, Lulu sics her dogs on him and marries Beverly. When she discovers that Beverly has another wife in the city, she sends him back to get a divorce, accompanied by her twelve-year-old son, Gerry.

After Beverly leaves, Nector goes to see Lulu to tell her he is leaving his wife for her, but he instead sets fire to her house, as recorded in "The Plunge of the Brave," "Flesh and Blood," and "The Good Tears." While rescuing her son Lyman from the burning house, Lulu loses her hair. (The incident is also referred to in chapters 5 and 14 of *The Bingo Palace*.) Lulu and her boys camp out on the site of the burned-out house for two months until the tribe finally builds her another house on better land.

In "The Good Tears," when Lulu is almost fifty she gives birth to her last child, her only daughter, Bonita, fathered by an unnamed Mexican migrant farm worker. "The Red Convertible" suggests that Bonita is born about 1963. In "The Good Tears," "The Red Convertible," and "Scales," Lulu suffers a series of heartaches with her sons. Shortly after Gerry graduates from high school, he is arrested and imprisoned for assault. Although he continually escapes, he is never a free man again. Then Henry Junior, after returning from Vietnam with psychological problems, drowns in 1974, and his half brother Lyman is so distraught that he stays depressed and drunk for a year.

When Lulu is around 65 she moves into the Senior Citizens. There she and Nector meet again, as recorded in "The Good Tears" and "Love Medicine." When the two embrace and begin to kiss, they are interrupted by Lipsha Morrissey, Lulu's grandson and Nector's foster son. At the time of Nector's death and funeral (1982), Lulu is in the hospital recovering from eye surgery. When she returns home, her old rival Marie Kashpaw helps care for her. In "The Tomahawk Factory" the two women become political allies in support of traditional culture and in opposition to Lyman's efforts to create a souvenir factory. Yet over time, the tension between them revives, and one day in 1983 an argument between them erupts into a riot that destroys the factory. In "Crossing the Water" (1984), Lulu tells Lipsha that he is her grandson, the child of her son Gerry and June Morrissey.

The Bingo Palace continues the story of Lulu's relationship with Lipsha and Gerry. In chapter 1 Lipsha is living aimlessly in Fargo when Lulu mails him a copy of a Wanted poster of his father, apparently as a warning. Lulu keeps the original poster in a picture frame in her apartment (chapter 10). According to chapter 4, Lulu feels that Marie has spoiled Lipsha, but in chapter 9 Lulu also tries to help him, registering him for tribal benefits. In chapter 7 Lulu is a regular patron of the bingo hall where Lipsha works, and he learns her businesslike approach to gambling. She persuades him to try his healing power on war veteran Russell Kashpaw and is disappointed when he fails. Lipsha goes to see Lulu briefly in chapter 11, when he is looking for Fleur. Lulu still does not talk about Fleur, but says that she does not hate her mother, merely understands her. In chapter 21 Lulu's efforts are responsible for a tribal request that Gerry be transported to a Minnesota prison. When he escapes from the transport flight, rumors surface in chapter 22 about Lulu's part in the affair, and she is questioned by federal marshals in chapter 25. After she plays cat and mouse with the marshals for hours, they arrest her for possession of the stolen Wanted poster. As she leaves her apartment in handcuffs, dressed in traditional regalia, she dances and trills the old woman's victory yell.

Lumber president. Man who, along with a military captain and the Indian agent, tries to convince the Chippewas to sell their land for cash in chapter 3 of *Tracks*. He is probably the president of the Turcot lumber company, which in chapters 5, 7, and 9 is buying up and logging reservation land, either upon agreement with the owners or after seizure by the government due to nonpayment of land fees. Chapter 7 especially hints at a conspiracy between the government agent, the lumber company, and certain tribal families, such as the Pukwans and the Morrisseys.

Lying Down Grass. Nanapush's first sexual partner, although not one of his three wives. Also known by her Indian name, Sanawashonekek, she is mentioned in chapters 3 and 9 of *Tracks*.

Lyman Lamartine. Son of Nector Kashpaw and Lulu Lamartine; Lulu's youngest son. Lyman is conceived during Nector and Lulu's five-year affair, 1952–1957, while Lulu is between husbands and Nector is married to Marie ("The Good Tears"). He is born about 1953. Lulu will not tell Nector absolutely that Lyman is his child, but in "The Plunge of the Brave" in *Love Medicine* Nector believes the boy looks like him, and in "The Good Tears" Lulu says he is "half Kashpaw." In 1957, when Nector sets fire to Lulu's house, young Lyman is alone in the house, sleeping ("The Good Tears"). Lulu rescues him but loses her hair in the fire.

We learn in chapter 11 of *The Bingo Palace* that Lyman is a skilled ladies' man from the time he is fourteen. He is also a natural entrepreneur. From age fifteen to sixteen, in "The Red Convertible" in *Love Medicine,* he owns and operates the Joliet Café for a year, until it is destroyed in a tornado. He is even financially savvy enough to have insured the café.

Of his seven half brothers, Lyman is particularly close to Henry Junior, born

Lyman Lamartine

in 1950 or 1951 ("Lulu's Boys"). He describes their relationship in "The Red Convertible" in *Love Medicine* and in chapter 14 of *The Bingo Palace*. When they travel the powwow circuit together, Lyman is always in Henry's shadow. The summer Lyman is sixteen (apparently 1969), he and Henry buy a red Oldsmobile convertible with the insurance money from the café. They spend the summer driving all over the northern Midwest, and even to Alaska. When they get back home, Henry becomes a Marine and, shortly after Christmas, is sent to Vietnam. (The family's first overseas letter from him arrives in 1970.) When Henry returns in 1973, Lyman tries to shake him out of his powerful depression by banging up the car so that Henry must repair it. The following spring (1974) Lyman and Henry drive the restored car to the Red River. Henry walks into the swift current and sinks, and, after an unsuccessful attempt to rescue him, Lyman sends the car in after him. When he returns home, Lyman tells his mother in "The Good Tears" that there has been an accident, that the car went out of control and into the river. (Lyman and Henry are also mentioned as brothers in "The Bridge" and "Love Medicine.")

In "The Tomahawk Factory" Lyman remains depressed and drunk for a year after Henry Junior's death, then becomes an ambitious administrator in the Bureau of Indian Affairs, eventually moving to Aberdeen. Nector dies in 1982, and Lyman asks Lulu about his father in "The Good Tears." According to "The Tomahawk Factory," sometime after Nector's death, Lyman moves back to the reservation to run the tribal souvenir factory that Nector had started to build. The factory is destroyed in 1983 in a brawl precipitated by his mother and Marie Kashpaw. Following the factory fight, he plans a future in Indian reservation gambling in "Lyman's Luck."

Lyman is an important character in *The Bingo Palace,* a book named after his business enterprise. In chapter 1, reservation gossip pegs him as a pleasant but scheming entrepreneur who, like his father, takes advantage of the government and mixes the interests of the tribe with his own ambition. When we first see him in chapter 2, he is at a powwow doing a traditional dance in his half brother Henry's outfit. Lyman is now financially successful and is semi-engaged to a beautiful young woman, Shawnee Ray Toose, of whose small son, Redford, he is the reputed father. Shawnee Ray is living with Lyman's half sister, Zelda Kashpaw, who is promoting their marriage. Lyman's rival for Shawnee Ray's affection is Lipsha Morrissey, the son of another of Lyman's half brothers, Gerry Nanapush.

When Lipsha takes Shawnee Ray out for dinner in chapter 4 and gets into trouble with the Canadian border guards, the influential Lyman rescues him in chapter 5. When he sees that Lipsha has Nector's ceremonial pipe, Lyman offers to buy it, but Lipsha refuses to sell. Lyman hires Lipsha to be a watchman-janitor at the bingo hall and is irritated in chapter 7 when Lipsha wins his advertising lure, the bingo van. Lyman continues his efforts to buy Nector's pipe in chapter 8. We learn in chapter 9 that Lyman manages to "borrow" the pipe by blackmailing Lipsha, but he also agrees to stop seeing Shawnee Ray. In chapter 8 Lyman travels to an Indian Gaming Conference in Reno where, in an all-night gambling spree, he loses the tribe's money and pawns the pipe. He is later able to redeem the pipe in chapter 9.

Lyman continues to see Shawnee Ray in chapter 9, despite his promise to Lipsha, yet the two men get along surprisingly well. Lyman has a new moneymaking scheme to build a larger casino beside an undeveloped lake on a piece of reservation land that he believes will soon revert to tribal ownership. He talks Lipsha into going in with him on this project by their opening a joint bank account. (Lyman tells Lipsha an anti-Indian joke in this chapter. Another version of the joke appears in chapter 20 of *The Antelope Wife*.)

We discover (along with Lipsha) in chapter 22 of *The Bingo Palace* that Lyman has withdrawn all of Lipsha's bingo winnings from their joint account. It becomes clear in chapters 17 and 20 that the lake property Lyman wants is none other than the Pillager land on Matchimanito. In chapter 13 Lyman has a vision in which Fleur Pillager repeats the words of Nanapush (recorded in chapter 3 of *Tracks*) regarding land as the only thing that lasts from generation to generation. Perhaps ironically, this message further encourages Lyman to acquire and develop Pillager land. It seems that Lyman is ultimately successful in seizing the land, for in the closing chapter of the novel, men come with signed papers to evict Fleur.

When Lipsha comes to Lyman for an uncle's spiritual advice in chapter 14, Lyman invites him to take part in a fast and vision quest under the direction of Xavier Toose (Shawnee Ray's uncle). Lyman reminisces about his half brother, Henry Junior, and tells Lipsha that he has gotten a court order to gain legal custody of his son, Redford. (Shawnee Ray has left Redford briefly with her alcoholic sisters, and as Zelda had warned her in chapter 10, Lyman is not happy with this arrangement.) Lipsha is furious with Lyman about the court order, and the two get into a fight in the local Dairy Queen. The result of Lyman's court order is revealed in chapter 15, when authorities seize Redford from the Toose sisters.

In chapter 17 the angry Shawnee Ray, who is once again living at Zelda's with Redford, informs Lyman that he may not, in fact, be Redford's father. She

Lyman Lamartine

adds that she will never marry him and warns him never to go to court again. Lyman's religious fast in chapter 18 culminates in his solitary dancing in the woods and a visionary conversation with the dead Henry Junior. In chapters 17 and 20 he sits in a circle with the other participants in the vision quest and tells them of his experience.

Lyman relinquishes the cherished ceremonial pipe in chapter 23, not returning it to Lipsha but giving it to Zelda as a way of conceding the failure of their alliance. From Shawnee Ray's thoughts in chapter 26, it is clear that Lyman has lost his battle with Lipsha for her affections.

In *Tales of Burning Love,* Lyman's efforts to realize his dream of a casino include getting the part-Chippewa contractor Jack Mauser, an old friend of one of Lyman's older brothers, involved in the project. In "Satin Heart" [12] he goes to Jack's supposed funeral convinced that Jack is not dead, and he speaks with Dot Nanapush Mauser, the wife both of Jack and of Lyman's half bother Gerry, who has just escaped from prison. Apparently, Lyman has spoken with Gerry after Gerry's escape from a snowbound car where Lipsha is still stranded. Lyman lets Dot know that Gerry will be at the B & B bar, and in "The Tale of the Unknown Passenger" [34] Gerry indicates that Lyman has gone out to try to rescue Lipsha.

In "The Owl" [17] Lyman calls Hegelstead, the Fargo banker who has made a now-defaulted loan to Jack. After a brief visit with Jack, Hegelstead calls Lyman back in "Mauser and Mauser" [39] and makes a deal: Lyman will pay off Jack's subcontractors, and Hegelstead will lend Jack (or Lyman) more money toward the construction of the casino, probably in return for a percentage of the profits. Besides the funding, Lyman wants Jack as chief contractor because he is an enrolled member of the tribe. Jack accepts Lyman's offer. In "A Last Chapter" [46] Lyman is referred to as Jack's casino partner.

Lynette Kashpaw. King Howard Kashpaw's white wife; mother of King Howard Kashpaw Junior. Lynette and King live in the Twin Cities. In "The World Greatest Fishermen" in *Love Medicine,* they come with their baby to a Kashpaw family gathering on the reservation in 1981, two months after the death of King's mother, June Morrissey Kashpaw. They are driving a new blue Firebird purchased with June's insurance money. That evening, King threatens Lynette and tries to drown her. "Crossing the Water" gives a glimpse of Lynette and King's dysfunctional family from the point of view of their now school-aged son. When Gerry Nanapush visits their apartment in 1984, Lynette is afraid of Gerry and insists that King sign over the registration of June's car to him and June's son, Lipsha Morrissey.

Margaret (Rushes Bear) Kashpaw

Magid. Ojibwa woman; daughter of Everlasting; lover of an Ivory Coast slave; forebear of Rozina Roy in chapter 3 of *The Antelope Wife.*

Man who takes Fleur's place. Unnamed man who, along with Jean Hat, saves Fleur Pillager from drowning when she is a child in chapter 2 of *Tracks.* They are the first of several men who take Fleur's place on death's road. Hat is run over by his surveyor's cart, and the unnamed man simply wanders off and disappears.

Man with frozen fingers. Recalled by Dot Mauser in "February Thaw" [40] in *Tales of Burning Love.* He was a man her mother knew on the reservation. See **Xavier Albert Toose.**

Many Women. See **George Many Women.**

Margaret (Rushes Bear) Kashpaw. Wife of the original Kashpaw (also known as Resounding Sky) and mother of twelve children, including Eli and Nector Kashpaw. From "The World's Greatest Fishermen" in *Love Medicine* and chapter 3 of *Tracks,* we learn that Margaret's husband, Kashpaw, dies sometime before 1913, apparently before the allotment of the reservation land, since Margaret receives the Kashpaw family allotment. When the allotments are made, Margaret's ten older children move to Montana, but the two youngest, Eli and Nector, stay on the reservation. She wants Eli, in particular, to stay with her and take care of her in her old age.

When Margaret first learns about Eli's relationship with Fleur Pillager in chapter 3 of *Tracks,* she is upset because she does not want Eli to leave. Nevertheless, in the spring of 1914 she assists at the birth of Fleur's daughter, Lulu, saving Fleur's life. When a drunk bear shows up at Fleur's cabin just before she delivers, Margaret marches straight up to it before realizing she has no gun. Because of this incident, she will later take the name "Rushes Bear" ("The Island" and "The Beads" in *Love Medicine*). When Eli refuses to return to his mother's home in chapter 4 of *Tracks,* Margaret and Nector often stay at Fleur's cabin. There, the Kashpaw and Pillager families join together into something of a clan, mixing Fleur's old religious ways with the Catholicism of Margaret, who often brings Lulu to Mass.

In the autumn of 1917 (chapter 4), when Fleur casts a spell on Sophie Morrissey, Margaret tries to be kind to the girl. Even so, in chapter 5, she becomes the target of Clarence Morrissey's vengeance. One night that winter Clarence and

Margaret (Rushes Bear) Kashpaw

Boy Lazarre tie up Nanapush and Margaret and shave her head. (This incident is also referred to in "The Tomahawk Factory" in *Love Medicine*.) When the men first grab Margaret, she utters a war cry and bites Lazarre's hand, a bite that results in blood poisoning and ultimately his death. Nanapush avenges the insult to Margaret by snaring Clarence, and he buys her a large coal-black bonnet, which she wears daily, earning herself the nickname "Old Lady Coalbucket." His gallantry softens her feelings toward him, and by Ash Wednesday 1918, they are keeping company, although their relationship continues to be prickly. Father Damien suggests that they be church married, but Nanapush declines.

In chapters 6 and 7 of *Tracks* Margaret comes to Fleur's aid again after her second baby is born prematurely in the winter of 1918–1919. During that famine winter, when the whole family is weak from starvation, in chapter 7 Margaret walks to town, and she and Father Damien return with government rations. She also helps the family raise money to pay Kashpaw and Pillager land fees and in the spring accompanies Nector to town to pay the agent. But it is revealed in chapter 9 that because the fees are higher than expected, unknown to Nanapush and Fleur, Margaret and Nector use all of the money to pay the fees on Kashpaw land and do not pay them on Pillager land.

Margaret is among the group on the shore of Matchimanito in the spring of 1919 (chapter 8) who are watching Pauline in the leaky boat. That fall (chapter 9) Fleur learns of Margaret and Nector's betrayal, and Margaret sends Nector to an off-reservation boarding school, partly to put him out of the way of Fleur's wrath. (Her sending Nector to school is also referred to in "The World's Greatest Fishermen" in *Love Medicine*.) Nanapush comes to live with Margaret, but Fleur refuses to do so.

After Fleur leaves the reservation, Margaret and Nanapush do the necessary paperwork to bring Lulu back from the government boarding school where Fleur has sent her. The story of Lulu's return in 1924 is found in chapter 9 of *Tracks* and in "The Island" in *Love Medicine*. Margaret, who now calls herself Rushes Bear, is irked by Lulu's presence and spends more time away from Nanapush at her own Kashpaw allotment. Nevertheless, years later in "The Good Tears," Lulu refers to Margaret as her grandmother and recalls her stories about the removal of the Chippewas from their ancestral lands. (In "The Island" Lulu twice refers to Margaret as Nanapush's "wife"; thus the genealogical charts for *Love Medicine* represents their relationship as a marriage.)

When Nector returns to the reservation in about 1934 ("Wild Geese" and "The Plunge of the Brave"), he lives with Margaret and Eli in the old Kashpaw place until he decides to marry Marie Lazarre. In "The Island" Margaret is angry that her son is marrying a member of the family that insulted her. As recorded in "The Beads," Margaret leaves Nanapush, stays for a time with her children in Montana, and then goes to her childhood home near Lake Superior. When she returns to the reservation in 1948, she moves in with Nector and Marie, who are now living in the Kashpaw house (see "The World's Greatest Fishermen" in *Love Medicine*). At first, she and Marie do not get along, but after she helps Marie through the difficult birth of Marie's last son that winter, the women bond with one another. Margaret has finally found a home and a daughter who takes care of her until her death. Years later, after Nector's death, in "Resurrection" Marie has a dream about the past that includes Margaret, and afterwards she thinks about the old Indian strengths that her mother-in-law had taught her.

Marie Lazarre Kashpaw. Daughter of Pauline Puyat and Napoleon Morrissey; supposed youngest daughter of Ignatius Lazarre, possibly adopted; wife of Nector Kashpaw. According to chapter 6 of *Tracks,* Marie is born in the summer of 1918. The chronology in "Saint Marie" in *Love Medicine,* however, suggests a birth date of about 1920. (Both this story's 1934 date and Marie's "I was near age fourteen" seem to refer to the same day—the primary, non-flashback event of the story—the day Marie goes up the hill to the convent to become a "saint.")

When Marie's mother, Pauline, discovers that she is pregnant in chapter 6 of *Tracks,* she wants to abort the child, but Bernadette Morrissey prevents her and later forcibly delivers Marie. Pauline abandons Marie at birth to join the reservation convent, and Bernadette takes care of the child. In chapter 7, Bernadette takes the baby Marie and moves to town when her children Sophie and Clarence bring their Lazarre spouses into Bernadette's house. Bernadette has contracted consumption, however, and we learn in chapter 8 that as she grows weaker, the slovenly Sophie increasingly cares for Marie. Marie grows up believing that she is a Lazarre, though her supposed Lazarre mother is probably not Sophie. Sophie's husband is Izear Lazarre and Marie's supposed father is Ignatius. (In "The Beads" in *Love Medicine* Marie refers to Ignatius as her father and Lucille Lazarre as her sister. The Lazarre woman she believes to be her mother is in 1948 an old drunk.)

In "Saint Marie" in *Love Medicine* Marie recalls growing up in the bush. The only times she and the other children come to town are for school and for Sunday Mass. At the Sacred Heart Convent school, Marie's teacher is Sister Leopolda, who makes it her mission to drive the devil from Marie. In 1934, "near age fourteen," Marie goes up to the convent hoping to become a "saint." Sister Leopolda is Marie's sponsor as a novice. The same day Marie arrives,

Marie Lazarre Kashpaw

Leopolda pours scalding water on her back and, after Marie kicks her into the oven, she stabs Marie's hand with a bread fork and knocks her out with a poker. When Marie regains consciousness, the sisters are kneeling at her bedside. Leopolda has told them that the wounds in Marie's hand are the miraculous stigmata. (This incident is also referred to, without naming Marie, in "Night Prayer" [6] in *Tales of Burning Love.*)

Marie is leaving the convent, her head and wounded hand wrapped in torn bed linen, when Nector Kashpaw grabs her in "Wild Geese" in *Love Medicine.* As they grapple, the encounter becomes sexual, and Nector discovers in amazement that he, who is in love with the charming Lulu Nanapush, wants this "dirty Lazarre."

The story of Marie and Nector's first two decades of marriage is told primarily in "The Beads" and "The Plunge of the Brave." They marry in 1934 or 1935, and the children begin to come: Gordie in about 1935 (see "Resurrection"), Zelda in 1941 (see "The World's Greatest Fishermen" and "Flesh and Blood"), Aurelia and Patsy in unspecified years, and Eugene in the winter of 1948–1949 ("The Beads").

Marie and Nector also lose two children, a boy and a baby girl who die in the same year (the girl is born around 1939 or 1940). Marie makes up for this loss by taking in other children. In 1948, while she is still pregnant with Eugene, Marie takes in the daughter of her adoptive sister Lucille Lazarre, June Morrissey, after Lucille dies. June is about nine, a little older than Marie's dead daughter would have been if she had lived. Later that year, June goes to live with Nector's brother Eli.

Also while Marie is pregnant with Eugene, Nector's mother, Margaret (Rushes Bear), comes to stay with them. Marie and Margaret have never liked each other, but when the baby is born that winter, Margaret, together with Fleur Pillager, helps Marie through her dangerous delivery. After that, the two women bond, and in Margaret, Marie at last finds the mother she never had. During this time, the family has little money, and Nector is often gone or drunk, yet Marie is determined to make him into something big on the reservation. He eventually begins to support his family, serves as tribal chairman, and even goes to Washington. What Marie does not know is that in 1952 he also begins a five-year affair with Lulu Nanapush Lamartine.

One day in 1957, in "Flesh and Blood" Marie takes her daughter Zelda to visit old Sister Leopolda, who seems to be dying. But the visit turns into a battle of insults and ultimately a physical struggle with Leopolda. When Marie and Zelda return home, Zelda finds a note from Nector under the sugar bowl, saying that he is leaving Marie for Lulu. While Zelda goes to bring Nector back, Marie washes the floor in her good dress, grieving. When Nector arrives home and is afraid to enter, Marie puts out her hand and pulls him in. She has replaced his note, now under the salt can, and never mentions it. (Marie will be remembered in chapter 14 of *The Bingo Palace* as one of the few people who was able to stay calm through the vicissitudes of love.)

The last child Marie takes in to raise is June's abandoned son Lipsha Morrissey, as we learn in "The World's Greatest Fishermen." Various versions of this adoption story are recorded in "Love Medicine" and "Crossing the Water" in *Love Medicine* and in chapter 5 of *The Bingo Palace*.

As Marie and Nector age, Nector becomes feeble-minded. Marie moves with him to the reservation's Senior Citizens, and Aurelia moves into their house on the Kashpaw allotment. Shortly after June's death in 1981, Marie and Nector join the rest of the family for supper at the old Kashpaw place in "The World's Greatest Fishermen" in *Love Medicine*. In "Love Medicine" (1982) Marie grieves that Nector, even with his failing mind, still loves Lulu, who also lives at the Senior Citizens. Marie asks Lipsha to make a love medicine to restore Nector's affection for her. Lipsha agrees, but uses a false medicine of turkey hearts. Marie chews and swallows her turkey heart, but Nector chokes on his and dies. Nector's spirit visits Marie, and Lipsha tells her that he visits because of his love for her, not because of Lipsha's medicine.

After Nector's death, Marie returns to the Kashpaw house in "Resurrection." While she is cooking and cleaning house, Gordie arrives—drunk, as he has remained since June's death. When Marie will not provide him with alcohol, Gordie drinks a can of Lysol. He apparently dies, for Marie senses that he is "chasing" his own death, and catches it.

Now that Nector is gone, Marie forms a friendship with Lulu Nanapush. Marie nurses her after eye surgery in "The Good Tears," and the two women become allies in supporting traditional Indian ways in opposition to Lyman Lamartine's commercialism in "The Tomahawk Factory." The friendship disintegrates, however, and their feuding escalates into an interfamily brawl that destroys Lyman's souvenir factory. By the next year, Marie and Lulu have apparently become allies again, as recorded in "Crossing the Water." The contrast between the two women is mentioned in chapter 11 of *The Bingo Palace*.

When Lipsha is confused after learning the truth of his parentage from Lulu, Marie tries to help him in "Crossing the Water" by virtually inviting him to steal her money. (In this story and in chapter 4 of *The Bingo Palace*, Marie is once again living in her apartment in the Senior Citizens.) Lipsha recalls this act of generosity in chapter 9 of *The Bingo Palace*. In chapters 1 and 4 of *The Bingo Palace,* Marie continues to be an indulgent "grandma" to Lipsha even after he

Marie Lazarre Kashpaw

is grown. In chapter 4 she gives him Nector's sacred ceremonial pipe. Marie is present in chapter 7 when Lipsha unsuccessfully attempts to use his "touch" to heal Russell Kashpaw and is also mentioned briefly in chapters 10 and 11. She remains calm in chapter 25 when federal marshals come to the Senior Citizens asking questions about the escaped Gerry Nanapush.

Marie Lazarre's aunt. Remembered by Marie as taking "us children" to Sunday Mass in "Saint Marie" in *Love Medicine.* The identities of this aunt and the **other children** are not specified, but since Marie was raised by Lazarres, the aunt is probably a Lazarre woman (either by birth or marriage). She may be Sophie Morrissey Lazarre, since Sophie is beginning to care for the toddler Marie in chapter 8 of *Tracks* and, according to chapter 7, she has numerous children and step-children.

Marie Lazarre's grandma. Remembered by Marie in "Saint Marie" in *Love Medicine* as the one person who knows as much about Satan as Sister Leopolda. The grandma, however, calls him by different names and is not afraid of him. Since Marie is mistaken about her parentage, this "grandma" is presumably a Lazarre rather than the mother of one of her birth parents, Pauline Puyat and Napoleon Morrissey (chapter 6 of *Tracks*). (Marie's comparison of this woman with Sister Leopolda takes on added significance for the reader of *Tracks,* chapter 8.)

Marlis Cook Mauser. Fourth wife of Jack Mauser and mother of John Mauser Jr. in *Tales of Burning Love.* In "Best Western" [28] Marlis says that she is Polish. Long before Marlis actually appears, the reader has formed impressions of this "most problematic" of Jack's wives. In "Jack's House" [9] Jack sees her as frightening—psychotic and manipulative. Eleanor Schlick Mauser despises her, referring to her as "that brain-dead Lolita" in "The Meadowlark" [7]. When Eleanor calls Marlis "Jack's slut" in "Satin Heart" [12], Candice Pantamounty defends her but admits that she is "bipolar." Jack also thinks about Marlis briefly in "The First Draw" [14], "The Garage" [15], and "The Owl" [17].

We learn in "The B & B" [16] that from the time she is twelve, Marlis wants to be a performer. Although she cannot sing, she takes piano lessons and devotes herself to transforming her originally plain appearance. In "Marlis's Tale" [27] we learn that she has a brother and a fifteen-year-old half sister. She says that her mother died young, that she herself is fresh out of Catholic school, and that her dad is rich but has kicked her out. In "Best Western" [28] Marlis recalls her father's anger and her hiding from him, and we learn that she goes by her mother's maiden name, Cook.

Marlis Cook Mauser

After leaving home, Marlis lives underneath the trailer house of her brother's ex-wife, Lindsay, although Lindsay's new husband, Dane, does not approve ("Marlis's Tale" [27]). She does not have a job, but lives off the settlements from two accidents. A third "accident" occurs in the summer of 1992 when Marlis grabs a live electrical cable in a store undergoing remodeling. Jack Mauser is there and resuscitates her, although imperfectly, so that she suffers nerve damage. She sues both the store and Jack, but Jack cures her.

A few weeks later (it is now August), Marlis runs into Jack in a bar, where she tells him that she is twenty-one. He shows her his huge loan check from the bank and reveals that he has just divorced. They get drunk and go to a motel, where Marlis steals the check. At the motel, she first claims to be twenty-five, then fifteen, and threatens to charge Jack with statutory rape if he does not buy her clothes and a car. The next day he buys her a whole new wardrobe.

That evening, in "Best Western" [28] Marlis takes Jack to her job at the Elkwood Lounge and gets him drunk again. That night she drives him to South Dakota, where they are married by a justice of the peace early the next morning. Back in Fargo later that day, she alters Jack's check and deposits it in her own bank account, showing the hesitant teller her marriage license as proof of identity. Marlis and Jack hide out a month in Eugene. (In September, Jack returns to his work in Fargo, as recorded in "The First Draw" [14].) Marlis convinces Jack to go on the road performing with her, he singing, she playing the piano.

Over the next two years Marlis and Jack book gigs in hotels and nightclubs in various cities across the northern Midwest. In Detroit at Christmastime 1993, Marlis realizes that she is pregnant. At a later engagement in Minneapolis–Saint Paul, Jack confronts her about the check. On their way to a performance in Billings, Montana, Marlis tells Jack that she is pregnant. At first he ignores her, then twists her arm, and later shoves her. His anger and her pain and fear remind her of her girlhood fear of her father. Marlis gets revenge in the Billings Best Western motel by tying Jack to the bed, subjecting him to some of the pain of being a woman, and then leaving.

In "Baptism River" [29] Marlis returns to Fargo. She gives half of Jack's money back to him, saving the rest to take care of the baby. Jack refuses to answer her calls and letters. That spring (1994), Candice Pantamounty, Jack's previous wife, invites Marlis to take a trip with her to a resort on Lake Superior, and Marlis agrees. At the second-rate motel where they stop for the night, Candice offers to help Marlis through the birth and then to adopt the baby. The woman in the adjacent room decides that Marlis and Candice are lovers, a notion the two find hilarious. The next morning, Marlis expresses her deepest misgivings

Marlis Cook Mauser

about Candice's proposal—she fears that if she gives the baby up for adoption, it will hate her all its life. Candice guesses, apparently correctly, that Marlis's mother had done the same thing with her.

Although Marlis tells her to stay away, in "The Waiting Room" [31] Candice shows up at Marlis's late-term check-up, attends Lamaze classes with her, visits in her apartment, and helps her through labor. Weeks after the birth of John Mauser Jr. (which is in or before June 1994, "Night Prayer" [6]), Marlis is still suffering severe postpartum depression. Candice moves into the apartment to take care of her and the baby, and the women become lovers.

Although Marlis continues to be depressed, she is determined to nurse the baby, promising Candice that she will not drink ("The B & B" [16]). For weeks she and Candice fight over custody. When Candice tells her to leave, Marlis refuses but does get a job dealing blackjack at the B & B in West Fargo. Candice hires a nanny to help take care of John Jr.

On the day of Jack's funeral, January 5, 1995, Marlis is drinking and acting as if Jack is not dead. She is working at the B & B that afternoon when Jack's other wives come to the bar-casino after his funeral. Later that evening, in "The Hitchhiker" [18] the wives all leave together in a blizzard, and on the way to Fargo the car becomes stuck in a snowdrift. As the stranded women argue about Jack in "Secrets and Sugar Babies" [19], Marlis and Candice get into a fight and then make up.

Marlis listens to Eleanor's and Candice's stories, engages in dialogue with them, and periodically helps clean snow from the tailpipe. In "Surviving Sleep" [24] she expresses her naturalistic view of life. After Candice's story, Marlis tells of her relationship with Jack in "Marlis's Tale" [27] and "The Best Western" [28]. Candice then picks up the thread of Marlis's story, recounting the development of her and Marlis's relationship. Marlis and Candice's memories in "The Waiting Room" [31] appear *not* to be told to the other women.

In "Rotating Wild" [32] Eleanor insults Marlis. Enraged, Marlis suggests that it is time to clean snow away from the tailpipe again and that it is Eleanor's turn. The women form a human chain, with Marlis holding Eleanor. When a strong gust of wind seizes her rival, Marlis lets go, allowing Eleanor to fly away into the storm. Overcome with fatigue and cold, in "The Tale of the Unknown Passenger" [34] Marlis and Candice sleep in each others' arms. "The Disappearance" [36] and "Two Front-Page Articles" [37] recount the wives' rescue by snowmobile. After being treated for frostbite at the hospital, Marlis and Candice are released.

While the women are at his funeral, in "Funeral Day" [23] Jack goes to Candice's house and kidnaps his son. After losing and then rescuing John Jr.,

Jack phones Candice and Marlis in "Mauser and Mauser" [39]. Marlis promises not to prosecute if Jack will bring the baby back immediately.

In "Spring Morning" [41] Marlis and Candice buy one of the houses in Jack's new subdivision, the Crest. One Saturday morning in March, Jack is at the house visiting Marlis and their son while Candice is at her office. Although Jack claims never to think about his relationship with her, Marlis tells him that she does, and when John Jr. is asleep, she seduces Jack. In "Spring Afternoon" [42] Marlis calls Candice at the office. The reader is not told, but suspects from what Candice says to Jack, that Marlis tells Candice about the morning's lovemaking.

Marlis Cook's brother. Ex-husband of Lindsay, under whose house trailer Marlis lives in "Marlis's Tale" [27] in *Tales of Burning Love.* He is apparently older than Marlis.

Marlis Cook's father. Man apparently responsible for much of Marlis's hatred and distrust of men, as revealed in her attitude toward Jack Mauser. In "Marlis's Tale" [27] in *Tales of Burning Love,* Marlis says that her father is rich, has kicked her out, and is a control-freak. In "Best Western" [28], when Jack twists her arm, she remembers her father's impulsive temper and her own fearful hiding as she listened to him search for her.

Marlis Cook's half sister. Fifteen-year-old whose driver's permit Marlis shows to Jack Mauser, pretending it is her own, in order to manipulate him with the threat of statutory rape charges, in "Marlis's Tale" [27] in *Tales of Burning Love.* We learn nothing more about who this girl is, but possibly she is the daughter of Marlis's father by a second marriage, since Marlis says that her mother died young.

Marlis Cook's mother. Woman who died young, according to Marlis in "Marlis's Tale" [27] in *Tales of Burning Love.* But Marlis's riddles about her origins—that she was made from "the clay her mother swallowed" and was "dragged in blue from a snowdrift"—may suggest a story not fully told. In "Baptism River" [29] Candice guesses that Marlis's mother gave her up at birth. The guess touches close enough to the truth to make Marlis weep, although it is possible that Marlis simply has experienced her mother's death as abandonment. In "Best Western" [28] we learn that the surname Marlis uses, Cook, had been her mother's maiden name.

Marshals. *Two marshals* are assigned to guard Gerry Nanapush as he is transported to a new prison facility in Minnesota in chapter 21 of *The Bingo Palace.*

Marshals

It appears that they die when their small plane crashes. The "Radio Bulletin" [11] in *Tales of Burning Love,* indicates that two men are confirmed dead in the accident, although one of these may be the pilot. In chapter 25 of *The Bingo Palace* a **group of marshals** comes to Lulu Lamartine's apartment to question her about the escaped Gerry, who is her son. In the end they handcuff and arrest her for stealing a Wanted poster of Gerry from the post office. In "Smile of the Wolf" [38] in *Tales of Burning Love,* another **group of marshals** comes to Dot Nanapush Mauser's house to arrest Gerry, who has come to visit his daughter, Shawn, but escapes as they arrive. Two of the marshals stay and question Shawn. One of them, **Ted,** is tall and impatient; the other is short and has a soft voice.

Martha May Davis. Woman who holds up a store and uses the money to buy an expensive wedding dress. Lipsha remembers the incident when thinking about the dangers of love in chapter 14 of *The Bingo Palace.*

Martin, Sister. See **Mary Martin de Porres, Sister.**

Martin Miller. Distraught father who in chapter 1 of *The Beet Queen* abducts the Adare baby from the Orphans' Picnic in Minneapolis in 1932. We learn in chapter 2 that he takes the child home to his wife, Catherine, to feed, because their own newborn son has just died. They decide to keep the Adare baby rather than return him to his rightful family, thus becoming kidnappers. According to chapter 5 Martin dies in 1944, and in 1950 Catherine writes to the Kozkas, confessing the abduction.

Marty. Gas-station attendant wearing a T-shirt that says "Big Sky Country" with whom Lipsha Morrissey trades insults in chapter 7 of *The Bingo Palace.* Lipsha later encounters him at a party. Marty and his friends pay Russell Kashpaw to tattoo a map of Montana on Lipsha's buttocks, and they vandalize Lipsha's new van. Lipsha tells Marty that he has a ***cousin named "Marty,"*** too.

Mary Adare. Daughter of Adelaide Adare and Mr. Ober; sister of Karl Adare and Jude Miller; niece of Pete and Fritzie Kozka. She is born about 1921.

   In chapter 1 of *The Beet Queen,* until Mary is eleven, she lives with her mother and older brother Karl in Prairie Lake, where Mr. Ober, who is not married to Adelaide, visits them regularly. Unlike Karl, Mary enjoys Mr. Ober's visits, because he pays special attention to her, calling her "Schatze" (a German word for "treasure" that can be used as a term of endearment). After Mr. Ober's death in 1932, the family, now destitute, moves to Minneapolis, where Adelaide gives birth to another boy. After their mother abandons them at the Saint Jerome's Orphans' Picnic and a stranger kidnaps the baby, Mary and Karl ride a freight

Mary Adare

train to Argus to stay with their aunt and uncle, Pete and Fritzie Kozka. Once in Argus, in "The Branch" Karl is frightened by a dog and runs back to the boxcar, but Mary runs to Kozka's Meats to find her family. Fritzie and Pete take her in, but her twelve-year-old cousin, Sita, is jealous of the attention Mary receives.

Mary further alienates Sita in chapter 2 when she "steals" Sita's best friend, Celestine James, and when she is moved ahead a year into Sita and Celestine's seventh-grade class at Saint Catherine's school. After an ice storm the following March, Mary breaks the ice at the foot of the playground slide with her face. To Mary, the pattern in the broken ice looks like Karl's face, but everyone else sees it as the face of Christ. Because of this apparent miracle, Mary is for a time the center of Argus attention. In chapter 3 Fritzie shows Mary a postcard from Adelaide asking about her children. Pretending to be Fritzie, Mary writes a card in reply, saying that all three of Adelaide's children "starved dead."

In chapter 4 Mary falls in love with Russell Kashpaw, Celestine's Indian half brother, who has returned home wounded from "a war" (for dating of this incident, see **Russell Kashpaw**). But Russell has no interest in Mary. When Fritzie and Pete decide to move south because of Fritzie's health in 1941, they leave the butcher shop to Mary, because Sita is not interested in it. (We learn in chapter 10 that Mary changes the shop's name to The House of Meats.) The night before Sita leaves home, Mary is involved in a second "miracle"—Sita and Mary wake in the middle of the night to see Mary's hands glowing blue. In 1950 (chapter 5) Mary forwards a letter to Sita in Fargo, not knowing that it contains information about her missing baby brother. Mary's other brother, Karl, thinks of Mary in chapter 6 when he suffers a serious back injury.

In chapter 7, Mary hires Russell to work on equipment for the butcher shop. Early in 1953, Sita invites Mary to the formal-dress grand opening of her new restaurant, Chez Sita. But when Mary, Celestine, and Russell show up, they have to help in the kitchen because the chef is suffering from food poisoning. Not long afterward, Karl comes to Argus looking for Mary, but he stays in town several weeks before seeing her. Mary, who has never liked Karl, is upset when he begins an affair with Celestine. Mary and Karl meet once for dinner, but simply get into a fight. (Karl remembers the incident in chapter 15.) The night Celestine phones Mary to say that she is pregnant, Mary has a vision of Celestine's baby, a girl with red curls like Mary's baby brother and with the stubbornness of Mary herself. In chapter 7 we also begin to see Mary's interest in fortune-telling and signs, which seems to have developed from her earlier "miraculous" experiences.

After Celestine's daughter, Wallacette Darlene, is born in January 1954, in chapter 9 Mary nicknames her Dot, and she assists at Dot's baptism. Mary

Mary Adare

is jealous of Celestine's close relationship with Dot in chapter 10, and she takes Dot's side whenever Celestine tries to discipline her. When Dot is in first grade, Mary believes her lie about her teacher's "naughty box," and she makes a fool of herself when she confronts the teacher. Because of this incident, Celestine refuses to speak to Mary until summer vacation. That summer (1961), however, Mary joins Celestine and Dot when they go to the reservation to take a wheelchair to Russell, now seriously paralyzed from a stroke.

After a fire at the butcher shop in 1964 (chapter 11), Mary moves in with Celestine and Dot through December. Her stay intensifies her and Celestine's jealousy over Dot. It is Mary whom Dot tells when she is in love with the boy playing half of the donkey in the Christmas play, but it is Celestine to whom Dot turns after the humiliating performance. When Mary learns about the "Jell-O" joke Celestine has played on her, her feelings are hurt. Because Dot's classmates are afraid of Mary, when Wallace Pfef throws an eleventh-birthday party for Dot in chapter 12 (1965), he attempts to subdue Mary by putting Everclear into her drinks. But the maneuver backfires. The drunken Mary turns the party into chaos. After everyone else is gone, Mary and Wallace talk, she reads his palm, and, for a very brief time, they seem to bond.

In 1972, when a brick is thrown through Mary's window in chapter 13, Mary, ever on the lookout for signs, predicts trouble. That night Celestine dreams about Sita, and Mary's interpretation the next morning is that Sita is ill and is calling for Celestine. In response, Mary, Celestine, and Mary's dog go to Blue Mound to stay with Sita, where Mary discovers Sita's hidden stash of pills. As Sita's health continues to deteriorate, Mary and Celestine's stay is prolonged. On the day of the Beet Festival (in July), Mary and Celestine return from their meat deliveries to pick up Sita, but find her dead in the front yard. They do not know what to do with her, since the undertaker is at the parade, so they take her with them to the festival. Mary is in the stands with Celestine, Karl, and Wallace in chapter 15, watching, stunned, as Dot flies off in a skywriting plane. Unknown to Mary, her "baby" brother, Jude Miller—now a priest—is also watching Dot's flight (chapter 14). Thus, for a brief moment, Mary is reunited with her brothers for the first time in forty years, again watching a red-haired Adare woman fly off in a plane. In chapter 16, Mary leaves the fairgrounds before Dot returns, to make arrangements for Sita at the funeral parlor.

Twelve years later, on a blistering June day in 1994 ("A Wedge of Shade" [3] in *Tales of Burning Love*), Dot returns to Argus to tell her mother and Aunt Mary about her sudden marriage to Jack Mauser. Dot and Celestine find Mary keeping cool in the meat locker. When Dot tells her about the marriage and

Mary Martin de Porres, Sister

Jack's financial problems, Mary offers to teach Jack the meat and grocery trade and perhaps to give the business to Dot and Jack.

Early the next year, in "February Thaw" [40] Mary is astute enough to play along with a ruse Dot has invented to protect her other husband, prison escapee Gerry Nanapush. Mary and Celestine take turns staying with Dot in the hospital while she recovers from hypothermia and exhaustion. When Dot comes to Mary's shop after her release from the hospital, Mary greets her in her usual matter-of-fact, emotionless manner, but Mary's love for Dot and relief at her recovery are clear.

Mary Adare's aunt and uncle. See **Fritzie Kozka** and **Pete Kozka**.

Mary Bonne. Woman who finds her husband in bed with another woman and cuts them both, as recalled in "Flesh and Blood" in *Love Medicine*.

Mary Fred Toose. Sister of Shawnee Ray and Tammy Toose. She is mentioned as a factory worker in "The Tomahawk Factory" in *Love Medicine*. In chapters 2 and 10 of *The Bingo Palace,* we learn that she and Tammy have a drinking problem. In chapter 10, Shawnee Ray misses her sisters, and, to get away from Zelda Bjornson, she takes her son Redford and goes to stay with them for a while. We learn from chapter 14 that Shawnee Ray leaves Redford with Mary Fred and Tammy while she attends a powwow and that Lyman Lamartine, the boy's presumed father, gets a court order to take Redford away from them. In chapter 15 Mary Fred tries to prevent tribal policeman Leo Pukwan, accompanied by Zelda and a social worker, from carrying out the order. She hides Redford and then attacks Pukwan with a large-buckled belt, but in the end Pukwan knocks her out and takes the child. (Shawnee Ray seems to be wearing that same belt in chapter 19.)

Mary MacDonald. Woman who pays Lipsha Morrissey ten dollars for treating her arthritis with his "touch" in the "Love Medicine" story in *Love Medicine*.

Mary Martin de Porres, Sister. Clarinet-playing nun at the Sacred Heart Convent in "Crown of Thorns" in *Love Medicine*. Playing late one night, she hears Gordie Kashpaw outside and through the open window takes his confession that he has killed his wife. When she goes out to investigate the death, she finds a dead doe in his car and breaks down weeping. In the morning the police and hospital orderlies come for Gordie. Later, in the story "Love Medicine" she kindly but firmly refuses to bless Lipsha Morrissey's love charm of turkey hearts.

Mary Pepewas. Sick girl who dies in Pauline Puyat's presence in chapter 4 of *Tracks.* Pauline has gone with Bernadette Morrissey to watch over the sick girl, and there is a suggestion that Pauline could have saved her but fails to do so.

Mary (I) Shawano and Josephette (Zosie I) Shawano. Twin daughters of Blue Prairie Woman and Shawano the younger who as infants are given to their grandmother Midass to raise, according to chapters 1 and 3 of *The Antelope Wife.* One of these women marries an unspecified Shawano man and gives birth to twins, Mary (II) and Zosie (II) Shawano. She also receives a land allotment on the Shawanos' reservation (chapter 18).

Mary (II) Shawano. Twin sister of Zosie (II) Shawano Roy in *The Antelope Wife.* We learn in chapter 3 that Mary and Zosie are the twin daughters of either Mary (I) or Zosie (I) Shawano, who are the twin daughters of Blue Prairie Woman. According to chapter 18, out of their family of six, the second Zosie and Mary are the sole survivors of a flu epidemic. They are living on a reservation "up north" from Minneapolis with their great-grandmother, Midass, when Augustus Roy II arrives in chapters 18 and 23.

After Augustus and Zosie marry, old Midass dies and the couple moves in with Mary, who is in love with Zosie's new husband. She and Augustus meet in secret, but after Zosie learns about their trysts, the twins conspire to confuse him. In an effort to keep them straight, Augustus marks Mary by burning her foot, and then Zosie by biting her ear. He then disappears without a trace. Rumor has it that the sisters, true to their windigo Shawano heritage, have eaten him. They are referred to as "murder suspects" in chapter 11. From their difficult experiences, according to chapter 18, the sisters learn to relish hard luck. Mary, in particular, appears years later as "unmarred" by her early experiences.

When Zosie gives birth to twin daughters, Rozina and Aurora, she and Mary raise the girls together. According to chapters 9 and 11, they refuse to tell the girls which of them is the mother. When the girls are five, Aurora dies of diphtheria (chapter 3).

According to chapter 11, both Zosie and Mary are "namers." Besides dreams and the wind, Mary also acquires names from **little frog woman.** When Rozin marries Richard Whiteheart Beads and gives birth to twin daughters, Deanna and Cally, both Mary and Zosie participate in the naming ceremony. Rozin and Richard move to Minneapolis when the girls are five (chapter 3). Mary and Zosie stay on the reservation but occasionally come down to baby-sit, as Cally recalls in chapter 6.

Either Mary or Zosie may be present when Cally saves the dog Almost Soup in chapter 8, because shortly afterward, he is taken to their reservation.

Mary Stamper

The dog is at their house when Rozin and eleven-year-old Cally return to the reservation in chapter 9, following the death of Deanna in March. When Cally becomes gravely ill during a blizzard the next February, Mary tries (at first unsuccessfully) to call an ambulance, and she forces the worried Rozin to rest.

By the time Cally is eighteen, Mary and Zosie have moved to Minneapolis, although they still spend most summers on the reservation, where they gather teas and bark (chapter 18). When Cally wants to move to the city in chapter 11, Rozin is unable to contact the grandmothers, and after Cally arrives, they continue to be elusive. About two years later, in chapter 14 Rozin moves to the city to live with her mothers and go to night school. Mary appears not to be present at Rozin's marriage to Frank Shawano, since after the wedding, in chapter 17 Zosie goes up north to fetch her.

The following December, in chapter 18 Mary and Zosie join the family for Christmas dinner at Frank and Rozin's apartment, bringing food and their picky eating habits. At the dinner table, the twins talk about morning sickness, difficult births, and their own funerals, to the discomfiture of their family. When Cecille Shawano challenges the sisters about the disappearance of Augustus Roy, the twins merely smile their "slightly windigo" smiles.

Mary Stamper. Mother of Jack Mauser. Mary is from the reservation, land that she calls "leftovers," which she nevertheless loves, as recorded in "Mauser and Mauser" [39] in *Tales of Burning Love*. Jack recalls spending at least part of his childhood there, and in "Jack's House" [9] he remembers some of her Ojibwa language. In "The Owl" [17], Mary is said to be descended from some wandering people who joined the Ojibwa but might have been a mixture of Cree, Menominee, Winnebago, and even French. *Mary's parents* apparently die when she is a child, and as an adult, she has periods of catatonia in which she re-experiences their loss. When Jack is six years old, his father leaves him with his German Aunt Elizabeth while his mother takes cold-water shock treatments for the "rigid silence" she falls into each autumn, presumably the season of her parents' death. (Jack tells his fourth wife, Marlis Cook, in "Best Western" [28] that his aunt had stolen him from his mother.)

Jack normally blocks out these painful memories, but shortly after his near-death by fire, he remembers his mother vividly, both her mental disturbance and her strength and tenderness. He remembers her staring at him for days with a hungry, wild expression, an expression similar to that of Sister Leopolda just before she dies in exaltation. As he is wandering, lost in the storm in "Blizzard Night" [35], he also remembers how she used to break a path for him to school in the winter.

Mary Stamper

There may be some secret connected with Mary's family beyond her own mental distress, for in "Easter Snow" [1] and "A Wedge of Shade" [3] Jack is reluctant to tell his mother's family name to June Morrissey and Celestine James, lest they be "wary" of him. Yet when Celestine learns his mother's name, she nods her acceptance and invites him in, since he is "a distant relative, after all."

Jack's "crazy mother" is also referred to in "The First Draw" [14]. In "The Stone Virgin" [44] he is not afraid when the statue of the Virgin falls on him, because in her face he sees, among others, that of his mother.

Massive Indian woman. Mysterious large woman who enters the B & B restaurant and casino out of a January blizzard in "The B & B" [16] in *Tales of Burning Love*. Dot Mauser seems to know her and orders her coffee and a pizza. After the strange woman has finished eating, she follows Dot down the hallway. Half an hour later, Dot returns alone. "The Tale of the Unknown Passenger" [34] reveals this person's true identity.

Matilda. See **Matilda Roy** and **Scranton Roy's mother.**

Matilda Roy. Firstborn daughter of Blue Prairie Woman; adopted daughter of Scranton Roy. Her story appears in chapters 1 and 6 of *The Antelope Wife.*

Before Matilda's birth, her mother has two husbands, first a deer man, then after his death, a human, Shawano the younger. The narrative does not specify which of these husbands is Matilda's father. In chapter 6, the reference to Blue Prairie Woman's "winters" (plural) with Shawano appears before its reference to the infant Matilda, suggesting that Shawano is her father. But these winters may occur after Matilda's birth. Matilda's reference to Scranton as "her human" and her later adoption by antelope people may suggest that the deer man is her father.

When the infant Matilda is still unnamed, Blue Prairie Woman is warned by a doe to leave the village. As she ties the baby's cradle board to a dog and starts to flee, the U.S. Cavalry attacks. The frightened dog runs onto the open prairie, a necklace of blue beads swaying from the cradle board. One of the soldiers, Scranton Roy, follows them. By the time he is able to untie the child three days later, she is desperate with hunger. The only way he can calm her is to let her suck at his nipple. After more days of traveling, Scranton finally stops and builds a sod house somewhere on the Great Plains. One morning as the baby is sucking, her faith is rewarded with milk. Scranton names his adopted daughter Matilda after his mother.

When Matilda is six, she goes to school, wearing her blue beads. The young schoolteacher, Peace McKnight, becomes Matilda's friend and soon, her step-mother. When Matilda sees her beloved father kiss Peace the first time, her confused feelings resolve into a new sense of self and freedom.

Peace becomes pregnant and then falls ill with a fever. Lying next to her one night, Matilda hears someone approach the house, then tap. Realizing that the woman who has come is her mother, she leaves Scranton a note and follows her. Matilda quickly falls ill with Peace's fever. As her mother cares for her, the two communicate in signs, and Blue Prairie Woman gives her child her own life-saving name, Other Side of the Earth. Matilda recovers, but her mother contracts the fever and dies within the day. Before dying, she kills and cooks the dog who accompanies them so that Matilda will have food. For two days Matilda sits and gazes west, singing her mother's dying song, until curious antelope come to investigate. Matilda is seven when she joins the antelope people, still wearing the blue beads.

Generations later, in chapter 2, when an old medicine man describes the forebear of Sweetheart Calico as a girl who lived with the antelope, he may be alluding to Matilda Roy. The subsequent history of Matilda's blue beads is related in chapter 18.

Maurice Morris. Resident of the Senior Citizens who sees the federal marshals coming to question Lulu Lamartine in chapter 25 of *The Bingo Palace*.

Mauser family. See **Aunt Elizabeth; Candice Pantamounty Mauser; Chuck Mauser; Dot Adare Nanapush Mauser; Eleanor Schlick Mauser; Jack Mauser; Jack Mauser's ancestors; Jack Mauser's father; Jack Mauser's grandfather; John Mauser Jr.; June Morrissey Kashpaw; Marlis Cook Mauser;** and **Mary Stamper.**

Maynard Moon. Lawyer whose son, Caryl Moon, Jack Mauser reluctantly hires in "Caryl Moon" [8] in *Tales of Burning Love*. Maynard is mentioned again in "Jack's House" [9] as the personal representative for the estate of John J. Mauser, deceased. He is apparently one of the lawyers who attend Jack's funeral—see **Moon, Webb, and Cartenspeil.** In "The Stone Virgin" [44] Maynard again coerces Jack into hiring his son.

Melvin. Child at the house in Bwaanakeeng who is sent to fetch the white puppy for soup in chapter 8 of *The Antelope Wife*.

Mexican man. Unnamed migrant farm worker who fathers Lulu Nanapush's last child, Bonita, in "The Good Tears" in *Love Medicine*.

Midass. Mother of Blue Prairie Woman in *The Antelope Wife*. According to chapters 3, Midass's full name is Midassbaupayikway, Ten Stripe Woman.

Midass

The only knowledge we have of Midass prior to her becoming Blue Prairie Woman's mother comes from the genealogy sketched by her great-great-granddaughter, Rozina Roy, in chapter 3. After mentioning the first generation of "south-looking" Shawanos—Shesheeb's sister who marries Henri Laventure—Rozin says that Midass marries into these people. The most straightforward reading of this paragraph would be that Midass marries a Shawano descendant of Shesheeb's sister and Laventure, and that Blue Prairie Woman is their daughter. (This reading is represented in Chart 21 in Part I of this guide.) If, on the other hand, we take Midass to be the name of Shesheeb's sister, then the marriage into the Shawano clan would be a later marriage, and Blue Prairie Woman would be Laventure's daughter. Midass must be either the descendant or wife of Laventure, since Rozin mentions him as a forebear.

According to chapter 6, Midass's daughter Blue Prairie Woman is first known as Apijigo Bakaday, So Hungry, because of her insatiable appetite. People warn that the girl may be a windigo, but Midass insists that there is nothing wrong with her. It is Midass who passes down the story of her daughter's deer husband. In chapter 1, the U.S. Cavalry raids their village shortly after Blue Prairie Woman's first daughter is born. One of the soldiers, Scranton Roy, kills either Midass's mother or her mother-in-law. Blue Prairie Woman later has twin daughters, Mary (I) and Josephette (Zosie I), whom she leaves with Midass to raise so she can search for her firstborn. One of these daughters also has twins named Mary (II) and Zosie (II). As we learn in chapter 18, out of their family of six, these second twins are the only survivors of a flu epidemic. Thus old Midass is left to raise her great-granddaughters as well.

In chapters 18 and 23, when the second Zosie and Mary are young women, Scranton Roy returns to the village, now situated on a reservation. He brings his grandson, Augustus (II), who falls in love with Zosie. The young man gives Midass red whiteheart beads in exchange for Zosie's hand and promises to take care of her sister, Mary. Midass uses the beads to decorate a blanket, a gift for a pregnant woman (whose son will be known as Whiteheart Beads). Midass dies shortly after the marriage of Augustus and Zosie.

Migwans girls. Girls at the trader's store who look longingly at the candy Fleur Pillager buys for the white boy in chapter 12 of *The Bingo Palace*.

Mille Lacs man. Man who is given the jingle dress by women who appear to him in a dream, mentioned in chapter 16 of *The Bingo Palace*. He is apparently Chippewa, because the jingle dress is said to be original to Chippewas.

Mindemoya. Name for Fleur Pillager in chapter 11 of *The Bingo Palace* meaning "old woman." See **Fleur Pillager.**

Mirage. Nanapush's father, whose Indian name is Kanatowakechin. In chapter 3 of *Tracks* he tells his son that the name Nanapush means trickery, living in the bush, and having a way with women. When Nanapush sees the deceased members of his family in chapter 9, he imagines himself with his father again, eluding soldiers through the thick snow that covers the bodies of his mother and sister.

Misshepeshu. Lake man (or monster, depending on one's point of view) of Matchimanito Lake. He and his power are intimately connected with the Pillager clan, who settle around the lake after their forced migration westward to the reservation just after the turn of the century. We learn in chapter 7 of *Tracks* that when the Pillagers arrive, Misshepeshu appears in the lake because of his connection with the Old Man, Fleur's father. To the Pillagers, he is benign, but others fear him. He is said to be waiting in hiding for the trespassing government surveyors in chapter 1, and in chapter 2 he is perhaps involved in the deaths of two of their guides. Margaret Kashpaw is concerned that he might take her when she crosses the lake in a leaky boat in chapter 3. It is seen as a sign of their desperation that the starving people ice fish on Matchimanito one famine winter, at the end of chapter 5, giving no thought to the lake man. Mothers warn their daughters in chapter 2 that he is particularly desirous of daring young girls and that he takes on different forms to lure them to their death by drowning.

Pauline Puyat believes that Fleur Pillager may be a lover to the water man. After Fleur's first child (Lulu) is born, in chapter 4 Misshepeshu seems to grow more benign, and Pauline thinks the child's eyes and skin resemble the lake man's. Later, in chapter 5, even Fleur's lover, Eli Kashpaw, believes for a time that the child of Fleur's second pregnancy is the lake man's. In chapter 8 Pauline equates the lake man with Satan and believes that Fleur is his agent. He appears to Pauline, or so she believes, and calls her to a confrontation, like Christ's temptation, in the "desert." She answers the call by going to Matchimanito to do battle with the copper-scaled monster of whom, she feels, Christ himself is afraid. There she believes that she kills the monster, but when dead, he turns into Napoleon Morrissey.

The lake man is mentioned once in *Love Medicine,* in the "Love Medicine" story, where his name is spelled "Missepeshu."

Misshepeshu also appears, though not by name, in *The Bingo Palace.* When Lipsha Morrissey engages in a religious fast and quest close to Matchimanito

Misshepeshu

in chapter 17, he thinks of the horned thing as an evil presence. In chapter 20, however, he realizes that it is the lake man who kept him alive as an infant at the bottom of the slough, where his mother had thrown him in a weighted gunnysack. It is significant to this account of Lipsha's salvation that Lipsha is himself a Pillager descendant and probably next in line to inherit the Pillager power—and presumably the special relationship with Misshepeshu—passed down to Fleur from her father.

Ojibwa lake creatures such as Misshepeshu are also referred to in chapter 8 of *The Antelope Wife*.

Montana guys. Young men who, along with Marty, take Lipsha Morrissey to Russell Kashpaw for an involuntary tattoo and who vandalize his bingo van in chapter 7 of *The Bingo Palace*. They are not all from Montana; one says he is from Kansas, another from South Dakota.

Montana Kashpaw. Husband of Regina Puyat Kashpaw and father of Russell and Isabel Kashpaw; apparently one of the older children of Kashpaw (Resounding Sky) and Margaret (Rushes Bear) Kashpaw who migrate to Montana when land allotments are made. Montana is only a place designation, not a name; no first name is given. The older Kashpaw children's migration is recorded in "The World's Greatest Fishermen" in *Love Medicine* and chapter 3 of *Tracks*. Regina's marriage to a Kashpaw is recorded in chapter 2 of *Tracks*, as are the facts that Russell is his son and that he is now living in Montana. Isabel's being the sister of Russell is recorded in chapter 2 of *The Beet Queen*.

The identity of the Montana Kashpaw is rendered somewhat ambiguous by *The Beet Queen*, in which Eli (a younger son of Margaret and Resounding Sky) is referred to as Russell's half brother (chapters 7 and 10). This would seem to suggest that it is the "original" Kashpaw, Margaret's husband and Eli's father, who marries Regina and then moves to Montana. The record of the Kashpaw family in *Tracks*, however, does not support such a reading. Chapter 2 of *Tracks*, set in 1913, indicates that Russell's father is currently living in Montana, while chapter 3 (1913–1914) indicates that Margaret's husband is dead and that it is her older children who have moved to Montana. The "half brother" designation for Eli and Russell in *The Beet Queen* may thus represent a general, rather than a specific, kinship, explainable by the fact that Eli may be closer in age to Russell than he is to his "Montana" older brother.

Moon, Webb, and Cartenspeil. Jack's representatives, who, along with virtually every other lawyer in the region, attend Jack's funeral in "Satin Heart" [12] in *Tales of Burning Love*. Jack owes each of these lawyers something. Although they each accept a chocolate from Dot Mauser, Jack's current wife, they do not want to appear appeased by this gesture and bury the candies among the palm and ficus tree roots in the visitation room. See also **Maynard Moon.**

Morrissey family. See **Bernadette Morrissey; Clarence Morrissey; Layla Morrissey; Lipsha Morrissey; Lulu Nanapush Morrissey Lamartine; Morrissey I; Morrissey II; Napoleon Morrissey; Philomena Morrissey; Sophie Morrissey;** and **Strict aunt in Grand Forks.** See also *Kyle Morrissey* in **Tomahawk factory workers.**

Morrissey I. Lucille Lazarre's companion and father of Lucille's daughter June Morrissey in *Love Medicine*. After Lucille's death, in "The Beads" Morrissey and an old drunk woman, who is apparently Lucille's mother, bring the nine-year-old June to Marie Lazarre Kashpaw (Lucille's supposed sister) for her to raise. Marie refers to him as "the whining no-good who had not church-married" her sister. After dropping off June, he is said in "The World's Greatest Fishermen" to have run off to the Twin Cities. Lulu Lamartine refers to June's father in "Crossing the Water."

Morrissey II. Lulu Nanapush's first husband. In "The Good Tears" in *Love Medicine* Lulu says that she married him for spite when her lover Moses Pillager would not come live with her in town. Nanapush's objections to the marriage are recorded in "The Island" in *Love Medicine* and in chapter 9 of *Tracks*. One of the purposes of the whole narration by Nanapush recorded in odd-numbered chapters of *Tracks* is to convince Lulu not to marry this Morrissey. She later admits that the marriage was a mistake, calling him riffraff in "The Good Tears." The children Lulu has while married to Morrissey she later renames Lamartine in "Lulu's Boys."

Morton, Mr. and Mrs. Neighbors of Dot Nanapush Mauser and Shawn Nanapush from whom Gerry Nanapush apparently steals a getaway snowmobile in "Smile of the Wolf" [38] in *Tales of Burning Love.* Shawn tells him about the snowmobile and where the key is hidden.

Moses Pillager. First lover of Lulu Nanapush; father of Gerry Nanapush and at least one older Nanapush son by Lulu.

Chapters 1 and 3 of *Tracks* and "The Island" in *Love Medicine* tell of Moses's infancy and boyhood. Moses (not his original name) is still a nursing child during the time of the first sickness that decimates the reservation tribe. Nanapush advises the child's family on how to fool death by making it seem that Moses is already dead. This strategy protects him from the sickness, but affects his

Moses Pillager

mind. In the later consumption epidemic of 1912, Moses and his distant cousin
Fleur are the only Pillagers who survive. After that epidemic, Moses, still a boy,
moves to the island on the far side of Matchimanito Lake, where he lives alone
with his cats and is protected by the lake creature. When Fleur returns to the
reservation with money in the fall of 1913, Moses helps her by going to town to
buy supplies. Fleur's daughter, Lulu Nanapush, remembers his stalking through
town as a wild boy but also his sitting under the trees with Nanapush, talking
in the old language about medicine ways.

Because of Moses's medicine knowledge, people on the reservation come to
him for help. In chapter 4 of *Tracks* he gives Pauline Puyat a love medicine;
in chapter 6 he is said to provide pregnant girls with medicine to induce
abortions; and in chapter 7 he helps Nanapush with a medicine ceremony
for Fleur after the death of her baby. When Pauline rolls in mud and leaves in
chapter 8, she compares herself to Moses. Moses seems to be Fleur's ally in her
resistance to the Turcot lumber company in chapter 9, for rumor has it that
he drowns two workers, and he is present when Fleur sabotages the company's
equipment.

Years later, Fleur's now-grown daughter, Lulu, comes to Moses's island in
"The Island" in *Love Medicine.* When they become lovers, Lulu pulls Moses
back into the circle of the living, and he tells her his real name. Lulu becomes
pregnant and needs to leave the island, but Moses will not go with her. Their
first son is probably born around 1935 or 1936. They have at least one other son,
Gerry, who is born about 1945. Because Moses will not follow her to town, in
"The Good Tears" Lulu marries Morrissey II for spite. We learn in "The Red
Convertible" that Moses is jealous of Lulu's later husbands and in "The Good
Tears" that he considers drowning to be the worst death for a Chippewa.

Chapter 14 of *The Bingo Palace* relates that Moses dies of desire on his island.
Even afterwards, his windigo love-howl rings across the lake, and in chapter 17,
he is said to haunt the island with the howls of cats. He is mentioned in chapter
27 as Fleur makes her death walk across the frozen lake to his island.

Moses also lives on in the traits he has passed down to his son and grandson.
According to "The Good Tears" and "Crossing the Water" in *Love Medicine*
and chapter 1 of *The Bingo Palace,* Gerry has inherited his ability to escape and
his Pillager grin from Moses, who in "Crossing the Water" is referred to as Old
Man Pillager.

Moses Pillager's grandfather. Man who, according to Margaret Rushes Bear
in "The Island" in *Love Medicine,* ate his own wife. She does not say whether
this is his Pillager grandfather or his mother's father.

Mud engineer. Oil field worker killed by a pressurized hose, whom June Kashpaw recalls hearing about in "The World's Greatest Fishermen" in *Love Medicine*. A mud engineer is the person at a drilling rig who is responsible for testing and correcting the composition of the "mud," viscous fluid used in drilling oil wells. Other characters who work as mud engineers are **Andy** and **Jack Mauser.**

N

Namer, Ojibwa. Powerful androgynous namer who secures an unused name for Blue Prairie Woman—Other Side of the Earth—in chapter 1 of *The Antelope Wife*.

Nanabozho. Chippewa trickster spirit mentioned in the story "Love Medicine" in *Love Medicine*. See also **Wenabojo.**

Nanapush. Last survivor in his family; adoptive father of Fleur Pillager and adoptive grandfather of Lulu Nanapush. Nanapush is born about 1862 (he is about fifty in the winter of 1912–1913 in chapter 1 of *Tracks*). We learn about Nanapush's early life from his memories in *Tracks*. In chapter 9 he recalls fleeing from soldiers through the snow with his father and seeing the snow cover the bodies of his mother and sister. In chapter 3 we learn that he receives the beginnings of a Jesuit education, enough to speak good English, read, and write. As a guide to white hunters and, for a time, a government interpreter (chapter 5), Nanapush gains a sophisticated knowledge of white ways, which all his life he uses to benefit his people. He is deeply rooted in traditional Indian ways, a holdout who will not sell or barter his land. His father tells him that his name means trickery, living in the bush, and having a way with women. As a young man, Nanapush is able to keep three wives satisfied. He and Kashpaw are friends and are notable for their amorous pursuits (even sharing some women between them, according to chapter 9). Nanapush is also friends with the Pillager clan. He visits Matchimanito Lake, where the Pillagers live, and in the early days of sickness (prior to the winter of 1912), he helps protect a Pillager child by giving him a false name, Moses.

Chapters 1 and 3 of *Tracks* tell of the consumption epidemic in the winter of 1912 that decimates the tribe and wipes out the last of Nanapush's family, including his three wives, a daughter, and a son (mentioned in chapter 9). Nanapush especially mourns his third wife, White Beads, and their daughter, Red Cradle, nicknamed Lulu. Nanapush himself, fifty at the time, is taken

Nanapush

ill but survives by telling a ceaseless story so that death cannot get a word in edgewise. In chapter 1 Nanapush rescues the seventeen-year-old Fleur Pillager, whose parents and three siblings have died in the epidemic. He nurses her back to life, then returns and buries her family. Even so, Nanapush and Fleur barely survive the winter. Near spring, Fleur leaves Nanapush to return to the Pillager cabin on Matchimanito Lake. (Nanapush's saving Fleur is also referred to by Pauline in chapter 2.)

Following on the heels of consumption, government agents and lumber companies are the next threat Nanapush must confront. In chapter 3 he refuses to sell or lease his allotment, arguing that land is the only thing that lasts. In the fall of 1913 Fleur returns to the reservation after spending the summer in Argus. Although she visits Nanapush and he considers her his daughter, she will not stay with him but returns to Matchimanito. Eli Kashpaw gets Nanapush's advice on how to win Fleur's love, and after he succeeds, Eli's mother Margaret Kashpaw complains to Nanapush. When the pregnant Fleur is ready to deliver the following spring, Nanapush gives Margaret a boat ride across the lake to assist her. He names Fleur's baby—giving her the nickname of his deceased daughter (Lulu) and his own surname. This is the only time during the early years that Nanapush allows his name to be written down.

After Lulu's birth, as we learn in chapter 4, Nanapush is often a visitor at Matchimanito, as is Pauline Puyat. Nanapush notices Pauline's emerging sexuality, teases her, and points her out to Napoleon Morrissey. In the fall of 1917 (chapter 5), after a lovers' quarrel with Fleur, Eli moves in with Nanapush. The two men share the famine of that winter, relieved for a time by Eli's shooting a moose, guided by Nanapush's spirit. That same winter Nanapush becomes involved in a feud between the Kashpaw family and the Morrissey and Lazarre families. Clarence Morrissey and Boy Lazarre capture Nanapush and Margaret and shave Margaret's head. Nanapush avenges her humiliation by snaring Clarence and nearly killing him. (There is no need for Nanapush to take vengeance on the Lazarre, since he dies as a result of being bitten by Margaret.) By Ash Wednesday Nanapush and Margaret are keeping company, although Nanapush declines Father Damien's suggestion that they be church married. The snow and famine continue, and at one point Nanapush nearly starves before Margaret comes to his cabin and revives him. They both move to Matchimanito until spring. When Pauline, now a religious fanatic, visits the Pillager cabin in chapter 6, Nanapush, whom she refers to as "the fiend," mocks and torments her.

The following winter (1918–1919) Nanapush and Margaret are at Margaret's house in chapter 7 when Nanapush finds Lulu outside, half frozen. Lulu has come for help for her mother, who has gone into premature labor. While Margaret goes to Fleur, Nanapush nurses Lulu's frozen feet, refusing to allow a white doctor to amputate. Finally, he transports her by toboggan to Fleur's cabin. The whole family again almost starves. Along with the government rations that save them comes the news that they are in danger of losing their land allotments because of nonpayment of land fees. The combined families raise money for fees on Kashpaw and Pillager land, but Nanapush loses his home to the hated Lazarres. Father Damien encourages Nanapush to take a leadership position in the tribe to help his people, and Nanapush reluctantly agrees to do so. Nanapush and Nector go to the Morrisseys' farm and force Clarence to give them part of a butchered cow. When Fleur's depression continues after the loss of her prematurely born baby, Nanapush and Moses Pillager conduct a healing ceremony for her.

That spring (1919, chapter 8), when in chapter 8 Pauline goes out onto Matchimanito Lake in a leaky boat to meet the devil, Nanapush tries to rescue her in a canoe. Later that year (chapter 9), Nanapush learns that Margaret and Nector, who have been entrusted with the land-fee money, have paid the fees only on Kashpaw and not Pillager land. After this betrayal, although Nanapush continues to live with Margaret on her Kashpaw land, he does not love her so well as before. Nanapush is present at Matchimanito when Fleur takes her dramatic, tree-felling revenge on the lumber company. Just before this incident occurs, he sees the deceased members of his family among the trees around Fleur's cabin. After Fleur leaves the reservation, Nanapush spends the next several years trying to get Lulu back home from the boarding school where Fleur has sent her. He has to become a bureaucrat himself to succeed.

Chapter 9 of *Tracks* and "The Island" in *Love Medicine* record Lulu's return in 1924. Nanapush takes her in to live with him and Margaret, although Margaret objects. (In "The Island" Lulu twice refers to Margaret as Nanapush's "wife"; thus the genealogical charts for *Love Medicine* represent their relationship as a marriage.) Nanapush tells Lulu that when he dies, he wants to be buried the old Indian way, even though Father Damien has won his spirit in a card game. When Lulu is a young woman and is determined to go to Moses Pillager on his island in Matchimanito Lake (in "The Island"), Nanapush gives her advice on how to deal with Moses. Later, when she is considering marrying a Morrissey man, Nanapush—as narrator in the odd-numbered chapters in *Tracks*—tells Lulu tales of family and tribal history: stories about Fleur, Eli, Nanapush, and Lulu herself and about their enemies, the Morrisseys and the Lazarres. Nanapush hopes with his narrative to persuade Lulu not to marry a Morrissey (chapter 7) and to help her understand Fleur's apparent abandonment of her (chapter 9).

Nanapush

It is unclear where Nanapush is living during this time. We know from chapters 7 and 9 of *Tracks* that in 1919 he loses his property—a pack of Lazarres move into his house—and he goes to live with Margaret on Kashpaw land. Yet when Lulu comes home in "The Island," he appears to be living on his own property, because whenever Margaret is angry with him, she is said to leave and go to the Kashpaw allotment, an hour's walk away. Also, when Fleur returns to the reservation in chapter 12 of *The Bingo Palace,* she stays for a time at Nanapush's house. Later, when Margaret leaves Nanapush and goes to live with her children, Fleur comes to stay with him. According to "The Beads" in *Love Medicine,* in 1948 Fleur is keeping house and caring for Nanapush somewhere deep in the brush where the woods have been logged—possibly on the Pillager land beside Matchimanito Lake.

By the "present" time of *The Bingo Palace* (which is sometime after 1984), Nanapush is dead but is remembered by various characters. In chapter 11 Lipsha Morrissey recalls stories of him as the healing doctor witch who was adoptive father to the now-old medicine woman Fleur. In Lyman Lamartine's vision in chapter 13, Fleur repeats Nanapush's words (from chapter 3 of *Tracks*) regarding land as the only thing that lasts. Gerry Nanapush hears Old Man Nanapush telling stories during a fevered vision in his solitary prison cell in chapter 21. On her death walk in chapter 27, among the Pillager ghosts Fleur sees Nanapush as a young man with clever hands, ceaselessly talking.

Nanapush family. Nanapush is the last surviving member of his family. For his deceased family members, see **Dove, the; Mirage; Red Cradle; Standing in a Stone; Unexpected, the;** and **White Beads.** His adoptive granddaughter, **Lulu Nanapush Morrissey Lamartine,** and three of her sons, including **Gerry Nanapush,** are not blood kin but wear the Nanapush name. See also *Billy Nanapush* in **Tomahawk factory workers.**

Napoleon Morrissey. Brother of Bernadette Morrissey, lover of Pauline Puyat, and father of Marie Lazarre. [A note about Napoleon's surname: Since Bernadette's children Clarence and Sophie bear the name Morrissey (chapters 5 and 7 of *Tracks*), this is apparently Bernadette's married name. She herself is a widow (chapter 4) and would presumably bear her deceased husband's name. Napoleon may be Bernadette's brother-in-law, or he may simply have taken the surname of his sister's family. Or, since his Morrissey surname appears only once, in Pauline's account in chapter 8, it may be that Pauline errs in applying the Morrissey family name to Napoleon.]

Napoleon comes to Argus with his sister Bernadette in chapter 4 of *Tracks,* and they take Pauline Puyat back to the reservation to live with them. After she has been with them for some time, Napoleon takes Pauline out to an old house in the woods, but leaves without having sexual intercourse with her. Later, however, Napoleon and Pauline have an ongoing sexual relationship. In chapter 6, when Bernadette learns that Pauline is pregnant by Napoleon, she banishes him to the barn. After giving birth to Napoleon's child, Marie, Pauline abandons the baby, leaving her with Bernadette.

In late winter of 1919 (chapter 7), when his niece Sophie and nephew Clarence bring their Lazarre spouses to the house and Bernadette leaves, Napoleon begins to drink steadily. One spring night, wandering drunk beside Matchimanito Lake, in chapter 8 Napoleon encounters the naked Pauline, who believes herself to be on a mission to confront Satan. Taking Napoleon to be the devil, Pauline chokes him to death and then drags his body into the woods behind Fleur Pillager's cabin. Fleur's young daughter, Lulu Nanapush, discovers a man's body in "The Good Tears" in *Love Medicine,* and this man is revealed in chapter 9 of *Tracks* to be Napoleon. After Fleur is forced off her land, surveyors find his decayed body, and Fleur is suspected of causing his death. The drunken Clarence even claims to have a "vision" in which Napoleon's ghost accuses her.

Nector Kashpaw. Youngest son of Margaret (Rushes Bear) and Kashpaw (Resounding Sky); husband of Marie Lazarre. Nector is born about 1908. In "The World's Greatest Fishermen" in *Love Medicine,* we learn that when reservation land is allotted and Margaret's older children move away, Nector and his brother Eli are the only children left at home. Chapter 3 of *Tracks* depicts Nector as having a natural aptitude for book learning and, apparently like his father, for business and politics. As a child, he is said to imitate Eli but to be very different from his woodsman brother. After Eli's wife, Fleur Pillager, gives birth to Lulu, in chapter 4 Nector and his mother stay for long periods at Fleur's cabin on Matchimanito Lake. They, along with Nanapush, spend much of the famine winter of 1917–1918 at Matchimanito (chapter 5), as well as the winter of 1919–1920 (chapter 6).

After Clarence Morrissey and Boy Lazarre shame Margaret in the winter of 1917–1918 (chapter 5), the nine-year-old Nector helps Nanapush make a snare for them in revenge. The snare catches, but does not kill, Clarence. Nector shows his awareness of issues concerning Indian land both in this chapter, as he asks Nanapush questions, and in chapter 7, in which he is the first to understand that unless the family pays its overdue land fees, the land will be auctioned off. At the end of chapter 7, Nector and Margaret take to the agent the money the family has raised to pay the fees, but there are hints that something is amiss. The nature of the problem is revealed in chapter 9. The money that was supposed to

Nector Kashpaw

pay fees for Kashpaw and Pillager land Nector and Margaret have used entirely to pay Kashpaw fees and late payment fines. The Pillager fees have not been paid, and the agent has sold Fleur's Matchimanito property. When Fleur tries to drown herself by walking into the lake and Eli rescues her, she curses Nector, saying that he will die in her place. In part to hide him from Fleur's wrath, Margaret sends Nector off to a government boarding school. He and Lulu leave the reservation on the same wagon, and in chapter 6 Pauline predicts that the government school will render these two young people blind and deaf to the Indian spiritual world.

Chapter 9 of *Tracks* reveals that after finishing eighth grade, Nector travels south to Oklahoma. In "The Plunge of the Brave" in *Love Medicine,* however, we learn that he goes to high school in Flandreau, where he plays football and the only book he reads is *Moby-Dick.* After Flandreau, he plays a bit part in a movie, works a year in the wheat belt, and poses virtually nude for a painting in Kansas. His experiences with the larger world persuade Nector to return to the reservation. There he again lives with his mother and brother, hunting geese with Eli and selling them for spending money ("Wild Geese"). Shortly after returning, he falls in love with Lulu and plans to marry her.

One summer evening in 1934, however, in "The Wild Geese" in *Love Medicine,* Nector's plans are turned aside by his confrontation with Marie Lazarre, who is coming down the hill from the reservation convent. Thinking that Marie has stolen linens from the convent, Nector tries to grab her. As they scuffle, the encounter becomes sexually charged.

The remainder of Nector's life is chronicled in several *Love Medicine* stories. When Nector's relationship with Marie becomes known in "The Island," Nanapush tells Lulu to forget about him. Margaret, who considers the Lazarres to be trash, is dismayed that Nector is going to marry Marie. "The Beads" and "The Plunge of the Brave" depict the next seventeen years of Nector's life as dominated by babies and work and ordered by Marie's firm, controlling hand. Nector tries to be a drunk, but Marie has other plans for him. She wants him to be someone big on the reservation, so she throws away his bottles and drags him home from bars. When Marie gives birth to their last baby, almost dying in childbirth, Margaret turns her affection from Nector, of whom she is ashamed, to Marie, whose stoicism she has come to admire. Over time, however, Nector becomes a stable provider for his family and the chairman of his tribe.

After seventeen years of marriage, in "The Plunge of the Brave" Nector reflects upon his life and wants Lulu again. In July 1952, delivering commodity butter on the hottest day of the year, Nector and Lulu begin an affair that lasts for five years. During those years, Lulu gives birth to Nector's son, Lyman, and

Nector Kashpaw

Nector works with the tribal council to get federal funding for a development project on the reservation, a factory. Nector becomes increasingly torn and exhausted from his double life. Matters come to a head in 1957 when Beverly Lamartine comes to court Lulu and Nector has to sign eviction papers forcing her off her land to make room for the factory. When Lulu receives the eviction notice, she is furious with Nector. She sics her dogs on him when he comes to visit that night and she marries Beverly ("The Good Tears").

In this crisis, Nector decides to leave Marie. One August afternoon, he leaves a letter for Marie on their kitchen table and goes to Lulu's house. While waiting for Lulu to return home, however, he starts a fire that burns down her house. (Nector's account in "The Plunge of the Brave" makes the house burning sound accidental, but Lulu's account in "The Good Tears" and Zelda's later recollection in chapter 23 of *The Bingo Palace* suggest that it was a direct result of his "burning" passion for Lulu.) In "Flesh and Blood," Zelda finds Nector's letter to Marie and comes to fetch him home. When he arrives at his house, uncertain whether he can enter, Marie reaches out and pulls him in.

In 1973 Nector is apparently still looked upon as the family patriarch, because Henry Lamartine Junior asks the runaway Albertine Johnson in "The Bridge" whether her grandfather Kashpaw knows where she is. By 1981, however ("The World's Greatest Fishermen"), Nector has become feeble-minded. His doctor attributes Nector's condition to diabetes, but in "Love Medicine," Lipsha Morrissey (Nector's adopted grandson) suggests that the old man's mental absence is willed. As Albertine indicates in "The World's Greatest Fishermen," his loss of memory may be a protection from the past.

In "Love Medicine" Nector, now living with Marie at the Senior Citizens in town, again hankers after Lulu, who also lives at the center. One day, Lipsha finds them embracing in the laundry room and decides to honor Marie's request that he make a love medicine to keep Nector's heart fixed on his wife. Lipsha's love medicine goes awry, however, when Nector chokes to death on the raw turkey heart Lipsha provides. All the scattered family members assemble for Nector's funeral. Afterwards, Marie senses the continuing presence of his spirit. In "The Good Tears" Nector's spirit also visits Lulu, who is in the hospital at the time of his funeral. In "Resurrection," when Marie moves back into the old Kashpaw place for a time, she remembers her years with Nector in that house.

Nector's spirit lives on in another way as well. His son Lyman Lamartine inherits Nector's aptitude for business and politics. In "The Tomahawk Factory," Lyman carries forward one of Nector's projects, a tribal souvenir factory. After the factory is ruined, Lyman hatches a grander scheme in "Lyman's Luck," a bingo hall and ultimately a casino. By the opening of *The Bingo Palace*, Lyman is

Nector Kashpaw

a successful bingo hall operator, and in chapter 1 the reservation folk compare his ambition and scheming to that of Nector. Lyman acknowledges his similarity to his father in chapter 13.

Lipsha also remembers his "Grandpa" Nector in chapters 11, 14, and 17 of *The Bingo Palace*. In chapter 4, as Marie gives Nector's ceremonial pipe to Lipsha, they remember the way Nector used to pray with the pipe—calmly, in the old language, eyes unfocused into the distance. We are told in chapter 5 that Nector had inherited this pipe from his own father, Resounding Sky. (Nector's pipe in also mentioned in chapters 8, 9, and 23.)

Zelda is haunted by a more troubling memory of her father. In chapters 5 and 23 of *The Bingo Palace* she recalls watching Nector burn the house of his lover, which she sees as an example of the dangers of love.

Ninimoshe. Name Klaus Shawano calls Sweetheart Calico in chapters 2 and 21 of *The Antelope Wife*. The word means "my sweetheart" and is used to refer to one's cross-cousin of the opposite sex, that is, a cousin not in one's patrilineal clan, hence a mother's brother's child or a father's sister's child. See **Sweetheart Calico.**

Nuns at Our Lady of the Wheat Priory. Nuns at the Argus convent where Sister Leopolda is living in 1994 in *Tales of Burning Love*. Mentioned briefly in "Night Prayer" [6], they reappear as background characters in "The Stone Virgin" [44]. The full name of the convent is given in "A Letter to the Bishop" [45].

In "White Musk" [4], Eleanor Mauser decides to ask the *Mother Superior* for permission to stay at the convent while she is doing research on Leopolda, a permission the nun grants. In "Night Prayer" [6], the Mother Superior gets Jack Mauser's highway construction workers to remove a cracked wooden statue of the Blessed Virgin. In "The Stone Virgin" [44], she persuades the road crew to help again, this time to transport the new stone statue to the convent.

Nuns at Sacred Heart Convent. Sisters at the convent on the hill overlooking the reservation township. In 1918–1919 Pauline Puyat lives with these nuns as a novice in chapters 6 and 8 of *Tracks,* taking her vows in the spring of 1919. See also **Anne, Sister Saint;** and **Superior.**

In 1932 Fleur Pillager leaves Karl Adare with these nuns after nursing him back to health in chapter 3 of *The Beet Queen*. They later send him to Saint Jerome's orphanage in Minneapolis. Two years later (1934) these sisters serve as mild and sane foils to the Satan-obsessed Sister Leopolda in "Saint Marie" in *Love Medicine.* They kneel beside the fourteen-year-old Marie Lazarre, who is lying on the **Mother Superior**'s couch after the supposed miraculous stigmata have appeared in her hand. Among those present on this occasion are **Sister Bonaventure, Sister Cecilia Saint-Claire,** and the **two French nuns** "with hands like paddles." These two call Marie "Star of the Sea" and, ironically, feel that she has unusual humility of the spirit. See also **Dympna, Sister; Leopolda, Sister;** and **Mary Martin de Porres, Sister.**

In chapter 5 of *The Bingo Palace* the **sisters** up on the hill are depicted as praying for the drunks who patronize Lyman Lamartine's bingo hall.

Nuns at Saint Catherine's school. Teachers who in 1932 witness Mary Adare's "miracle" in chapter 2 of *The Beet Queen* and who, almost thirty years later, have to deal with her niece, Dot Adare. They are said not to know what to do with Dot in chapter 11, and in chapter 12 they have to stop the school Christmas play when Dot knocks down another child. See also **Hugo, Sister; Leopolda, Sister;** and **Seraphica, Sister.**

Nuns at Saint Jerome's orphanage. Nuns who apparently take care of Karl Adare after he is sent to the orphanage from Sacred Heart Convent in chapter 3 of *The Beet Queen*. Several of the nuns are present at the Orphans' Picnic on the day Karl returns to visit in chapter 4, among them **Sister Ivalo, Sister Mary Thomas, Sister Ursula,** and **Sister George.**

Nuns at Sobieski. Teachers at a Catholic school that Marlis Cook attends before she comes to Fargo, as recorded in "Marlis's Tale" [27] in *Tales of Burning Love*. They are referred to in "Best Western" [28] as having taught Marlis the basics of piano playing.

Nurses. The *morning nurse* during Karl Adare's stay in the hospital in Minneapolis becomes a friend to Wallace Pfef in chapter 9 of *The Beet Queen*, and Wallace continues to correspond with her. The *nurse in the state mental hospital* in chapter 10 has strict instructions not to read Sita Tappe's lips or her notes.

The *nurse in the Argus hospital* who leads Jack and Dot Mauser to Eleanor Mauser's room in "The Meadowlark" [7] in *Tales of Burning Love* criticizes Jack for bringing wine into the hospital, but she seems relieved to have him come to take "Mrs. Mauser" home. In "Best Western" [28] Marlis Cook Mauser recalls the *school nurse* (who seems also to be a counselor) who had said that Marlis was obsessed because she was constantly falling in love with all sorts of men. *Maternity nurses* attend the birth of Marlis's baby in "The Waiting Room" [31]. The *nurse in the Fargo hospital* is grumpy with Dot in "February Thaw" [40] when Dot is recovering after nearly freezing to death in the blizzard. A *nurse in the Argus hospital* cleans Jack Mauser's cuts and bandages him after a

Nurses

falling statue nearly crushes him in "The Stone Virgin" [44]. Jack tells her how beautiful and gentle she is.

When Cally Roy becomes gravely ill in chapter 9 of *The Antelope Wife*, **nurses at the IHS** (Indian Health Service) help care for her.

Ober, Mr. Lover of Adelaide Adare; father of Karl and Mary Adare and Jude Miller in *The Beet Queen*. In chapter 1 Mr. Ober is described as a tall man with a neat black beard. He is possibly German, since his term of endearment for his daughter is "Schatze," a German word that means "treasure" or "sweetheart." He owns a large Minnesota wheat farm and has a wife, but he keeps a separate household in Prairie Lake with Adelaide. He dies in 1932, smothered in a grain-loading accident. Suicide is suspected, since he has borrowed heavily against his land during the Great Depression. His death leaves the pregnant Adelaide and her children homeless and destitute.

Ogimaakwe. Indian name of Fleur Pillager's mother, Boss Woman, used in chapters 1 and 9 of *Tracks*. See **Boss Woman.**

Ojibwa villagers. People in the ancestral Shawano village somewhere south of their original Canadian homeland (chapter 3) in *The Antelope Wife*. In chapter 6, some of these villagers call Apijigo Bakaday a windigo because she is continually eating. After the death of Apijigo Bakaday's deer husband, the people rename her Blue Prairie Woman, and her women relatives accept her into their number. When the U.S. Cavalry attacks in chapter 1, old men, women, children, and a few warriors are present in the village, which loses its store of food in the raid and suffers famine through the next winter. In the spring, the elders hold a feast for the survivors, and they secure a new name for Blue Prairie Woman. Sometime later, in chapter 23, the remaining villagers are confined to the reservation "up north" where the granddaughters and great-granddaughters of Blue Prairie Woman will grow up. (For notes about the location of this reservation, see **Rozina [Rozin] Roy Whiteheart Beads Shawano.**)

Old drunk woman. Purported mother of Marie Lazarre; mother of Lucille Lazarre and wife of Ignatius Lazarre (Marie's presumed sister and father). She shows up at Marie's door in 1948 with Lucille's daughter, June, and June's father, Morrissey I, in "The Beads" in *Love Medicine.*

Since Sophie Morrissey Lazarre seems to be the one taking care of Marie in infancy (chapter 8 of *Tracks*), we might conjecture that this drunk woman is

Sophie. A problem with this reading is that Sophie's husband in chapter 7 of *Tracks* is Izear Lazarre, while in "The Beads" Marie's father is presumed to be Ignatius.

Old Lady Blue. Nosy woman in *Love Medicine* who needles Marie Kashpaw in "The Beads" about Marie's husband's drinking and his brother Eli's too frequent visits to Marie's house. At the mission bundle sales, Marie fights with her for a Stetson hat in "Crossing the Water."

Old Lady Pillager. Name Lipsha Morrissey uses for Fleur Pillager in the "Love Medicine" story in *Love Medicine* and in chapters 11 and 14 of *The Bingo Palace*. See **Fleur Pillager.**

Old Man Bunachi. Man who receives a mistaken thousand-dollar Social Security credit. Lulu Lamartine knows about the money without being told and asks for a loan in "Crossing the Water" in *Love Medicine.*

Old Man LaGrisaille. Man who brings Marie Kashpaw ripe corn to can in "Resurrection" in *Love Medicine.*

Old Man Pillager. Name used to refer to Fleur Pillager's father in chapter 9 of *Tracks* and to Moses Pillager in "Crossing the Water" in *Love Medicine.* Fleur's father is also called Old Pillager in chapter 2 of *Tracks* and the Old Man in chapter 7. See **Moses Pillager** and **Pillager.**

Old rancher. Man whom Marlis propositions at a gas station in "Best Western" [28] in *Tales of Burning Love.* He takes her to a motel but decides she is too young and drives her back. His kindness serves in her mind as a telling contrast to Jack Mauser's opportunistic crassness.

Old rich woman. Artist who uses the almost nude Nector Kashpaw as the model for her painting "The Plunge of the Brave" in *Love Medicine.*

Old Swedish widow and her daughter. Referred to in "Satin Heart" [12] in *Tales of Burning Love.* The widow owns a basement apartment where as a young man Jack Mauser eats cookies. It is not clear whether he is just visiting or whether he lives there as a tenant. Jack proposes to the daughter. Years later, the daughter, now a tax lawyer, attends Jack's funeral.

Old woman killed by Scranton Roy. See **Blue Prairie Woman's grandmother I.**

Omar, The Great. Airplane stunt pilot and sometime bootlegger. In chapter 1 of *The Beet Queen* Omar is performing stunts at the Orphans' Picnic in

Omar, The Great

Minneapolis in 1932 when he takes Adelaide Adare for a ride. She flies off with him, abandoning her children Karl, Mary, and an unnamed infant. In chapter 3 Karl imagines, mistakenly, that his mother has not willfully abandoned him, but that Omar has abducted her against her will. Also in this chapter we learn that Omar and Adelaide are living in Florida and that Omar believes she has left a life of comfort to be with him. Omar has a serious accident with Adelaide as his passenger, but they both survive. Jealous that she may think more about her children than about him, Omar leaves beside her hospital bed a postcard that Mary has sent from Argus, falsely announcing that all of Adelaide's children have died of starvation.

In chapter 11 Omar and Adelaide are apparently still in Florida where they operate a "birdorama." One morning he is feeding the birds when he hears glass breaking in the house. When he goes in, he sees that Adelaide has had one of her periodic fits of rage and is standing with her feet bloody in the broken glass.

Orderlies. *Orderlies* come to the hotel in Minneapolis to take Karl Adare to the hospital after he has injured his back in chapter 6 of *The Beet Queen*. The young **orderly in the psychiatric hospital** where Sita Kozka Tappe is staying in chapter 10 takes her to the phone so she can call her husband Louis and report that she is "cured" of her speech impediment. An **orderly from the American Legion** helps to dress Russell Kashpaw for the Beet Parade in chapter 13.

Original Dog. Mythic female ancestor to whom Almost Soup attributes much of his survival wit in chapter 8 of *The Antelope Wife*. Original Dog was companion to Wenabojo, trickster creator of humans.

Other Side of the Earth. Name given to Blue Prairie Woman when she seems to be dying of grief after the disappearance of her first child, in chapter 1 of *The Antelope Wife*. When Blue Prairie Woman finds her lost daughter (Matilda Roy) and the girl falls ill, the mother gives her the same life-restoring name.

According to chapter 18, Zosie Shawano Roy acquires this name in a dream by gambling with the spirit of Blue Prairie Woman. Zosie later gives the name to her granddaughter, Deanna Whiteheart Beads.

There also seems to be an allusion to this name in chapter 18 when Cally Roy says of Sweetheart Calico that she has been to "the other side of the earth," where she has seen Blue Prairie Woman.

Ozhawashkwamashkodeykway. Ojibwa word for Blue Prairie Woman, found in chapter 1 of *The Antelope Wife*. According to chapter 11, this is also Cally Roy's spirit name, given to her by her Grandma Zosie, who won it from the original Blue Prairie Woman. See **Blue Prairie Woman** and **Cally Whiteheart Beads Roy.**

Partying woman. Woman in the room next to Candice Pantamounty Mauser and Marlis Cook Mauser in the Mariner Motel in Minnesota, as recounted in "Baptism River" [29] in *Tales of Burning Love.* She invites them to her solitary twenty-fourth birthday celebration and later assumes that they are lesbians.

Patsy Kashpaw. She and Eugene are the youngest of Marie and Nector Kashpaw's five children. Patsy is the older of the two, since, as recorded in "The Beads" in *Love Medicine,* Marie's youngest is a boy, born in 1948. Their sister Aurelia takes care of Patsy and Eugene in "Flesh and Blood" (1957) when Marie takes their other sister Zelda to visit Sister Leopolda. Patsy is nearby as Marie reads the letter from Nector that says he is leaving her.

Pauline Puyat. Daughter of a mixed-blood father and half-white mother. As a child, in chapter 10 of *The Beet Queen,* Pauline and her cousins Isabel and Russell Kashpaw seek out Eli Kashpaw on the reservation because he is good company.

Pauline is the narrator of the even-numbered chapters in *Tracks,* but because of the increasingly bizarre nature of her accounts and the fact that she herself reports her lies, the reader doubts her reliability as narrator. In chapter 2, in the spring of 1912 Pauline leaves the reservation to go to Argus because she wants to be like her pure Canadian grandfather and her light-skinned mother. Living with her father's sister, Regina Puyat Kashpaw, Pauline takes care of Regina's son, Russell, and helps at the butcher shop where Regina's companion, Dutch James, works. The first winter she is there, a great many reservation Indians die of consumption. Pauline is not able to learn whether her parents and sisters have died or have moved north to avoid the sickness. The following June (1913), Fleur Pillager arrives in Argus and also begins working at the butcher shop. The fifteen-year-old Pauline watches each night as Fleur wins money in card games with the three butcher shop employees, Dutch, Lily Veddar, and Tor Grunewald. When Pauline and Russell witness the men's attack on Fleur one hot August night, Pauline does not try to stop them. The next morning a tornado—which Pauline believes Fleur has called up in revenge—wrecks the town, but particularly the butcher's shop. Lily, Tor, and Dutch take shelter in the meat lockers, and Pauline locks them in. After several days, the townspeople pull

Pauline Puyat

away the rubble covering the lockers and find the men inside frozen—Tor and Lily dead, and Dutch so frostbitten that he loses his ears and parts of his limbs.

Chapters 3 and 4 tell of Pauline's return to the reservation, first from Nanapush's point of view and then, in more detail, from her own. Pauline wants to leave Argus because of her nightmares of the three frozen men, intensified by watching Dutch rot piece by piece. In December (1913) Bernadette Morrissey comes to town and agrees to take her in. On the reservation, Pauline lives with Bernadette, her brother Napoleon, son Clarence, and two daughters Sophie and Philomena. Pauline begins to assist Bernadette as she sits with the dying and prepares the bodies of the dead. When Mary Pepewas dies, Pauline is alone with her. There is a suggestion that Pauline could have saved the girl, but does not. Afterward, Pauline believes that she herself mutates into a scavenger bird, and the next morning she is found asleep in a high tree. Thereafter, her nightmares cease until Margaret Kashpaw induces her to tell about the Argus activities of Fleur, who has returned to the reservation with money and is perhaps pregnant. Fleur claims that Pauline's account is a lie. When Fleur's baby, Lulu, is about to be born in the spring of 1914, Pauline fetches Margaret to help. Just before Fleur gives birth, Pauline shoots a drunk bear who has entered the cabin.

As chapter 4 continues, Pauline wants a husband. She agrees to a rendezvous in the woods with Napoleon, but they do not consummate this first sexual encounter. Later, on one of her visits to Fleur's cabin, Pauline is attracted to Eli, who refuses her. In revenge, Pauline uses a love medicine to make Eli have relations with the fourteen-year-old Sophie. (In a perhaps-Freudian slip, after recounting this incident, Pauline refers to herself as "Pauline Kashpaw.") In retaliation, Fleur casts a spell on Sophie, which is broken by a statue of the Blessed Virgin. Pauline is present on this occasion and believes that she is sole witness to a miracle—the statue's weeping. By the close of chapter 4 Pauline has become Napoleon's lover. Her revenge against Eli is complete in chapter 5, when Fleur rejects him because of his escapade with Sophie.

In chapter 6 Pauline has decided to become a nun, but she is pregnant with Napoleon's child. She tries to abort the baby, but Bernadette prevents her. Even in labor, Pauline tries to keep from giving birth, so that Bernadette must forcibly deliver the baby. After the birth, Bernadette keeps the baby girl, Marie, and Pauline enters the convent. According to *Tracks,* the year is 1918. (The "Saint Marie" story in *Love Medicine* suggests a slightly different birth date. See **Marie Lazarre Kashpaw.**)

At this point in the narrative two patterns begin to emerge that will continue and intensify through the remainder of *Tracks:* Pauline offers her pain to God in recompense for her sins, and she has visions in which Christ—or Satan—

Pauline Puyat's mother and sisters

speaks to her. In chapter 6 she is called to hunt down and defeat the devil in the form of Misshepeshu, the scaled, gold-eyed creature of Matchimanito Lake, whose human connection is Fleur Pillager. In response to this call, Pauline begins to make regular visits to Fleur's cabin by the lake. One night, when only Pauline and Lulu are with her, Fleur, pregnant with Eli's child, begins to miscarry. She needs Pauline to help her, but Pauline is inept, and Fleur's baby is born prematurely. Five-year-old Lulu goes out into the winter night for help. In anger Fleur throws a knife at Pauline. Pauline's death vision follows. In it, Fleur gambles with the dead for the lives of her baby and Lulu. She loses the baby's life but wins Lulu's. When Margaret arrives at Fleur's cabin, she blames Pauline for the baby's death and spits on her.

In spring of 1919 (chapter 7) Pauline of *Tracks* Pauline interferes with a healing ceremony Nanapush is conducting for Fleur and, in the process, burns her hands badly. She returns to the convent in chapter 8, where Superior cares for her hands. In her ensuing fever, Pauline sees a figure who she decides is Lucifer and who calls her to meet him "in the desert." In a second vision, Pauline understands this to mean that she must go to Matchimanito and confront the lake creature. When her hands are healed, Pauline goes to Matchimanito and steals Nanapush's leaky boat (in chapter 9 Nanapush claims that Pauline has ruined his boat). She drifts out and anchors the boat in the middle of the lake, planning to stay forty days, or until she is able to confront the lake devil and kill him with her crucifix. Pauline rejects the shouts of people on the shore and Nanapush's attempt to save her, but finally the anchor rope breaks and the boat drifts ashore. She strips off all of her clothes, armed only with her rosary to confront the demon. On the shore, the lake monster appears, they grapple, and she finally chokes him to death with her rosary. Once dead, however, the demon transmutes into the body of Napoleon Morrissey, which Pauline drags into the woods behind Fleur's house. (Reservation gossip accuses Fleur of killing Napoleon.)

As Pauline takes her vows as a nun, she receives both an assignment to teach school in Argus and a new name—Leopolda. Her story continues under this new name in *The Beet Queen, Love Medicine,* and *Tales of Burning Love.*

Pauline Puyat's mother and sisters. Pauline's mother is a light-skinned, half-white woman, daughter of a Canadian man and an Indian woman, according to chapter 2 of *Tracks.* She and the rest of Pauline's family disappear during the consumption epidemic in 1912, while Pauline is living in Argus (the account of the epidemic appears in chapter 1). Pauline is not able to learn whether they die or go north to escape the sickness. She misses her mother and sisters and dreams that they are buried high in the trees. Bernadette Morrissey, who

Pauline Puyat's mother and sisters

knows Pauline's mother, in chapter 4 appears to believe that the family has moved, leaving Pauline behind. Pauline sees her mother in her death vision in chapter 6.

Pausch, Sheriff. Summoned by the paranoid Sita Tappe to arrest her cousin Karl Adare for stealing her jewelry in chapter 8 of *The Beet Queen*. The sheriff comes, frisks Karl, but finds no evidence of theft. Pausch is a former botany teacher and a friend of Sita's biologist husband, Louis Tappe.

Peace McKnight. Wife of Scranton Roy; mother and grandmother respectively of Augustus Roy I and II in *The Antelope Wife*. Peace is a sturdily built but graceful Scot from Aberdeen (in east-central Dakota territory), who moves onto the Great Plains to teach school after her father's business fails. Her few pupils are unpromising until the six-year-old Matilda Roy arrives. Peace becomes friends with Matilda and moves in with the child and her adoptive father, Scranton Roy. She and Scranton soon become a couple. But Peace is put off by the discomfort of her husband's bed and sleeps with the poultry instead. Finding herself pregnant, she further rejects her husband sexually, especially after her illness with a fever. During this illness, the seven-year-old Matilda disappears in the night, leaving a note that she has gone with her mother. After three agonizing days in labor during a blizzard, Peace dies after giving birth to the son she has already named Augustus.

Peace McKnight's father. Aberdeen sheep farmer and button-seller in chapter 1 of *The Antelope Wife*.

Peace McKnight's students. Three grown *Swedish sisters,* dying of consumption, and one *angry German boy,* in chapter 1 of *The Antelope Wife*. All are virtually unteachable.

Pembina woman. Woman wearing the necklace of northwest trader blue beads whom Zosie Shawano sees as a child, according to chapter 18 of *The Antelope Wife*. Later, when Zosie is pregnant, she sees the Pembina woman again in a dream, wearing the beads. Zosie gambles with her and wins both her beads and her two names. The dream woman turns out to be Zosie's grandmother, Blue Prairie Woman.

The fact that the women with blue beads are described as Pembina possibly suggests that the reservation "up north" (chapters 6 and 8) where Blue Prairie Woman's descendants live may be in the Pembina region, that is, far northeast North Dakota.

Pepewas boy. Fat little boy, apparently Mary Pepewas's brother, sent to fetch Bernadette Morrissey when Mary is sick with consumption in chapter 4 of *Tracks.*

Pepperboy. Candice Pantamounty's dog in *Tales of Burning Love.* According to "Candice's Tale" [25], this plain but rakish stray dog shows up at Jack Mauser's construction site. When Jack tries to tame him, the dog bites him several times, so Jack takes him to the Fargo city dump to shoot him. Candice intervenes and adopts the dog, whom she names Pepperboy. Candice and Pepperboy become devoted to each other, and when Candice and Jack marry he becomes a point of contention. Following a hunting trip in "The Wandering Room" [26], Pepperboy is tied in the back of Jack's pickup. Unaware that Pepperboy jumped out at a stoplight, Jack accidentally drags him to his death. Kneeling beside him as he dies, Candice sees forward to the end of her marriage.

Pete Kozka. Husband of Fritzie Kozka and father of Sita Kozka. In chapter 2 of *Tracks,* as owner of the butcher shop in Argus, Pete employs Lily Veddar, Tor Grunewald, Dutch James, Pauline Puyat, Pauline's young cousin Russell Kashpaw, and—in the summer of 1913—Fleur Pillager. Pete occasionally plays cards with his male employees after closing, rubbing his good-luck talisman, the lens of a cow's eye. When Fleur comes to work for Pete, she joins the men's card games, but Pete is gone to Minnesota when his employees attack Fleur and the butcher shop is demolished by a tornado.

Pete is still operating Kozka's Meats when the abandoned child Mary Adare, Fritzie's niece, comes to stay with the Kozkas in chapter 1 of *The Beet Queen.* Pete and Fritzie are kind to Mary, and Pete gives her his lucky cow's lens, which angers his daughter Sita.

After Fritzie collapses with a pulmonary hemorrhage in 1941 (chapter 4), she and Pete move south for her health, leaving the butcher shop to Mary. About ten years later, the suntanned Pete and Fritzie attend Sita's wedding to Jimmy Bohl in chapter 5. Pete's junk collection still remains in the backyard of the butcher shop in chapter 7. By the 1960s (chapter 11), because of the new supermarkets, the butcher shop is not doing as well as it had when Pete ran it. Shortly before her death in 1972, in chapter 13 Sita thinks about her father—that he had liked Jimmy's beer lamps and how much he would have loved to have had a grandchild.

Years later, in 1995 (in "A Wedge of Shade" [3] in *Tales of Burning Love*), Mary recalls Pete and Fritzie's leaving the butcher shop to her, although she does not mention them by name.

Philomena Morrissey

Philomena Morrissey. Youngest child of Bernadette Morrissey and sister of Clarence and Sophie Morrissey. According to Pauline Puyat in chapter 4 of *Tracks,* Philomena is sweet and fat, but she is apparently not so messy as Sophie, who is four years older. Both girls have dainty French ways, the product apparently of their mother's education in Quebec. When Pauline comes to stay, she sleeps with the sisters and kicks them in her nightmare-ridden sleep. In chapter 6 Philomena grows thinner and is seen dancing wildly with Sophie. Bernadette takes Philomena and leaves home in chapter 7 when Sophie and Clarence both marry Lazarres and bring them to the house.

Pillager. Father of Fleur Pillager. In *Tracks* he is called Old Pillager (chapter 2), the Old Man (chapter 7), and Old Man Pillager (chapter 9). In chapter 3 of *The Bingo Palace* we learn that Pillager's mother is Four Soul, a healer who is among the original group of Chippewas who come west to the reservation. Chapter 7 of *Tracks* tells us that Misshepeshu, the spirit-man who lives in Matchimanito Lake, on whose shores the Pillagers settle, first appears in the lake when the family arrives because Pillager has a special connection with him. The lake man seems to be integrally connected with the family's medicine power, which Pillager apparently inherits from his mother and then passes on to his eldest daughter, Fleur.

   In the consumption epidemic that ravages the reservation in the winter of 1912 (chapter 1), Pillager dies, along with most of his family, survived only by the seventeen-year-old Fleur. They are buried when the snow recedes, but their spirits remain to haunt the land around Matchimanito. Pillager is one of the spirits who appear to Nanapush in Fleur's clearing in chapter 9. In chapter 27 of *The Bingo Palace* he is one of the ghosts who wait for Fleur on the island in Matchimanito as she makes her death walk across the frozen lake.

Pillager family. Through several generations the Pillagers are holdouts who will not part with their land, refusing to smoke the pipe in the treaty with the U.S. government (chapter 5 of *The Bingo Palace*). Pillager land around Matchimanito Lake is considered to have a special sanctity and power, as indicated in chapters 1 and 7 of *Tracks* and chapters 7, 17, and 20 of *The Bingo Palace.* For the family's relationship with the lake man of Matchimanito, see **Misshepeshu.** For the medicine power of the Pillager clan, see **Fleur Pillager.** See also **Baby Pillager; Boss Woman; Chokecherry Girl; Gerry Nanapush; He Is Lifted By Wind; Lulu Nanapush Morrissey Lamartine; Moses Pillager; Moses Pillager's grandfather; Pillager; Pillager woman;** and **Small Bird.** Three other Pillagers about whom we have no knowledge, but who are listed in the records of the Pillager clan written down by Father Damien (chapter 3 of *The Bingo Palace*) are **Comes from Above, Strikes the Water,** and **Unknown Cloud.**

Pillager woman. One Shawano man stops with this woman as his clan is migrating from the north (probably Canada) to the south (probably the Dakotas) in chapter 3 of *The Antelope Wife.*

Pilot. Man who pilots the small airplane transporting Gerry Nanapush to a new prison facility in Minnesota in chapter 21 of *The Bingo Palace.* The "Radio Bulletin" [11] in *Tales of Burning Love* indicates that two men are confirmed dead in the accident, but since there are also two federal marshals aboard, we do not know if the pilot is one of the dead.

Postmaster and postmistress. Nosy husband-and-wife operators of the Argus post office who spread gossip about Karl Adare's letters and packages to his daughter Dot in chapter 10 of *The Beet Queen.*

Priests. In *Love Medicine* one of Nector Kashpaw's high school teachers, a **priest in Flandreau,** teaches him *Moby-Dick* all four years, as he recalls in "The Plunge of the Brave." The **priest at the Sacred Heart Convent** in 1982 refuses to bless Lipsha's turkey hearts in "Love Medicine." (His name is not given, but he may be Father Damien.)

In chapter 2 of *The Beet Queen* the **priest at Saint Catherine's school** proclaims the face in the ice on the school playground to be an image of Christ. He may be the same as the **priest who baptizes Dot Adare** in chapter 9. **Father Mullen** and **Father Bonaventure** are priests at Saint Jerome's orphanage in Minneapolis who are present when Karl Adare returns to the Orphans' Picnic in chapter 4. Father Mullen had apparently called Karl the devil while Karl was living at Saint Jerome's. Catherine Miller's spiritual advisor, **Father Flo,** counsels her in chapter 5 to write a letter to the rightful family of Jude Miller, the baby she and her husband had abducted eighteen years earlier.

We learn in chapter 1 of *Tracks* that the **first priest on the reservation** dies of consumption in the epidemic of 1912. He is replaced by the young Father Damien. The **priest in Argus** lives in a residence attached to the church when Fleur Pillager comes to Argus in 1913. In chapter 2 the priest or someone at his residence secures a job for Fleur at Pete Kozka's butcher shop.

A **reservation priest** is referred to in "Night Prayer" [6] in *Tales of Burning Love* as having documented a stigmata miracle at which Sister Leopolda was present. The incident is probably Marie Lazarre's "miracle" (related in "Saint Marie" in *Love Medicine*) and the priest is probably Father Damien.

Priests

At the request of Klaus Shawano, the **Father at the recovery lodge** tries unsuccessfully to calm the sobbing Richard Whiteheart Beads in chapter 15 of *The Antelope Wife*. See also **Damien Modeste, Father; Jude Miller;** and **Retzlaff, Bishop.**

Psychiatrists and therapists. The *psychiatrist treating Sita Tappe* is convinced that Sita is faking her speech impediment and puts her into a psychiatric hospital (chapter 10 of *The Beet Queen*). After one night there, Sita is "cured." **Doctor Hakula** is the therapist in *Tales of Burning Love* who, after Candice Pantamounty's hysterectomy, helps her to deal with her psychological and addiction problems in "Candice's Tale" [25]. Some years later, in "The Waiting Room" [31] Candice arranges for a *psychiatrist to treat Marlis Mauser* for postpartum depression. **Dr. Fry,** whose card Rozina Whiteheart Beads holds in chapter 7 of *The Antelope Wife,* is probably a psychiatrist.

Puffy Shawano. Brother of Frank, Klaus, and Cecille Shawano in *The Antelope Wife*. The reference to his mother's "children" (plural) prior to Klaus's birth (chapter 13) may suggest that Puffy is older than Klaus. (Frank is the only child named in this chapter.)

According to chapter 16, Puffy is a tribal judge. When Frank marries Rozina Roy, Puffy provides some of the meat that is cooked for the reception. As the family makes preparations, Puffy watches the four-months-sober alcoholic Klaus struggle to stay away from the cold beer. Later, when Richard Whiteheart Beads interrupts the cliffside ceremony, Puffy and Klaus restrain Frank from pushing him over the cliff. That afternoon, after Klaus hits Richard with a frozen turkey, judge Puffy remarks that a frozen turkey would make a perfect murder weapon.

Pugweyan. Uncle of Klaus Shawano who comes to see the German that Klaus's father (probably Pugweyan's brother) has kidnapped in chapter 13 of *The Antelope Wife*. Pugweyan reasons with the angry Asinigwesance, who wants to kill the prisoner.

Pukwan family. See **Edgar Pukwan; Edgar Pukwan Junior;** and **Leo Pukwan.** See also *Felix Pukwan* in **Tomahawk factory workers.**

Puyat family. Mixed-blood family, skinners for their clan, usually quiet (except for Pauline), referred to in chapters 2 and 3 of *Tracks*. Pauline Puyat's immediate family consists of her father, **Puyat,** her half-white mother, and her sisters. She has a **Canadian grandfather,** presumably her mother's father. In the spring of 1912, Puyat allows her to leave the reservation and stay with his sister, Regina Puyat Kashpaw, in Argus. See also **Pauline Puyat; Pauline Puyat's mother and sisters;** and **Regina Puyat Kashpaw James.**

Rancher. See **Old rancher.**

Ray. Friend of Lyman Lamartine who helps conceal the photograph of Henry Lamartine Junior in "The Red Convertible" in *Love Medicine.*

Red Cradle. Daughter of Nanapush and White Beads who dies as a young child; nicknamed Lulu. According to chapter 3 of *Tracks* her Indian name is Moskatikinaugun. Of all his dead family members, Nanapush seems to grieve most for her and her mother. Years later, Nanapush names Fleur Pillager's first child after Red Cradle's nickname, Lulu. Red Cradle is also referred to in chapter 9 of *Tracks* and chapter 3 of *The Bingo Palace.*

Redford Toose. Son of Shawnee Ray Toose and (probably) Lyman Lamartine in *The Bingo Palace.* Redford is mentioned in chapter 1, and we first see him at the powwow in chapter 2. He and his mother live with Zelda Kashpaw, Lyman's half sister, who plays the part of a controlling grandmother. We are not told Redford's age, but he seems to be a toddler. In chapter 2 Zelda is holding him, and when he is put down, he runs to his mother. Chapter 10 shows him just barely beginning to talk, and in chapter 15 he is old enough to understand where his mother is and why she is away, but we do not hear him speak.

Redford is ill the night Lipsha Morrissey wins the bingo van (chapter 7). When Lipsha visits Shawnee Ray at Zelda's house in chapter 9, Redford is with Zelda at church. In chapter 14 Shawnee Ray leaves Redford with her sisters, Mary Fred and Tammy, while she is gone to a Montana powwow. While he is staying with his aunts, in chapter 15 Redford dreams that a huge metal crushing "thing" is coming for them. He awakes as tribal policeman Leo Pukwan, social worker Vicki Koob, and Zelda arrive to take him back to Zelda's house. They have a court order granting Lyman custody of his son.

In chapter 14 Redford and his mother are again living with Zelda. Redford has always been subject to nightmares (chapter 9), but after his abduction from the Toose house, these apparently increase in intensity (chapter 23). He also becomes more timid and reluctant to leave his mother, as he demonstrates when Albertine Johnson comes to visit in chapter 19. Lyman thinks of Redford as the heir to Lyman's acquisitive talents in chapter 13, but in chapter 17 Shawnee Ray warns him never to try to get custody of Redford again. She says that because she had other boyfriends at the time of Redford's conception, Lyman cannot be sure that he is the boy's father. Using her powwow winnings and money from Lipsha, Shawnee Ray finally takes Redford and escapes from Zelda's house. In

Redford Toose

chapter 26 Redford and his mother are living in drafty housing at the university where she is enrolled.

Regina (in *The Antelope Wife*). Companion to Shawano the ogitchida and mother of Frank, Puffy, Klaus, and Cecille Shawano. According to chapter 13, Regina refuses to marry her children's father or to take his windigo family name. Regina may have some African American ancestry. (It is not clear whether Klaus is speaking of his maternal or paternal heritage in his chapter 2 reference to his "Buffalo Soldier" blood.)

When, shortly after his return from World War II, Shawano the ogitchida kidnaps a young German, Regina is far along in her pregnancy with Klaus. Frank and at least one other of her children are with her in the kitchen as she watches the German cook the blitzkuchen. When she eats the magical cake, she communicates with her unborn son.

In chapter 16, Frank, now a middle-aged man, recalls the smells associated with his mother and loves Rozina Roy in part because her scent reminds him of Regina.

Regina Puyat Kashpaw James. Mother of Russell and Isabel Kashpaw by a Montana Kashpaw, and of Celestine James by Dutch James; aunt of Pauline Puyat. In chapter 2 of *Tracks* we learn that Regina is the sister of Puyat, Pauline's father, and that the Puyats are mixed-blood. Chapter 7 of *The Beet Queen* indicates that one trait of Regina's family is that their teeth look fierce when they grin (a trait shared with the Pillager clan). Chapter 2 of *Tracks* indicates that Regina marries a Kashpaw who later goes to live in Montana. He is thus apparently one of Margaret and the original Kashpaw's older children who must move to Montana when land allotments are assigned, as related in "The World's Greatest Fishermen" in *Love Medicine* and chapter 3 of *Tracks*. (This detail appears to conflict with *The Beet Queen*'s references to Margaret's and Regina's sons as half brothers, implying that Margaret and Regina marry the same Kashpaw man. See **Montana Kashpaw**.)

In chapter 2 of *Tracks*, after Regina's Kashpaw husband goes to Montana, she meets the white man Dutch James, and she and Russell go to live with him in Argus. In the spring of 1912, Regina takes in her niece Pauline to live with them. The following summer, in chapter 4, Dutch nearly freezes to death in the butcher shop's meat locker, where he has taken refuge during a summer tornado. No one realizes—and oddly Regina does not mention—that he is missing until he has been trapped in the locker for several days. Nevertheless, when he is found, Regina cares for him as he rots away piece by piece with gangrene, and for the first time they seem actually to love each other. By the time cold weather comes, he is more or less healed, and he and Regina get married. That winter Pauline returns to the reservation. Pauline says in chapters 2 and 4 that she herself chooses to leave Argus (she claims that Regina beats her). According to Nanapush in chapter 3, however, it is Regina who sends Pauline back after the girl begins to act strange.

In chapter 2 of *The Beet Queen* we learn that, in addition to her son Russell, Regina has an older daughter by Kashpaw named Isabel and a younger daughter, Celestine, fathered by Dutch James and born a month after her marriage to him. According to this chapter, after her marriage to Dutch, Regina brings down three other children from the reservation that Dutch "hadn't known about." This account does not jibe with the account in *Tracks,* which indicates that Russell and Pauline are already living with Regina in Argus before she and Dutch marry and which makes no mention of Isabel. There is also some confusion about the identity of the "three other children." In chapter 2 of *The Beet Queen,* these three are said to carry the last name Kashpaw and never to have been court-adopted by James, implying that all three are Regina's children, although only Russell and Isabel Kashpaw are named. Chapter 10 of *The Beet Queen* refers to Isabel, Pauline, and Russell's being on the reservation together, which suggests that these are the three children referred to in chapter 2. We know, however, that Pauline is not a Kashpaw but a Puyat, Regina's niece rather than her daughter.

From chapter 2 of *The Beet Queen* we learn that Regina dies when Celestine is still young and from chapter 10 that Eli Kashpaw and Fleur Pillager come down to Argus for her funeral.

Reservation girl. Girl whose hands bleed, a stigmata manifestation referred to in "Night Prayer" [6] in *Tales of Burning Love.* See **Marie Lazarre Kashpaw.**

Resounding Sky. See **Kashpaw.**

Retzlaff, Bishop. Receives Jude Miller's letter concerning some seemingly miraculous events at the convent in Argus, which hints that that Sister Leopolda may be eligible for sainthood in "A Letter from the Bishop" [45] in *Tales of Burning Love.*

Reverend. Female minister who marries Rozina Roy and Frank Shawano in chapter 16 of *The Antelope Wife.* When Rozin's ex-husband Richard Whiteheart Beads arrives at the cliffside ceremony and tries to leap from the cliff, the Reverend holds on to his ankle until others can pull him back.

Richard Whiteheart Beads. First husband of Rozina Roy and father of Deanna and Cally Whiteheart Beads in *The Antelope Wife.* According to chapter

Richard Whiteheart Beads

23, Richard's surname comes from the original Whiteheart Beads, who was named for a bead-embroidered blanket given to his mother by Midass, great-great-grandmother of Richard's wife, Rozina.

We learn in chapter 16 that as a young man Richard is slim and smartly dressed and has a promising future in tribal politics, but he is obsessive. He marries Rozina Roy on an Ojibwa reservation somewhere "up north" of Minneapolis. According to chapter 7, Richard is an idealistic student at the time and is proud of marrying a girl with Roy blood. (We know from chapters 1, 18, and 23 that the Roy ancestors were educated men and women.) According to chapter 16, however, Richard's obsessive love maddens Rozin, and she tries to leave three times. Twice, he persuades her to stay. The third time, she stays because she is pregnant with twins. The reader wonders if Richard may suggest an abortion, since he later recalls Rozin's insistence, "*No abortion*" (chapter 7). Their twin daughters, Deanna and Cally, are born probably in the mid-1970s.

By the time the girls are five, Rozin insists that the family leave the reservation because Richard's job has become too dangerous and political (chapter 7). They move to Minneapolis in chapter 3, where Rozin teaches school and Richard pursues his scheme of large-scale garbage disposal on reservation land. While Richard is busy meeting with environmental engineers, however, Rozin is falling in love with a different sort of man, the baker Frank Shawano.

In chapter 4, Richard appears entirely successful. He is a leading player in the nation's first Native-owned waste-disposal business, and he has won the company's top prize of a paid vacation to Hawaii. Over the next months and years, however, the problems created by his obsessions will destroy his life, both professionally and personally, and he will often plan suicide (chapter 7). The exact sequence of his business and family crises is left vague, but the events are as follows:

In business, the obsessively ambitious Richard illegally dumps toxic waste and takes a payoff, which he uses to buy a lake cabin (chapter 18). At the company party in chapter 4, Richard gives his Hawaii trip to Klaus Shawano, along with his I.D. Klaus notes his nervousness at the party, but misinterprets it. Richard, apparently aware that he is in trouble, is setting Klaus up. On the trip, law-enforcement officials assume that Klaus is Richard and arrest him for the company's dumping violations. But Richard does not entirely escape the consequences. Although he still seems to have a job in chapter 7, we learn in chapter 18 that he is prosecuted for his violations.

In his family, both Richard's obsessive love and Rozin's affair with Frank work to sour their relationship. One afternoon in early June when Deanna and

Cally are still small (chapter 6), Richard takes the girls to the city park, where they see a woman who looks like Rozin walking with an athletic-looking man. Richard insists that she is not Rozin, but his grave manner seems to belie his words. When Richard comes home one day, he senses that Frank has been there. Two days later, he searches the house and finds signs of the affair. His subsequent confrontation with Rozin ends the affair, but in her grief, she grows to hate him.

Richard and Rozin's troubled relationship reaches a crisis when their daughters are eleven. The snowy March morning in chapter 7 seems to Richard to be the beginning of an ordinary day. But when the girls go to school, Rozin stuns him with the announcement that her old lover, Frank, has terminal cancer and that she is leaving Richard to be with him. Richard goes to the office and tries unsuccessfully to recapture a sense of normalcy. He returns home early and fights with Rozin, verbally and then physically, but she is implacable. After drinking himself to sleep, he wakes in the night, determined to kill himself. But Richard's efforts to die of carbon monoxide poisoning in his pickup truck are foiled by his own bumbling until he finally changes his mind. The next morning, as we learn in chapter 9, he discovers Deanna behind the truck's seat, dead.

According to chapter 17, Richard wants to bury the whole truck with his daughter. He tries to care for Rozin in the early days of their grief, but she cannot forgive him (chapter 16). In chapter 9, she takes Cally and moves back to the reservation to stay with her "mothers," Zosie Roy and Mary Shawano. Both Rozin and Cally reject their relationship with Richard, changing their surname to Roy (chapters 14 and 11). Seven years later, the eighteen-year-old Cally still says that she never wants to see him again.

Guilt over Deanna's death, the loss of Rozin, and perhaps the failure of his financial schemes all contribute to Richard's undoing. In chapter 10 he is a drunken bum—wandering the streets with Klaus, drinking Listerine and cheap wine, and accepting handouts from strangers. Seven years after Deanna's death, in chapter 11 Richard walks into Frank's bakery and seems to see her behind the counter (it is actually Cally). In horror, he staggers out the door and runs down the street.

Richard and Klaus eventually join a recovery program, but according to Klaus in chapter 15, Richard is more obnoxious sober than drunk, indulging in uncontrollable crying binges. Instead of taking responsibility for Deanna's death, however, Richard weeps for imaginary pasts he has invented. Once when Richard has been crying for two days, Klaus confronts him with reality. Richard responds by confronting Klaus with his own crimes.

Richard Whiteheart Beads

In chapter 16, Richard is still in and out of recovery programs. His final crisis comes when Rozin decides to marry Frank, a wedding he attempts to disrupt in a variety of ways. He calls Cally the night before; he tells Cecille Shawano that he is coming to the wedding; and he interrupts the ceremony with a suicide attempt and the reception with a claim that he has poisoned the cake. That night, although Rozin tries to stop him, he shoots himself in the head at the door of her and Frank's hotel room. In chapter 17, he dies in the hospital.

In chapter 17 memories of Richard haunt Rozin. His suicide gives rise to her own death wish, for she feels that his ghost is inescapable. Yet with Frank's help, Rozin puts aside Richard's uneasy ghost and rejoins the living. Cally is also somewhat haunted by her father during the Christmas dinner in chapter 18. He seems incarnate in the visage and grip of his nephew Chook, and as Cally listens to the family's conversation, she sees her father's bloody head and feels his tears in her own hands.

Rift-In-A-Cloud. Illiterate Chippewa landholder whom Nanapush advises not to put his thumbprint on a treaty in chapter 5 of *Tracks,* apparently because the treaty would take away the man's land.

Ronald Lovchik. See **Lovchik.**

Rooming house residents. Assorted *veterans* and pensionless retired *farm-hands* who live in the rooming house where Marlis Cook stays for a month in "Marlis's Tale" [27] in *Tales of Burning Love.* Marlis is talking to the oldest of the residents, an *eighty-seven-year-old man,* when Jack Mauser comes to see her.

Royce. Liquor dealer who reluctantly delivers wine on credit to Gordie Kashpaw in "Crown of Thorns" in *Love Medicine.* Gordie refers to him as "cousin," but the word may not indicate a blood relationship.

Roy family. Family in *The Antelope Wife* that includes non-Indians **Augustus Roy I; Augustus Roy II; Peace McKnight; Scranton Roy; Scranton Roy's father;** and **Scranton Roy's mother;** and Shawano Ojibwas **Aurora Roy; Cally Whiteheart Beads Roy; Deanna Whiteheart Beads; Matilda Roy** (by adoption); **Rozina (Rozin) Roy Whiteheart Beads Shawano;** and **Zosie (II) Shawano Roy.** In addition to these Ojibwa women, chapter 16 also refers to (apparently Ojibwa) *Roy men,* but their identity is not clarified. For the ancestry of this family, see also **Shawano family.**

Rozin. See **Rozina (Rozin) Roy Whiteheart Beads Shawano.**

Rozina (Rozin) Roy Whiteheart Beads Shawano. Daughter of Zosie (II) Shawano Roy and Augustus Roy II; mother of Deanna and Cally Whiteheart Beads in *The Antelope Wife*. The Roy blood mixed with her Ojibwa ancestry gives Rozin wavy hair and lightened skin (chapter 3). Chapter 14 records her Ojibwa name, Waubanikway (Dawn Woman). She is the narrator of chapter 3.

Rozin grows up on an Ojibwa reservation. Although its precise location is not revealed, the narrative does give a few hints. It is said to be "up north"—north of both Minneapolis (chapter 6) and the prairie country "out in Bwaanakeeng" (i.e., Dakota-land) where the dog Almost Soup is born (chapter 8). The dog's prairie birthplace may be near the region referred to in chapter 1 as the "vast carcass of the world west of the Otter Tail River," that is, the Wahpeton area in southeastern North Dakota, into which Almost Soup's ancestor flees. The reservation, then, would be north of this area. Also, the woman wearing Blue Prairie Woman's beads whom Zosie (II) sees as a child is referred to in chapter 18 as a "Pembina woman," indicating perhaps that Blue Prairie Woman's descendants live in the Pembina region, in far northeast North Dakota.

The marriage of Rozin's parents is ill-fated (chapter 18), and by the time of Rozin and Aurora's birth, her father has apparently disappeared. They are probably born in the 1940s or 1950s. (By the end of the novel, which seems to be in the mid-1990s, Rozin has a twenty-two-year-old daughter.) Rozin's mother, Zosie, and Zosie's twin sister, Mary, raise Rozin and Aurora, and they will not tell the girls which of them is their mother (chapters 9 and 11). When the girls are five, Aurora dies of diphtheria, and according to chapter 3, she must be pried from Rozin's arms.

Rozin seems still to be living on the reservation when she marries Richard Whiteheart Beads, who according to chapter 16 is a young tribal leader. We learn in chapters 7 and 16 that Rozin chafes at Richard's possessive love. (As she looks back in chapters 3, 9, 16, and 17 on her marriage and the subsequent catastrophes, she wishes that she had kept to the old-time ways and never become involved with Richard, although her anger is mixed with love.) From the first year of marriage, Rozin plots her escape, and she tries to leave three times. Twice Richard persuades her to stay. The third time she stays because she discovers, to her joy, that she is pregnant. Her twin girls, Deanna and Cally, are born probably in the mid-1970s.

When life on the reservation becomes too dangerous and political, Rozin insists that they leave. The family moves to Minneapolis in chapter 3, where Rozin teaches school and Richard pursues his scheme of creating a big-time garbage-disposal business. Shortly after they arrive, when the twins are five, Rozin sees Sweetheart Calico in front of Frank Shawano's bakery. Rozin enters

Rozina (Rozin) Roy Whiteheart Beads Shawano

the bakery and meets Frank, and they begin seeing one another. Because she loves Richard and the girls, Rozin grieves to find herself falling in love with Frank. They first consummate their relationship in a woods near a playground. One June afternoon, unknown to Rozin, Richard and the girls see her and Frank walk through the city park in chapter 6. To young Cally, her mother's companion appears as a deer man, like the deer husband of their forebear, Apijigo Bakaday.

Frank also comes to Rozin's house, bringing cookies. Richard eventually confronts Rozin about the affair, and it ends. But in her sadness, she grows to hate Richard. (The duration of Frank and Rozin's affair is uncertain. In chapter 7 Richard refers to the "years" she was Frank's lover.)

One snowy March day when the twins are eleven, in chapter 7 Rozin tells Richard that Frank is dying of cancer and that she is leaving Richard to be with him. The depressed Richard tries to commit suicide through carbon monoxide poisoning, but fails. Deanna, who surreptitiously climbs into Richard's truck, dies instead.

Rozin is overwhelmed with grief. Richard tries to take care of her, but according to chapter 16 she cannot forgive him. Blaming both Richard and her own love for Frank, in chapter 9 Rozin goes to live with her twin mothers on the reservation. Her grief for Deanna makes Rozin absent-minded and careless with Cally. After playing outside one sunny but freezing February day, nearly a year after Deanna's death, Cally becomes gravely ill. Rozin, Zosie, and Mary nurse her for three days, but a blizzard prevents their getting medical help, and Cally almost dies before the ambulance arrives. After Cally recovers, Rozin realizes that Cally can read her mind. Rozin continues to brood over her anger and love for Richard and to worry about what he has become. As we learn in chapters 10 and 11, he has become a drunken bum.

When Cally is eighteen, Rozin wants her to stay up north and go to the tribal college. She sees, however, that Cally is determined to leave, and in chapter 11 Rozin tries to contact her mothers, who have moved to Minneapolis. She is not able to reach them, so Cally goes to stay with cancer survivor Frank Shawano instead.

By the time Cally is twenty, in chapter 14 Rozin moves to the city to go to night school to become a lawyer. She stays with her mothers and works in a food co-op. She has taken back her maiden name, Roy, and also uses her Ojibwa name, Waubanikway. One August evening Frank shows up at Rozin's checkout counter saying that he needs her. He continues to phone her until she agrees to go with him to the state fair. There, after a frightening ride on the Gravitron, Rozin allows herself to fall in love with Frank again. According to chapter 16, she is attracted by both his strong physical bearing and their ability to be honest with one another.

Rozin and Frank's wedding, recorded in chapter 16, is in the autumn. (Since Cally buys supplies for the wedding six months in advance, their wedding date must be at least a year after the Gravitron incident.) Many family members come to Frank's bakery to help with the preparations, and an even larger family group goes out to the cliffside site of the ceremony. Richard interrupts the ceremony with another botched suicide attempt and disrupts the reception with a letter to Rozin claiming that he has poisoned the wedding cake—a lie, as he admits to her. At the reception, Frank, Rozin, and the wedding guests eat the not-poisoned cake. That evening, however, Richard shows up again—at Rozin and Frank's hotel room. He knocks at their door, puts a gun to his own head, and although the naked Rozin rushes to stop him, shoots.

In chapter 17, Rozin withdraws to her mothers' apartment, where the new grief merges with her old griefs. She hears Deanna's voice and prepares a meal for her daughter's ghost. For ten days Rozin refuses company and food and struggles with dreams about Richard, Frank, and a windigo stranger who is a gateway to death. Finally Frank gets into the apartment, refuses to leave, and cares for her.

Afterward, Rozin and Frank are apparently able to begin a normal married life. The following December (chapter 18) the family gathers at their bakery shop apartment for Christmas dinner. As Cally and other dinner guests observe, the new couple are deeply in love, and Rozin is unperturbed when her mother tries to embarrass her about their obvious affection. The next autumn, in chapter 22 Frank and Rozin each try to think of a way to celebrate their upcoming anniversary. Frank would prefer something private; Rozin would like a big party. Putting the other ahead of self, however, Rozin devises a private sexy encounter, and Frank makes elaborate plans for a surprise party. Their plans collide into an ending that catches everyone, including the reader, by surprise.

Rozin's cousins. Women who put Rozina Roy Shawano into the shower to wash off the blood after Richard Whiteheart Beads's suicide in chapter 16 of *The Antelope Wife.* They may be Ruby and Jackie.

Ruby. One of Rozina Roy's two oldest cousins, close in age to her sister Jackie, who helps with the preparations for Rozin's wedding in chapter 16 of *The Antelope Wife.* She and her sister may be the cousins who put Rozin into the shower after Richard Whiteheart Beads's suicide.

Rushes Bear. See **Margaret (Rushes Bear) Kashpaw.**

Russell Kashpaw

Russell Kashpaw. Son of Regina Puyat Kashpaw and a Montana Kashpaw; younger brother of Isabel Kashpaw and older half brother of Celestine James. As children, Russell, Isabel, and their cousin Pauline Puyat seek out Eli Kashpaw on the reservation to get to know him, as related in chapter 10 of *The Beet Queen*. (Throughout *The Beet Queen*, Eli is called Russell's half brother, but the genealogy in *Love Medicine* and *Tracks* indicates that Eli is the younger brother of Russell's father. See **Montana Kashpaw.**)

We learn in chapter 2 of *Tracks* that after Russell's father goes to Montana, he and his mother move to Argus to live with Dutch James. (Chapter 2 of *The Beet Queen* gives a variant account of the timing of Russell's move to Argus.) As a boy Russell helps out in the butcher shop where Dutch works, joined in 1912 by his cousin Pauline and in 1913 by Fleur Pillager. Although Pauline takes care of Russell, he prefers Fleur, whom he follows around the shop. One August night, he and Pauline see Dutch, Lily Veddar, and Tor Grunewald attack Fleur. Russell throws himself on Dutch in an attempt to stop the attack, but Dutch cuffs him off. When a tornado strikes the next day and the three men take refuge in the meat locker, Russell and Pauline lock them in, although Pauline acknowledges in chapter 4 that she, not Russell, is the one responsible for this deed. In chapter 8 she recalls Russell's reaction to the incident. Tor and Lily freeze to death, and Dutch loses parts of his limbs to frostbite.

After Dutch somewhat recovers, he marries Regina and thus becomes Russell's stepfather, although Russell never takes the James surname. According to chapter 2 of *The Beet Queen*, Russell's half sister Celestine is born a month later, and Regina and Dutch die when Celestine is still small.

About twenty years later (1932), in chapter 2 of *The Beet Queen*, Russell is still living with Celestine and his older sister, Isabel, on Dutch James's homestead just outside Argus. When Sita Kozka and her cousin Mary Adare come to visit Celestine, Russell mocks them. But after Mary's "miracle," when the face of Christ appears in the ice, Russell kneels beside the image and blesses himself.

In chapter 4, Russell goes off to war, and when he returns home a "second time," he has been wounded. The dating of this incident is problematic, because it appears in a chapter dated 1941, but Mary, who is narrating, says that Russell is back "from Korea." Russell's wounding and return could be a flash-forward to the Korean War, but aspects of the narration suggest otherwise. This chapter indicates that Fritzie and Pete move south for Fritzie's health in about 1941, and yet when Russell comes home wounded, Fritzie and Pete are still living in Argus. In addition, chapter 7, set in 1953, seems to refer to a later war and wounding when its narrator, Celestine, says that Russell has returned "from his latest war, Korea," with "even more wounds." After his chapter 4 return, he is

Russell Kashpaw

handsomely scarred, gets a job, and seems in control of his life, whereas after his chapter 7 return, he is listless, limping, and almost animal-like in appearance. Celestine also says in chapter 7 that Russell had his earlier "more attractive" scars "when he came back from Germany." Perhaps in mentioning Korea in chapter 4, Mary gets her wars confused. Even so, the early dating remains problematic, since the United States did not enter World War II until the end of 1941.

In chapter 4, while Russell is recovering in a Virginia hospital, Mary sends him a get-well card, but he does not respond. When he returns to Argus, he is considered a hero and gets a job at the bank. Mary sees him, falls in love with his scars, and asks Celestine to invite him to dinner. During dinner Russell is mostly cold toward Mary, but eventually lets her touch his scars.

In chapter 5 Russell is drinking in the bar that Sita Kozka Bohl enters after being kidnapped from her wedding dance (about 1950). When he returns home from Korea in 1952 or 1953 (chapter 7), there is talk of honoring him as North Dakota's most-decorated hero. Hearing that his sister Isabel has died violently, he goes to South Dakota to find out about her but is unable to learn anything. Back in Argus, the unemployed Russell mopes and drinks until Mary hires him to work on the butcher shop's equipment. He goes with Celestine and Mary to the grand opening of Sita's restaurant, Chez Sita, where he, Celestine, and Mary help in the restaurant's kitchen after the chef becomes ill. When Karl Adare moves in with Celestine, Russell disapproves, particularly when Celestine becomes pregnant. He leaves the house and goes to stay with Eli Kashpaw on the reservation.

That winter (1953–1954), in chapter 8 Russell has a stroke while ice fishing that leaves him largely paralyzed. (The account of his condition in chapter 10 makes clear that he cannot walk or dress himself, and his speech is seriously impaired.) Seven and a half years later, in chapter 10 Celestine makes her daughter, Dot Adare, give Russell the wheelchair Dot's father had sent her. Dot mentions other visits to her Uncle Russell and Eli in chapter 12, and in chapter 14 one of her various dreams of the future is to live with them on the reservation. We learn in chapter 11 that Dot sleeps in the room of the James house that used to be Russell's. In chapters 13, 15, and 16 Russell participates in the 1972 Beet Festival and is honored as the town's most-decorated hero. Just before the parade begins, Dot notices that Russell is thirsty and makes his attendants give him some water. During his ride on a parade float, he sees his sister Isabel on the old Chippewa road of death and thinks that he himself has died. He is jerked back into life when he laughs.

In these later chapters of *The Beet Queen* (1972), Russell appears to be unable even to pin on his medals, put on his hat, or ask for a drink of water. By the

Russell Kashpaw

time of *The Bingo Palace,* however, (sometime after 1984) although he is still wheelchair-bound and suffering from his multiple strokes and shrapnel wounds, his condition has obviously improved, since he is now a tattoo artist. In chapter 7 Lipsha Morrissey tries unsuccessfully to use his healing power to ease Russell's pain. Later, Lipsha is forcibly taken to Russell's tattoo parlor by some Montana men, but after the abductors leave, Russell is kind to him. We learn in chapter 17 that Russell works with Xavier Toose, apparently in religious ceremonies.

S

Satan. Variously called Lucifer, the Dark One, and the Devil, he appears to Pauline Puyat in chapters 6 and 8 of *Tracks*—or so she believes. According to these chapters and chapter 2, Pauline believes that the lake creature Misshepeshu is one of his manifestations, that Fleur Pillager and Nanapush are his agents, and that it is Satan, not Napoleon Morrissey, that she kills on the lake shore. She also seems to think that Satan is the father of her child, Marie, and—in the form of the lake monster—of Fleur's child, Lulu.

As Sister Leopolda, Pauline continues her battle with Satan in "Saint Marie" in *Love Medicine.* Marie, however, affirms in "Saint Marie" and "Flesh and Blood" that the devil is in Sister Leopolda and loves her best. Marie does not believe he has touched the abandoned child June Morrissey in "The Beads."

Scranton Roy. Adoptive father of Matilda Roy; father of Augustus Roy I and grandfather of Augustus Roy II in *The Antelope Wife.*

In chapter 1, Scranton Teodorus Roy is born in a small Pennsylvania community to a Quaker father and poet mother. As a young man, he is stung by the scorn of a traveling drama-troupe woman, follows her west, and enlists in the U.S. Cavalry at Saint Paul, Minnesota. Farther west, his company attacks an Ojibwa village (probably in autumn). Surprised by his sudden hatred, Scranton kills two children and an old woman. He sees a dog fleeing into the open spaces west of the Otter Tail River (i.e., Dakota territory) with a baby tied to its back, and he follows them. After three days, Scranton is finally able to approach the dog and remove the child, a girl. He can find nothing to feed her and ultimately stops her crying by putting her to his nipple. The three continue farther into the wilderness until, somewhere on the Great Plains, Scranton stops and builds a sod house. One morning as the child is sucking, Scranton's milk lets down, and she is fed. He names his adopted daughter Matilda after his mother.

An educated man who writes poetry, Scranton apparently teaches Matilda to write. When she is six, she becomes fast friends with the young schoolteacher,

Peace McKnight. At Matilda's request, Scranton lets Peace stay at their house, and shortly thereafter he makes her his wife. When Peace becomes pregnant, however, she refuses to sleep with him, especially after her illness with a fever. While Peace is ill, Scranton experiences another loss. One morning, there is no Matilda in the bed beside Peace, only a note indicating that the seven-year-old has gone with her mother, who came for her in the night. Peace dies after giving birth to their son, Augustus. Scranton revives the unbreathing child and puts him to his breast. Augustus may die shortly after his own son (also named Augustus) is born, because in chapter 23 Scranton raises Augustus II alone.

Many years later, Scranton falls ill and is visited by the spirit of the old woman he killed. After a hundred days of fever and seizures, he offers to find the woman's village and try to make amends. Taking his grandson, Scranton makes his way east with supplies and finds the remnant of villagers, now on a reservation. Here, Scranton experiences yet another loss. Augustus falls in love with a young Ojibwa woman, Zosie Shawano, the great-great-granddaughter of the woman Scranton killed. Sometime after his marriage to Zosie, Augustus disappears without a trace.

Scranton Roy's father. Intelligent Quaker who establishes a small community in Pennsylvania in chapter 1 of *The Antelope Wife*. Scranton rejects his father's pacifist ways when he enlists in the U.S. Cavalry.

Scranton Roy's mother. Reclusive woman named Matilda who writes poetry in chapter 1 of *The Antelope Wife*. When Scranton disappears into the west, his mother burns her poetry and dies in mourning. Scranton names his adopted daughter after her.

Senior Citizens, residents of the. Nosy neighbors of Marie Kashpaw and Lulu Lamartine. Lulu is their favorite topic of gossip and Josette Bizhieu their chief informant. They seem to be the "we" narrating chapters 1 and 25 of *The Bingo Palace,* in which Lulu steals the Wanted poster of her son Gerry Nanapush and, after refusing to cooperate with the marshals looking for Gerry, is arrested for that theft. As the marshals lead Lulu away, these residents join in Lulu's old-lady trill, a victory yell.

Seraphica, Sister. Tall "dreamy" nun at Saint Catherine's school in Argus who plays the organ and directs choir. In chapter 10 of *The Beet Queen,* Mary Adare says that Sister Seraphica is to be Dot Adare's second-grade teacher.

Shawano, first. Referred to in the headnote to part 3 of *The Antelope Wife* as the great-grandson of Sounding Feather. He is presumably the same person as the original Shawano, below.

Shawano, original

Shawano, original. Windigo man whom the long-ago Shawano brothers accept into their family in the north, in chapter 17 of *The Antelope Wife.* (See also **Windigo stranger.**) He is presumably the same person as the first Shawano, above. There is some evidence that this original Shawano may also be Shesheeb of chapter 3: both are windigos; the clan begins to be called Shawano shortly after Shesheeb's capture; and the people are still living in the north in both accounts.

Shawano brothers. Shawano family members who long ago in the far north accept the "original" Shawano, a windigo, into their family, according to chapter 17 of *The Antelope Wife.*

Shawano family. Clan name of the "south-looking" people in *The Antelope Wife,* as well as surname of certain families within that clan. (The name means "south" or "people of the south.")

The *clan* name Shawano begins about the time of the windigo **Shesheeb** and **Shesheeb's sister,** who marries the Frenchman **Henri Laventure** (chapter 3). Shesheeb may be the man referred to as "original Shawano" and "first Shawano" (see **Shawano, original;** and **Shawano, first**). Shesheeb's people originally live in the north, probably Canada, but after Shesheeb is captured, they begin migrating south and are called "those people who had just left for the south," or "Shawano." Virtually all of the Indian characters in *The Antelope Wife* are descendants of this south-looking people, including the **Roy family** and probably the **Whiteheart Beads family.** Forebears of this clan in the generations prior to Shesheeb include the **Ivory Coast slave** and **Magid;** Magid's father, **Everlasting;** and the great-grandmother of the first Shawano, **Sounding Feather.**

The Shawano *family* surname is used by several family units:
(1) the **Shawano brothers,** who take in the original Shawano.
(2) **Shawano the younger,** who marries **Blue Prairie Woman.** Their descendants include **Mary (I) Shawano and Josephette (Zosie I) Shawano; Mary (II) Shawano** and **Zosie (II) Shawano Roy; Aurora Roy** and **Rozina (Rozin) Roy Whiteheart Beads Shawano; Deanna Whiteheart Beads;** and **Cally Whiteheart Beads Roy.** Blue Prairie Woman's (and possibly Shawano the younger's) descendants also include **Matilda Roy** and perhaps, through Matilda, **Sweetheart Calico.**
(3) **Shawano father of Mary (II) and Zosie (II).**
(4) **Shawano the ogitchida** and his children, **Frank Shawano, Puffy Shawano, Klaus Shawano,** and **Cecille Shawano.**

The Shawano clan is fundamentally Ojibwa. But as Cally Roy says in chapter

11, it is like "mixed party nuts," characterized by a wide mixture of bloods, including African (chapters 2, 3, and 16), French (chapters 3 and 16), Irish (chapters 11 and 18), German, Cree, Winnebago, Lakota, and Brazilian (chapter 16). Shawano ancestry includes both windigos (chapters 1, 3, 6, 13, 17, and 18) and deer or antelope people (chapters 1 and 6; also chapter 2). Present-day members of the clan represent all walks of life, from professors and politicians to blue-collar workers and alcoholic bums (chapter 11).

Shawano father of Mary (II) and Zosie (II). According to chapter 11 of *The Antelope Wife,* he is the cousin of Shawano the ogitchida, Klaus and Frank Shawano's father. Thus when Zosie's daughter Rozin marries Frank, she is marrying a kinsman.

Shawano the ogitchida. Father of Frank and Klaus Shawano; cousin of the Shawano father of Mary (II) and Zosie (II) (chapter 11) in *The Antelope Wife.* In chapter 13 Shawano is referred to as the ogitchida (i.e., "warrior") because he fights on the German front in World War II. After returning home in 1945, Shawano discusses with *clansmen* who are meeting in the house of *his uncle* how to avenge the death of *his cousin.* That night he kidnaps the young German prisoner of war Klaus, who will bake the blitzkuchen and subsequently be adopted into the clan.

Shawano the younger. Second husband of Blue Prairie Woman in *The Antelope Wife.* After the deer husband of Apijigo Bakaday is killed and her name is changed to Blue Prairie Woman in chapter 6, she marries the human man Shawano, even though he is descended from windigos. The couple spends winters away from the village, on the trapline with *Shawano's father* and *brothers.* When the U.S. Cavalry attacks the village in chapter 1 (probably in autumn), Shawano the younger is away harvesting wild rice. When he returns, he and his wife become "windigo" (i.e., insatiable) lovers. On his next return after a winter of trapping, however, his pregnant wife is indifferent to him.

Shawnee Ray Toose. Daughter of Irene Toose; mother of Redford Toose; lover of Lyman Lamartine and Lipsha Morrissey in *The Bingo Palace.* Chapters 1 and 2 introduce us to Shawnee Ray. After her father dies in a threshing accident, her mother remarries and moves to Minot. The teenage Shawnee Ray becomes pregnant, presumably by Lyman, and remains on the reservation to finish high school, living with Zelda Kashpaw, Lyman's half sister. Zelda is trying to promote a marriage between Shawnee Ray and Lyman. Although Shawnee Ray does not really object to the idea, she does have plans of her own. Chapters 7 and 9 reveal that she is going to the local junior college and has a

Shawnee Ray Toose

dream of creating Chippewa-accented fashion designs and ultimately opening a boutique.

When Lipsha Morrissey returns to the reservation in chapter 2, he sees Shawnee Ray dancing at the powwow and immediately falls in love with her. In chapter 4 he finally gets the courage to ask her out. On their way to a restaurant in Canada, they are stopped at the border and mistakenly taken into custody for drug possession. Lyman arrives to clear up the misunderstanding. In chapter 7 Shawnee Ray encounters Lipsha at the laundry. They go for a drive with some friends but are dropped off at a motel where they make love for the first time. Shawnee Ray borrows money from Lipsha to help her launch her fashion design enterprise.

The rivalry between Lipsha and Lyman for Shawnee Ray's love is intense, as is clear in chapters 8, 11, 13, and 14. The ceremonial pipe of Nector Kashpaw, who is Lipsha's foster father and Lyman's actual father, becomes a kind of symbol of that rivalry. Shawnee Ray is uncomfortable with the pressure to decide between her two suitors. She continues to be attracted to Lipsha but in chapter 9 tells him to give her some time so she can get her bearings. Lipsha honors her request for a short time, but then drives to Zelda's house to see her while Zelda and Redford are gone. They argue, Lipsha begs for another chance, and they make love on Shawnee Ray's bedroom floor. In chapter 10 Shawnee Ray feels confused. She had pictured herself marrying a stable man like Lyman, but she is in love with the still-directionless Lipsha. With the aid of Lipsha's money, she decides to get away from Zelda for a while, to stay with her sisters in the bush and try to make some money on the powwow circuit.

In her efforts to raise money for college, where she wants to study art, in chapter 14 Shawnee Ray enters a big powwow in Montana, leaving Redford with her sisters, Tammy and Mary Fred Toose. Since Lyman and Zelda do not approve of this arrangement, Lyman files a court order for custody of Redford, and in chapter 15 Zelda and the authorities come take him from his aunts by force. At the powwow in chapter 16, as Shawnee Ray prepares for the final dance, the jingle dress, she reminisces about her father.

After placing second in the powwow, Shawnee Ray returns to Zelda's house in chapter 17. She violently rejects Lipsha's marriage proposal, but she is most angry with Lyman because of the court order. She suggests that Lyman may not really be the father of Redford and says that she will never marry him. When Zelda's daughter, Albertine Johnson, comes to visit, she takes Shawnee Ray's side against Zelda. Privately, Shawnee Ray tells Albertine she is going to leave Zelda for good. In chapter 20, Albertine emphasizes to her friend Lipsha that he should leave Shawnee Ray alone until he gets his own life in order.

In chapter 22 Shawnee Ray regains custody of Redford, leaves the reservation, and enrolls at the university. Lyman concedes the failure of his pact with Zelda in chapter 23 by leaving Nector's pipe on her kitchen counter. That winter, in chapter 26 Shawnee Ray and Redford are living in poorly insulated university housing. The morning after a January blizzard, she and Redford play in the snow, and then while he sleeps, she works on a ribbon shirt for Lipsha—interest on the money he has loaned her. As she sews the shirt, she thinks of Lipsha with an ache and considers buying two wedding bands. The scene is made poignant by knowledge that the reader, but not Shawnee Ray, possesses: Lipsha is snowbound in the blizzard and, as the book ends, his fate is uncertain.

Shawn Nanapush. Daughter of Gerry Nanapush and Dot Adare. According to "Scales" in *Love Medicine,* Shawn is conceived in the visiting room of a state prison, where Gerry is held for assault and repeated escapes. Gerry escapes once while Dot is pregnant with Shawn. He is recaptured but escapes again in order to be present at Shawn's birth in October 1980. Four years later, Dot and Shawn seem to be living in Canada, where the newly escaped Gerry is headed so that he can see them in "Crossing the Water."

As a thirteen-year-old in *Tales of Burning Love,* Shawn is athletic and tomboyish, and a much kinder, easier child than Dot had been at the same age. The summer after Shawn's thirteenth birthday, Dot marries Jack Mauser without divorcing Gerry. From brief references in "A Wedge of Shade" [3] and "Trust in the Known" [5], as well as their teasing and amiable jousting in "The Meadowlark" [7], it is clear that Shawn and Jack like each other. Even after Dot leaves Jack and moves with Shawn into an apartment in "Jack's House" [9], he wants to see Shawn in "February Thaw" [40]. But Shawn's affection for Jack does not come close to the attachment and longing she feels for her own father, Gerry. We learn in "Funeral Day" [23] that she keeps a framed photograph of Gerry on her bureau.

In his prison cell in chapter 21 of *The Bingo Palace,* Gerry also longs to be with his daughter. When, newly escaped from prison, he visits her early one January morning in "Smile of the Wolf" [38] in *Tales of Burning Love,* Shawn is overcome with emotion. In her seeming small talk, she tells Gerry about her neighbor's snowmobile and where the key is hidden. When marshals break down the door looking for him, he has already escaped again, presumably on the snowmobile. When two of the marshals question her, Shawn denies that she has seen her father and pretends that she and her mother are afraid of him.

Shesheeb. Court-convicted windigo brother of Henri Laventure's oldest wife in chapter 3 of *The Antelope Wife.* Shesheeb is an Ojibwa whose people live

Shesheeb

in the north, but after he is caught they begin moving south. Since the clan begins to be called Shawano after Shesheeb's capture, Shesheeb may be the man referred to as the "original Shawano" in chapter 17. Both are windigos, and in both stories the people are still living in the north.

Shesheeb's sister. Oldest wife of the Frenchman Henri Laventure and forebear of Rozina Roy in chapter 3 of *The Antelope Wife*.

Shumway, Mrs. Dot Adare's first-grade teacher at Saint Catherine's school in Argus who is forced into the classroom toy box in chapter 10 of *The Beet Queen* by a raging woman she does not know. She calls the police, and Officer Ronald Lovchik discovers that Mary Adare is the culprit and that she had been motivated by Dot's lie. Mrs. Shumway is also present at the Christmas pageant in chapter 11.

Sioux vet. Old war veteran who talks with Lipsha Morrissey in the border-town hotel in "Crossing the Water" in *Love Medicine.* He says he was at Iwo Jima with Ira Hayes. When he accidentally hits Lipsha in the head with an empty Old Grand Dad bottle, Lipsha has a vision that his father is about to escape from prison. Lipsha recalls the incident in chapter 14 of *The Bingo Palace,* although there he remembers the bottle as a wine bottle.

Sita Kozka Bohl Tappe. Daughter of Pete and Fritzie Kozka. Sita is introduced in chapters 1 and 2 of *The Beet Queen* (1932) as a twelve- or thirteen-year-old living in her parents' house, which is attached to their butcher shop in Argus. She is beautiful, although almost frail, and, as the Kozkas' only child, she is accustomed to having her own way. When her eleven-year-old cousin, Mary Adare, comes to live with them, Sita dislikes having to share with Mary her room, her parents, and, especially, her best friend Celestine James. Sita's criticism of Fritzie's smoking is mentioned in chapter 3. In chapter 4 (1941) Sita is twenty-one or twenty-two and wants to move away from Argus. Two incidents precipitate her leaving: her parents' move to the Southwest for Fritzie's health and Mary's hands' mysteriously glowing in the dark one night. Sita moves to Fargo to work in the DeLendrecies department store, hoping to marry a well-off young professional.

Nine years later, in chapter 5, Sita is still living in Fargo and modeling for DeLendrecies. She has had a three-year affair with a married doctor and is now (1950) dating Jimmy Bohl, who operates a steak house in Argus. She receives a letter, addressed to her parents but forwarded to her, from Catherine Miller, the woman who had raised Mary Adare's kidnapped infant brother, now named Jude Miller. Sita goes to Minneapolis for Jude's February 18 ordination, but she has no contact with the Millers. While in Minneapolis, she redeems from a pawn shop the garnet necklace of her aunt, Mary's mother Adelaide. Back in Fargo, she writes to Mrs. Miller, but never mails the letter, and she marries Jimmy Bohl. As a cruel prank, Jimmy's brother and cousins abduct her from the wedding dance and deposit her near a bar on the Indian reservation.

The year 1953 is eventful for Sita. In chapter 7 she is operating The Poopdeck Restaurant in Argus with her husband, Jimmy. When they divorce, in the settlement Sita gets their house and the restaurant, which she remodels and reopens as Chez Sita, her attempt at creating a fine restaurant. The grand opening of Chez Sita is a near-disaster, however, and business soon dwindles to nothing. Because of several cases of food poisoning, the state health inspector visits the restaurant, and he and Sita begin dating. We learn from accounts at the end of chapter 7 and the beginning of chapter 8 that Sita marries the health inspector, a man named Louis Tappe. She sells the restaurant, he sells his house and takes a job as county extension agent, and they move to the big house in Blue Mound that Jimmy Bohl had built. As chapter 8 opens, Sita is bordering on a nervous breakdown. When her cousin Karl Adare shows up in her garden, she imagines that he steals her jewelry and hallucinates that he sinks down into the earth. In chapter 9, Wallace Pfef blames Mary Adare for Sita's mental problems.

At some unspecified time, as recorded in chapter 10, Louis has Sita committed to a mental hospital. She has decided that she is unable to speak, and the psychiatrists and nurses insist that Louis must stop humoring her. After spending only one night as roommate to a self-proclaimed cannibal, Sita is "cured." The next morning she can speak. (The dating of this incident is problematic, because the TV programming while Sita is in the hospital suggests a date of 1968 or later, but the chapter 12 reference to her hospital stay indicates a pre-1965 date.)

In chapter 12 Wallace invites Louis and Sita to Dot's eleventh-birthday party in January 1965. Sita, still high-strung, has thinned and aged since her stay in the hospital, and her condition has been a strain on Louis. At the party Sita is hit in the face by a flying birthday cake.

By 1972, chapter 13, Sita's husband Louis is dead. (Sita would be in her early fifties.) One night Celestine has a dream about Sita, which Mary interprets as meaning that Sita is ill and is asking for Celestine. The two women, along with Mary's dog, drive to Sita's house in Blue Mound. At first they find little evidence of Sita's illness, but then they discover the orange pills hidden in a canister of flour, painkillers or tranquilizers to which she has become addicted. Because Sita continues to grow weaker, Celestine and Mary stay for weeks, even though Sita does not want them there.

Sita Kozka Bohl Tappe

One night, Mary accidentally hits Sita in the head with a brick. After this incident, Sita loses the use of her left arm and continues to weaken, but she has less pain. She stays in the basement, sleeping on the pool table and hiding her few remaining pills in the toilet tank. On the morning of the Beet Festival, while Celestine and Mary are gone, Sita swallows the remaining half-bottle of pills, dresses carefully, fixes her hair and face, and puts on Adelaide's garnet necklace. When Celestine and Mary return to take her to the parade, Sita is standing in the front yard, propped up in the yew bushes, dead. Since the funeral home is closed for the parade, the two women load Sita's body into the passenger seat of their truck and take her with them to the fairgrounds. On the way, in a scene of macabre humor, Sita is greeted by her former suitor, Officer Lovchik, and is accidentally included in the Beet Parade. Celestine and Mary leave her body in the truck while they attend the festival.

Sita continues to outlive her own death in chapters 14 and 15. In response to her twenty-year-old letter to Catherine Miller, which Celestine had found and mailed in chapter 13, Jude Miller comes to Argus on the day of the Beet Festival in chapter 14. Then in chapter 15 Karl Adare rests in the truck for a few minutes and speaks to Sita, not realizing that she is dead. After the Beet Queen ceremonies are over, in chapter 16 Mary takes Sita's body to the funeral parlor.

Skinners. Desperately poor family about whom Marie Kashpaw dreams in "Resurrection" in *Love Medicine.* They had lived a mile up the trail from Marie and Nector's house and used to eat her cast-out potato peelings.

Skunk. Appears to Lipsha Morrissey twice in *The Bingo Palace.* When Lipsha goes on a vision quest beside Matchimanito Lake in chapter 17, one morning he wakes to find a large female skunk sleeping on top of him. When she opens her mouth Lipsha sees her pointy teeth and hears the words, "This ain't real estate." She then smiles and sprays him. The next night in his bed, in chapter 20 Lipsha again sees the skunk, who repeats her admonition and sends him a vision of what it would mean to commercialize sacred Pillager land.

Several details seem to connect the skunk to Fleur Pillager: her proximity to Matchimanito, her respect for the land, her gender, and her toothy smile, reminiscent of the dangerous Pillager grin. Furthermore, Fleur is a channel for animal spirits. In chapter 11 of this novel, she takes the form and voice of a bear. In chapter 3 of *Tracks* Nanapush hears all the Manitous of the woods speak through her—Turtle, Loon, Otter, and others.

Slick Lamartine. Elder brother to Henry and Beverly Lamartine in "Lulu's Boys" in *Love Medicine.* The three brother are inseparable in high school and all go into the military, but Slick is killed at boot camp.

Small Bird. Sister of Fleur Pillager. Also known as Bineshii and Josette, she dies of consumption in chapter 1 of *Tracks*. She is mentioned again in chapter 9 of *Tracks* and chapter 3 of *The Bingo Palace*.

Sophie Morrissey. Middle child of Bernadette Morrissey; sister of Clarence and Philomena Morrissey. According to Pauline Puyat in chapter 4 of *Tracks,* Sophie at age fourteen is tall and beautiful, but lazy and slovenly. Both she and her younger sister have dainty French ways, the product apparently of their mother's education in Quebec. When Pauline comes to stay with the Morrisseys, she kicks the sisters in her nightmare-ridden sleep. In revenge for Eli Kashpaw's rejection of her, Pauline uses a love medicine to bewitch Sophie and Eli into making love while Pauline's spirit enters Sophie's body. Bernadette beats Sophie and tries to send her away from the reservation, but she escapes and goes to Fleur Pillager's house. There Fleur casts a spell on her that roots her to the ground, rigid, for two days. Sophie's brother, Clarence, steals a statue of the Virgin Mary to break the spell, and Pauline sees the statue cry frozen tears. In chapter 5 Clarence avenges Eli's liaison with his sister by shaving the head of Eli's mother, Margaret Kashpaw.

Sophie grows thinner and wilder in chapter 6 and is seen dancing with Philomena. In chapter 7 she marries Izear Lazarre, who already has six children by a previous wife whom he is rumored to have killed. Sophie's new family, along with Clarence and his Lazarre wife, move into Bernadette's house. Disgusted with their behavior, Bernadette takes Philomena and the foster child Marie (Pauline's baby fathered by Sophie's uncle Napoleon) and moves to town, after which the once-prosperous Morrissey household quickly deteriorates into a slum. Sophie is soon pregnant with the first of her many children. As Bernadette grows weak from consumption, in chapter 8 the slovenly Sophie Lazarre is increasingly the caretaker of her cousin Marie, who grows up thinking she is a Lazarre. (This raises the question of whether Sophie is either the **Old drunk woman** in "The Beads" in *Love Medicine,* whom Marie thinks is her mother, or **Marie Lazarre's aunt** in "Saint Marie.")

Sorrow. Female dog who as a puppy nurses at Blue Prairie Woman's breasts in chapter 1 of *The Antelope Wife*. She is a puppy of the bitch who carries Blue Prairie Woman's baby (Matilda Roy) on her back (chapter 6). Sorrow follows Blue Prairie Woman in her search for this lost child and becomes the food that enables Matilda to survive. One of her descendants is Almost Soup, the dog saved in chapter 8 by Cally Roy, Blue Prairie Woman's great-great-granddaughter.

Sorrow's mother. Bitch who carries the infant Matilda Roy into the open spaces west of the Otter Tail River in chapter 1 of *The Antelope Wife*. When

Sorrow's mother

she flees the village, the bitch is young and swift and according to chapter 6, has **six fat puppies.** Of these puppies, only Sorrow survives. One of the soldiers attacking the village, Scranton Roy, follows the fleeing dog. After three days he is able to lure her with food and remove the baby from her back. The bitch follows Scranton to the place where he settles on the Great Plains. By the time Matilda is six, this Indian dog may be dead, because a **hound** has taken her place.

Sounding Feather. Great-grandmother of first Shawano. In the headnote to part 3 of *The Antelope Wife,* Sounding Feather dyes feathers in a mixture of copper and her own urine. The final color is affected by her treatment of **her mother, her child, her sisters,** and **her husband,** and she is frightened by the purity of the blue created after she has done wrong.

Stacy Cuthbert. Woman who kills a rival by hitting her with a shovel. Lipsha Morrissey recalls the incident as he is musing on the "beautiful sickness" of love in chapter 14 of *The Bingo Palace.*

Standing in a Stone. Son of Nanapush and White Beads, mentioned in chapter 9 of *Tracks.* His Indian name is Asainekanipawit, and he is also known as Thomas. He apparently dies when still a child, along with his sister, Red Cradle.

Stan Mahng. Young Indian who commits suicide over a lost love. After his **girlfriend** leaves him, marries **another man,** and has **Stan's baby,** Stan visits them and holds his son. Then he goes to Matchimanito Lake, cuts a hole in the ice, ties stones to his feet, and slips through the hole into the freezing lake. Lipsha Morrissey recalls Stan when he is himself despairing over his unrequited love for Shawnee Ray Toose in chapter 14 of *The Bingo Palace.* Stan may have been a cousin of Fleur Pillager or Xavier Toose, because we are told that his cousin's house was on Matchimanito Lake.

State health inspector. See **Louis Tappe.**

State trooper. Man Gerry Nanapush is said to have killed on the Pine Ridge reservation in "Scales" in *Love Medicine.* While Gerry's son, Lipsha Morrissey, is driving him to Canada after his 1984 escape, Lipsha asks his father whether he really killed the trooper. Gerry apparently replies, but Lipsha refuses to tell readers Gerry's answer.

Stationmaster. Former employee of Jack Mauser who does not recognize him when he rushes into the Fargo train station in "Funeral Day" [23] in *Tales of Burning Love.*

Statue of the Virgin at Argus. Near-human Italian stone statue given to Our Lady of the Wheat Priory in *Tales of Burning Love,* which in "The Stone Virgin" [44] falls on Jack Mauser, nearly crushing him. An *anonymous benefactor* donates the money for the statue (this donor is also mentioned in "A Letter to the Bishop" [45]). An *Italian stonecutter* rough-cuts the statue, and an *Italian sculptor* fine-carves it. The *sculptor's wife* had recently lost a baby, their long awaited *son,* and he carves the statue with an expression of repressed passion and wild grief.

Although not a character in the usual sense, the stone Virgin does appear to kiss Jack, to have an independent will, and later to sweat blood. Jack recognizes in her face all the women he has ever loved, and he believes that the accident fulfills Sister Leopolda's prophecy in "Night Prayer" [6] that he would be crushed by a woman, who would "snap his bones" and "throttle him with her kiss." The Virgin is gracious, however, for Jack is miraculously unharmed. The miracles surrounding the statue are detailed by Father Jude Miller in "A Letter to the Bishop" [45].

Statue of the Virgin on the reservation. Plaster statue that seems to come to life and weep frozen tears in chapter 4 of *Tracks.* Only Pauline Puyat sees the tears.

Strict aunt in Grand Forks. Relative to whom Bernadette Morrissey tries to send her daughter Sophie after Sophie's sexual encounter with Eli Kashpaw in chapter 4 of *Tracks.* Sophie, however, never leaves the reservation because she jumps off the cart and runs to Fleur Pillager's cabin.

Superior. Mother nun of the Sacred Heart Convent in *Tracks.* In chapter 6 (1918–1919) she seems to think that Pauline Puyat is a saintly novice and is pleased when Pauline says (falsely) that she has no Indian blood. Superior is troubled, however, by Pauline's overly severe asceticism. She dresses Pauline's burned hands in chapter 8 and helps to feed her while she is recovering. When Pauline takes her vows as a nun, she draws from Superior's hand a scrap of paper declaring her new name: Leopolda.

Susy. Hitchhiking girl whom Henry Junior and Lyman Lamartine take home to Chicken, Alaska, during their long summer trip in "The Red Convertible" in *Love Medicine.* Her family befriends the brothers, who stay with them for a while before returning home.

Swede Johnson. First husband of Zelda Kashpaw; father of Albertine. As recounted in "The World's Greatest Fishermen" in *Love Medicine,* he impregnates and then marries Zelda, joins the Army, goes AWOL from boot camp,

Swede Johnson

and disappears. Albertine knows him only by his pictures. Eli recalls feeding him and Zelda skunk for dinner. Swede is also mentioned in chapter 3 of *The Bingo Palace.*

Sweetheart Calico. Present-day "antelope wife" of the novel *The Antelope Wife;* lover of Klaus Shawano. We are not told her true name. Klaus calls her Ninimoshe, which means "my sweetheart" and is used to refer to a cross-cousin of the opposite sex, that is, a different-clan cousin whom one can marry. (In chapter 15, however, Klaus guesses that he and Sweetheart Calico may be from the same clan, possibly suggesting that their relationship is taboo.) Klaus's family in Minneapolis sometimes calls her Auntie Klaus, but most often Sweetheart Calico, for the cloth Klaus uses to capture and bind her (chapter 11).

Sweetheart Calico may be descended from the Shawano deer-antelope women Blue Prairie Woman and Matilda Roy. Jimmy Badger's story in chapter 2 about Sweetheart Calico's ancestor, the girl who lived with the antelope, is congruous with the stories of both Matilda Roy in chapter 1 and Blue Prairie Woman (as Apijigo Bakaday) in chapter 6. This association is strengthened toward the end of the novel when we learn in chapter 18 that Sweetheart Calico is the owner of Blue Prairie Woman's necklace of blue beads, which Matilda is wearing when she joins the antelope herd.

Sweetheart Calico remembers running beside her mother in chapter 5. In chapter 21, she recalls being knocked into a horse pasture by a speeding car at age nine.

Klaus first encounters Sweetheart Calico and her three daughters in chapter 2 at a powwow in Elmo, Montana, where he has a trader's booth. Several details in the initial description of these women suggest their connection with the antelope people: their doeskin clothing, their effortless movement, and the mother's feathers from the red-tailed hawk, the bird that follows the antelope. Klaus attracts their attention by flicking a piece of sweetheart calico. He then tricks the girls into taking a nap, gives the mother a soporific tea in his van, and when she falls asleep, kidnaps her. When they stop in Bismarck, North Dakota, she realizes that he has trapped her. She fights to get free and breaks her teeth on the edge of the bathtub, but Klaus takes her home to Minneapolis. At night, he sometimes ties her to himself with a strip of sweetheart calico cloth. Making excuses for his possessive love, Klaus blames her wiles. Klaus and others refer to her as his wife, but this designation may simply reflect Klaus's rationalization for a relationship that is essentially bondage. Although he appears not to believe Jimmy Badger's account of her ancestry, Klaus continues to think of Sweetheart Calico as his antelope woman (see chapters 2, 4, 10, 15, and 21).

In Minneapolis, Sweetheart Calico watches television, dials phone numbers all over the state of Montana, eats junk food, drinks, and even (according to Klaus) tries to kill him with sex (chapter 2). What she does not do is talk. From the time Klaus meets her at the powwow, through her captivity, she says nothing. Klaus records her thoughts, but these are only his subjective interpretations. (A fairly elaborate example of Klaus's reading meaning into her expressions and gestures appears in chapter 4.)

Over the next several years, Sweetheart Calico lives a yo-yo existence. According to chapter 5, she keeps trying to escape the city, but is unable to do so. Chapter 11 notes that she walks sometimes for days, then returns with a pitiful, baffled look and sleeps for a week. Although she leaves Klaus again and again, she keeps coming back. His need, like the calico cloth, has tied her to a stake in the Minnesota soil (chapter 5); in his eyes she sees only an "ungated fence" (chapter 19); and she feels that she is "drowning" in him (chapter 18).

Our knowledge of Sweetheart Calico's life in the city is sketchy and the chronology is unclear. In chapter 3 Rozina Roy sees her begging for money and eating a pastry in front of the bakery belonging to Klaus's brother Frank Shawano. Rozin says that Sweetheart Calico drives Klaus crazy and that he disappears for four years, leaving her behind for his family to take care of. Cally Roy says in chapter 11 that Klaus and Sweetheart Calico both disappear for four years and that when Klaus returns, he has become a drunk and a bum. Thirteen years after the day Rozin sees her begging in front of Frank's bakery, Sweetheart Calico is living in rooms above the shop with Frank and his sister, Cecille.

Sometime between Sweetheart Calico's arrival in Minneapolis and Klaus's final return as a bum, while she is still living with him off and on, the two take a trip to Hawaii in chapter 4, using tickets given to them by Richard Whiteheart Beads. But on this ill-fated trip, the couple is shadowed by two government agents, who ultimately arrest Klaus, mistaking him for Richard. This incident is apparently the beginning of the end of their relationship, since a year later Klaus insists that Richard is responsible for his losing Sweetheart Calico. (Klaus seems to hint in chapters 4 and 10 that he thinks Sweetheart Calico and Richard are lovers.)

Another incident that takes place sometime before Sweetheart Calico moves in with Frank and Cecille, probably after the Hawaii trip, is alluded to in chapter 5. There is apparently an explosion where she is staying, and she is thrown through the window into the snow, covered with a melted plastic shower curtain. Street people take her to a shelter and clothe her.

When the eighteen-year-old Cally Roy moves to Minneapolis in chapter 11, Sweetheart Calico is already living in the rooms above the bakery. Cally is

Sweetheart Calico

unnerved by the silent "Auntie Klaus," with her fixed stare and jagged grin, fearing that this strange woman wants to steal her. Sweetheart Calico, however, seems to see Cally as a possible mode of escape. She wants the younger woman to join her on her multi-day wanderings, which Cally will not do. One day Klaus, now a street bum, walks into the bakery, speechless with thirst. Sweetheart Calico, in a kind of "savage mercy," brings him a cup of water. Their eyes lock as he drinks, and afterward they walk out the door with arms around each other. If the accounts in chapters 11 and 12 are in chronological order, then Sweetheart Calico leaves Klaus after the cup-of-water incident, returns, and leaves again.

Some three or so years after Cally's move to Minneapolis, Frank marries Cally's mother, Rozina Roy, in chapter 16. Both Sweetheart Calico and Klaus, who has been sober for four months, attend the wedding. When Richard Whiteheart Beads interrupts the cliffside ceremony and tries to leap from the cliff, Sweetheart Calico lunges forward and helps the Reverend hold onto his legs. As she holds on, she smiles her dreamy, jagged-tooth smile.

The following Christmas, recorded in chapter 18, Sweetheart Calico does not seem to be living at Frank's any longer, but she is present at the family gathering. After dinner, she is in the kitchen as Cally washes dishes. One of Cally's comments as she talks to the silent woman suggests a relationship between Sweetheart Calico and Cally's great-great-grandmother, Blue Prairie Woman. She says that Sweetheart Calico has been to "the other side of the earth" and has seen Cally's namesake, Blue Prairie Woman.

When Cally's grandmother, Zosie Shawano Roy, joins them in the kitchen, the three women drink coffee as Zosie tells the story of Blue Prairie Woman's necklace of northwest trader blue beads. After hearing the story, Cally wants to know more about the beads, and Zosie reveals that Sweetheart Calico is their owner. If Cally wants them, she must trade with the antelope woman. To Cally's astonishment, Sweetheart Calico draws the string of beads from her mouth, where she has been hiding them. These beads are the reason Sweetheart Calico has never spoken. Now, more than fifteen years after being kidnapped, she speaks, offering Cally her terms for trade—the beads in exchange for her freedom. At last Cally agrees to accompany Auntie Klaus on her long ramble through the city, walking north beyond the river. On their walk and through the night as Cally dozes, Sweetheart Calico releases her pent-up words. When Cally wakes before the first light, the antelope woman is gone.

Sweetheart Calico's first sensations of freedom are recorded in chapter 19, but her full freedom requires that Klaus choose to release her. In chapter 20, he makes a decision to do so, and in chapter 21, he carries it out. When he sees her, Sweetheart Calico is not full of antelope life, but walks hesitantly, her once-vivid eyes and hair (see chapter 2), now lifeless. He ties their hands together with the old strip of sweetheart calico. They walk north and west along the river, and finally due west. Where they sleep that night, they see the skeleton of a dog chained to a shed, a mirror of Sweetheart Calico's life-defeating captivity. The next morning they reach the vast open spaces to the west. When Klaus unties the strip of cloth and tells her to go, she does not bound off, as he expects, but wearily makes her way west. Once or twice she attempts to run—leaps and falls—until finally she disappears at the horizon.

Sweetheart Calico's daughters. Polite, demure women who dance with their mother at the Elmo, Montana, powwow in chapter 2 of *The Antelope Wife.* Each girl ties up her hair differently as she dances. The trader Klaus Shawano tricks the girls into taking a nap so that he can kidnap their mother. Sweetheart Calico makes numerous long-distance calls to Montana from Minneapolis, apparently trying to find them. She dreams about them in chapter 5.

According to Jimmy Badger in chapter 2, the women are descended from a girl who lived with the antelope, and they seem to have special powers. After their mother's abduction, they are angry, causing the tribe's luck to change for the worse. Much later, the alcoholic Klaus sees a vision of them in chapter 10. Richard Whiteheart Beads warns Klaus in chapter 15 that the daughters will "get" him for destroying their mother.

Sweetheart Calico's mother. Seemingly an antelope woman. In chapter 5 of *The Antelope Wife,* Sweetheart Calico recalls running beside her.

Sweetheart Calico's sisters. In the alcoholic Klaus Shawano's vision in chapter 10, the twenty-six sisters are antelope women, galloping with Sweetheart Calico and her daughters.

Tammy Toose. Sister of Shawnee Ray and Mary Fred Toose. In chapters 2 and 10 of *The Bingo Palace,* we learn that Tammy and Mary Fred have a drinking problem. In chapter 10, Shawnee Ray misses her sisters, and, to get away from Zelda Kashpaw, she takes her son, Redford, and goes to stay with them for a while. We learn from chapter 14 that Shawnee Ray leaves Redford with Tammy and Mary Fred while she attends a powwow and that Lyman Lamartine, the boy's presumed father, gets a court order to take Redford away from them. When a social worker, the tribal policeman, and Zelda come for Redford in chapter 15, Tammy tries unsuccessfully to turn them away.

Tatro. See **Jewett Parker Tatro.**

Thomas Nanapush. See **Standing in a Stone.**

Three fires people. Term used to refer to Rozina Roy's distant ancestors in chapter 3 of *The Antelope Wife*. (Three Fires was the name of a confederation of three Algonquian tribes, including the Ojibwa.)

Tillie Kroshus. Nanny of John Mauser Jr., infant son of Jack Mauser and Marlis Cook Mauser, hired by Candice Pantamounty in *Tales of Burning Love*. Mrs. Kroshus shows up first in "Memoria" [10] taking care of the baby at Jack's funeral. After the funeral, in "The B & B" [16] she takes John Jr. home to Candice's house. There, in "Funeral Day" [23] she has to deal with a stranger at the door, who claims to be Jack's brother and asks to see the baby and to borrow Candice's car. (The "brother" is actually Jack.) Mrs. Kroshus tries unsuccessfully to outsmart him and escape with the baby. Jack ties her up and steals the car with John Jr. strapped inside. The incident is retold in "Two Front-Page Articles" [37], in which Mrs. Kroshus accuses Jack of faking his own death.

Titus. Bartender in Lyman Lamartine's bingo hall. He brings Lipsha Morrissey a hamburger in chapter 8 of *The Bingo Palace* and warns him to be alert in dealing with Lyman. He is also mentioned as Lipsha's friend and coworker in chapters 14, 20, and 22.

Tol Bayer. Man who has all the symptoms of an alcoholic but never drinks, referred to in chapter 13 of *The Beet Queen*.

Tomahawk factory workers. Reservation inhabitants employed in Lyman Lamartine's tribal business, Anishinabe Enterprises, in "The Tomahawk Factory" in *Love Medicine*. These workers are members of various reservation families and include **Norris Buny, Agnes Deer, Eno Grassman, Bertha Ironcloud, Kyle Morrissey, Billy Nanapush,** and **Felix Pukwan.** See also **Lipsha Morrissey; Lulu Nanapush Morrissey Lamartine; Marie Lazarre Kashpaw;** and **Mary Fred Toose.**

When these workers' employment is threatened because of low-volume sales of their products, an interfamily brawl precipitates a riot in which the workers destroy the factory.

Tom B. Peske. Pilot hired by Wallace Pfef in chapter 14 of *The Beet Queen* to skywrite "Queen Wallacette" at the Beet Queen coronation. Dot Adare herself (that is, Wallacette) is an unexpected passenger on the flight, as recorded in chapters 15 and 16.

Toose. First husband of Irene Toose and father of Shawnee Ray, Mary Fred, and Tammy Toose. We learn in chapter 15 of *The Bingo Palace* that he dies in a threshing accident. It is clear from his daughters' memories of him that they loved and miss him. In chapter 15 the tribal police officer tries to weaken Mary Fred by speaking of her dead father because he knows the memory will sadden her. Before the jingle dance competition of an important powwow in chapter 16, Shawnee Ray remembers that her father helped her learn the steps to this dance, and she recalls an incident from her childhood. When she was eight or nine, her father rubbed the yellow-orange powder of butterfly's wings on her skin, told her to ask the butterfly for help and grace, and then threw her into the air.

Toose family. See **Irene Toose; Mary Fred Toose; Redford Toose; Shawnee Ray Toose; Tammy Toose; Toose;** and **Xavier Albert Toose.**

Tor Grunewald. Employee at Pete Kozka's butcher shop in *Tracks.* In chapter 2 Tor plays cards with Lily Veddar, Dutch James, and Fleur Pillager in the evenings after work. One hot night in August 1913, enraged at Fleur's winnings, Tor participates in an attack on Fleur. The next day the three men take shelter from a tornado in the meat locker, and Pauline locks them in. When they are found several days later, Tor has frozen to death. He reappears in Pauline Puyat's death vision in chapter 6, again playing cards with Fleur.

Twins, beading. Mythical twins in the headnotes to parts 1 and 2 of *The Antelope Wife,* also alluded to in chapter 23, who sew the pattern of the world, one working with light beads, the other with dark. Each tries to add one more bead than her sister, thereby upsetting the balance of the world. In the headnote to part 4, the *second twin* gambles everything for ruby-red whiteheart beads. When *her children* swallow the beads, she pursues them with a knife.

The beading of Zosie Roy, Mary Shawano, and Rozina Roy in chapters 9 and 18 mirrors the pattern-creation of the mythic twins.

Two guys in suits. Large, pony-tailed government agents who shadow Klaus Shawano and Sweetheart Calico on their Hawaii trip and arrest Klaus in chapter 4 of *The Antelope Wife.*

Two Hat. Man under whose window a fox barks. The incident is referred to in chapter 12 of *The Bingo Palace* as possible evidence for the occult doings of Fleur Pillager. The context seems to associate the fox's barking, as well as the appearance of an owl, with Fleur's designation of people to take her place on death's road. Jean Hat, possibly related to Two Hat, had been one of the first to take Fleur's place. See also **Hat family** and **Jean Hat.**

Uncle Chuck

Uncle Chuck. See **Chuck Mauser.**

Unexpected, the. Nanapush's second wife, mentioned in chapters 3 and 9 of *Tracks.* Her sexual desires are said to live up to her name. Her Indian name is Zezikaaikwe.

Veteran. See **Sioux vet.** See other war veterans by their given names, such as **Henry Lamartine Junior** and **Russell Kashpaw.**

Vicki Koob. Social worker who helps take Redford Toose away from Tammy and Mary Fred Toose. In chapter 15 of *The Bingo Palace* she comes with Zelda Kashpaw and tribal police officer Leo Pukwan to the Toose home, where Shawnee Ray Toose has left her son, Redford, while she is away at a powwow competition. The abduction is prompted by a court order secured by Redford's presumed father, Lyman Lamartine, giving him custody. In order to justify what she knows is a questionable action, Koob takes notes on the squalor she sees in the Toose house but chooses to overlook the love.

Vietnamese woman. Bleeding woman whom Henry Lamartine Junior remembers in "A Bridge" in *Love Medicine.* In a cheap hotel in Fargo, Henry, who has recently returned from Vietnam and is now drunk, momentarily confuses Albertine Johnson with the dying woman.

Waldvogel, Mrs. Sita Tappe's elderly roommate in the state mental hospital who believes herself to be a cannibal in chapter 10 of *The Beet Queen.* Mrs. Waldvogel shows Sita photographs of her family—including *her son,* a *baby,* and someone named *Markie*—and implies that she has eaten one of them.

Wallace Pfef. Argus community leader and promoter of the beet industry in *The Beet Queen.* In chapter 9 we learn his full name, Wallace Horst Pfef, and something of his family background and his involvement in the Argus community. To deflect curiosity about the fact that he has never married,

Wallace keeps in his living room a picture of a girl he doesn't know, telling the townsfolk that she is his *"**poor dead sweetheart**."* (She is also referred to obliquely in chapter 6.) In 1952 Wallace attends the Crop and Livestock Convention in Minneapolis, as recounted in chapters 6 and 9, where he learns about the sugar beet as a successful cash crop. While there, he meets Karl Adare and has his first homosexual experience. After Karl injures his back, Wallace visits him in the hospital. On his way home Wallace stops beside the road and converses with Ronald Lovchik about his vision of Argus's future wealth from the sugar beet industry.

As chapter 9 continues, over the next year Wallace tries to forget about Karl, although frequenting the butcher shop of Karl's sister, Mary, makes this more difficult. On one of these visits to the butcher shop, Wallace gives Mary and Celestine James invitations to the opening of the restaurant Chez Sita (chapter 7). One spring evening in 1953, Karl phones Wallace and then shows up at Wallace's house the next night. They live together for two weeks, when Karl suddenly disappears. Following a stray dog one evening about a week later, Wallace finds Karl sitting in his underwear in Celestine's backyard. (This dog is mentioned in chapter 13 as later belonging to Wallace.) The following January (1954), stranded in a blizzard, Celestine gives birth to Karl's baby in Wallace's living room. Grateful for his help, Celestine names the baby girl Wallacette, although everyone except Wallace calls her by her nickname, Dot.

As Dot grows up, chapters 9 and 12 record that she and Wallace are close. Once, when she runs away from home, she goes to Wallace's house. In 1964, she invites him to come see her in the school Christmas play and borrows his old bathrobe for her costume. During the performance, dressed in the bathrobe that Karl once wore, Dot is transformed in Wallace's eyes into Karl himself. Thus, when she comes to his house after the ill-fated play, he refuses to let her in. After this incident, Wallace feels guilty, and Dot will hardly speak to him. Finally, when he gives her a party in January for her eleventh birthday, they are friends again.

As a rebellious teenager in chapter 14, Dot at times shares her feelings with Wallace, and he tries in a variety of ways to help her. When she is eighteen, he dreams up the idea that Argus should hold a Beet Festival that will include coronation of a Beet Queen—namely Dot. Wallace throws himself completely into the yearlong preparations, and to ensure Dot's triumph, he rigs the vote. Already exhausted, when Wallace learns that Karl is coming to the festival, he is near collapse. The events the day of the Beet Festival are recorded in chapters 14, 15, and 16. After Dot overhears people gossiping about Wallace's vote-rigging, she takes revenge by dunking him in the dunking tank. When Wallace collapses

Wallace Pfef

in the tank, Karl saves him from drowning. Wallace, Karl, Celestine, and Mary watch from the grandstand as Dot runs away from the Beet Queen coronation and flies off in the skywriting plane. That evening Karl's car is parked in front of Wallace's house.

Wallacette Darlene Adare. See **Dot Adare Nanapush Mauser.**

Wenabojo. Trickster spirit who creates humans. According to chapter 8 of *The Antelope Wife,* Original Dog is Wenabojo's companion. See also **Nanabozho.**

White Beads. Third and most-loved wife of Nanapush, mentioned in chapters 3, 5, and 9 of *Tracks.* Her Indian name is Wapepenasik. They have a daughter, Red Cradle, and a son, Standing in a Stone. By the winter of 1912, White Beads and her children have died, leaving Nanapush with no living family. In chapter 3 Nanapush gives Eli Kashpaw some of her personal belongings for Eli to use as a love gift to Fleur Pillager, and in chapter 5 he tells Eli to fall to his knee and clutch Fleur's skirt, as he himself used to do to soften the heart of White Beads.

Whiteheart Beads family. According to chapter 23 of *The Antelope Wife,* this family name originates because of a blanket decorated with red whiteheart beads that Midass gives to a *pregnant woman.* The woman's son so loves the decoration that he is called *Whiteheart Beads.* The *Whiteheart Beads ancestors* are also referred to in chapter 16. This family is probably part of the Shawano clan, since the original Whiteheart Beads lives in the same village as the Shawanos.
    See **Cally Whiteheart Beads Roy; Deanna Whiteheart Beads; Richard Whiteheart Beads;** and **Rozina (Rozin) Roy Whiteheart Beads Shawano.**

Windigo Dog. Dog or dog spirit that visits the drunken Klaus Shawano after Sweetheart Calico leaves him in *The Antelope Wife.* In chapter 12 Windigo Dog tells Klaus a dirty dog joke about a *Ho Chunk Winnebago dog,* a *Sioux dog,* and an *Ojibwa dog.* In return, Klaus tells him the story of the original Klaus (chapter 13). In chapter 20 Windigo Dog tells Klaus an anti-Indian story about *three dogcatchers* and their *trucks full of dogs.* (Lyman Lamartine tells Lipsha Morrissey another version of this story in chapter 9 of *The Bingo Palace.*) Windigo Dog verbally abuses Klaus, but at least once also gives him advice (chapter 15). He seems also to be the *stray dog* who sacrifices himself to save Klaus's life in chapter 20.
    There may be a connection between Klaus's Windigo Dog and Cally Roy's dog, Almost Soup. "Windigo Dog" is the subtitle of Almost Soup's chapter

8; both dogs are white; and both are ultimately willing to sacrifice themselves for their humans. Nevertheless, there are important differences. Although he narrates two chapters, Almost Soup is a real dog who stays on the reservation when Cally comes to the city. Klaus's Windigo Dog lives in Minneapolis and seems more metaphysical than physical. He is the "bad spirit of hunger" that overpowers Klaus in Sweetheart Calico's absence (chapter 12). As such, he mirrors Klaus's insatiable, destructive passion. When Windigo Dog disappears in chapter 20, Klaus is finally able to master his windigo cravings.

Windigo stranger. Man in Rozina Roy's dream who invites her to pass to the next life through his icy body in chapter 17 of *The Antelope Wife.* (In the myths, Windigo is a bad ice spirit, possessed of an insatiable, often cannibalistic, hunger. Erdrich at times uses this figure to represent any excessive, possessive passion.) See also **Shawano, original.**

Winnebago prisoners. Prison inmates who, according to King Howard Kashpaw in "Crossing the Water" in *Love Medicine,* spread false rumors that King had betrayed the confidences of Gerry Nanapush.

Woman in labor two weeks. Woman in the story Zosie Roy and Mary Shawano tell at Christmas dinner in chapter 18 of *The Antelope Wife.* The woman lives, but *her baby* dies.

Wristwatch. Lulu Nanapush's cousin in the "Love Medicine" story in *Love Medicine.* He is said to wear his dead father's broken wristwatch, which miraculously starts running again the moment he dies after a meal at Lulu's house.

Xavier Albert Toose. Uncle of Shawnee Ray, Mary Fred, and Tammy Toose in *The Bingo Palace.* Xavier is referred to as Shawnee Ray's uncle in chapter 4, apparently her father's brother. According to the "tale of burning love" recounted by Zelda Kashpaw in chapter 5, thirty years after the fact, as a young man the handsome Xavier courts Zelda for a year. She consistently refuses him, because she wants a city life and Xavier is an old-time Indian devoted to the traditional religious ceremonies. One winter night he says he will wait outside until she admits that she loves him. As a result of his freezing vigil, he loses the fingers on one hand. (Without naming Xavier, Dot Mauser recalls this incident in "February Thaw" [40] in *Tales of Burning Love.*) Although Zelda marries two other men, both white, Xavier is the only man she ever loves.

Xavier Albert Toose

Chapter 3 indicates that she names her daughter, Albertine, after Xavier, and in chapter 19 Albertine confronts Zelda with the fact that she has never gotten over him.

In chapter 10 Xavier continues his devotion to traditional Chippewa ways and passes his knowledge on to his nieces. Shawnee Ray has learned from him the Chippewa way to make moccasins. He has studied the old-time medicine and is conducting sweat lodge ceremonies with Mary Fred to cure her alcoholism. It is to Xavier that Lipsha Morrissey and Lyman Lamartine turn when they want to do a vision quest in chapter 14, and in chapter 17, Xavier guides them through the attendant ceremonies. One night, thirty years after her rejection of Xavier, in chapter 23 Zelda realizes that she has never stopped loving him. When she goes to see him the next day, without any exchange of words, he understands and escorts her into his house.

Z

Zelda Kashpaw Johnson Bjornson. Oldest living daughter of Nector and Marie Kashpaw. According to Nector in "The World's Greatest Fishermen" in *Love Medicine,* Zelda is born September 14, 1941. In 1948 ("The Beads") Zelda prevents her sister and brother, Aurelia and Gordie, from hanging their cousin, June Morrissey. That same year, when their grandmother Margaret (Rushes Bear) comes to stay with the family, Margaret bedevils the children and pulls Zelda's hair. In "Flesh And Blood" (1957) Marie takes sixteen-year-old Zelda to show off to Sister Leopolda, Marie's former teacher and adversary. Upon returning from that visit, Zelda finds Nector's letter saying that he is leaving Marie. She hands the letter to her mother, goes after her father—who has just set fire to Lulu Lamartine's house—and brings him home. Zelda's coming to fetch her father is told from Nector's point of view in "The Plunge of the Brave." As Zelda grows up, she is haunted by the memory of her father's burning his lover's house, an incident she views as evidence of the dangers of love. As a result, according to chapters 1, 5, and 23 of *The Bingo Palace,* she closes her heart to love.

While Zelda is still a young woman, the handsome Xavier Toose courts her, as recounted in chapter 5 of *The Bingo Palace.* Zelda is in love with him, but he is a traditional Indian and she wants a city life with a white man. Thus she rejects him, even though he freezes his fingers courting her. (This incident seems to occur not long after Nector's burning of Lulu's house, since chapter 23 of *The Bingo Palace* places both incidents thirty years in the past.) After rejecting Xavier,

Zelda Kashpaw Johnson Bjornson

Zelda is said in chapter 14 to lose her "love-luck." At one point, she aspires to become a nun, but instead allows herself to become pregnant by a white man, Swede Johnson, whom she then marries, as recounted in "The World's Greatest Fishermen" in *Love Medicine*. But before their daughter is born in 1958, Swede goes AWOL from boot camp and is never seen again. According to chapter 3 of *The Bingo Palace,* Zelda names the child Albertine after Xavier, whose middle name is Albert.

"The World's Greatest Fishermen" indicates that after her daughter is born, Zelda moves into a trailer near Marie and Nector and works as a bookkeeper. She blames Albertine for her lost opportunities, and Albertine repays her by being a difficult child, even running away as a teenager. (See also "A Bridge" and chapter 19 of *The Bingo Palace.*) In 1981 Zelda has a new white husband, Bjornson, who has a wheat farm on the edge of the reservation, and her daughter is a responsible young woman in nursing school. But Zelda and Albertine still do not get along. Zelda's conversations with Aurelia in "The World's Greatest Fishermen" and with Lipsha Morrissey in "Love Medicine" also demonstrate that she is as controlling and critical with other members of the family as she is with her daughter.

In *The Bingo Palace* Bjornson is never mentioned, and according to chapters 4 and 9, Zelda is now living at the old Kashpaw house. She has taken in Shawnee Ray Toose and her son, Redford, and is attempting to control their lives. Her ultimate goal is for Shawnee Ray to marry Zelda's half brother, Lyman Lamartine. She is thus an obstacle to Lipsha's courtship of Shawnee Ray, as chapters 9 and 19 make clear. There are hints in chapters 11 and 14 that Zelda is not above manipulating tribal records to achieve her goals: she seems to have written in Lyman as Redford's father, and she may be hindering Lipsha's efforts to become enrolled. To get her to lighten up on Shawnee Ray, in chapter 5 Lipsha slips gin into his Aunt Zelda's tonic water at the bingo parlor. Stimulated by the gin, she tells Lipsha about Xavier and about her rescue of Lipsha as an infant.

In chapter 10 Zelda tries unsuccessfully to keep Shawnee Ray from going to stay with her sisters, Tammy and Mary Fred Toose. When Shawnee Ray is away at a powwow, in chapter 15 Zelda goes with a social worker and tribal police officer to take Redford from the Toose sisters. Shawnee Ray returns to Zelda's house in chapter 17, but in chapter 19 she decides to leave for good. Albertine confronts Zelda about her attempts to control Shawnee Ray, striking a nerve when she asks Zelda about Xavier.

One afternoon after Shawnee Ray leaves, in chapter 23 Zelda finds her father's ceremonial pipe in her kitchen, a token from Lyman conceding that

Zelda Kashpaw Johnson Bjornson

their pact has failed. That night, believing that she is having a heart attack, Zelda thinks back over her life. She regrets her lifelong rejection of passion and realizes that she has always loved Xavier. With the realization comes a kind of repentance. The next day she goes to see Xavier, thinking they will only smoke the pipe together. But when Xavier accepts her into his house, the pipe stays in the car—it appears that they have become lovers at last.

Zelda Kashpaw's brothers. Mentioned without names in chapter 5 of *The Bingo Palace*. See **Eugene Kashpaw** and **Gordie Kashpaw.**

Zosie (I). See **Mary (I) Shawano and Josephette (Zosie I) Shawano.**

Zosie (II) Shawano Roy. Twin sister of Mary (II) Shawano; granddaughter of Blue Prairie Woman; mother of twins Rozina and Aurora Roy in *The Antelope Wife.*

We learn in chapter 3 that Zosie and Mary are the twin daughters of either Mary (I) or Josephette (Zosie I) Shawano, who are the twin daughters of Blue Prairie Woman. They live on an Ojibwa reservation "up north," on an allotment belonging to their mother (chapter 18). (For notes about its location, see **Rozina [Rozin] Roy Whiteheart Beads Shawano.**) According to chapter 18, out of their family of six, the second Zosie and Mary are the sole survivors of a flu epidemic (possibly the epidemic of 1918–1919). They are living with their great-grandmother, Midass, when Augustus Roy II arrives in chapters 18 and 23. Augustus is smitten with the silent but sly Zosie and gives Midass red whiteheart beads in exchange for her.

When Midass dies, Augustus and Zosie move in with Mary, producing a bizarre love triangle. After Zosie learns that her husband is sleeping with her sister, the twins conspire to confuse him. In an effort to keep them straight, Augustus marks Zosie by biting her ear. He later disappears without a trace. Rumor has it that the sisters, true to their windigo Shawano heritage, have eaten him. They are referred to as "murder suspects" in chapter 11. According to chapter 18, from their difficult experiences, the sisters learn to relish hard luck, but the difficulties wear more heavily on Zosie than Mary.

Zosie, now pregnant with twins, sees Blue Prairie Woman in a dream, wearing northwest trader blue beads (chapter 18). Zosie gambles with the spirit of her grandmother, winning both her beads and her two names. Years later, she will give the names to her own granddaughters. (Since the beads later show up in the possession of Sweetheart Calico, Zosie may not win the actual beads, but a vision of their blueness.) Zosie's twins, Rozina and Aurora, are born probably in the 1940s or 1950s. She and Mary raise them together and, according to

Zosie (II) Shawano Roy

chapters 9 and 11, will not tell the girls which of them is the mother. When the girls are five, Aurora dies of diphtheria (chapter 3).

Rozin is apparently still living on her mother's reservation when she marries Richard Whiteheart Beads. When Rozin's twin daughters, Deanna and Cally, are born, according to chapter 11 Zosie and Mary both participate in the naming ceremony. Rozin and her family move to Minneapolis when the girls are five. Zosie and Mary stay on the reservation, but they occasionally come down to baby-sit. Recounting one of these occasions in chapter 6, Cally recalls Zosie's beading and her telling the story of their windigo forebear, Apijigo Bakaday, who married a deer man. Zosie allows the girls to dance naked in the rain, since they are "part deer."

Either Zosie or Mary may be present when Cally saves the dog Almost Soup in chapter 8, because shortly afterward he is transported to their reservation. He is at their house when Rozin and eleven-year-old Cally return to the reservation in chapter 9, following the death of Deanna in March. During the long nights of the following winter, Zosie reads all the summer news. When Cally becomes gravely ill during a February blizzard, Zosie helps care for her, cuts wood for the fire, and shovels snow from the road so the ambulance can get through.

By the time Cally is eighteen, Zosie and Mary have moved to Minneapolis, which they call Mishimin Odaynang, Apple Town. They still spend most summers on the reservation, where they gather teas and bark (chapter 18), and in the fall, Zosie harvests wild rice in a canoe (chapter 17). When Cally wants to move to Minneapolis in chapter 11, Rozin is unable to contact the grandmothers. After Cally comes to stay with Frank Shawano, Zosie and Mary continue to be elusive and Cally manages only one brief phone visit with one of them. One day, however, Zosie walks into Frank's bakery, and Cally gives her a piece of Frank's blitzkuchen.

About two years later, in chapter 14 Rozin moves to Minneapolis to live with her mothers and go to night school. When Rozin marries Frank and Richard shoots himself after the wedding, Rozin isolates herself in her mothers' apartment in chapter 17. Zosie calls her from the hospital to say that Richard has died. When Rozin continues to withdraw, Zosie goes up to the reservation to get Mary, apparently to help heal their daughter.

The following December, in chapter 18 Zosie and Mary join the family for Christmas dinner at Frank and Rozin's apartment. Since Zosie is self-conscious about her appearance, Cally compliments her looks. Zosie participates in the banter at the table, calling Richard's nephew Chook a "windigo boy," discussing death and funerals (including her own), attempting to embarrass Rozin, and responding to Cecille Shawano's accusation that she ate her own husband with

Zosie (II) Shawano Roy

only a "slightly windigo" smile. After dinner, Zosie tells Cally the story of her dream of Blue Prairie Woman and the blue beads. In telling the story, she also reveals that she, not Mary, is Rozin's mother.

Zosie's father. See **Shawano father of Mary (II) and Zosie (II).**

Miscellaneous Minor Characters

Minor characters who do not appear in the alphabetized dictionary are given in **boldface** below. We have divided this portion of the dictionary by novel and have placed the characters into something of a running narrative to help readers see how they fit into the larger story. As would be expected, novels set largely in towns and cities have more of such "extras" than those set primarily on the reservation.

LOVE MEDICINE

When the young Lulu Nanapush is considering going out to Moses Pillager's island in "The Island," Nanapush tells her about Moses's history, including the fact that he stole his cats from an **old Frenchwoman.** Lulu takes Moses both some nickels she has earned scrubbing floors for a **teacher in town** and her smile, which she says has won barley sugar from the **trader.**

On the day she goes to see Sister Leopolda in 1957, in "Flesh and Blood" Marie Kashpaw (and for a while her daughter Aurelia) is watching the **baby** of a **young girl** who lives across the road. While Aurelia is watching the baby, her brother Gordie is out hunting with a **boy down the road,** who is Gordie's friend and whom Aurelia likes. Marie holds onto the baby when she finds her husband Nector's letter saying that he is leaving.

In "The Bridge" an **airport guard** searches Henry Lamartine Junior on his way home from Vietnam in 1973, after the shrapnel in Henry sets off the metal detector. On the streets of Fargo the fifteen-year-old runaway Albertine Johnson sees an **Oriental man,** a **woman in a tiger-skin shirt,** and **two Indian men** dragging a **dazed woman.** A **night clerk** signs Albertine and Henry Junior into the Fargo hotel where they sleep together.

Eight years later Albertine is away at nursing school, and she hears the vacuum cleaner of her **white landlady** while thinking about her dead aunt, June Morrissey ("The World's Greatest Fishermen").

The **clerk at the Rudolph Hotel** in a border town asks Lipsha Morrissey and an old Sioux vet to leave the lobby when he discovers that they are drinking in "Crossing the Water." Just outside the hotel, Lipsha has a small vision predicting his father's prison break.

THE BEET QUEEN

In chapter 1, at the 1932 Orphans' Picnic in Minneapolis there are **nuns** and **vendors** selling items and a **crowd** buying their wares and watching the aeronaut Omar. People in the crowd urge Mary Adare to let Martin Miller take her baby brother home for his wife to feed. In chapter 2 an Argus **newspaper photographer** takes Mary's picture after her playground accident causing the face of Christ to appear in the ice. **Farmers** from around Argus drive for miles to see the miracle. The **Kozka Meats customers** in chapter 4 include Germans, Poles, and Scandinavians who visit and eat with Fritzie and Pete Kozka in the kitchen of the butcher shop and who are not bothered by watching an animal be slaughtered.

In chapter 5 (1950) the **postman** brings a letter to the Fargo apartment of Sita Kozka containing the news that Mary's lost baby brother, now eighteen and named Jude Miller, is about to be ordained. Sita recalls hearing her mother, Fritzie, and **Fritzie's friends** talk about the child's disappearance. (Sita will recall the women's conversations again in chapter 13.) Sita makes a trip to Minneapolis to see Jude's ordination. While she is there, an **elevator operator** offers to take her up to the top floor of the Foshay Building (she does not go), and a **shopgirl** in a department store helps her with a dress. At Jude's ordination, a **bishop** presides and an **aged nun** plays the organ. Afterward a **cab driver** takes her to a pawnshop, where a **young pawnbroker named John** sells her the garnet necklace her aunt, Adelaide Adare, had pawned to his father, **John Senior,** in 1932.

Also in chapter 5, following Sita's wedding to Jimmy Bohl, Jimmy is dancing with the **waitresses from the Poopdeck Restaurant** while his brother and cousins kidnap Sita. When the kidnappers drop her off on the reservation, **seven old men and two loud women,** along with Russell Kashpaw, are drinking at the Indian bar as Sita blows in.

When Sita transforms the Poopdeck Restaurant into Chez Sita in chapter 7, her fancy **chef and his helpers** come down with food poisoning just before the restaurant's grand opening. The **waiters and waitresses,** young people from Argus, must cope with the fiasco. They have sworn not to reveal the behind-the-scenes problems, but this is a promise they will not keep. Despite the crisis, the **customers** leave satisfied. The **hostess** that evening, a simpering woman in a prom dress, takes Celestine James, Mary Adare, and Russell Kashpaw to their table.

In chapter 6 a **waitress in the hotel bar** serves Karl Adare and Wallace Pfef a drink when they are in Minneapolis for the Crop and Livestock Convention. A **bellhop** brings dinner to Karl's room after he and Wallace make love. During one of the bitter winters recorded in chapter 10, an **old man** freezes beneath his clothesline, his arms full of clothes. When Eli Kashpaw comes to the hospital to fetch Russell Kashpaw after his stroke, a **cousin** is working at the hospital desk. In the same chapter Sita is disgusted by the crudeness and poor grooming of her fellow **patients in the state mental hospital.** The **Birdorama customers** in Florida are subdued by Adelaide Adare's snapping voice and eyes in chapter 11.

In chapter 12 Wallace Pfef visits with the **school principal** after the disastrous Christmas pageant at Saint Catherine's school. In the same chapter the **waitress at the Flickertail** serves breakfast to Karl Adare, Celestine James, and Dot Adare at their first family gathering in fourteen years. While Karl is working for Elmo's Landscape Systems in Texas (chapter 14), in chapter 15 the **contractors** who use their services are sometimes amused, sometimes disturbed by his singing. When **one of the managers** of the business sneers at him for bragging about his daughter, Dot, Karl quits and returns to Argus to see Dot crowned as Beet Queen.

Numerous people are involved with the July 1972 Argus Beet Festival that closes the novel. Argus **chamber of commerce members, club presidents,** and **other town leaders** enthusiastically endorse Wallace's idea of having such a festival, although when a drought cripples the beet crop that summer, some want to cancel it (chapter 14). People quote the Fargo weatherman **Dewey Berquist** as they talk about the drought. Even so, many townspeople pitch in to help. A **former contestant for Miss North Dakota** (now a gym teacher) teaches Dot and the other **Beet Queen princesses** how to wave and smile from their parade float (chapter 16). **National guardsmen** organize the **Beet Parade participants,** which include a group of **senior citizens,** dressed outlandishly and playing off-key music (chapter 16). **Members of the American Legion** salute military veteran Russell Kashpaw (chapter 13), who is riding on their float, and one **Legionnaire** finally gives Russell a drink of water (chapter 16). In chapter 16 Dot says that her three friends driving the cars pulling Beet Parade floats, **P. J., Eddie,** and **Boomer,** are "half buzzed" at parade time. The **mayor, police chief, sheriff,** and **members of the town council** each take a turn at the dunking booth in chapter 14. In chapter 16 an **emcee** on a bullhorn urges people to the grandstand for the Beet Queen coronation. The mayor presides over this ceremony (chapters 15 and 16), while the **Legion post commander** stands by (chapter 15).

Others from the surrounding area and the state who are asked to participate in the festival include the **governor and his wife, nine high school marching bands, rock bands, polka bands,** a **motorcycle-riding team, car show drivers,** and **tractor drivers.**

Huge **crowds,** mentioned in chapters 13, 14, 15, and 16, attend the festival. They are said to wave at Mary and Celestine's car during the Beet Parade, squeeze against Jude Miller, and later swelter in the grandstand. One **shrill woman** watching the parade says that Russell Kashpaw looks stuffed (chapter 13). When Dot and her court overhear a **group of spectators** discussing Dot's rigged election as Beet Queen (chapter 16), the other princesses are resentful and mock her. When Jude Miller arrives in Argus the day of the festival, he talks to the **train conductor** and asks the **ticket agent** for information (chapter 14).

TRACKS

In chapter 5 of *Tracks* a **trader** buys mink furs from Eli Kashpaw, who uses the money to buy flour, a blanket, and—for his daughter, Lulu—a pair of fancy dance shoes. In chapter 7 Father Damien finds a **child** who has been neglected by **drunken parents,** encased in snow and leaves and frozen to death. In the same chapter, the Kashpaws and Pillagers sell cranberry bark to the **Pinkham's dealer** (presumably for Lydia E. Pinkham's tonic) to raise money to pay the families' land fees.

THE BINGO PALACE

Patrons of the bingo palace mentioned by Lipsha Morrissey in chapter 5 include young and old, women and men, road workers, French-Cree businessmen, and Scandinavian farmers. (Bingo players are also mentioned in chapter 7.) Two **bingo callers** are working the night Lipsha wins the bingo van in chapter 7, one male, the other female. In chapter 20 Lipsha imagines the **bingo caller, dealer,** and **customers** at the new casino Lyman Lamartine plans to build. In chapter 7 Lipsha and

Shawnee Ray Toose get a ride to Hoopdance with some **friends,** who let the couple off at the motel where they make love for the first time.

At a casino in Reno, Nevada, where Lyman Lamartine attends the Indian Gaming Conference in chapter 8, he notices **trim hostesses** smelling of chlorine from the swimming pool and **two elderly women** playing the slot machine. A **room service waiter** brings a large order to Lyman's hotel room, but instead of staying to eat, he goes down to the casino, where he plays blackjack with **other players.** The **dealer** tries to get rid of him when he is winning. An **elderly man** accidentally knocks Lyman's chips to the floor, temporarily interrupting his gambling spree. When Lyman begins losing and runs out of money, a **pawnshop clerk** gives him a hundred dollars for Nector Kashpaw's ceremonial pipe.

When Lipsha and Lyman begin to fight at the Dairy Queen in chapter 14, the other **Dairy Queen customers** get involved in the melee. Just before Shawnee Ray dances in the final round of the Montana powwow in chapter 16, she watches the **other dancers** and a **boy spraying water** in the arena to settle the dust.

While Lipsha is playing games in Art's Arcade in Fargo in chapter 22, waiting for his father, Gerry Nanapush, **other arcade patrons** come in—drop-outs and hooky-players. Some of them watch Lipsha play his last game, and when he stops, one kid takes over the game. In the Fargo public library, Lipsha is still looking for Gerry when he is approached by a **librarian** asking if he can help Lipsha. When Lipsha steals a stuffed toucan in chapter 24, the **manager of Metro Drug** begins to chase him, followed by a **policewoman** and a **crowd,** including mall-sitters and passersby. When Lipsha and Gerry steal a car, the crowd continues its pursuit until the car's owner rolls off the trunk and bowls them over. A few miles out of town a **smoky** (highway patrol officer) takes up the pursuit. His high-speed chase ends abruptly when the stuffed toucan breaks loose from the escape car and crashes through his windshield.

When federal marshals arrest Lulu Lamartine in chapter 25, **newspaper photographers** from all the North Dakota newspapers are on hand to record the event, along with **local tribal officials** and **Chippewa police** to question the marshals' jurisdiction.

TALES OF BURNING LOVE

Two circus watchers die in the lightning storm in "Eleanor's Tale" [20] that takes the life of Harry Kuklenski, Anna's first husband. Other **men** put out the tent fire with their jackets. A **rescuer** breaks Anna's arm and knocks her unconscious in his attempts to help her, and she is taken to a hospital operated by **Franciscans.** Years later, when Anna's second husband, Lawrence Schlick, is looking for her in a poor part of Fargo ("The Red Slip" [21]), he is approached by an eager **missionary** and a **drunk man** asking for a quarter.

When Anna's teenage daughter, Eleanor Schlick, grinds Jack Mauser's hand in broken glass in DeLendrecies, a **store clerk** and **several customers** stare at them, and the **manager** tries to pull her away. A **girlfriend** of Eleanor takes an art photograph of her lying on a couch in a red satin slip. Eleanor gives the picture to Jack in "The Red Slip" [21]. Eleanor tells her parents she is going to visit a **girlfriend in Minneapolis,** but she actually goes to Florida and marries Jack. At their Florida hotel a **room service waiter** brings them breakfast.

When Jack marries June Morrissey in a Williston bar in 1981 ("Easter Snow" [11]), a drunken, card-carrying **reverend** performs the ceremony. Jack's buddy and sometimes roommate acts as **best man,** while the bar patrons serve as **witnesses.** The next morning, local and state **police officers** help Jack find June Morrissey's body.

As a young woman, Candice Pantamounty has a **friend in Baltimore** who helps her join a class-action suit against the makers of the Dalkon shield ("Candice's Tale" [25]). On her first lunch date with Jack, a **solid-hipped waitress** flips Jack the finger. A **car driver** in "The Wandering Room" [26] signals to Jack that he is dragging a dog with his pickup truck. The dog, Candice's Pepperboy, dies.

Before Marlis Cook meets Jack, a **man opening his car door** accidentally clips her ("Marlis's Tale" [27]). She lives for a time on the money from the out-of-court settlement. In August 1992 the **waitress at the Library** bar brings Jack a hamburger and five beers the day he celebrates getting the first check of his huge bank loan in "The First Draw" [14]. The combination of Jack's fifth beer and his meeting Marlis in the bar changes his life. That night, the **host at the Treetop** restaurant seats Jack and Marlis by a window overlooking the "twin towns" of Fargo-Moorhead. A **piano player** at the Treetop plays popular old songs while Jack and Marlis drunkenly sing along. That night in the motel, Jack finds a picture of an unidentified **elderly woman** in Marlis's wallet. Two days later, a female **justice of the peace** sleepily performs Jack and Marlis's early morning marriage ceremony in "Best Western" [28].

Also in "Best Western" [28], while Marlis and Jack are staying for a month at the Garden Court in Eugene, Jack notices a group of

young people with orchestra instruments, apparently attending a convention. Jack admires one of them, a **long-legged blond girl** with a violin, but he is worried about whether they will be noisy. On the way to Billings, Montana, just after Jack wrenches Marlis's arm at a highway rest stop early in 1994, she catches the eye of a **woman walking a dog.** An **elderly woman at a gas station** stares at them as they fight. The woman is shocked when Marlis offers a condom to an old rancher. That spring, in "Baptism River" [29] the **desk clerk at the Mariner Motel** in Minnesota where Candice and Marlis spend the night also doubles as its **café waitress.** A **Lamaze instructor** teaches Marlis natural childbirth techniques in "The Waiting Room" [31].

In "A Wedge of Shade" [3] (June 1994), the **farmer** who lives next to Celestine James in Argus has just sold his field for a subdivision, probably to Jack Mauser. Employees of Jack's construction company are mentioned several times in the novel: A **truck driver** drops Jack off in Argus in "Hot June Morning" [2] so that he can meet the mother of his new wife, Dot Adare Nanapush. As the women wait for Jack to show up in "A Wedge of Shade" [3], his **construction workers** are moving in the background. A few days later in "Night Prayer" [6], the Mother Superior at Our Lady of the Wheat Priory asks the **foreman of the construction crew** to remove the old wooden statue of the Virgin Mary. The following April, these workers help install the new stone statue in "The Stone Virgin" [44]. (These workers are also present in an earlier [1992] incident, as recorded in "The First Draw" [14].)

When Dot begins paperwork that fall to divorce both Jack and Gerry Nanapush in "Caryl Moon" [8], her **lawyer** thinks she is crazy. As Jack's house is burning down in December 1994 ("Jack's House" [9]), he recalls that his **insurance agent** had tried to sell him additional coverage, but he had declined to buy. The **guests at Jack's funeral** a few days later in "Satin Heart" [12] include assorted farmers, gambling entrepreneurs, restaurant owners, and police officers, as well as people with whom he has done business—bankers, building inspectors, unpaid suppliers, dissatisfied clients, and especially lawyers.

When Jack's wives go to the B & B in West Fargo after his funeral ("The B & B" [16]), other customers include a group of **blackjack players,** one of whom, a morose **man in a tractor hat,** speaks to several of the wives. The **blackjack dealers** are all blonde women. That evening, the **TV weatherman** comments in "The Hitchhiker" [18] that the developing storm is a "lollapalooza." Earlier, neither he nor various **other weather prognosticators** (local farmers and state meteorologists) had predicted the storm. There had once been a rumor, however, among the present generation's **Scandinavian and German grandmothers** that the end of the world would come in the middle of a terrible winter and that the doom would begin in January, the month of Saint Paul's conversion. The **manager of the B & B** cooks a pizza for the massive Indian woman who sweeps into his restaurant out of the blizzard ("The B & B" [16]). He and the **cocktail waitress** argue over whether they should serve this woman.

An **airport watchman** and a **rental car agent** discover the nearly frozen Eleanor Mauser when she takes refuge from the storm in the airport terminal in "A Conversation" [33]. The watchman is mentioned again in "Two Front-Page Articles" [37] as having alerted the Fargo police and fire departments to the plight of Jack Mauser's other wives, who are still snowbound in a car. In "The Disappearance" [36] a **snowmobile rescue squad** rescues the wives Dot, Marlis, and Candice and a hitchhiker. One of the rescuers is distraught because he lets the fourth "woman" fall off his snowmobile. The missing passenger, who is Gerry Nanapush, visits his daughter, Shawn, in "Smile of the Wolf" [38], and Shawn tells him about a **neighbor woman** who has a cat named Uncle Louie.

The next month, while Dot is walking Mary Adare's dog in "February Thaw" [40], she sees a **man with a dog** just disappearing around a corner. The longing of Mary's dog for the other animal takes on significance in the context of Dot's own longing for Gerry.

In "The Stone Virgin" [44] a **delivery truck driver** brings the stone statue to the Argus convent. After Jack is nearly crushed by the falling statue, a **store clerk** brings five hundred dollars' worth of new clothes to him in the Argus hospital. Following his release from the hospital, Jack tells a local **newspaper reporter** that he had "recognized her" (i.e. the statue). In "A Letter to the Bishop" [45] Jude Miller writes about the **janitorial workers** who clean Jack's blood from the statue. The blood, however, reappears, and the **manager of the janitorial company,** a Lutheran, says that it seems "as though the stone itself were sweating blood."

THE ANTELOPE WIFE

At the Elmo powwow in chapter 2, Klaus Shawano's neighbors next to his trading store are a **family from Saskatoon.** When he goes to see old Jimmy Badger about catching an antelope, the **gamblers** whom the old man has beaten are folding their chairs and grumbling. Back in Minneapolis, Klaus is jealous when **men in bars** approach his antelope wife, Sweetheart Calico. The **old women** say that any man who follows an antelope woman, as Klaus has, is lost forever.

When Rozina Roy and Frank Shawano make love the first time in chapter 3, they can hear **children** on the playground nearby.

In chapter 4, Klaus tries to change his and Sweetheart Calico's seating for their flight to Hawaii, but the **airport check-in person,** a heavily made-up woman with long fingernails, says that she cannot help them. Back in Minneapolis, when Sweetheart Calico is thrown through a window by an explosion in chapter 5, the **street people** get clothes for her, including the silk blouse of a **rich lady.**

As the alcoholic Klaus wanders the streets in chapter 10 with Richard Whiteheart Beads, several people give them money: a **Korean or Mexican woman, two men,** and a **group of people,** all exiting an art museum, and later a **woman leaving an antique store.** When Klaus tries to drink from the lawn sprinklers, the **museum guard** and a **large woman** tell them to leave. A **grocery store security guard** and a **liquor store clerk** also will not give him a drink of water. Seeing images of the Blue Fairy in his mind, Klaus recalls watching *Pinocchio* eight or ten times with different **nieces and nephews, their friends,** and **relatives of their friends.** In chapter 15 Klaus and Richard have checked into a recovery lodge, where they live with **three other recovering alcoholics.** When Klaus goes to get the priest to stop Richard's crying, he puts on the pants of his **counselor.**

In chapter 8, Cally Roy visits **relatives** in Bwaanakeeng. She is playing with a **boy cousin** when she rescues the dog Almost Soup. After Almost Soup relates the story of his rescue, he mentions the names of several humans who die by drowning, causing other people to offer dogs as a sacrifice to the lake spirit. The drowning victims include **Fatty Simon; Agnes Anderson,** who dies after an accident on a bridge; **Alberta Meyer** and the **Speigelrein girls,** who drown in the lake; old **Kagewah,** who dies after falling through the ice one spring; and **Morris Shawano,** the track star who disappears from **his dad**'s boat. Almost Soup has refused to be a sacrificial offering for any of them.

According to chapter 11, there is a photo of **Cally's one-time boyfriend** taped to the wall of her room on the reservation. After she moves back to Minneapolis at age eighteen, Cally works in Frank

Shawano's bakery, and **passersby** glance in at the display of breads and cakes. The **kung fu clients** from Cecille Shawano's studio next door come in after their workouts for pastries.

Rozin and Frank's **wedding guests** in chapter 16 include a diverse assortment of Shawano and Roy family members. Some of them help with preparations before the wedding; they attend the cliffside ceremony; and at the reception they eat Frank's blitzkuchen. When Richard Whiteheart Beads tries to leap from the cliff at the ceremony, **ambulance technicians** take him away. **Police** come to the reception to investigate Richard's letter claiming to have poisoned the cake, and a **police sergeant** dusts the letter for fingerprints. That night **medics** remove Richard from Rozin and Frank's hotel after he shoots himself in the head. A year later Frank invites all the wedding guests to a surprise anniversary party (chapter 22).

When Sweetheart Calico begins talking in chapter 18, she tells about seeing a vision of the economic oppression of **children in China** and **young virgins.**

Bibliography

Louise Erdrich has drawn a great deal of scholarly attention. This section is designed to list the most important interviews, bibliographic aids, and scholarly studies that have appeared in print. In the references below *American Indian Culture and Research Journal* is shortened to *AICRJ* and *Studies in American Indian Literatures* is shortened to *SAIL*.

BOOKS BY LOUISE ERDRICH

Imagination. Westerville, Ohio: Merrill, 1981.
Jacklight. New York: Holt, Rinehart & Winston, 1984.
Love Medicine. New York: Holt, Rinehart & Winston, 1984; New and Expanded
    Version, New York: Holt, 1993.
The Beet Queen. New York: Holt, 1986.
Tracks. New York: Holt, 1988.
Baptism of Desire. New York: Harper & Row, 1989.
The Crown of Columbus. By Erdrich and Michael Dorris. New York: Harper-
    Collins, 1991.
Route Two. By Erdrich and Michael Dorris. Northridge, Calif.: Lord John,
    1991.
The Bingo Palace. New York: HarperCollins, 1994.
The Blue Jay's Dance: A Birth Year. New York: HarperCollins, 1995.
Tales of Burning Love. New York: HarperCollins, 1996.
Grandmother's Pigeon. New York: Hyperion, 1996.
The Antelope Wife. New York: HarperCollins, 1998.

INTERVIEWS

Louise Erdrich has granted a large number of interviews, many of which have been transcribed and published. Some twenty-three of them, not listed separately here, have been gathered into the Chavkins' *Conversations with Louise Erdrich and Michael Dorris* volume listed below. We also list, alphabetically, three other notable interviews that are not in that volume.

Berkley, Miriam. "Louise Erdrich." *Publisher's Weekly*, August 15, 1986, 58–59.

Bonetti, Kay. "An Interview with Louise Erdrich and Michael Dorris." *Missouri Review* 11, no. 2 (1988): 79–99. Reprinted in *Conversations with American Novelists: The Best Interviews from* The Missouri Review *and the American Audio Prose Library,* ed. Kay Bonetti, Greg Michalson, Speer Morgan, Jo Sapp, and Sam Stowers, 76–91. Columbia: University of Missouri Press, 1997.

Chavkin, Allan, and Nancy Feyl Chavkin, eds. *Conversations with Louise Erdrich and Michael Dorris.* Jackson: University of Mississippi Press, 1994.

George, Jan. "Interview with Louise Erdrich." *North Dakota Quarterly* 53, no. 2 (1985): 240–46.

BIBLIOGRAPHIC AIDS

The scholarship on Erdrich's work has grown so fast that bibliographers, right from the start, have felt called upon to provide guidance for students and other scholars. Here are some of the most important bibliographical articles and books dealing with Erdrich's poetry and fiction.

Bataille, Gretchen M., and Kathleen M. Sands. *American Indian Women: A Guide to Research.* New York: Garland Publishing, 1991.

Beidler, Peter G. "Louise Erdrich." In *Native American Writers of the United States,* ed. Kenneth M. Roemer, 84–100. Vol. 175 of the *Dictionary of Literary Biography.* Detroit: Gale Research, 1997.

Brewington, Lillian, Normie Bullard, and R. W. Reising. "Writing in Love: An Annotated Bibliography of Critical Responses to the Poetry and Novels of Louise Erdrich and Michael Dorris." *AICRJ* 10, no. 4 (1986): 81–86.

Burdick, Debra A. "Louise Erdrich's *Love Medicine, The Beet Queen,* and *Tracks*: An Annotated Survey of Criticism through 1994." *AICRJ* 20, no. 3 (1996): 137–66.

Chavkin, Allan, and Nancy Feyl Chavkin. "Selected Bibliography." In *The Chippewa Landscape of Louise Erdrich,* ed. Allan Chavkin, 189–99. Tuscaloosa: University of Alabama Press, 1999.

"Louise Erdrich: A.S.A.I.L. Bibliography #9: Poems and Short Stories." *SAIL* 9, no. 1 (1985): 37–41.

Pearlman, Mickey. "A Bibliography of Writings by Louise Erdrich" and "A Bibliography of Writings about Louise Erdrich." In *American Women Writing Fiction: Memory, Identity, Family, Space,* ed. Mickey Pearlman, 108–12. Lexington: University Press of Kentucky, 1989.

Ruoff, A. LaVonne Brown. *American Indian Literatures: An Introduction, Biblio-*

graphic Review, and Selected Bibliography, 84–88. New York: Modern Language Association of America, 1990.

CRITICISM

The scholarship on Erdrich's work is rich and complex. Almost all of it focuses on her fiction, particularly the novels set in and around her fictional Chippewa reservation in North Dakota. Her poetry and nonfiction have been all but ignored by scholars. With a few exceptions, the following list does not include reviews.

Ainsworth, Linda. [Louise Erdrich's *Love Medicine.*] *SAIL* 9, no. 1 (1985): 24–29. Reprinted in *Critical Perspectives on Native American Fiction,* ed. Richard F. Fleck, 274–76 [Ainsworth's name is omitted]. Washington, D.C.: Three Continents Press, 1993.

Aldridge, John W. "Medium without Message (Bobbie Ann Mason, Mary Robison, Louise Erdrich)." Chap. 3 in *Talents and Technicians: Literary Chic and the New Assembly-Line Fiction,* 79–100. New York: Scribner's, 1992.

Bak, Hans. "Circles Blaze in Ordinary Days: Louise Erdrich's *Jacklight.*" In *Native American Women in Literature and Culture,* ed. Susan Castillo and Victor M. P. Da Rosa, 11–27. Porto, Portugal: Fernando Pessoa University Press, 1997.

———. "The Kaleidoscope of History: Michael Dorris and Louise Erdrich's *The Crown of Columbus* (with a Coda on Gerald Vizenor's *The Heirs of Columbus*)." In *Deferring a Dream: Literary Sub-Versions of the American Columbiad,* ed. Gert Buelens and Ernst Rudin, 99–119. Basel: Birkhäuser Verlag, 1994.

———. "Toward a Native American 'Realism': The Amphibious Fiction of Louise Erdrich." In *Neo-Realism in Contemporary American Fiction,* ed. Kristiaan Versluys, 145–70. Amsterdam: Rodopi, 1992.

Barak, Julie. "Blurs, Blends, Berdaches: Gender Mixing in the Novels of Louise Erdrich." *SAIL* 8, no. 3 (1996): 49–62.

Barnett, Marianne. "Dreamstuff: Erdrich's *Love Medicine.*" *North Dakota Quarterly* 56, no. 1 (1988): 82–93.

Barry, Nora, and Mary Prescott. "The Triumph of the Brave: *Love Medicine's* Holistic Vision." *Critique: Studies in Contemporary Fiction* 30, no. 2 (1989): 123–38.

Bataille, Gretchen M. "Louise Erdrich's *The Beet Queen*: Images of the Grotesque on the Northern Plains." In *Critical Perspectives on Native American Fiction,* ed. Richard F. Fleck, 277–85. Washington, D.C.: Three Continents Press, 1993.

Beidler, Peter G. "Louise Erdrich." In *Native American Writers of the United States,* ed. Kenneth M. Roemer, 84–100. Vol. 175 of the *Dictionary of Literary Biography.* Detroit: Gale Research, 1997.

———. "Three Student Guides to Louise Erdrich's *Love Medicine.*" *AICRJ* 16, no. 4 (1992): 167–73.

Berninghausen, Tom. " 'This Ain't Real Estate': Land and Culture in Louise Erdrich's Chippewa Tetralogy." In *Women, America, and Movement: Narratives of Relocation,* ed. Susan L. Roberson, 190–209. Columbia: University of Missouri Press, 1998.

Bird, Gloria. "Searching for Evidence of Colonialism at Work: A Reading of Louise Erdrich's *Tracks.*" *Wicazo Sa Review* 8, no. 2 (1992): 40–47.

Bloom, Harold, ed. "Louise Erdrich." In *Native American Women Writers,* 24–37. Philadelphia: Chelsea House, 1998. [Contains excerpts from articles included in this bibliography by Schneider, Van Dyke ("Questions"), Cornell, Friedman, Peterson ("History"), Walsh and Braley, Pittman, and Purdy ("Building Bridges").]

Bowers, Sharon Manybeads. "Louise Erdrich as Nanapush." In *New Perspectives on Women and Comedy,* ed. Regina Barreca, 135–41. Philadelphia: Gordon and Breach, 1992.

Brady, Laura A. "Collaboration as Conversion: Literary Cases." *Essays in Literature* 19, no. 2 (1992): 298–311. [See especially pp. 306–9.]

Brehm, Victoria. "The Metamorphoses of an Ojibwa *Manido.*" *American Literature* 68, no. 4 (1996): 677–706.

Breinig, Helmbrecht. "(Hi)storytelling as Deconstruction and Seduction: The Columbus Novels of Stephen Marlowe and Michael Dorris/Louise Erdrich." In *Historiographic Metafiction in Modern American and Canadian Literature,* ed. Bernd Engler and Kurt Müller, 325–46. Paderborn: Ferdinand Schöningh, 1994.

Brogan, Kathleen. "Haunted by History: Louise Erdrich's *Tracks.*" *Prospects* 21 (1996): 169–92. Reprinted [with slight revision] as "Ghost Dancing: Cultural Translation in Louise Erdrich's *Tracks,*" in *Cultural Haunting: Ghosts and Ethnicity in Recent American Literature,* 30–60 (Charlottesville: University Press of Virginia, 1998).

Brown, Dee. [Louise Erdrich's *Love Medicine.*] *SAIL* 9, no. 1 (1985): 4–5. Reprinted in *Critical Perspectives on Native American Fiction,* ed. Richard F. Fleck, 264–65. Washington, D.C.: Three Continents Press, 1993.

Carr, Susan. "The Turtle Mountain/Yoknapatawpha Connection." *Bulletin of the West Virginia Association of College English Teachers* [West Virginia Institute of Technology] n.s. 16 (fall 1994): 18–25.

Castillo, Susan Perez. "The Construction of Gender and Ethnicity in the Poetry of Leslie Silko and Louise Erdrich." In *Visions in History,* ed. Gerald Gillespie; *Visions of the Other,* ed. Margaret R. Higonnet and Sumie Jones, 637–45. Vol. 2 of *The Force of Vision,* ed. Earl Miner and Haga Toru. Tokyo: International Comparative Literature Association and University of Tokyo Press, 1995.

———. "The Construction of Gender and Ethnicity in the Texts of Leslie Silko and Louise Erdrich." *Yearbook of English Studies* 24 (1994): 228–36.

———. "Postmodernism, Native American Literature, and the Real: The Silko-Erdrich Controversy." *Massachusetts Review* 32, no. 2 (1991): 285–94.

———. "A Woman Constantly Surprised: The Construction of Self in Louise Erdrich's *The Blue Jay's Dance.*" *European Review of Native American Studies* 11, no. 1 (1997): 39–41.

———. "Women Aging into Power: Fictional Representations of Power and Authority in Louise Erdrich's Female Characters." *SAIL* 8, no. 4 (1996): 13–20. Reprinted in *Native American Women in Literature and Culture,* ed. Susan Castillo and Victor M. P. Da Rosa, 29–36 (Porto, Portugal: Fernando Pessoa University Press, 1997).

Catt, Catherine M. "Ancient Myth in Modern America: The Trickster in the Fiction of Louise Erdrich." *Platte Valley Review* 19, no. 1 (1991): 71–81.

Chavkin, Allan. Introduction to *The Chippewa Landscape of Louise Erdrich.* Tuscaloosa: University of Alabama Press, 1999.

———. "Vision and Revision in Louise Erdrich's *Love Medicine.*" In *The Chippewa Landscape of Louise Erdrich,* ed. Allan Chavkin, 84–116. Tuscaloosa: University of Alabama Press, 1999.

Cid, Teresa. "Wanting America Back: *The Crown of Columbus* as a Tentative Epic in an Age of Multiculturalism." In *The Insular Dream: Obsession and Resistance,* ed. Kristiaan Versluys, 342–49. Amsterdam: VU University Press, 1995.

Clarke, Joni Adamson. "Why Bears Are Good to Think and Theory Doesn't Have to Be Murder: Transformation and Oral Tradition in Louise Erdrich's *Tracks.*" *SAIL* 4, no. 1 (1992): 28–48.

Cooperman, Jeannette Batz. *The Broom Closet: Secret Meanings of Domesticity in Postfeminist Novels by Louise Erdrich, Mary Gordon, Toni Morrison, Marge Piercy, Jane Smiley, and Amy Tan.* New York: Peter Lang, 1999.

Cornell, Daniel. "Woman Looking: Revis(ion)ing Pauline's Subject Position in Louise Erdrich's *Tracks.*" *SAIL* 4, no. 1 (1992): 49–64.

Cox, Jay. "Dangerous Definitions: Female Tricksters in Contemporary Native American Literature." *Wicazo Sa Review* 5, no. 2 (1989): 17–21.

Cox, Karen Castellucci. "Magic and Memory in the Contemporary Story

Cycle: Gloria Naylor and Louise Erdrich." *College English* 60, no. 2 (1998): 150–72.

Crabtree, Claire. "Salvific Oneness and the Fragmented Self in Louise Erdrich's *Love Medicine.*" In *Contemporary Native American Cultural Issues,* ed. Thomas E. Schirer, 49–56. Sault Ste. Marie, Mich.: Lake Superior State University Press, 1988.

Daniele, Daniela. "Transactions in a Native Land: Mixed-Blood Identity and Indian Legacy in Louise Erdrich's Writing." *RSA Journal* [Florence, Italy] 3 (1992): 43–58.

Davis, Rocío G. "Identity in Community in Ethnic Short Story Cycles: Amy Tan's *The Joy Luck Club,* Louise Erdrich's *Love Medicine,* Gloria Naylor's *The Women of Brewster Place.*" In *Ethnicity and the American Short Story,* ed. Julie Brown, 3–23. New York: Garland, 1997.

Desmond, John F. "Catholicism in Contemporary American Fiction." *America,* May 14, 1994, 7–11. [See especially p. 9.]

Downes, Margaret J. "Narrativity, Myth, and Metaphor: Louise Erdrich and Raymond Carver Talk about Love." *MELUS* 21, no. 2 (1996): 49–61.

"Erdrich, Louise." In *Contemporary Authors,* new revision series, vol. 41, ed. Susan M. Trosky, 124–28. Detroit: Gale Research, 1994.

Faris, Wendy B. "Devastation and Replenishment: New World Narratives of Love and Nature." *Studies in the Humanities* 19, no. 2 (1992): 171–82.

Flavin, James. "The Novel as Performance: Communication in Louise Erdrich's *Tracks.*" *SAIL* 3, no. 4 (1991): 1–12.

Flavin, Louise. "Gender Construction amid Family Dissolution in Louise Erdrich's *The Beet Queen.*" *SAIL* 7, no. 2 (1995): 17–24.

———. "Louise Erdrich's *Love Medicine*: Loving over Time and Distance." *Critique: Studies in Contemporary Fiction* 31, no. 1 (1989): 55–64.

Friedman, Susan Stanford. "Identity Politics, Syncretism, Catholicism, and Anishinabe Religion in Louise Erdrich's *Tracks.*" *Religion and Literature* 26, no. 1 (1994): 107–33.

Gaughan, Sara K. "Old Age, Folk Belief, and Love in Stories by Ernest Gaines and Louise Erdrich." *Louisiana Folklore Miscellany* 10 (1995): 37–45.

Gish, Robert F. "Life into Death, Death into Life: Hunting as Metaphor and Motive in *Love Medicine.*" In *The Chippewa Landscape of Louise Erdrich,* ed. Allan Chavkin, 67–83. Tuscaloosa: University of Alabama Press, 1999.

Gleason, William. " 'Her Laugh an Ace': The Function of Humor in Louise Erdrich's *Love Medicine.*" *AICRJ* 11, no. 3 (1987): 51–73.

Grödal, Hanne Tang. "Words, Words, Words." *Dolphin* 18 (1990): 21–26.

Hafen, P. Jane. "Sacramental Language: Ritual in the Poetry of Louise Erdrich." *Great Plains Quarterly* 16, no. 3 (1996): 147–55.

Hansen, Elaine Tuttle. "What If Your Mother Never Meant To? The Novels of Louise Erdrich and Michael Dorris." Chap. 4 in *Mother without Child: Contemporary Fiction and the Crisis of Motherhood,* 115–57. Berkeley and Los Angeles: University of California Press, 1997.

Hanson, Elizabeth I. "Louise Erdrich: Making a World Anew." Chap. 6 in *Forever There: Race and Gender in Contemporary Native American Fiction,* 79–104. New York: Peter Lang, 1989.

Hendrickson, Roberta Makashay. "Victims and Survivors: Native American Women Writers, Violence against Women, and Child Abuse." *SAIL* 8, no. 1 (1996): 13–24.

Hessler, Michelle R. "Catholic Nuns and Ojibwa Shamans: Pauline and Fleur in Louise Erdrich's *Tracks." Wicazo Sa Review* 11, no. 1 (1995): 40–45.

Holt, Debra C. "Transformation and Continuance: Native American Tradition in the Novels of Louise Erdrich." In *Entering the Nineties: The North American Experience,* ed. Thomas E. Schirer, 149–61. Sault Ste. Marie, Mich.: Lake Superior State University Press, 1991.

Hornung, Alfred. "Ethnic Fiction and Survival Ethics: Toni Morrison, Louise Erdrich, David H. Hwang." In *Ethics and Aesthetics: The Moral Turn of Postmodernism,* ed. Gerhard Hoffmann and Alfred Hornung, 209–20. Heidelberg: Universitätsverlag C. Winter, 1996.

Howard, Jane. "Louise Erdrich: A Dartmouth Chippewa Writes a Great Native American Novel." *Life,* April 18, 1985.

Jaskoski, Helen. "From Time Immemorial: Native American Traditions in Contemporary Short Fiction." In *Since Flannery O'Connor: Essays on the Contemporary American Short Story,* ed. Loren Logsdon and Charles W. Mayer, 54–71. Macomb: Western Illinois University, 1987.

Khader, Jamil. "Postcolonial Nativeness: Nomadism, Cultural Memory, and the Politics of Identity in Louise Erdrich's and Michael Dorris's *The Crown of Columbus." ARIEL* 28, no. 2 (1997): 81–101.

Kloppenburg, Michelle R. "The Face in the Slough: Lipsha's Quest for Identity in Louise Erdrich's *Love Medicine* and *The Bingo Palace." European Review of Native American Studies* 11, no. 1 (1997): 27–34.

Kolmar, Wendy K. " 'Dialectics of Connectedness': Supernatural Elements in Novels by Bambara, Cisneros, Grahn, and Erdrich." In *Haunting the House of Fiction: Feminist Perspectives on Ghost Stories by American Women,* ed. Lynette Carpenter and Wendy K. Kolmar, 236–49. Knoxville: University of Tennessee Press, 1991.

Kroeber, Karl. [Louise Erdrich's *Love Medicine*.] *SAIL* 9, no. 1 (1985): 1–4. Reprinted in *Critical Perspectives on Native American Fiction,* ed. Richard F. Fleck, 263–64. Washington, D.C.: Three Continents Press, 1993.

Lansky, Ellen. "Spirits and Salvation in Louise Erdrich's *Love Medicine.*" *Dionysos: The Literature and Addiction TriQuarterly* 5, no. 3 (1994): 39–44.

Larson, Sidner. "The Fragmentation of a Tribal People in Louise Erdrich's *Tracks.*" *AICRJ* 17, no. 2 (1993): 1–13.

Le Guin, Ursula K. [Louise Erdrich's *Love Medicine*.] *SAIL* 9, no. 1 (1985): 5–6. Reprinted in *Critical Perspectives on Native American Fiction,* ed. Richard F. Fleck, 265. Washington, D.C.: Three Continents Press, 1993.

Lee, A. Robert. "Ethnic Renaissance: Rudolfo Anaya, Louise Erdrich, and Maxine Hong Kingston." In *The New American Writing: Essays on American Literature since 1970,* ed. Graham Clarke, 139–64. New York: St. Martin's Press, 1990.

Lincoln, Kenneth. " 'Bring Her Home': Louise Erdrich." Chap. 6 in *Indi'n Humor: Bicultural Play in Native America,* 205–53. New York: Oxford University Press, 1993.

———. Preface to *Native American Renaissance.* Berkeley and Los Angeles: University of California Press, 1985 [paperback edition].

"Louise Erdrich." In *Contemporary Literary Criticism,* vol. 54, ed. Daniel G. Marowski and Roger Matuz, 164–73. Detroit: Gale Research, 1989.

Ludlow, Jeannie. "Working (in) the In-Between: Poetry, Criticism, Interrogation, and Interruption." *SAIL* 6, no. 1 (1994): 24–42.

Magalaner, Marvin. "Louise Erdrich: Of Cars, Time, and the River." In *American Women Writing Fiction: Memory, Identity, Family, Space,* ed. Mickey Pearlman, 95–108. Lexington: University Press of Kentucky, 1989.

Manley, Kathleen E. B. "Decreasing the Distance: Contemporary Native American Texts, Hypertext, and the Concept of Audience." *Southern Folklore* 51, no. 2 (1994): 121–35.

Maristuen-Rodakowski, Julie. "The Turtle Mountain Reservation in North Dakota: Its History as Depicted in Louise Erdrich's *Love Medicine* and *Beet Queen.*" *AICRJ* 12, no. 3 (1988): 33–48.

Maszewska, Jadwiga. "Functions of the Narrative Method in William Faulkner's *Absalom, Absalom!* and Louise Erdrich's *Tracks.*" In *Faulkner, His Contemporaries, and His Posterity,* ed. Waldemar Zacharasiewicz, 317–21. Tübingen: Francke, 1993.

Matchie, Thomas. "Building on the Myth: Recovering Native American Culture in Louise Erdrich's *The Bingo Palace.*" In *American Indian Studies: An*

Interdisciplinary Approach to Contemporary Issues, ed. Dane Morrison, 299–312. New York: Peter Lang, 1997.

———. "Exploring the Meaning of Discovery in *The Crown of Columbus.*" *North Dakota Quarterly* 59, no. 4 (1991): 243–50.

———. "Flannery O'Connor and Louise Erdrich: The Function of the Grotesque in Erdrich's *Tracks.*" In *Papers Presented to the Linguistic Circle of Manitoba and North Dakota: 1989–1993,* ed. Harold J. Smith and Gaby Divay, 67–78. Fargo: Center for Writers, North Dakota State University, 1996.

———. "Louise Erdrich's 'Scarlet Letter': Literary Continuity in *Tales of Burning Love.*" *North Dakota Quarterly* 63, no. 4 (1996): 113–23.

———. "*Love Medicine*: A Female *Moby-Dick.*" *Midwest Quarterly* 30, no. 4 (1989): 478–91.

McCafferty, Kate. "Generative Adversity: Shapeshifting Pauline/Leopolda in *Tracks* and *Love Medicine.*" *American Indian Quarterly* 21, no. 4 (1997): 729–51.

McCay, Mary A. "Cooper's Indians, Erdrich's Native Americans." In *Global Perspectives on Teaching Literature: Shared Visions and Distinctive Visions,* ed. Sandra Ward Lott, Maureen S. G. Hawkins, and Norman McMillan, 152–67. Urbana, Ill.: National Council of Teachers of English, 1993.

———. "Louise Erdrich." In *American Women Writers: A Critical Reference Guide from Colonial Times to the Present,* vol. 5: supplement, ed. Carol Hurd Green and Mary Grimley Mason, 131–34. New York: Continuum, 1994.

McKenzie, James. "Lipsha's Good Road Home: The Revival of Chippewa Culture in *Love Medicine.*" *AICRJ* 10, no. 3 (1986): 53–63.

Medeiros, Paulo. "Cannibalism and Starvation: The Parameters of Eating Disorders in Literature." In *Disorderly Eaters: Texts in Self-Empowerment,* ed. Lilian R. Furst and Peter W. Graham, 11–27. University Park: Pennsylvania State University Press, 1992.

Meisenhelder, Susan. "Race and Gender in Louise Erdrich's *The Beet Queen.*" *ARIEL* 25, no. 1 (1994): 45–57.

Mermann-Jozwiak, Elisabeth. "'His Grandfather Ate His Own Wife': Louise Erdrich's *Love Medicine* as a Contemporary Windigo Narrative." *North Dakota Quarterly* 64, no. 4 (1997): 44–54.

Mitchell, David. "A Bridge to the Past: Cultural Hegemony and the Native American Past in Louise Erdrich's *Love Medicine.*" In *Entering the Nineties: The North American Experience,* ed. Thomas E. Schirer, 162–70. Sault Ste. Marie, Mich.: Lake Superior State University Press, 1991.

Morace, Robert A. "From Sacred Hoops to Bingo Palaces: Louise Erdrich's

Carnivalesque Fiction." In *The Chippewa Landscape of Louise Erdrich,* ed. Allan Chavkin, 36–66. Tuscaloosa: University of Alabama Press, 1999.

Nelson-Born, Katherine A. "Trace of a Woman: Narrative Voice and Decentered Power in the Fiction of Toni Morrison, Margaret Atwood, and Louise Erdrich." *LIT* 7, no. 1 (1996): 1–12.

Owens, Louis. "Acts of Recovery: The American Indian Novel in the Eighties." *Western American Literature* 22, no. 1 (1987): 53–57.

———. "Erdrich and Dorris's Mixedbloods and Multiple Narratives." Chap. 7 in *Other Destinies: Understanding the American Indian Novel,* 192–224. Norman: University of Oklahoma Press, 1992.

Pasquaretta, Paul. "Sacred Chance: Gambling and the Contemporary Native American Indian Novel." *MELUS* 21, no. 2 (1996): 21–33.

Pellerin, Simone. "An Epitome of Erdrich's Art: 'The Names of Women.'" *European Review of Native American Studies* 11, no. 1 (1997): 35–38.

Peterson, Nancy J. "History, Postmodernism, and Louise Erdrich's *Tracks.*" *PMLA* 109, no. 5 (1994): 982–94.

———. "Indi'n Humor and Trickster Justice in *The Bingo Palace.*" In *The Chippewa Landscape of Louise Erdrich,* ed. Allan Chavkin, 161–81. Tuscaloosa: University of Alabama Press, 1999.

Pittman, Barbara L. "Cross-Cultural Reading and Generic Transformations: The Chronotope of the Road in Erdrich's *Love Medicine.*" *American Literature* 67, no. 4 (1995): 777–92.

Purdy, John [Lloyd]. "Against All Odds: Games of Chance in the Novels of Louise Erdrich." In *The Chippewa Landscape of Louise Erdrich,* ed. Allan Chavkin, 8–35. Tuscaloosa: University of Alabama Press, 1999.

———. "Betting on the Future: Gambling against Colonialism in the Novels of Louise Erdrich." In *Native American Women in Literature and Culture,* ed. Susan Castillo and Victor M. P. Da Rosa, 37–56. Porto, Portugal: Fernando Pessoa University Press, 1997.

———. "Building Bridges: Crossing the Waters to a *Love Medicine* (Louise Erdrich)." In *Teaching American Ethnic Literatures: Nineteen Essays,* ed. John R. Maitino and David R. Peck, 83–100. Albuquerque: University of New Mexico Press, 1996.

———. "Karen Louise Erdrich." In *Dictionary of Native American Literature,* ed. Andrew Wiget, 423–29. New York: Garland, 1994. Reprinted as *Handbook of Native American Literature.* New York: Garland, 1996.

Rainwater, Catherine. *Dreams of Fiery Stars: The Transformations of Native American Fiction.* Philadelphia: University of Pennsylvania Press, 1999.

———. "Ethnic Signs in Erdrich's *Tracks* and *The Bingo Palace.*" In *The Chippewa*

Landscape of Louise Erdrich, ed. Allan Chavkin, 144–60. Tuscaloosa: University of Alabama Press, 1999.

———. "Reading between Worlds: Narrativity in the Fiction of Louise Erdrich." *American Literature* 62, no. 3 (1990): 405–22.

Rayson, Ann. "Shifting Identity in the Work of Louise Erdrich and Michael Dorris." *SAIL* 3, no. 4 (1991): 27–36.

Rosenburg, Ruth. "Louise Erdrich." In *American Novelists since World War II, Fourth Series,* ed. James R. Giles and Wanda H. Giles, 42–50. Vol. 152 of the *Dictionary of Literary Biography.* Detroit: Gale Research, 1995.

Ruoff, A. LaVonne Brown. Afterword to *The Chippewa Landscape of Louise Erdrich,* ed. Allan Chavkin, 182–88. Tuscaloosa: University of Alabama Press, 1999.

Ruppert, James. "Celebrating Culture: *Love Medicine.*" Chap. 8 in *Mediation in Contemporary Native American Fiction,* 131–50. Norman: University of Oklahoma Press, 1995. [This chapter is a somewhat altered version of Ruppert's *NDQ* article, below.]

———. "Mediation and Multiple Narrative in *Love Medicine.*" *North Dakota Quarterly* 59, no. 4 (1991): 229–42.

Sanders, Scott R. [Louise Erdrich's *Love Medicine.*] *SAIL* 9, no. 1 (1985): 6–11. Reprinted in *Critical Perspectives on Native American Fiction,* ed. Richard F. Fleck, 265–68. Washington, D.C.: Three Continents Press, 1993.

Sands, Kathleen M. [Louise Erdrich's *Love Medicine.*] *SAIL* 9, no. 1 (1985): 12–24. Reprinted in *Critical Perspectives on Native American Fiction,* ed. Richard F. Fleck, 268–73. Washington, D.C.: Three Continents Press, 1993.

Sarris, Greg. "Reading Louise Erdrich: *Love Medicine* as Home Medicine." In *Keeping Slug Woman Alive: A Holistic Approach to American Indian Texts,* 115–45. Berkeley and Los Angeles: University of California Press, 1993.

Sarvé-Gorham, Kristan. "Power Lines: The Motif of Twins and the Medicine Women of *Tracks* and *Love Medicine.*" In *Having Our Way: Women Rewriting Tradition in Twentieth-Century America,* ed. Harriet Pollack, 167–90. *Bucknell Review* series vol. 39, no. 1. Lewisburg, Pa.: Bucknell University Press, 1995.

Scheick, William J. "Narrative and Ethos in Erdrich's 'A Wedge of Shade.'" In *The Chippewa Landscape of Louise Erdrich,* ed. Allan Chavkin, 117–29. Tuscaloosa: University of Alabama Press, 1999.

———. "Structures of Belief/Narrative Structures: Mojtabai's *Ordinary Time* and Erdrich's *The Bingo Palace.*" *Texas Studies in Literature and Language* 37, no. 4 (1995): 363–75.

Schiavonne, Michelle. "Images of Marginalized Cultures: Intertextuality in Marshall, Morrison, and Erdrich." *Bulletin of the West Virginia Association of College English Teachers* [West Virginia Institute of Technology] n.s. 17 (fall 1995): 41–49.

Schneider, Lissa. "*Love Medicine*: A Metaphor for Forgiveness." *SAIL* 4, no. 1 (1992): 1–13.

Schultz, Lydia A. "Fragments and Ojibwe Stories: Narrative Strategies in Louise Erdrich's *Love Medicine*." *College Literature* 18, no. 3 (1991): 80–95.

Schweninger, Lee. "A Skin of Lakeweed: An Ecofeminist Approach to Erdrich and Silko." In *Multicultural Literatures through Feminist/Poststructuralist Lenses,* ed. Barbara Frey Waxman, 37–56. Knoxville: University of Tennessee Press, 1993.

Secco, Anna. "The Search for Origins through Storytelling in Native American Literature: Momaday, Silko, Erdrich." *RSA Journal* [Florence, Italy] 3 (1992): 59–71.

Sergi, Jennifer. "Storytelling: Tradition and Preservation in Louise Erdrich's *Tracks*." *World Literature Today* 66, no. 2 (1992): 279–82.

Shaddock, Jennifer. "Mixed Blood Women: The Dynamic of Women's Relations in the Novels of Louise Erdrich and Leslie Silko." In *Feminist Nightmares, Women at Odds: Feminism and the Problem of Sisterhood,* ed. Susan Ostrov Weisser and Jennifer Fleischner, 106–21. New York: New York University Press, 1994.

Shechner, Mark. "Until the Music Stops: Women Novelists in a Post-Feminist Age." *Salmagundi* 113 (1997): 220–38. [See especially pp. 223–27.]

Silberman, Robert. "Opening the Text: *Love Medicine* and the Return of the Native American Woman." In *Narrative Chance: Postmodern Discourse on Native American Indian Literatures,* ed. Gerald Vizenor, 101–20. Albuquerque: University of New Mexico Press, 1989. Reprint, Norman: University of Oklahoma Press, 1993.

Silko, Leslie Marmon. "Here's an Odd Artifact for the Fairy-Tale Shelf." *SAIL* 10, no. 4 (1986): 178–84. Originally published in *Impact Magazine, Albuquerque Journal,* October 8, 1986, 10–11.

Sims-Brandom, Lisa. "Smoked Jerky vs. Red Pottage: Native American Tradition and Christian Theology in Louise Erdrich's *The Bingo Palace*." *Publications in the Arkansas Philological Association* 21, no. 2 (1995): 59–69.

Slack, John S. "The Comic Savior: The Dominance of the Trickster in Louise Erdrich's *Love Medicine*." *North Dakota Quarterly* 61, no. 3 (1993): 118–29.

Sloboda, Nicholas. "Beyond the Iconic Subject: Re-Visioning Louise Erdrich's *Tracks*." *SAIL* 8, no. 3 (1996): 63–79.

Smith, Jeanne Rosier. "Comic Liberators and Word-Healers: The Interwoven Trickster Narratives of Louise Erdrich." Chap. 3 in *Writing Tricksters: Mythic*

Gambols in American Ethnic Literature, 71–110. Berkeley and Los Angeles: University of California Press, 1997.

———. "Transpersonal Selfhood: The Boundaries of Identity in Louise Erdrich's *Love Medicine.*" *SAIL* 3, no. 4 (1991): 13–26.

Stripes, James D. "The Problem(s) of (Anishinaabe) History in the Fiction of Louise Erdrich: Voices and Contexts." *Wicazo Sa Review* 7, no. 2 (1991): 26–33.

Tanrisal, Meldan. "Mother and Child Relationships in the Novels of Louise Erdrich." *American Studies International* 35, no. 3 (1997): 67–79.

Tharp, Julie. "Women's Community and Survival in the Novels of Louise Erdrich." In *Communication and Women's Friendships: Parallels and Intersections in Literature and Life,* ed. Janet Doubler Ward and JoAnna Stephens Mink, 165–80. Bowling Green, Ohio: Bowling Green State University Popular Press, 1993.

Towery, Margie. "Continuity and Connection: Characters in Louise Erdrich's Fiction." *AICRJ* 16, no. 4 (1992): 99–122.

TuSmith, Bonnie. "Native American Writers." Chap. 4 in *All My Relatives: Community in Contemporary Ethnic American Literatures,* 103–36 [see esp. 129–32]. Ann Arbor: University of Michigan Press, 1993.

Van Dyke, Annette. "Of Vision Quests and Spirit Guardians: Female Power in the Novels of Louise Erdrich." In *The Chippewa Landscape of Louise Erdrich,* ed. Allan Chavkin, 130–43. Tuscaloosa: University of Alabama Press, 1999.

———. "Questions of the Spirit: Bloodlines in Louise Erdrich's Chippewa Landscape." *SAIL* 4, no. 1 (1992): 15–27.

Velie, Alan R. "American Indian Literature in the Nineties: The Emergence of the Middle-Class Protagonist." *World Literature Today* 66, no. 2 (1992): 264–68.

———. "Magical Realism and Ethnicity: The Fantastic in the Fiction of Louise Erdrich." In *Native American Women in Literature and Culture,* ed. Susan Castillo and Victor M. P. Da Rosa, 57–67. Porto, Portugal: Fernando Pessoa University Press, 1997.

———. "The Trickster Novel." In *Narrative Chance: Postmodern Discourse on Native American Indian Literatures,* ed. Gerald Vizenor, 121–39 [*Love Medicine* mentioned on 121–23]. Albuquerque: University of New Mexico Press, 1989. Reprint, Norman: University of Oklahoma Press, 1993.

Walker, Victoria. "A Note on Narrative Perspective in *Tracks.*" *SAIL* 3, no. 4 (1991): 37–40.

Walsh, Dennis M., and Ann Braley. "The Indianness of Louise Erdrich's *The Beet Queen*: Latency as Presence." *AICRJ* 18, no. 3 (1994): 1–17.

Wiget, Andrew. "Singing the Indian Blues: Louise Erdrich and the Love that Hurts So Good." *Puerto del Sol* 21, no. 2 (1986): 166–75.

Winsbro, Bonnie. "Predator, Scavenger, and Trickster-Transformer: Survival and the Visionary Experience in Louise Erdrich's *Tracks*." Chap. 3 in *Supernatural Forces: Belief, Difference, and Power in Contemporary Works by Ethnic Women*. Amherst: University of Massachusetts Press, 1993. 52–81.

Wong, Hertha D. "Adoptive Mothers and Thrown-Away Children in the Novels of Louise Erdrich." In *Narrating Mothers: Theorizing Maternal Subjectivities,* ed. Brenda O. Daly and Maureen T. Reddy, 174–92. Knoxville: University of Tennessee Press, 1991.

———. "Louise Erdrich's *Love Medicine*: Narrative Communities and the Short Story Sequence." In *Modern American Short Story Sequences: Composite Fictions and Fictive Communities,* ed. J. Gerald Kennedy, 170–93. New York: Cambridge University Press, 1995.

Wong, Hertha D. Sweet, ed. *Louise Erdrich's* Love Medicine*: A Casebook*. New York: Oxford University Press, 1999.

Woodward, Pauline G. "Chance in Louise Erdrich's *The Beet Queen*: New Ways to Find a Family." *ARIEL* 26, no. 2 (1995): 109–27.

Zeck, Jeanne-Marie. "Erdrich's *Love Medicine*." *The Explicator* 54, no. 1 (1995): 58–60.

Index

Note: The names of the characters are not listed in this index because they are listed alphabetically in Part II. References to the individual novels in the introduction and Part I are listed here, but not those in Part II, where they are given to guide readers to novels in which each character appears.